T0357280

Jim

BLACK LIVES

———

Yale University Press's Black Lives series seeks to tell the fullest range of stories about notable and overlooked Black figures who profoundly shaped world history. Each book is intended to add a chapter to our larger understanding of the breadth of Black people's experiences as these have unfolded through time. Using a variety of approaches, the books in this series trace the indelible contributions that individuals of African descent have made to their worlds, exploring how their lives embodied and shaped the changing conditions of modernity and challenged definitions of race and practices of racism in their societies.

Jim

———

THE LIFE
AND AFTERLIVES OF
HUCKLEBERRY FINN'S
COMRADE

———

Shelley Fisher Fishkin

———

Black Lives

Yale University Press | New Haven and London

Yale University Press books may be purchased in quantity for
educational, business, or promotional use. For information,
please email sales.press@yale.edu (US office) or
sales@yaleup.co.uk (UK office).

Spike Lee's Huckleberry Finn by Ralph Wiley c/o Heygood Images
Productions, Inc. Copyright © 2025 Estate of Ralph Wiley.
Reprinted with permission.

Set in Freight Text Pro type by Integrated Publishing Solutions.
Printed in the United States of America.

Library of Congress Control Number: 2024952454
ISBN 978-0-300-26832-4 (hardcover : alk. paper)

A catalogue record for this book is available from the British Library.

This paper meets the requirements of ANSI/NISO Z39.48-1992
(Permanence of Paper).

10 9 8 7 6 5 4 3 2 1

Frontispiece (p. xii): *Jim*. Wood engraving from the Pennyroyal Press
edition of *Adventures of Huckleberry Finn*, 1984, by Barry Moser.

CONTENTS

———

EXPLANATORY

————

AMERICA'S MOST NOTORIOUS racial slur figures prominently in *Adventures of Huckleberry Finn*, a word that has
been used for centuries in the United States to vilify and
stigmatize Black people. Spoken by a non-Black individual, the
word immediately identifies the speaker with the ideology of white
supremacy and with it the history of dehumanization, disparagement, and defamation to which Black people have been subjected
from the beginnings of racial slavery through the present.

As a writer, Mark Twain sought to represent the authentic
speech of his characters on the page as accurately as he could—a
challenge he undertook "pains-takingly" (as he says in the "Explanatory" note that precedes the first page of the novel).[1] As
Twain wrote in a later essay, "When the personages of a tale deal
in conversation, the talk shall . . . be such talk as human beings
would be likely to talk in the given circumstances."[2] The epithet
was commonly used by white people to disparage Black people
in the time and place in which the novel is set. Mark Twain also
understood that the toxic word denied the humanity of the people it was used to describe and recognized that it embodied and
enabled society's racist norms.[3] No character in the novel chal-

lenges those norms directly. But Twain is not one of those characters, and none of them represents him. Rather, Twain makes those norms the object of his lacerating satire in order to push the reader to recognize and reject them. Out of respect for the care with which Twain crafted his characters' speech, as well as out of respect for his recognition of the role the word played in sustaining and normalizing racism, I have retained the book's original language in my discussion of it.[4]

For more than a century, many critics—Black as well as white—have treated the slur as if it were a part of Jim's name. It is not. Twain never used that appellation, and neither should we.

While racist preconceptions may have led some readers to mistakenly call Jim by a name Twain never used, antiracist impulses have led some to try to ban the novel in part because of the presence of this word or, in some cases, to rewrite the book by excising the racially charged language. These practices both dishonor the author and the history of racial oppression the book engages and distort readers' understanding of Jim and the world in which he lives.

Let me be clear: in my view, given the pain that the word inflicts there is no need to read the word aloud in the classroom. But neither should it be sanitized when it appears in books or be erased from the historical record.[5] The word is offensive. So, too, are slavery and racism. Twain used the word in his writing for the same reason that I do not say it: we both understand its destructive force. Keeping the word on the page helps convey the odious nature of both the world of the novel and the history that it reflects. We can no more hide from this painful word than we can from America's painful past. America has a racist history, but it also has an antiracist history—and Twain's work, in its original form, helps us understand that. Only if readers, teachers, and citizens confront the word and the racist worldview that under-girds it might the racist attitudes that it embodies and empowers be relegated to the past, paving the way for a future in which the word has no place.

Jim

INTRODUCTION

J IM ENTERED THE WORLD with the debut of Mark Twain's most celebrated novel, *Adventures of Huckleberry Finn*, in 1885.[1] A shrewd and self-aware enslaved man seeking his freedom in a world determined to keep him enslaved, he is also one of the first Black fathers in American fiction. He has been viewed as an emblem both of Mark Twain's alleged racism and of Twain's opposition to racism; a diminished character inflected by minstrelsy and a powerful challenge to minstrel stereotypes; a reason for banning *Huckleberry Finn* and a reason for teaching it. Jim has figured centrally in debates about the limits and potential of Black English. He has been Exhibit A in discussions of the risks and rewards of dramatic irony. He has been both an embarrassment and a source of pride for Black readers.

I argue in this book that Samuel Clemens, writing as Mark Twain, crafted Jim as a smart and enormously admirable man whose movements and behavior are constrained by his status as an enslaved person in a morally bankrupt society where human beings are regularly bought and sold as property. His companion Huck, the titular hero of the story and the book's narrator, does not see Jim that way. Nor does Huck recognize the moral failings of those around him—much as Sam Clemens had not condemned the world of his childhood when he himself was a child. But by the time Mark Twain wrote *Huckleberry Finn*, his understanding of that world had radically changed. His travels and his marriage into the abolitionist Langdon family helped spark his growing awareness of what was wrong with a world where people who thought of themselves as upstanding, God-fearing citizens could support and benefit from an indefensible status quo. Although *Huckleberry Finn* is supposedly narrated by a boy who, like young Sam Clemens, did not question the justice of the world in which he lived, the novel was written not by Huck but by Mark Twain the adult author who, by 1885, was ready to challenge norms that he had accepted as a child.*

Mark Twain was an accomplished author when he published this book, respected for both serious and humorous fiction and nonfiction written in standard English. But his decision to write *Huckleberry Finn* entirely in Huck's voice was startling and unprecedented: American letters had never met an "author" like Huck—an ebullient nonstop talker, a grade-school dropout who never managed to learn the niceties of proper grammar, a gifted liar who half-learned the half-baked pieties his guardians tried to instill in him, a simultaneously hilarious and humorless scamp who is oblivious to all that he misconstrues about the world around him. Ernest Hemingway claimed in 1935 that "all modern American literature comes from one book by Mark Twain called *Huckleberry Finn*," and Jorge Luis Borges averred that *Huckleberry Finn* "taught the whole American novel to talk."

---

* Throughout this book I will refer to "Sam Clemens" when discussing chapters of the author's life before he took the pen name of "Mark Twain" in 1863. From 1863 on, the dividing line between "Sam Clemens" and "Mark Twain" grows increasingly blurred, with the author signing letters as either "Sam" or "Mark," and being addressed by either name in person. In discussing the author's work, as well as his personal life after 1863, I will generally refer to him as "Mark Twain."

Huck—a child, as Twain put it, "with a sound heart and a deformed conscience"—is convinced that he is doing wrong when he acts in ways that the reader recognizes as right: violating the norms of his slaveholding society by trying to help his friend reach freedom. In the more than forty thousand books and articles written about the novel, Huck's language and crisis of conscience have figured prominently. But, with a few exceptions, Jim has generally gotten short shrift.

Jim has been hiding in plain sight. The first Black father in a novel by a white male American author, Jim has been disparaged, demeaned, and dismissed by many critics for more than a century. But he is more complex and multilayered than meets the eye. Paying him the attention that he deserves opens up new ways of understanding the history of race and racism in America. It shines a spotlight on the lives of the real individuals who shaped Twain's portrayal of him. And it offers distinctive insights into the challenges of representing Black intelligence, emotion, and creativity in a world that denied their existence—a challenge shouldered, not only by Twain himself, but also by scores of writers, Black and white, who followed. A biography of one of the most important Black lives in American letters deserves a place in a biography series devoted to "Black Lives."

This book examines Jim's origins, impact, and afterlives in seven interconnected sections.

Chapter 1: Contexts and Conditions probes the world of slavery in antebellum Missouri that Jim entered—one in which he enjoyed the same rights as his mistress's cows and chickens.[2] It was a world in which, as Twain notes in his autobiography, "the local pulpit taught us that God approved of [slavery], that it was a holy thing, and that the doubter need only look in the Bible if he wished to settle his mind—and then the texts were read aloud to us to make the matter sure."[3] It was a world in which enslaved people were prohibited from learning to read or write and therefore couldn't find out that there were verses in the Bible other than "Servants, obey thy masters."

It was a world in which slave catchers lurking along the Illinois shore made the possibility of escape highly dangerous and in which runaways were severely punished. In addition, anyone who helped slaves try to escape risked being sentenced to the state penitentiary. Although wanton cruelty was frowned on and nominally prohibited by law, it was common nonetheless: a slave, for instance, could receive up to thirty-nine lashes just for directing insulting language to a white person. An enslaved person's mobility, social interactions, speech, and deportment were greatly constrained in many other ways as well.

Slave traders were a familiar presence and coffles of slaves were a common sight in antebellum Missouri, a place where every enslaved person lived with the awful knowledge that someone they loved could be taken from them suddenly, at any time. It was a place where parents could be sold away from their children on a whim. Mark Twain was born into this world in 1835. Fifty years later, he would become the first white male writer to portray a Black slave determined to be a father—and a surrogate father—even to a white child. (This chapter builds on Terrell Dempsey's pioneering research on slavery in Hannibal, Missouri.)

Chapter 2: Myths and Models explores the cultural conversation about race that Twain entered when he created Jim as a character and the aspects of it that he subverted by creating Jim as he did. I begin by laying out the racist myths and stereotypes about Black people that were widely accepted in Twain's time, promulgated not only in popular culture but also in so-called scientific theories of the day. A view of African Americans as unintelligent, insensible to pain, and uncreative, dating at least back to Thomas Jefferson, was deployed to defend slavery before and during the Civil War; after the war these myths helped rationalize restrictive Black codes and segregation in the era of Jim Crow. In this chapter I describe eight individuals in Twain's life who prompted him to reject these racial myths: two enslaved men Twain knew well during his childhood, one of whom was a gifted storyteller and the other of whom introduced him to satire as a tool of social criticism; an erudite Black guide Twain met in Venice during his first European tour, who ran circles around all the other guides on the trip; a Black friend whose quick thinking and heroic actions prevented members of Twain's family from losing their lives in a carriage accident; the astute and talented Black butler in Twain's home in Hartford, Connecticut; the brilliant Black public intellectual whom Twain first met through his in-laws; a talented Black painter whose work Twain admired and promoted; and a formerly enslaved woman whose riveting story of being separated from her youngest child on the auction block and reunited with him after the war inspired Twain's first ex-tended use of Black vernacular speech in his writing. These in-dividuals blasted to smithereens the myth that Black people had no ability to think rationally, imagine creatively, or feel pain and grief, and each contributed in distinctive ways to Twain's charac-terization of Jim. In addition, three of them were fathers of daugh-ters who mattered deeply to them, as Twain himself was when he was writing the novel.

Chapter 3: The Debates examines controversies that have swirled around Jim since his debut. In one of the most antholo-gized essays written on the novel, Leo Marx wrote in the *American Scholar* in 1953 that "Jim has been made over in the image of a flat stereotype: the submissive stage-Negro," and ever since, many scholars have repeated the charge, seeing in Jim a caricatured racist stereotype created for the enjoyment of white audiences.[4]

In 1985, for example, Fredrick Woodard and Donnarae MacCann wrote in the *Mark Twain Journal* that "Twain's use of the minstrel tradition undercuts serious consideration of Jim's humanity beyond those qualities stereotypically attributed to the noble savage; and Jim is forever frozen within the convention of the minstrel darky."[5] But writers and scholars from Sterling Brown and Ralph Ellison to David Bradley, Jocelyn Chadwick, Robert Paul Lamb, Hilton Obenzinger, Forrest Robinson, David L. Smith, Ralph Wiley, and myself give Twain—and Jim—more credit. I build on this interpretive tradition in this chapter: every example cited to show that Jim embodies minstrel stereotypes, I contend, may instead be recognized as an example of his strategies of self-preservation and self-empowerment, and passages that allegedly ridicule him turn out instead to reveal his intelligence. This is not just a question of interpretation, for I argue that these passages are shaped by literary and cultural sources far beyond the racial (and racist) politics of minstrelsy.

The chapter also focuses on debates about Jim's speech, looking at the care Twain used in crafting Jim's words and the pains he took to differentiate them from the caricatured, made-up dialect one might hear in a minstrel show—echoing controversies surrounding Black vernacular speech to this day. Twain produced a novel in which characters with the most educated and elevated speech and the most impeccable grammar are the most morally reprehensible in the book. As I argue, Twain saw Black English as a viable mode of speech for expressing arguments, insights, and emotions in a range of registers. Jim's words, then, become a vehicle for Twain to upend entrenched racial hierarchies in the antebellum world where the novel is set and the post-Reconstruction world in which it was written and published.

Chapter 4: Jim's Version: An Interpretive Exercise is a response to the question of what Jim's story would be like if he had told it himself. *Huckleberry Finn* is narrated by Huck, and everything the reader sees is from Huck's angle of vision. But what did Jim think about it all? The chapter retells the story from Jim's perspective. Without adding anything that cannot be plausibly inferred from the book Twain wrote, this chapter explores the narrative through Jim's eyes, conveying emotions and ideas he likely felt and thought but couldn't afford to express. This section was indelibly shaped by the late Ralph Wiley's inspired yet unproduced screenplay *Spike Lee's Huckleberry Finn*, in which Huck's words—as Twain wrote them—provide the voiceover narration while the camera registers what is happening through Jim's eyes. I have done my best to retain Jim's characteristic manner of speaking throughout this section, on the level of both syntax and diction, exactly as Twain wrote it. I have not added any offensive racial epithet to the narrative at any point, nor have I cut any that appear in Jim's speech in the original, in keeping with Twain's commitment to realism.[6]

The novelist Percival Everett embarked on an analogous experiment in his virtuoso novel *James*, which appeared when this book was already in production.[7] Although the literate, erudite James that Everett presents *sounds* completely different from the Jim I present in this chapter, the two have much in common; they are, indeed, kindred spirits.

The final chapters explore Jim's afterlives in three contexts: on stage and screen, in translation, and in the high school classroom.

Chapter 5: Afterlives: Jim on Stage and Screen explores how thirteen Black actors interpreted Jim's character on stage and screen between 1920 and 2012. They include the longest reigning world light heavyweight champion of all time, a bodybuilder who held the title of the "world's most muscular man," and an African geology student studying in Moscow. As they pushed rafts down the Dnieper River in Ukraine, the Danube River in Romania, and the Sacramento, Ohio, and Mississippi Rivers in the United States, these actors brought to the role their own experiences with racism and their own distinctive insights into who Jim was and why he did what he did. Their portrayals of Jim were also shaped by the scripts and directors as well as by geopolitics and national ideologies. How did these actors variously develop, demean, deepen, diminish, and distort Jim in these plays and films? Did they present Jim as a smart and resourceful man with intelligence and agency, or was he cast as a stock figure from minstrelsy or the "plantation tradition" romanticizing the antebellum South? Was the racism of the world in which he lives presented or elided? As they inhabited and embodied Jim as a character, how did each of these actors contribute to Jim's life as a national and global touchstone for American racism and the portrayal of Black men on stage and screen?

Chapter 6: Afterlives: Jim in Translation analyzes how Jim has fared during his global travels from the nineteenth century to the present, exploring how translators have treated Jim in sixteen of the sixty-seven languages into which the novel has been translated: Arabic, Chinese, Czech, Danish, French, German, Hindi, Japanese, Korean, Norwegian, Persian, Portuguese, Russian, Slovenian, Spanish, and Swedish. How do these translations present his character? How do they render his speech? Some translators decided to eliminate portions of the book in which Jim figures prominently, dramatically changing the reader's understanding of his character in the process. Some have him say lines that Twain never wrote. The translators' choices reflect not only their understanding (or lack thereof) of Twain's satiric critique of his society but also dimensions of bigotry, ethnocentrism, and marginalization in the translators' own countries, along with their nations' anxieties related to religion and challenges to authority. An examination of their efforts to translate Jim can teach us valuable lessons about the dynamics of racism around the world.

Chapter 7: Afterlives: Jim in the High School Classroom examines some of the controversies involving Jim that have led *Huckleberry Finn* to be denounced as unsuitable for use in American high schools in more than twenty states over the past seven decades. Parents have charged that Jim is not the kind of role model they prefer for their children; that he is an embarrassing, inferior, childlike figure who perpetuates racial stereotypes; and that encountering him in the classroom is a painful experience for Black students. I argue that they are correct—if the book is taught as it is often taught.

No teacher should be forced to bring Jim into their classroom if they are not prepared to engage the history of American racism that informs the novel and that continues to derail American ideals of equality—or if they are not prepared to help students understand the irony of Twain's decision to satirize racism by telling the story through the eyes of a child too innocent to call out the flaws of the racist society in which he lives. Jim can be a powerful, transformative presence for students to encounter— but only if they are guided by teachers with the preparation and the confidence to deal with the thorny historical, literary, and social issues that the novel raises. Here, I concentrate on how students responded to Jim in the classrooms of two teachers who rose to this challenge: Ann Lew in a multiethnic, minority-majority public high school in San Francisco and John Pascal in a private Catholic boys' preparatory school in New Jersey, where nonwhite students make up about a third of the school. Although I do suggest in the Appendix some strategies that may be helpful to teachers (including ways of addressing the ubiquity of an offensive racial epithet in the book), my focus here is on the students' interesting and, indeed, sometimes rather startling responses to

Jim—an example of all we can gain by asking students and teachers to reckon with Jim and his world.

My focus in this book is on Jim in the novel Mark Twain published in 1885. Because Twain's novel has produced a host of spinoffs and satires, as well as more than a century of heated debate, it's worth saying what this book is not. First, limits of time and space prevent me from exploring the more than two dozen sequels and spinoffs of *Huckleberry Finn*. These include, in addition to Percival Everett's novel noted above, novels, short stories, poems, and plays by Gerry Brenner, E. E. Burke, Jon Clinch, Robert Coover, Tim DeRoche, Wil Haygood, Scott Kaiser, John Keene, Norman Lock, Gina Logan, Greg Matthews, Edward Morgan, Lee Nelson, Phong Nguyen, Nancy Rawles, Bernard Sabath, Sam Sackett, Martí Sales, John Seelye, Julie Smith, Mark Time, Dan Walker, David Walker, Robert Wells, Clement Wood, and Twain himself.[8]

Second, I do not deal with well-meaning but misguided expurgated versions of the novel by John Wallace or Alan Gribben (in which offensive epithets embodying the racism of the society are eliminated); and by the same token I do not deal with creative parodies of those versions such as the "Robotic *Huck Finn*," in which the word "*robot*" is used in every place where an offensive epithet appears and where a robot replaces Jim in the illustrations; or the "Zombie *Huck Finn*," in which Jim the human is replaced by Jim the zombie.[9]

Last, and most important, this is not a book about the question of whether Mark Twain was a racist. This somewhat reductive question is the least interesting and most narrow way to address Jim and to approach Twain's novel. I have traced the evolution of Twain's thinking about race elsewhere.[10] Suffice it to say that during his youth in Hannibal as well as his adulthood in Hartford and Elmira, New York, and during his travels around the world, Twain was exposed to what a centuries-old belief in white supremacy had birthed into America and the world. He began to question the legitimacy of that idea in his thirties and continued to do so for the rest of his life. Did he consistently challenge that belief and the bigotry it engendered? Did he succeed in eradicating all racist attitudes in his own life? Did he eliminate them in the entire body of his work as a writer? The answer to these questions is no.

Twain did go further in his writing and his life than most of his peers when it came to dismantling the underpinnings of racism in American society. But despite the distance he had traveled on this topic, he had his blind spots and lapses, his moments of insensitivity and failures of nerve; and he could, on occasion, be inattentive, sloppy, or not at the top of his game. For example, Twain (unlike his neighbor and sometime coauthor *Hartford Courant* editor Charles Dudley Warner) supported higher education for African Americans and put his money where his mouth was. Nonetheless, in 1907, when he went to Oxford to get an honorary degree and white Rhodes scholars consulted him about their decision to snub the first Black Rhodes scholar, Alain Locke, Twain failed to criticize them, claiming that it was their right to associate with whomever they wished.[11] Twelve years after *Huckleberry Finn* was published, Twain quipped that "there are many humorous things in the world; among them the white man's notion that he is less savage than the other savages."[12] Yet in some of his works (including some sequels Twain himself wrote to *Huckleberry Finn*), racist caricatures may be found. Indeed, one might argue that Twain wasn't above playing to the prejudices of his audiences now and then—as when he performed excerpts from *Huckleberry Finn* during his lecture tours that, taken out of the context of the book as a whole, could strike audiences as redolent of minstrelsy and win their approval in the process. And, of course, as Kerry Driscoll has shown in *Mark Twain among the Indians and Other Indigenous Peoples,* to a large extent Twain maintained a blind spot all his life when it came to racism toward Native Americans.[13] But these lapses and blind spots are not the subject of this book. Jim, the central Black character in the novel Twain published in 1885—and responses to him in Twain's time and ours—is.

This book is about Jim in *Huckleberry Finn:* who he was, how Mark Twain portrayed him, and how the world has responded to him. It endeavors to unseat some of the misconceptions and erroneous judgments that have impeded how we understand Jim. The persistence of a substratum of racist assumptions in our own time has helped prevent us from fully appreciating one of the most fascinating Black lives in American literature, a character many observers—Black and white—believe to be "not only the most noble character of the book but also" one of the first Black heroes in American fiction.[14]

CHAPTER 1

Contexts and Conditions

ONE TWENTY-FIRST CENTURY historian has called Jim "the most well known, albeit fictional, Missouri slave."[1] Who was Jim, and where did he come from?

When we meet Jim in *Huckleberry Finn*, he is living in St. Petersburg, a fictional village modeled on Hannibal, the northeast Missouri town on the Mississippi River in Marion County where Mark Twain grew up. Historians call the thirteen-county region that includes this county Little Dixie, since it was settled by migrants from the hemp- and tobacco-growing districts of Virginia, central Kentucky, and Tennessee who brought their slaves with them, creating a culture similar to that of the Upper South. Unlike slaveholding on the large cotton, rice, sugar, and indigo plantations of the Deep South, slaveholding in Missouri was on a small scale, with most households owning or renting a handful of slaves to raise wheat, corn, barley, rye, oats, flax, hemp, and fruit; tend hogs and cows; mind children; and do carpentry, cooking, cleaning, washing, gardening, and ironing. Jim's principal duty is handling the cattle.

We don't know where Jim came from originally—only that the Widow Douglas's sister, Miss Watson, brought him with her when she came to live with her sister some time before the Widow adopted Huck. But we know that when he was growing up, Jim knew his father and had lived with or near him when his father became ill and died. Jim had also lived with or near his grandmother, who shared her folk wisdom. As Albert Raboteau has observed, the "rich tradition of folk belief and practice" that the enslaved brought from Africa—such as "conjure, herbalism, ghost lore, witchcraft, and fortunetelling"—helped them make sense of some of the inexplicable phenomena life offered, including "illness, misfortune, and evil." It also offered some buffers against the psychological as well as physical assaults of a system in which enslaved people's humanity was denied and their collective agency was severely limited.[2] Both Black and white witnesses affirmed that individuals believed to possess special powers were familiar figures in antebellum slave communities in the South. As William Wells Brown, a formerly enslaved writer who grew up in Missouri, noted, it was common to find on a plantation at least one practitioner "who laid claim to be a fortune teller, and who was granted with more than common respect by his fellow slaves." Jim came to play that role in his community.[3]

The world where he gained this knowledge was actually one in which whites believed in signs and superstitions as fully as Black people did. Indeed, Jim's belief that it was bad luck to count things you cook for supper, see the moon over your left shoulder, handle a snakeskin, and shake tablecloths after sundown, as well as his conviction that a hairy chest was a sign that one would be rich, were all superstitions widely held among white people of the region as well as Blacks. These beliefs, along with the idea that there were witches who rode their victims at night, originated in Europe rather than Africa. (Indeed, the only folk belief in the book not of European origin is the idea of telling fortunes with a hairball from the stomach of an ox, a belief that has its roots in voodoo, a set of religious practices originating in West Africa.)[4]

But while these superstitions in the Mississippi River valley were shared by Blacks and whites, other dimensions of the spiritual worldview of enslaved people had distinctive African roots; these blended with Christian beliefs to form the folk religion that engaged the majority of enslaved people in the region, including Jim. For many people with African roots in the South, as Alexis Wells-Oghoghomeh notes, West African cosmological frameworks led many to believe in a world "animated by spirits and governed by relationships among the embodied, the formerly embodied, and the incorporeal . . . in which aspects of the known sense world interacted with and shaped invisible domains." Rather than ending in death, life continues in a spirit world; those in the spirit world have supernatural powers over the living, and the living have various obligations to the dead. These rituals aimed to supplicate the spirits of the dead to stop them from coming back to haunt the living. In some communities it was traditional to kill a white chicken "to offer 'a last good meal' for the deceased's spirit," or to kill a hog at a funeral "in order to satisfy the mourners and 'so that the spirit have plenty at the last.'" "Like their West African forebears," she notes, "enslaved southerners acknowledged the materiality of spirits," sometimes placing objects on the grave "to satisfy the spirit and keep it from following you back to the house." These beliefs help explain Jim's comment that he always did all that he could for dead people—so that, we can infer, they will not haunt the living.[5]

We know that before he was taken to the Widow Douglas's, Jim lived with his wife and two children in a small cabin, probably on his owner's farm. Like most cabins where enslaved people lived in Missouri, it would have been built of logs, with beds made of ticking filled with grass, straw, or corn husks placed on ropes stretched over a log base on the dirt floor.[6] It was in his cabin one day that Jim had ordered his four-year-old daughter, 'Lizabeth, to shut the door, only to find that she ignored him—twice. Infuriated, he punished her with a slap that sent her sprawling. But when the wind slammed the door with a loud "ker-*blam!*" and she never moved, Jim realized to his horror that scarlet fever had left her deaf. Ever since, he has been filled with remorse.[7]

Since Huck tells us—when he and Jim are on the river—that Jim hadn't been away from home before, we might presume that Jim previously lived nearby, although Huck did not know his owner. In any event, when Miss Watson brought Jim with her to live with the Widow Douglas, he was separated from his family. (His wife lives on a nearby farm; the location of his children is not specified.)

As an enslaved man in Missouri in the 1830s and 1840s, Jim would have had the same rights as his owner's cattle and would have been treated as just another kind of chattel, though the animals were not invited to attend religious services. The first time the enslaved people who lived in the household of the Widow Douglas and Miss Watson are mentioned, we learn that they are being called in for evening prayers, where Jim would have been exposed to a smattering of Bible verses. Enslaved people in the region recalled that the verses shared with them most frequently were "Servants, obey thy masters," "Thou shalt not steal," and variations on the theme that slavery was the will of God.[8] As Twain noted in his autobiography, local preachers argued that God approved of slavery.

Enslaved people accounted for a significant portion of the community's wealth and were taxed just as other property was taxed, with the revenue thus raised helping to fund state and local governments. In 1847, such assessments accounted for more than 10 percent of state taxes generated by Marion County.[9]

Although the whip and the lash were part of Missouri slaves' world, Jim does not experience either directly during the time that we know him.[10] Miss Watson, his owner, is not abusive. But she is as susceptible as any slaveholder in the town to the seductions of wealth, and when a slave trader offers her eight hundred dollars for Jim, she finds it hard to resist. Although like many Missouri slaves, Jim has an "abroad marriage"—one in which slaves and their spouses live in different households—he knows exactly where his wife lives, and presumably where his children live as well; Jim can't bear the thought of being sold, since that would mean further separation from them, perhaps forever. Miss Watson intended to sell him to a slave trader who was going to take him down the river to New Orleans into the heart of the hellish slavery of the Deep South. And so Jim takes off.

Jim is deeply aware of the precarity of his own and his family's condition as enslaved people, and he is determined to save himself and those he loves from the potential terrors that fate might hold for them. His principal goal in life—that which drives everything he does from the moment he realizes that Miss Watson is planning to sell him—is to seek his own freedom and that of his family. Jim's passionate pursuit of this goal comes from his awareness of the harm he and his family face by remaining enslaved. Given the intense shame Jim feels over having hit his daughter for not "minding" him before he realized she was deaf, the potential violence she might face while enslaved likely helped fuel his determination to secure her freedom, as well as that of her brother and mother.

As Twain once argued, slavery in Missouri was not "the brutal plantation article," but as his own recollections suggest, it was fairly brutal nonetheless. When Twain was ten, he had watched a white man strike and kill a slave with a piece of iron on one of Hannibal's main streets. "I knew the man had a right to kill his slave if he wanted to," Twain wrote, "& yet it seemed a pitiful thing & somehow wrong, though why wrong I was not deep enough to explain. . . . Nobody in the village approved of that murder, but of course no one said much about it." On another occasion he recalled the community's response to the death of a slave at the hands of a white man: "Everybody seemed indifferent about it as regarded the slave—though considerable sympathy was felt for the slave's owner, who had been bereft of valuable property by a worthless person who was not able to pay for it."[11] Testimony gathered from Missouri slaves amply attests to the harsh physical and psychological trauma they had to endure. Mary Armstrong recalls, for example, that her owner "whipped my little sister what was only nine months old, . . . jus' cause she cry like all babies do, an' it killed my sister." Emma Knight remembered that in the winter, "our feet would crack open from de cold and bleed." Her father was "put on a block and sold 'cause de master wanted money to buy something for de house."[12]

As Emma Knight found out, slave families could be casually separated when financial exigencies or whims (such as the desire for a new piece of furniture) made it convenient to sell off family members. Permanent family separations were often the result of such sales. Bill Simms remembers that his "oldest sister was sold on the block with her children. She sold for eleven hundred dollars, a baby in her arms sold for three hundred dollars. Another sold for six hundred dollars and the other for a little less than that. I have never seen her since."[13] As Twain himself noted, the slave trader was "loathed by everybody. He was regarded as a sort of human devil who bought and conveyed poor helpless creatures to hell—for to our whites and Blacks alike the Southern plantation was simply hell; no milder name could describe it."[14]

Even enslaved people owned by "good" masters could be sold away from their families, and as Terrell Dempsey notes, "respectable people gladly sold slaves" when they needed money.[15] John Quarles, Sam Clemens's favorite uncle and by all reports a kindly master, gave the son of a slave he had known from birth to his own son as a gift: John Quarles's son, Ben, sold Daniel Quarles's son, Harvey, for a piece of land. Harvey Quarles, whose father, Daniel, would be a model for Jim in *Huckleberry Finn,* was thereby separated from his family in Missouri and relocated to Texas. When Sam Clemens's father, John Marshall Clemens, traveled to Mississippi to collect an old debt, he found the financial straits of the Mississippi debtor so moving that (as he wrote home) he "could not have the conscience" to demand repayment. He had no qualms, however, about selling a slave he had brought with him. He sold Charley for about forty dollars' worth of tar—the same amount that the king and the duke get for Jim when they sell him in the novel. And when John Marshall Clemens won a verdict against a man named William Beebe who owed him money, he had the sheriff seize an enslaved nine-year-old girl and sell her at public auction to satisfy the judgment.[16] Jim's steely determination to buy or steal his wife and children out of slavery comes from living in this precarious world.

Slave traders were a familiar presence in Hannibal, where there was always a brisk market in slaves. Clay (Carrie) Smith, a slave from Hannibal, recalled that her aunt Harriet "was sold on de block down on Fourth Street right here in Hannibal." Indeed, slave trading regularly took place at Melpontian Hall—about four blocks from the house where the Clemens family lived—a building that also served as the place where the town voted on election day.[17]

Hannibal was part of a booming national slave-trading network whose workings are partially reflected in advertisements slave traders placed in the *Missouri Courier* while Sam Clemens worked there as a printer's apprentice. One slave trader named Joseph Dudding, for example, placed an ad that said, "50 Negroes wanted. The subscriber will at all times pay the highest prices in CASH for

"SALE OF SLAVES" NOTICE, April 9, 1858, Clay County, Missouri.
Shawshots/Alamy Stock Photo.

likely negroes. He may at all times be found in the city of Hannibal." Another slave dealer named Francis Davis, who advertised in
the newspaper Sam's brother Orion Clemens published, offered
"Cash for Negroes! I TAKE this method of informing the people

that I am prepared at all times to pay the highest cash prices for NEGROES, and can at all times be found at the stable of Shoot and Davis." A local livery barn served as the "headquarters for the slave trade" in Hannibal, according to a young man from Michigan named Franklin Harriman who took a job there. Enslaved people would be brought to the barn by their owners to be sold "the same as we would up North bring horses or cattle into town for sale," Harriman recalled. The local slave trader, William Perry Owsley, would look them over, jail them, and eventually "put handcuffs on them or chain them together and put them on board a boat going south & would go down to some southern state and dispose of them."[18]

It was a coffle of slaves like the one Harriman described that left such a lasting impression on Sam Clemens: "I vividly remember seeing a dozen Black men and women chained to one another, once, and lying in a group on the pavement, awaiting shipping to the Southern slave market. Those were the saddest faces I have ever seen." William Wells Brown, who was hired out by his master to be a waiter on a steamboat, describes how familiar the sight of a slave coffle was in Hannibal: "The boat took on board, at Hannibal, a drove of slaves, bound for the New Orleans market. They numbered from fifty to sixty, consisting of men and women from eighteen to forty years of age. A drove of slaves on a southern steamboat, bound for the cotton or sugar regions, is an occurrence so common, that no one, not even the passengers, appear[s] to notice it, though they clank their chains at every step."[19]

Families too poor to own slaves often rented them, garnering the social capital that came with having slaves in the household. "A little slave boy" named Sandy from the Eastern Shore of Maryland, for example, had been "brought away from his family and friends halfway across the American continent and sold" to a man in Hannibal, who then rented him to the Clemens family. He slept on a pallet on the floor in the Clemens's home. On at least one occasion, Clemens saw his father whip Sandy for some "trifling little blunders and awkwardnesses." (But when Sam Clemens recalled this incident and wrote it up in *Following the Equator*, his wife, Olivia [known as Livy], wrote in the margin, "I hate to have your father pictured as lashing a slave boy." Clemens response was to change *lash* to *cuff.* He told his wife, "It's out, and my father is whitewashed.") On another occasion, Clemens saw his father whip Jennie, a young enslaved woman he owned, with a cowhide after she had snatched the whip from his wife's hand, fearing a whipping herself.[20]

A Missouri slave named Charlie Richardson recalled, "We never had no jails. Your back was the jail. When you done something serious Marster Warren called in the 'whuppers' and they made your back bleed and then rubbed salt into the skin. After that they chained you to a tree and let you suffer." Wanton cruelty was frowned on and nominally prohibited by law, but it was common nonetheless. But as harsh as their treatment at the hands of local slaveowners might be, Missouri slaves were nonetheless terrified by the prospect of being sold farther south, where they knew it was common for slaves to be simply worked to death, as well as disciplined even more harshly by the lash.[21]

The world in which Jim lived in the 1830s and 1840s—the era when the novel is set—was one in which an enslaved person's mobility, social interactions, speech, and deportment were greatly constrained. When the first board meeting of the newly organized town of Hannibal met in 1839, one of its first acts was passing "An Ordinance Respecting Slaves, Free Negroes, and Mulattoes," mandating that "not more than five slaves or free Negroes or mulattoes could assemble at any one place at the same time within the Town of Hannibal, except in discharge of their duties to their masters, owners, or overseers." (The only exceptions were for worship services with a white minister or a Black minister who had the permission of the town's trustees.) The penalty for violating this "unlawful assembly" rule was thirty-nine lashes. The general assembly directed county courts to appoint patrols to "visit negro quarters, and other places suspected of unlawful assemblages of slaves." The patrols were allowed to give up to ten lashes to a slave found "strolling about from one plantation to another, without a pass from his master, mistress, or overseer." Free negroes were prohibited from entering the state.[22]

Up to thirty-nine lashes could be given to any Black person, enslaved or free, "for using insulting language" to a white person.[23] As justice of the peace in Hannibal, John Marshall Clemens was often charged with administering these punishments mandated by law. When Huck callously toys with Jim's very real grief and relief after the two are separated during the fog and then reunited, Jim's decision to shame and rebuke Huck by calling him "trash" is all the more remarkable, given the penalties that existed for insulting a white person.

In 1847, the Missouri General Assembly prohibited the education of Black people, free or enslaved. (Laws like this were partly in response to the literacy and intelligence of Nat Turner, who led a slave rebellion in Virginia that had sent shock waves across the country the previous decade.) Anyone teaching a Black person to read was to be fined five hundred dollars and imprisoned for six months.[24] Jim is subjected to an enforced ignorance, but his lack of education should not be confused with a lack of intelligence: time and time again, as Huck reads to him, Jim demonstrates that he is more than capable of not just comprehension but bringing unexpected insights to the texts Huck shares.

Jim is also aware of the behavior expected of him and of behavior likely to summon trouble. For example, he knows the value of a nickel and is delighted to pocket the nickel that Huck and Tom leave in payment for the candles that they steal (an anachronism, by the way: nickels were not made until 1866). But Jim also knows that a slave with a nickel is immediately suspect: he needs an excuse for how he came by it. It occurs to him that absent a plausible excuse, a wildly over-the-top implausible one might do instead. For that reason, he concocts the story of being ridden by witches and chased by the devil. His story, for all its strangeness, conforms to stereotypes common among whites about the superstitious nature of enslaved people. (Two or three decades after the action of the novel takes place, members of the Ku Klux Klan would play on these stereotypes by using sheets to disguise themselves as ghosts as they terrorized Black communities at night.) Instead of potentially being whipped for theft, Jim is lionized in the slave community as a storyteller and paid for telling and retelling his story again and again; in short, he has converted himself into a creative artist who gets paid for telling an engaging story—like Mark Twain himself.

Missouri's proximity to free states made efforts to escape bondage not uncommon, and Jim may well have been aware of Hannibal slaves who had headed east or north to freedom. He would also have been aware of the risks involved. During the 1840s the Missouri General Assembly instituted a reward system for any citizen who apprehended a runaway slave, defined as any slave found more than twenty miles from their home or place of employment. The reward for slaves captured within Missouri's borders was $25 in 1840—the equivalent of about $900 today. Slaves captured within the county from which they escaped or in adjoining counties brought a reward of $5 to $10 (between $180 and $360 today). Rewards like these led people like the husband of Mrs. Judith Loftus in the novel and his friends to avidly hunt for Jim. The rewards for capturing a runaway Missouri slave out-

From One **Thousand** Dollars
REWARD!

RANAWAY from the subscribers living 12 miles West of Springfield, Greene county, Missouri, on the night of the 21st ult., two negroes described as follows:

ARCHA, belonging to James L. Alexander, is a molatto man, some 24 years old, or upwards, some 5 feet 6 inches high, has grey eyes, and plays the fiddle well.

JOHN, belonging to John A. Miller, is rather a dark complected man, some 28 years old, about 6 feet high, heavy built, Weighs some 180 pounds, has rather a positive way of affirming or denying.

We will give the following rewards for the apprehension and delivery of said negroes to us in Greene county, Mo., or if confined in any jail so that we get them back to Missouri, that is to say: Twenty dollars each, if taken in Greene county, Missouri, 50 dollars each, if taken out of Greene county and in the State of Missouri, and 250 dollars each, if taken in a free State or Territory and delivered as above, and $500 for legal conviction and after sentence to the Penitentiary, for the white man who has given said negroes free papers or aided in getting them off.

    JAMES L. ALEXANDER, by his
    Agent, **S. C. NEVILL,**
    J. A. MILLER.

November 4, 1854.

Notice of reward for capture and delivery of runaway slaves, Greene County, Missouri. Used with permission of the Greene County Archives and Records Center, Springfield, Missouri.

side Missouri were even greater: $100 if the slave was over the age of twenty, $50 if the slave was under twenty (the equivalent of $3,600 and $1,800, respectively, today).[25] This reward structure helped make the Illinois shore a risky and dangerous destination for runaways and helps explain why Jim does not just cross the river from Jackson's Island into Illinois. Even without these rewards, however, anti-Black hostility was rife in Illinois. In 1848, 70 percent of Illinois voters expressed their approval of an amendment to the state constitution that "made it illegal for African Americans, slave or free, to settle permanently in Illinois."[26] These attitudes were encoded in the Black Law of 1853, which formally made it illegal for Blacks to enter and stay in Illinois, mandating that "a Negro could be seized by a sheriff and his services auctioned off" for a time before he was expelled from the state.[27]

Some Missouri runaways hid out in the woods, islands, and smaller rivers in the area, living off the land as Jim does when he first arrives at Jackson's Island. Having run off without a plan, Jim is open to the idea of improvising one with Huck. Runaways who got caught were sometimes subjected to public whippings to scare others off from similar behavior. They were also sometimes tortured in private. Clemens had a childhood memory of hearing the "loud and frequent groans" of a runaway slave captured in Florida, Missouri, "by six men who took him to an empty cabin, where they threw him on the floor and bound him with ropes." In 1847, when Clemens was eleven, a runaway slave who belonged to a man named Neriam Todd swam across the river and hid in the swampy thickets of Sny Island, on the Illinois side of the Mississippi. A boy Twain knew named Benson Blankenship found him and brought him scraps of food instead of giving him up for a reward. (Bence Blankenship's behavior would become a model for aspects of Huck's behavior in *Huckleberry Finn*.) Some woodchoppers chased the man into a part of the swamp called Bird

Slough, where he disappeared; several days later, Sam Clemens and a few of his friends who had crossed the river to fish and forage for berries found his mutilated body. Yet courage persisted in the face of cruelty and danger. Indeed, slaves escaped with just enough frequency that insurance companies advertised policies to help protect slave owners from the financial loss involved.[28]

Huck may be only a child, but he is a white child and as such can offer Jim a small measure of protection by posing, at various points, as his owner. As it turns out, Jim can offer Huck things he desperately needs as well: care and companionship, affection and acceptance, and the kind of tough, loving discipline only a parent can give but that Huck never got from his own alcoholic, abusive father.

Huck actually risks more than being called "a low down abolitionist" when he decides to go on the run with Jim. "In those old slave-holding days," Clemens recalled,

> the whole community was agreed as to one thing—the awful sacredness of slave property. To help steal a horse or a cow was a low crime, but to help a hunted slave, or feed him or shelter him, or hide him, or comfort him, in his troubles, his terrors, his despair, or hesitate to promptly betray him to the slave-catcher when opportunity offered was a much baser crime, & carried with it a stain, a moral smirch which nothing could wipe away.

The penalty for helping a slave to escape was a five-to-ten-year sentence at the state prison. Indeed, Sam Clemens's father served on a jury that sent three abolitionists from Illinois to the state penitentiary. In that trial—the biggest criminal case in Marion County—the judge had instructed the jury that even if the defendants who had enticed the slaves to run away had not planned to keep the slaves themselves—even if they simply intended to "steal" the slaves in order to give them their freedom—nonetheless both they and the runaways were guilty of theft. As Dempsey notes, "It was a twisted but logical idea—property could own itself. A runaway slave was stealing from his master to give himself to himself." This context informs Jim's comment in chapter 8 that "I owns mysef, en I's wuth eight hund'd dollars." In addition to violating various laws involving slavery, by stealing himself Jim was depriving his mistress of valuable property. Certain punishment awaited any Missouri slave who was returned to his master after escaping to Iowa or Illinois; he was likely to be whipped, jailed, and possibly sold.[29]

Jim had not planned to try to escape: Miss Watson may "peck on" him all the time and treat him "pooty rough," but he occupied a position of respect—even celebrity—among his fellow slaves. Only the prospect of being sold led him to "run off." But then an unfortunate coincidence occurs: Huck Finn disappears the same night that Jim runs off and is presumed murdered. While hiding under the shavings in a nearby copper shop the day he escapes, Jim overhears some terrifying gossip: the town thinks that he is the one who killed Huck. The fact that Jim finds himself likely to be accused of murder makes it all the more imperative for him to disappear. Missouri law stipulated that any slave who lifted his hand against a white person—except in self-defense—would be punished with up to thirty-nine lashes.[30] Murdering a white person was a capital offense, and Missouri law did not allow slaves to testify on their own behalf in court.

When Twain's novel ends, Jim is free because Miss Watson sets him free in her will. What would a Black man in his position in Missouri at the time have been likely to encounter? Presumably, Jim would have had to return to St. Petersburg to get his certificate of freedom or free papers from the local authority that had executed Miss Watson's will. Without such papers, he could not prove that he was free and could be sold and reenslaved by anyone. But he was outside Missouri when he found out that he was free, and in the 1840s, Missouri prohibited the entry of free Black people into the state unless they were in the service of a white man or just passing through. If Jim could have somehow obtained legal evidence that he was free before he returned to Missouri (and it is unclear how he might have done that), *and* if the law barring free Blacks from immigrating to the state were not invoked (he might have had to have either Huck or Tom claim that he was their servant), Jim would have had to get a license from the state of Missouri if he wanted to remain there for any period of time.[31]

Getting a license would not have been easy. To get such a license, he would have had to "produce satisfactory evidence" that he was "of good character and behavior." Presumably the doctor he helped when Tom was wounded would have been happy to provide that. But Jim also would have had to post a bond of up to a thousand dollars as "security for good behavior," an astronomical sum effectively designed to deter applicants. A Hannibal ordinance would have required him to pay an annual fee of five dollars, a cash bond in addition to producing "evidence of good moral character and behavior" to get the license. Free Black people who failed to have a license could face up to twenty lashes and fines up to one hundred dollars, as well as arrest, jail time, and expulsion from the state. (Sam Clemens showed his awareness of the license law as early as 1855, when he included in a letter to the Muscatine *Tri-Weekly Journal* the story of a free young Black woman who "had entered the State without a license, and was passing as a slave to avoid the consequences of this breach of the law.")[32]

But the license was only one of the problems Jim would face when he returned: even more serious was the fact that he was an alleged murderer, a possible felon who had allegedly committed a crime that was punishable by death and then fled the state. The only way Jim could prove his innocence would be to produce Huck. A living, breathing Huck is Jim's only alibi. Jim would need to produce Huck himself to avoid being jailed and executed— or perhaps he might produce Tom Sawyer, who could testify to Huck's being alive. Even if Jim could legally prove his freedom, his testimony that Huck was actually alive would be no good to him in Hannibal: free Blacks, like slaves, couldn't testify in Missouri courts.

Jim had told Huck that he planned to purchase his wife and children as soon as he was free himself. It is unclear whether they were in or near St. Petersburg/Hannibal or somewhere else. The person who owned them may or may not have been willing to sell them. Jim's plan to hire an abolitionist to steal them if that were the case was risky to say the least. The precarity of his position is underlined by the experience of an enslaved man in Missouri who would have been his contemporary—a man named Dred Scott.

Dred Scott was born in Southampton County, Virginia, around 1799 and was taken by his owner, Peter Blow, to Alabama, then later to Missouri in 1830. When Blow died, Scott was purchased by Dr. John Emerson, a surgeon in the US Army, who took Scott with him to the Wisconsin Territory, where, under the Missouri Compromise, slavery was outlawed. Scott also accompanied Emerson to posts in Illinois and Fort Snelling, an area that would become Minnesota—also a place that prohibited slavery. In Fort Snelling, Scott married Harriet Robinson, who was also enslaved; the two began to raise a family. In 1843 Emerson died, and Scott and his family became the property of his widow, Irene Emerson. Scott tried many times to purchase his own freedom from Emerson's widow, but she refused.

In 1846 both Scott and Harriet decided to sue for their freedom in court on the basis of their having lived for significant periods in a territory and a state where slavery was outlawed, citing a statute that said that any person taken to a free territory became free and could not be reenslaved on returning to a slave state. The case moved through the courts for the next decade, finally landing on appeal at the Supreme Court. There, in a notorious decision penned in 1857 by Chief Justice Roger B. Taney, the court held that Scott was not a US citizen under the Constitution and for that reason not entitled to sue for freedom in federal court. Despite Scott's residence in a free state and territory, the court ruled that he had never been free and had to remain enslaved. Furthermore, the court ruled that Congress had exceeded its authority over private property when it crafted the antislavery provision of the Missouri Compromise. Scott and his wife were returned as slaves to Irene Emerson, who had remarried; she and her new husband, an abolitionist, returned the Scott family to one of the adult children of Scott's original owner, who granted them their freedom two months after the court ruling in May 1857. Dred Scott died a year later, in 1858.[33]

How might Jim have known enough about the work of abolitionists to think he'd hire one to steal his children if their master wouldn't sell them? He would probably have been aware of the Reverend Dr. David Nelson, the founder of the First Presbyterian Church of Hannibal, where Sam Clemens attended Sunday school as a boy. Nelson, who was open about his opposition to slavery, was forced to flee Hannibal for Illinois after violence arose against abolitionists' activities.[34] (As Twain would write in "A Scrap of Curious History": "In that day, for a man to speak out openly and proclaim himself an enemy of negro slavery was simply to proclaim himself a madman. For he was blaspheming against the holiest thing known to a Missourian, and could not be in his right mind.")[35]

Whether or not Jim's plan to purchase his wife and children or have an abolitionist steal them panned out, if they had remained in Missouri decades after the action of the novel, all of them would have been freed on January 11, 1865, when the Missouri state convention passed an emancipation ordinance that immediately freed all slaves in the state. Their freedom beyond Missouri's borders was guaranteed later that month, on January 31, when the US Congress passed the Thirteenth Amendment banning slavery.

Jim and his wife probably would have been cheered by the fact that, although their marriage during slavery was not recognized by law, in 1865 the Missouri General Assembly passed legislation that allowed them to be married legally in front of a justice of the peace. The clerk would note the names of 'Lizabeth and Johnny as well, legitimizing their children in the process.[36] It is likely that they would have been delighted two years later when Missouri ratified the Fourteenth Amendment, which guaranteed that they would have the same rights as whites under the law. And they would have welcomed the Fifteenth Amendment, passed three years after that, in 1870, which gave Jim the same right to vote that white men had. Jim and his wife had never been taught to read or write, and neither had 'Lizabeth or Johnny, since teaching slaves to read had long been against the law. But Jim might well have gotten friends and neighbors who could read and write to teach him and his family, his appetite whetted by those afternoons when Huck read to him on the raft.

As he sat on his front porch surrounded by people he loved and watched the sun set over the hills, Jim might have sighed contentedly in those early days: he was free, and his family was free. And freedom, after all, meant everything. Or did it?

The Radical Republicans who had dominated Missouri's Constitutional Convention in 1865 passed a new constitution that freed the state's slaves and gave them civil rights. It also excluded ex-Confederates from voting and holding civil offices. But in the election of 1870, the former Confederates won back the right to vote. A new state constitution soon mandated segregated schools. White people in Hannibal lost no opportunity to remind Black people that they didn't really count for much, free or not. Fannie Barrier Williams was the sister-in-law of the first Black teacher hired at the three-room school for Black children at 924 Rock Street in Hannibal founded in 1870, called the Douglasville School. Williams had grown up in Brockport, New York, and when she was twenty-one, she decided to head south with the idealistic goal of helping Black children. But the intimidation, physical assaults, and myriad forms of discrimination she encountered in Hannibal gave her an education she never expected. Looking back on her time there years later, she wrote that until she went to Hannibal,

I had never been reminded that I belonged to an "inferior" race. . . . No one but a colored woman, reared and educated as I was, can ever know what it means to be brought face to face with conditions that fairly overwhelm you with the ugly reminder that a certain penalty must be suffered by those who, not being able to select their own parentage, must be born of a dark complexion.

What a shattering of cherished ideals![37]

Barrier left the town after two years, but her encounter with racism and discrimination in Hannibal prompted her to embark on a lifelong fight for equality that would make her one of the most prominent civil rights leaders in the country.[38]

If Jim had stayed in Missouri, he and his family would also have lived in the shadow of the many lynchings in the state during the decade following the Civil War. For example, George Bryan was lynched in Livingston County in 1873, Edmund Moore in

Charleston County in 1875, and Raphael Williams in Platte County in 1876.[39] (Mark Twain was deeply disturbed by the proliferation of lynchings and at one point planned to write a book about them before abandoning the idea.)[40]

Jim and his family would have watched rights they had won during Reconstruction eviscerated during the following decade, when the Supreme Court struck down the Civil Rights Act and when rights that had been guaranteed by the Fourteenth and Fifteenth Amendments were "practically of no force or effect," as Frederick Douglass noted in 1880 in a speech he gave in Elmira, New York, when Twain was in that city.[41] In the 1890s and early 1900s, Jim would have seen his grandchildren subjected to Jim Crow laws that mandated "whites only" railroad cars, schools, waiting rooms, water fountains, hospitals, morgues, cemeteries, and even Bibles for witnesses in courtrooms. Jim and his wife would not have lived to see the indignities their children and grandchildren would continue to suffer well into the twentieth century.

Those indignities are eloquently documented in the display cases in Jim's Journey: The Huck Finn Freedom Center, a Black history museum opened four blocks from the Mark Twain Boyhood Home in 2013 by Faye Dant, herself the descendant of enslaved people in the state, and in *Hannibal's Invisibles*, a book Dant published in 2024.[42]

The museum tells the story of Daniel Quarles, a man crucial to Sam Clemens's becoming the storyteller he grew to be. It tells the story of other families with roots in slavery, such as that of Dant herself. The museum shares the history of Hannibal's segregated restaurants, waiting rooms, funeral homes, and American Legion posts. It displays scores of photos of the small, proud segregated Douglass High School—close to the old Douglasville School site— that gave generations of Hannibal's Black children the skills to make their way in a world run by whites who assumed they'd never amount to very much. (Douglass graduates proved them wrong by becoming outstanding teachers, doctors, and lawyers; talented musicians and athletes; officers in the military; and successful businesspeople—even the deputy librarian and chief operating officer of the Library of Congress.) The museum also tells the story of how, at a time when African Americans were classified as inferior specimens of humanity by pseudoscientists and so-called educators, Mark Twain's awareness of Black individuals of courage and talent impelled him to challenge this characterization in fiction, nonfiction, quips, quotes, and unpublished meditations that he wrote from the 1870s until his death.

Dant's book, *Hannibal's Invisibles*, filled with photographs of Hannibal's Black past, tells the story of two brothers who served in the only African American infantry division to see combat in Europe during World War II, only to find that the GI Bill's promise of educational training turned out to be for "whites only" in their hometown. She also tells the story of Hannibal resident Fannie Griffin, who trained at the respected Homer G. Phillips Hospital in St. Louis only to find that "Black nurses were not welcome in Hannibal hospitals." Jim's descendants would have found—as Faye Dant herself did—that they had to sit in a segregated balcony in the local movie theater, that they wouldn't get served at a number of local eateries, and that they could skate at the local rink only on "Negro Skate Nite."

Dant tells the story of people who lived their lives under the long shadow of slavery and Jim Crow, who were constrained but not crushed by the racism they had to negotiate on a daily basis; of people who, in the face of daunting challenges, established a supportive community that helped its members survive and, in many cases, thrive. It's the story of parents employed by the town's white families as domestics, laundresses, yardmen, janitors, and chauffeurs who managed to care for their own children with devotion and determination, advocate for them, and help guide them to careers in medicine, law, education, business, and other fields. It's the story of people who had to endure endless small and large humiliations and insults—such as the father who, when asked by his child why he allowed white people to call him "son" and "boy," responded, "I do this so we can eat." But it is also the story of people who lived, learned, worked, and played in spite of those humiliations and insults and who created self-contained neighborhoods to which they could retreat with dignity and without fear.

Jim's Journey: The Huck Finn Freedom Center and *Hannibal's Invisibles* both foreground a chapter of Hannibal's past that until recently had been erased or ignored. The story of Hannibal's Black residents was not a story that "America's Hometown" had much of an interest in preserving. "America's Hometown" celebrated *Tom Sawyer* and whitewashed fences but disregarded the Mark Twain who was a critic of racism—including the racism of his hometown—and eliminated most physical traces that remained of the Black community that had lived in Hannibal continuously from the time of slavery to the present, a community that had shaped Mark Twain's work in indelible ways.

Jim, unlike Black Hannibal, has not been forgotten or ignored. But, like the individuals whose stories emerge in Dant's museum and book, he has not received his due. He has been stereotyped and disparaged. He has been dismissed as a "poor role model," a buffoon, a minstrel clown, an embarrassment. Like many of the Black people in Twain's world and our own, he has been gratuitously insulted and maligned. He deserves better. So do we.

CHAPTER 2

———

Myths and Models

RACIST BELIEFS in America characterizing African Americans as inferior to whites date back at least to Thomas Jefferson, who had conjectured in *Notes on the State of Virginia* (1785) that Blacks were less capable than whites at using reason, feeling grief, and exercising their imagination.[1] The idea that Black people were unintelligent, insensible to pain, and uncreative became increasingly entrenched in American culture as slaveholders used it to justify slavery. After the Civil War the widespread persistence of attitudes such as these garnered support for Black codes and segregation.[2] These myths and stereotypes about Black people dominated not only popular culture but also so-called scientific theories about race.

These racist views pervaded Mark Twain's society for the entirety of his life. Indeed, Huck Finn buys into all of them in the novel that bears his name, as we will see, paralleling Twain's own beliefs through his adolescence and early adulthood.[3] But during the years leading up to *Huckleberry Finn*, personal encounters with a number of Black individuals made clear to Twain the distance between those myths and stereotypes and reality, prompting him to challenge and subvert both as he crafted his most famous Black character. ("What is the most rigorous law of our being?" Twain asked in 1887. "Growth. No smallest atom of our moral, mental, or physical structure can stand still a year. . . . In other words, we change—and must change, constantly, and keep on changing as long as we live.")[4]

Throughout his life Mark Twain often found that prejudices held by those around him toward specific ethnic groups or races dissolved when he got to know individuals belonging to those groups. For example, as a child, Sam Clemens imbibed Hannibal's negative stereotypes of Jews and viewed them as proper objects of scorn; Sam and his friends even chased and threw stones at the two little Levin boys—the only Jewish children in town.[5] But some years later on the Comstock Lode in Nevada, Clemens met a brilliant and public-spirited Jewish engineer and inventor named Adolph Sutro and was so impressed by the man that he permanently revised his view of Jews.[6] As he wrote a friend in 1885, "Twenty years ago I knew Adolph Sutro well (of Sutro Tunnel)—a fine, manly beautiful character; and I have always found something of Sutro in all the Jews whom I have personally known since; and part of Sutro is sufficient equipment for an average man."[7] As a result of this personal experience, Twain rejected his early prejudices and became a staunch advocate for the Jews.[8]

Twain's personal experience often led him to challenge bigotry that was widely accepted by those around him. In San Francisco in the 1860s, for example, he watched the police ignore gratuitous violence directed against innocent Chinese and also heap abuse on the Chinese themselves. Seeing this led Twain to criticize the police and write with sympathy about the plight of the unoffending foreigners (a decision that incurred the ire of the police and made it prudent for him to leave the city).[9] Whether he was meeting a Jew whose character belied the anti-Semitic beliefs his society widely accepted or encountering instances of Chinese men unjustly persecuted for the color of their skin,

Twain's inclination—at least from his thirties on—was to allow what he saw and heard with his own eyes and ears to trump stereotypes widely accepted by those around him, remaining always open to the idea that we grow and change, and "keep on changing as long as we live."

A similar dynamic characterized his response to the prevalent myths and stereotypes about Black people—myths and stereotypes he would devote a substantial body of work to dismantling. Those stereotypes—and the personal encounters that undermined them for Mark Twain—are the subject of this chapter.[10]

The Myth of Black Mental Inferiority

In 1833, in an antiabolitionist tract published in New York titled *Evidence against the Views of the Abolitionists, Consisting of Physical and Moral Proofs, of the Natural Inferiority of Negroes*, Richard H. Colfax averred that "the acknowledged meanness of the negroe's [*sic*] intellect . . . renders it improper and impolitic, that he should be allowed the privileges of citizenship in an enlightened country."[11] In 1839 Samuel George Morton's well-known and (at the time) respected *Crania Americana* claimed to offer evidence that Blacks had smaller brains than whites.[12] The noted physician Samuel A. Cartwright reiterated the "smaller brains" theory to the Medical Association of Louisiana in 1851.[13] And in 1856 surgeon Josiah Clark Nott arranged to have portions of French theorist Arthur de Gobineau's thousand-page *Essai sur l'inégalité des races humaines* [*Essay on the Inequality of the Human Races*] translated into English. A founding text in the tradition of what is now called "biological racism," Gobineau's treatise was published that year in the United States with an appendix by Nott, including a section that argued that Blacks had developed abnormal physical traits to compensate for their stupidity.[14]

In the United States, the "stupidity" myth was promulgated

in such works as *Southern Institutes; or, An Inquiry into the Origin and Early Prevalence of Slavery and the Slave-Trade* (1858) by Louisiana attorney George S. Sawyer, which asserted that "the social, moral and political as well as the physical history of the negro [*sic*] race . . . furnishes the most undeniable proof of their mental inferiority."[15]

These ideas represented the conventional wisdom in the world in which Twain grew up, pervading medical science, history, and the received wisdom of white American and European scholars, doctors, and professionals. But on his first trip abroad in 1867, Twain would meet a Black person who was clearly superior to all the white people he had ever met in the same line of work. Twain would write about this man in the book that came out of that trip, *The Innocents Abroad* (1869).

While a Grand Tour of Europe had been the prerogative of elites for more than a century—a monthslong trip giving a rich young man an aesthetic, cosmopolitan education—the nation's first grand European tour for a group of middle-class, ordinary Americans took place in 1867. Mark Twain had the good fortune to go along on the *Quaker City* as resident scribe, sending regular reports home to the *Daily Alta California*, the *New York Herald*, and the *New York Tribune*. Throughout the trip he voiced a steady patter of complaints about the stupidity, arrogance, and irritating manner of all the tour guides the group met. Each of the guides in Gibraltar, for example, inflicted on the tourists "a tiresome repetition of a legend that had nothing very astonishing about it, even in the first place." In Paris, their guide "was always hungry; he was always thirsty; he could not pass a restaurant; he looked with a lecherous eye on every wine shop," and "he was always wanting us to buy things. On the shallowest pretenses he would inveigle us into shirt stores, boot stores, tailor shops, glove shops" where the shopkeepers paid him "a percentage of the sale." The guides in Paris, Twain wrote, "deceive and defraud every American" who goes there for the first time. His ire only increased as the trip progressed. "Perdition catch all the guides," he vented in Genoa, where the guide showed them "the birthplace of Columbus" only to confess after the tourists stood in silent awe for fifteen minutes that it was actually "the birthplace of Columbus' grandmother." In Milan, Twain complained about the fractured and incomprehensible "guide-English" that "make[s] life a burden to the tourist." The guides' "tongues are never still. . . . They interrupt every dream, every pleasant train of thought with their tiresome cackling." But then in early August 1867, they arrived in Venice.[16]

Here in Venice, Twain tells us that whenever he encountered a painting that genuinely appealed to him, "in every single instance the guide has crushed out my swelling enthusiasm with the remark, 'It is nothing—it is of the Renaissance.'"

I did not know what in the mischief the Renaissance was, and so I always had to simply say "Ah! So it is—I had not observed it before."

I could not bear to be ignorant before a cultivated negro, the offspring of a South Carolina slave. But it occurred too often for even my self-complacency, did that exasperating, "It is nothing—it is of the Renaissance." I said at last:

"Who is this Renaissance? Where did he come from? Who gave him permission to cram the Republic with his execrable daubs?"

We learned, then, that Renaissance was not a man; that renaissance was a term used to signify what was at best but an imperfect rejuvenation of art. The guide said that after Titian's time and the time of the other great names we had grown so familiar with, high art declined; then it partially rose again—an

inferior sort of [painter] sprang up, and these shabby pictures
were the work of their hands. . . .

Twain praises the guide's knowledge, skill, and style, which stand
out all the more in contrast to the insufferably ignorant and rude
previous guides:

> The guide I have spoken of is the only one we have had yet
> who knew any thing. He was born in South Carolina, of slave
> parents. They came to Venice while he was an infant. He has
> grown up here. He is well educated. He reads, writes, and
> speaks English, Italian, Spanish, and French with perfect
> facility; he is a worshipper of art and thoroughly conversant
> with it; knows the history of Venice by heart and never tires of
> talking of her illustrious career. He dresses better than any of
> us, I think, and is daintily polite. Negroes are deemed as good
> as white people in Venice, and so this man feels no desire to go
> back to his native land. His judgment is correct.[17]

One would be hard pressed to find as admiring a description of
any Black person by any white writer at this time.

When Twain published this in *The Innocents Abroad* in 1869,
this section was the longest passage he had written up to this point
about a "negro." The terse four words with which this passage
concludes sum up the travesty of the ideology of white superiority. The Black guide in Venice is not "as good as" any of the white
guides Twain has encountered on the trip: he is vastly superior
to them. His very existence—the child of two South Carolina
slaves—made the "stupidity" myth dissolve into thin air.

Five months after his account of the erudite Black man in
Venice appeared in print, Twain became reacquainted with another extremely intelligent Black man: author, editor, publisher,

and abolitionist Frederick Douglass. Twain's father-in-law, Jervis Langdon, had aided the formerly enslaved Douglass on his flight to freedom, and Douglass had remained a family friend. It is not clear when Twain and Douglass first met, but when they ran into each other, probably in Boston in December 1869, they were both very glad to see each other again. Twain wrote to his fiancée, Livy: "Had a talk with Fred Douglas [sic] to-day, who seemed exceedingly glad to see me—& I certainly was glad to see him, for I do so admire his 'spunk.'")[18]

In the years that followed, particularly during the decade when he wrote *Huckleberry Finn*, the financial support Twain gave to Black students in American universities, including Warner T. McGuinn, one of the first Black law students at Yale, provides further evidence that he had thoroughly rejected the myth of Black mental inferiority.[19] It was not a universal perspective, even among his avowedly liberal peers. Some influential friends of Twain's, such as *Hartford Courant* editor Charles Dudley Warner, argued that higher education for African Americans encouraged idleness among them.[20] Twain disagreed.

Twain may have met the brilliant Black guide in Venice and the extraordinary Frederick Douglass during the decade before he began writing *Huckleberry Finn*, but he didn't need to mine memories like these to find a model of Black intelligence: he had daily contact with a tremendously smart Black man during the years he was writing the novel. This man was also the person to whom Twain read chapter drafts as he worked on the book.

George Griffin began to work for the Clemens family in their Hartford home some time before the end of 1874 and would remain with them until the summer of 1891, when financial woes forced the family to close the house and move to Europe to save on living costs.[21] Griffin was nominally their butler, although he was much more than that: he was Twain's sounding board, billiard companion, and literary adviser. Although he had a wife and a Hartford home of his own, most of the time when the Clemens family was in Hartford, Griffin stayed in a room off the third-floor billiard room where Twain did all of his writing during the autumn, winter, and spring (in summer the family would relocate to Elmira, New York). Twain often commented on Griffin's intelligence, noting that "he had a remarkably good head" and "an acute financial eye," both of which would enable him to become a relatively wealthy man at a time when Twain himself and many of his peers were in deep financial trouble. Twain called Griffin "smart and diligent," "shrewd" and "wise," resourceful, and quick-thinking. "There was nothing commonplace about George," Twain wrote.[22]

Twain's lengthiest description of Griffin appears in "A Family Sketch," written in the early 1900s:

> George was an accident. He came to wash some windows, and remained half a generation. He was a Maryland slave by birth; the Proclamation set him free, and as a young fellow he saw his fair share of the Civil War as body servant to General [Charles] Devens. He was handsome, well-built, shrewd, wise, polite, always good-natured, cheerful to gaiety, honest, religious, a cautious truth speaker, devoted friend to the family, champion of its interest, a sort of idol to the children.[23]

Griffin indulged the children in their play, giving them rides as a horse or elephant or camel, as their imaginations required, and they adored him. He tricked them into believing that the family cat showed great intelligence, and they credited the cat from then on, never suspecting Griffin's behind-the-scenes maneuvers. He was a gifted fabricator who lied mainly to protect Twain and his wife from uninvited visitors and unwanted attention. His laugh was a familiar sound when the family was at dinner (he was often the first to laugh at Twain's jokes—sometimes anticipating the punch lines).

An easy camaraderie and trust developed between Griffin and Twain, and Griffin became a sounding board and first audience for pages Twain wrote across the hall from the room Griffin occupied. It is not surprising, therefore, as others have suggested, that aspects of Griffin made their way into Jim, the first fully drawn Black character Twain created. As Arthur G. Pettit has observed, Griffin and Jim were both "large physically, intelligent, argumentative, sentimental, deeply religious and loyal to their friends."[24] Scholars have recently determined that the mysterious "Per Order of G.G., Chief of Ordnance" that follows the famous "Notice" with which the novel begins ("Persons looking for a moral will be banished," and so on) most likely refers to George Griffin.[25]

Twain tells us that Griffin "was deacon and autocrat of the African Methodist Church. He ruled his race in the town, he was its trusted political leader, and (barring election eve accidents) he could tell the Republican committee how its vote would go, to a man, before the polls opened on election day. His people sought his advice in their troubles, and he kept many a case of theirs out of the court by settling it himself."[26] It was not only the city's Black population, however, whose trust and friendship Griffin earned: "He was well and creditably known to the best whites in the town, and he had the respect and I may say the warm friendly regard of every visiting intimate of our house." Griffin sagely turned this goodwill into more than social capital: he managed to wrest from it what was in those days a sizable chunk of financial capital as well by gathering information that would allow him to place smart political bets.

Griffin managed to turn these political bets into a major source of income—but they required that he conduct meticulous research if he wanted to be successful. In order for Griffin to be able "to bet intelligently upon State and National elections," he had to be "exhaustively posted in a wide array of details competent to affect results," Twain writes. Griffin was "methodical, systematic, pain-staking, thorough" in his investigations.

> Before he risked a dollar on a candidate or against him, he knew all about the man and his chances. He searched diligently, he allowed no source of information to escape a levy. For many years several chief citizens arrived at our house every Friday evening in the home-season, to play billiards— Governor [sic][Henry] Robinson, Mr. Edward M. Bunce, Mr. Charles E. Perkins, Mr. Sam. Dunham, and Mr. [Franklin] Whitmore. As a rule, one or two of the team brought their wives, who spent the evening with Mrs. Clemens in the library. These ladies were sure to arrive in that room without their husbands: because they and the rest of the gentlemen were in George's clutches in the front hall, getting milked of political information. Mrs. Clemens was never able to break up this scandalous business, for the men liked George, they admired him, too, so they abetted him in his misconduct and were willing to help him the best they could.[27]

The kind of research he had to undertake to place his successful election bets led Griffin to appreciate the "brain work" in which he saw Twain engaged—something he had not appreciated previously. Twain notes that Griffin told Livy Clemens,

> "When I used to see Mr. Clemens setting around with a pen and talking about his 'work,' I never said anything, it warn't my place, but I had my opinions about that kind of language, jist the same. But since I've took up with the election business I reconnize 't I was ignorant and foolish. I've found out, now,

that when a man uses these" (holding out his big hands), "it's—
well, it's any po' thing you've a mind to call it; but when he uses
these" (tapping his forehead), it's *work*, sho's you bawn, and
even *that* ain't hardly any name for it!"[28]

(Twain's efforts to capture Griffin's manner of speaking do not
imply any disrespect; Twain fully appreciates his recognition
that "brain work," through different from physical labor, can be
exhausting and challenging in its own right.) Griffin's own agile
brainwork saved him from many a financial disaster. He and
Twain remained close after the family left Hartford.

Twain was also friends with another Black man during these
years whose quick thinking saved the lives of several members of
his family: John T. Lewis, a free-born Black tenant at Quarry Farm
in Elmira where the Clemens family spent summers, who was
exactly the same age as Twain. When a photo shoot for a *Ladies'
Home Journal* interview in 1903 featured a picture of Twain and
Lewis, Twain said he and Lewis had been friends for thirty-four
years. He noted that forty years ago, Lewis had been his father-
in-law's coachman and that he remained a neighbor. Twain wrote
that he had "not known an honester man nor a more respectworthy
one." He told the *Journal* that "twenty-seven years ago, by the
prompt & intelligent exercise of his courage, presence of mind,
& extraordinary strength, he saved the lives of relatives of mine
whom a runaway horse was hurrying to destruction."[29]

Twain and other members of his family had watched in horror
one evening in 1877 as the new high-stepping gray horse pulling
the buggy carrying Twain's sister-in-law, Ida Langdon, her daughter Julia, and a nursemaid named Norah began galloping out of
control. The carriage was picking up alarming speed as it drove
down the hill, heading toward what seemed certain disaster at an
upcoming turn in the road. "The buggy seemed to fly. It would

strike obstructions & apparently spring the height of a man from the ground," Twain would write in a letter to a friend.[30] Twain and his brother-in-law

left the shrieking crowd behind & ran down the hill bare-headed & shouting. A neighbor appeared at his gate—a tenth of a second too late!—the buggy vanished past him like a thought. My last glimpse showed it for one instant, far down the descent, springing high in the air out of a cloud of dust, & then it disappeared. As I flew down the road, my impulse was to shut my eyes as I turned them to the right or left, & so delay for a moment the ghastly spectacle of mutilation & death I was expecting.

I ran on & on, still spared this spectacle, but saying to my-self[,] "I shall see it at the turn of the road; they never can pass that turn alive."

But when they arrived at what they thought would be the devastating spot, they were astonished to find two wagons where they expected to see one and, miraculously, no one hurt. "A miracle had been performed—nothing less," Twain believed.

"How this miracle was ever accomplished at all, by human strength, generalship & accuracy, is clear beyond my comprehension," Twain wrote, "& grows more so the more I go & examine the ground & try to believe it was actually done." John Lewis's "prompt & intelligent exercise of his courage, presence of mind, & extraordinary strength" had accomplished the miracle. Lewis, driving a load of manure up the hill in his own buggy, "saw the frantic horse plunging down the hill toward him, on a full gallop," Twain recalls, "throwing his fore-feet breast-high at every jump. So Lewis turned his team diagonally across the road just at the 'turn,' thus forming a V with the fence—the running horse could

Mark Twain with John T. Lewis, tenant farmer and friend of
Twain's at Quarry Farm, where Twain and his family spent summers.
Lewis's quick thinking and heroic action stopped a runaway horse
from killing members of Twain's family and a family servant.
Courtesy The Mark Twain House & Museum, Hartford, Connecticut.

not escape that, but must enter it. Then Lewis sprang to the
ground & stood in this V." Lewis summoned all his strength and
with perfect aim seized "the gray horse's bit as he plunged by, &
fetched him up standing!" "It was down hill, mind you," Twain
writes, and "ten feet *further* down hill neither Lewis nor any other
man could have saved them, for they would have been on the
abrupt 'turn' then." Twain concluded: "I know one thing *well;* if
Lewis had missed his aim he would have been killed on the spot
in the trap he had made for himself, & we should have found the
rest of the remains away down at the bottom of the steep ravine."
The enormous strength Lewis had summoned to stop the runaway horse was necessary but not sufficient to do what had to be

done: it was the combination of that strength with his intelligence and quick thinking that allowed him to save people Twain loved from certain death.

As Jocelyn Chadwick has observed, Lewis's lowly status—a farmer pulling a "load of manure"—makes some Black readers uncomfortable, for some of the same reasons some Black readers are uncomfortable with Jim. "For some African Americans, John Lewis and his 'load of manure' represent the core of what we wish to deny, if not escape entirely." But Twain's genuine and profuse admiration for Lewis cannot be denied. Nor can it be separated from the person Lewis is: with his "rickety wagon, and his team of horses" pulling the truckload of manure, this humble, hardworking farmer "elects—freely and consciously—to place his own life in jeopardy to save another's." Lewis, Chadwick writes, "commands and demands respect as a folk hero of substantial dimensions."[31] This unassuming yet heroic man will prove to be another model for the character traits that Twain will assign to Jim.

Twain's encounter with the gifted Black guide in Venice, his close relationship with the perceptive and clever George Griffin, and his friendship with the quick-thinking John T. Lewis—not to mention his acquaintance with the brilliant Frederick Douglass—helped Twain reject the myth of Black stupidity. The existence of these models of Black intelligence undergirds Twain's decision to make Jim smart and savvy, a man who understands the world around him and how it works better than the white boy with whom he travels.

The Myth That Black People Do Not Experience Grief and Pain the Way White People Do

In Thomas Jefferson's view, Black people did not feel things as deeply as white people did. "Their griefs," he wrote, "are transient. Those numberless afflictions, which render it doubtful whether heaven has given life to us in mercy or in wrath, are less felt and sooner forgotten with them." The belief that Black people did not feel the same depth and breadth of emotions as white people— that they were relatively inured to personal loss and tragedy— helped justify the practice of separating families when doing so was in a slaveholder's financial interest.[32]

Indeed, at the start of "A True Story, Repeated Word for Word as I Heard It," Twain's first contribution to the *Atlantic Monthly*, a "Misto C—" (a stand-in, as readers would assume, for "Mr. Clemens") presents himself as someone who casually accepts Jefferson's belief about Black people being relatively immune to emotional pain. "Misto C—" introduces "Aunt Rachel"—the name Twain gave Mary Ann Cord, the cook at Quarry Farm on whom the story is centered—in the story as "a cheerful, hearty soul," telling us that "it was no more trouble for her to laugh than it is for a bird to sing. She was under fire, now, as usual when the day was done. That is to say, she was being chaffed without mercy, and was enjoying it. She would let off peal after peal of laughter, and then sit with her face in her hands and shake with throes of enjoyment which she could no longer get breath enough to express."[33] At this point a thought occurs to Misto C— and he says, "Aunt Rachel, how is it that you've lived sixty years and never had any trouble?" The question stops Aunt Rachel in her tracks:

> She stopped quaking. She paused, and there was a moment of silence. She turned her face over her shoulder toward me, and said, without even a smile in her voice:
>
> "Misto C—, is you in 'arnest?"

Misto C— tells the reader that "it surprised me a good deal; and it sobered my manner and my speech, too." He explains that he believed that she "can't have had any trouble" because, he says,

"I've never heard you sigh, and never seen your eye when there wasn't a laugh in it." Aunt Rachel now faces him "full of earnestness" and repeats—incredulously—the view he has just expressed: "Has I had any trouble? Misto C—, I's gwyne to tell you, den I leave it to you." What follows is the tremendously moving story of how she was separated from her husband and all seven of their children on the auction block in Richmond, Virginia. Aunt Rachel tells the story in her own distinctive voice, represented on the page as Black vernacular dialect. When the piece appeared in November 1874, it was the first time Black dialect had been used for anything but comic effect in the pages of the *Atlantic Monthly*.

She begins by describing her husband's deep love for her and their love for their seven children:

> I was bawn down 'mongst de slaves; I knows all 'bout slavery, 'case I ben one of 'em my own se'f. Well, sah, my ole man— dat's my husban'—he was lovin' an' kind to me, jist as kind as you is to yo' own wife. An' we had children—seven chil'en—an' we loved dem chil'en jist de same as you loves yo' chil'en. Dey was black, but de Lord can't make no chil'en so black but what dey mother loves 'em an' would n't give 'em up, no, not for anything dat's in dis whole world.

At the start of Misto C—'s description of what transpired the evening Aunt Rachel told him her "true story," he and his family are seated on the porch, while Aunt Rachel is "sitting respectfully below our level, on the steps,—for she was our servant, and colored." But as she begins to limn her experience on the auction block in Richmond, her position changes. Twain writes that she "had gradually risen, while she warmed to her subject, and now she towered above us, black against the stars." The story she tells is heart-wrenching:

"Dey put chains on us an' put us on a stan' as high as dis po'ch,—
twenty foot high,—an' all de people stood aroun', crowds an'
crowds. An' dey'd come up dah an' look at us all roun', an'
squeeze our arm, an' make us git up an' walk, an den say, 'Dis
one don't 'mount to much.' An' dey sole my ole man, an' took
him away, an' dey begin to sell my chil'en an' take dem away,
an' I begin to cry; an' de man say, 'Shet up yo' dam blubberin',
an' hit me on de mouf wid his han'. An' when de las' one was
gone but my little Henry, I grab' him clost up to my breas' so,
an' I ris up an' says, 'You shan't take him away,' I says; "I'll kill
de man dat tetches him!' I says. But my little Henry whisper
an' say, 'I gwyne to run away, an' den I work an' buy yo' freedom.' Oh, bless de chile, he always so good! But dey got him—
dey got him, de men did; but I took and tear de clo'es mos' off
of 'em, an' beat 'em over de head wid my chain."

Twain's decision to devote significant space in the piece to the
wrenching pain Aunt Rachel suffered is all the more bold when
we realize that the norm in the *Atlantic*, as well as other mass
magazines, during this era was not to acknowledge Black grief.
For most white Americans during the last quarter of the nineteenth century, the pain African Americans suffered under slavery
was displaced by tales of ex-slaves nostalgic for the old plantation,
insanely loyal to their former masters—individuals for whom freedom was a burden and a curse.[34]

In an era when scenes of slavery in popular culture tended to
be racist, feel-good confections far removed from reality, Mark
Twain intervened by signifying to those demeaning and misleading falsities by revisiting the slave past for very different ends:
to make real the pain that African Americans had endured under
slavery and to honor the fortitude, creativity, and courage that
had enabled them to survive—and using himself as the foil against

which this tale unfolds, a stand-in for white Americans unable or unwilling to hear the stories such as Mary Ann Cord's.[35] Twain's focus in "A True Story" and *Huckleberry Finn* on the painful reality of the slave South ran directly counter to the plantation tradition and its cultural apologists. Contrast Twain's images of the slave past with this piece by an anonymous author who identified himself as "A South Carolinian," appearing in the *Atlantic* two and a half years after Twain's story:

> The old plantation days are passed away, perhaps forever. My principles now lead me to abhor slavery and rejoice at its abolition. Yet sometimes, in the midst of the heat and toil of the struggle for existence, the thought involuntarily steals over me that we have seen better days. I think of . . . visits to the plantation, with its long, broad expanse of waving green, dotted here and there with groups of industrious slaves; . . . of the "Christmas gif', Massa," breaking your slumbers on the holiday morn; of the gay devices for fooling the dignified old darkies on the first of April; of the faithful old nurse who brought you through infancy, under whose humble roof you delighted to partake of an occasional meal; of the flattering, foot-scraping, clownish, knowing rascal to whom you tossed a silver piece when he brought up your boots; of the little darkies who scrambled for the rind after you had eaten your water-melon on the piazza in the afternoon,—and, . . . I feel the intrusive swelling of the tear of regret.[36]

At a time when the reigning racial ideology of the day assumed that "negroes were relatively insensible to pain," Mary Ann Cord's description of what she felt at her separation from her children on the auction block was moving proof of the myopic fallacy of this assumption. Aunt Rachel then goes on to describe her jubilant reunion with her youngest child, Henry. The child, who had gone north via the Underground Railroad, became a manservant to a colonel in the Union Army, and was part of the successful effort to take the city of New Bern, North Carolina. When the Union soldiers have a ball at the home of Aunt Rachel's owner in New Bern, she recognizes her son and is joyfully reunited with him. The story concludes with her repeating back to Misto C— his original words, the words that prompted her to tell her story. But she repeats them with a signifying wink that makes clear that she means the opposite of what she says: "Oh, no, Misto C—, I hain't had no trouble. An' no joy!" The story that Cord told with such "vigorous eloquence," as Twain put it, was all the more meaningful to Mark Twain because he had known both her and her son, Henry, for years, although he hadn't known their story: Henry Washington had been his barber in Elmira since Twain first came to that community.[37]

Twain claims to have written down Cord's words "before they were cold." In fact, he made a number of changes before submitting the story for publication. But it remained, at its core, the story that she had told him. Recalling Cord's "gift of strong & simple speech" a quarter century later, Twain wrote that her story was "a curiously strong piece of literary work to come unpremeditated from lips untrained in the literary art."[38] Hearing it helped make him aware of the power of a vernacular narrator—a lesson that would be central to the novel he would begin writing two years later. Cord's story left a deep impression on Twain and marked an important milestone in his career as a writer. Although it confounded readers, who expected humor when they saw the byline "Mark Twain," the story won him the lifelong respect of the *Atlantic*'s editor, William Dean Howells, who found it "extremely good and touching." Howells later wrote him that it "delights me more and more: I wish you had about forty of 'em!"[39] In the book

Mary Ann Cord, a formerly enslaved woman who worked as a cook at Quarry Farm, where Twain and his family spent summers, told Twain the powerful story of her being separated from her children on the auction block and reunited with her son, Henry, after the Civil War. Her artful and compelling storytelling helped Twain recognize the potential power of Black vernacular speech and inspired his first contribution to the *Atlantic Monthly*, "A True Story, Repeated Word for Word as I Heard It." Mary Ann Cord, ca. 1875–85, Leon Washington Condol Papers, Courtesy Special Collections and University Archives, University of Maryland Libraries.

Twain would begin to write in 1876, Jim will reprise Cord's exact words when he says, speaking through the "hair-ball" to advise Huck on his future in chapter 4 of the novel: "You gwyne to have considable trouble in yo' life, en considable joy." Her words would also echo in Jim's poignant expressions of grief over his separation from his own children and Huck's response to them; her comment about how much she loved her children foreshadows Huck's comment about Jim's love of his own children: "I do believe he cared just as much for his people as white folks does for their'n."

Although Jefferson's *Notes on the State of Virginia* may have been the earliest American text to promulgate the myth that Black people didn't feel pain the way white people did, the myth was alive and well in the pages of one of the leading reference books published in the 1870s—an encyclopedia on which Twain generally relied for accurate information. In the entry under "Negro" in *The American Cyclopædia: A Popular Dictionary of General Knowledge*, published by D. Appleton and Company between 1873 and 1876, readers learned that "Negroes . . . are comparatively insensitive to pain."[40]

But other books that nestled on Twain's shelves alongside the *Cyclopædia* countered that assertion, as did his own personal experience. Two such books that Twain owned and read were Charles Ball's *Slavery in the United States: A Narrative of the Life of Charles Ball* (1837) and James Pennington's *Fugitive Blacksmith; or, Events in the History of James W. C. Pennington . . . Formerly a Slave in the State of Maryland* (1849).[41] These two slave narratives documented in graphic detail the physical and psychological pain that slaveholders inflicted on slaves and that their slaves felt.

An incident in Twain's personal experience forced him to recognize the pain endured by the child as well as the parent in separations like these. Twain recalled in his autobiography that in his home when he was growing up,

> We had a little slave boy whom we had hired from some one, there in Hannibal. He was from the eastern shore of Maryland and had been brought away from his family and his friends halfway across the American continent and sold. He was a cheery spirit, innocent and gentle, and the noisiest creature that ever was, perhaps. All day long he was singing, whistling, yelling, whooping, laughing—it was maddening, devastating, unendurable. At last, one day, I lost all my temper and went raging to

my mother and said Sandy has been singing for the past hour
without a single break and I couldn't stand it and wouldn't she
please shut him up.[42]

His mother would not "shut him up." Instead, Twain tells us,

> The tears came into her eyes trembled and she said something
> like this: "Poor thing, when he sings it shows that he is not
> remembering and that comforts me; but when he is still I am
> afraid he is thinking and I cannot bear it. He will never see his
> mother again; if he can sing I must not hinder it, but be thank-
> ful for it. If you were older you would understand me; then
> that friendless child's noise would make you glad.

These models shaped Twain's portrayal of Jim as a father devas-
tated by separation from his children.

In addition, Twain was acquainted with three Black fathers
who may have influenced his portrayal of Jim as a father. One was
Daniel Quarles, an enslaved man he got to know on his uncle's
farm in Florida, Missouri, where he spent two or three months
every summer during his childhood, whom he cites as an inspiration for Jim in *Huckleberry Finn*. Born in Virginia in 1798, Quarles
was brought to Missouri when he was thirty-six by his master,
John Quarles, in 1834, the year before Twain was born. He was
married to an enslaved woman named Hannah (although slave
marriages were not recognized by law), and together they had at
least three children. Twain had ample opportunity to see Daniel
Quarles interact with his own children as well as those of his
master. Another Black father he got to know was John T. Lewis,
the tenant farmer at Quarry Farm who had selflessly stopped the
runaway carriage. Lewis and Twain both had daughters named
Susie born in 1872 (Twain's family spelled it "Susy"), and Lewis

and his wife and daughter were a familiar presence at Quarry Farm when Twain was there.[43] The third Black father Twain got to know was Frederick Douglass. When Twain ran into Douglass in Boston in 1869 (possibly at the offices of their mutual lecture agent, James Redpath), Douglass told him a poignant story about his daughter Rosetta. As Twain recounted in a letter to his fiancée, "He told the history of his child's expulsion from Miss Tracy's school, & his simple language was very effective. Miss Tracy said the pupils did not want a colored child among them—which he did not believe, & challenged the proof. She put it at once to a vote of the school, and asked 'How many of you are willing to have this colored child with you?' And they *all* held up their hands! Douglas[s] added: 'The children's hearts were right.' There was pathos in the way he said it."[44]

Twain, of course, was a father himself at the time he created Jim in *Huckleberry Finn*. He was also a father who did not need to imagine the guilt a father might feel about his behavior toward his child: he felt it himself. Although Twain had three cherished daughters at the time he wrote the novel, his only son, Langdon, born prematurely in 1870, had died of diphtheria when he was nineteen months old. Twain unjustly blamed himself for the child's death, thinking that he had neglected to keep him sufficiently warm during a carriage ride. (Lewis had also lost an infant son.)[45] Twain's contact with these Black fathers, as well as his own experience as a grieving father, probably helped him craft Jim as a father in *Huckleberry Finn*—and helped him understand both the pain Jim felt at separation from his children and the guilt he felt about his treatment of his daughter.

The Myth That Black People Were Uncreative

In *Notes on the State of Virginia*, Jefferson wrote, "Never yet could I find that a black had uttered a thought above the level of plain narration," adding that he had never seen "even an elementary trait of painting or sculpture." "In imagination," he stated, "they are dull, tasteless, and anomalous."[46] While throughout the nineteenth century, many Americans dismissed the idea of Black creativity as cavalierly as Jefferson did, Mark Twain had the good fortune to get to know several individuals whose creative storytelling and artistic talents challenged these assumptions.

One was Daniel Quarles, According to Twain, "Uncle Dan'l," as he was known on the farm, was "a faithful and affectionate good friend, ally, and adviser," as well as an inspiration for Jim in *Huckleberry Finn*.[47] Daniel's storytelling was legendary, and hearing his stories was a high point of Twain's stay at his uncle's farm every summer. Twain remembered fondly "the look of Uncle Dan'l's kitchen as it was on the privileged nights, when I was a child, and I can see the white and black children grouped on the hearth, with the firelight playing on their faces and the shadows flickering upon the walls," as they listened to "Uncle Dan'l telling the immortal tales" to his enthralled audience. He recalled "the creepy joy which quivered through me when the time for the ghost story was reached—and the sense of regret, too, which came over me, for it was always the last story of the evening and there was nothing between it and the unwelcome bed."[48] That young white child listening to stories in Daniel's kitchen had no way of predicting that storytelling would be central to his own future career, but when he became a storyteller himself, he presumably hoped to engage his readers as fully as Daniel Quarles's stories had engaged him.

If Daniel Quarles had a deep impact on Twain's sense of how to tell a story, it was another enslaved man, Jerry, who introduced him to satire as a tool of social criticism. As Twain recalled in "Corn-Pone Opinions" in 1901:

Fifty years ago, when I was a boy of fifteen and helping to
inhabit a Missourian village on the banks of the Mississippi,
I had a friend whose society was very dear to me because I
was forbidden by my mother to partake of it. He was a gay
and impudent and satirical and delightful young black man—
a slave—who daily preached sermons from the top of his master's woodpile, with me for sole audience. He imitated the
pulpit style of the several clergymen of the village, and did it
well, and with fine passion and energy. To me he was a wonder.
I believed he was the greatest orator in the United States.

Twain tells us that he "listened to the sermons from the open
window of a lumber room at the back of the house." Jerry evidently "interrupted his preaching, now and then, to saw a stick of
wood; but the sawing was a pretense—he did it with his mouth;
exactly imitating the sound the bucksaw makes in shrieking its
way through the wood. But it served its purpose; it kept his master
from coming out to see how the work was getting along." Twain's
mother forbade him to listen to Jerry's satirical sermons, but that
made him listen to them all the more. "The black philosopher's
idea," Twain writes in "Corn-Pone Opinions," "was that a man is
not independent, and cannot afford views which might interfere
with his bread and butter. If he would prosper, he must train with
the majority; in matters of large moment, like politics and religion,
he must think and feel with the bulk of his neighbors, or suffer
damage in his social standing and in his business prosperities."[49]

This "gay and impudent and satirical . . . young black man"
preaching daily sermons from the top of the woodpile with this
attentive white boy as his sole audience signified on the sermons
of the local preachers while signifying on his own text at the same
time. He is making the case for the irresistible pull of conformity

as he himself is performing a nonconformist rhetorical tour de force for an audience of one. But what an audience of one that was! The audacious doubleness of Jerry's verbal brilliance thrilled Twain, as did its attention to the gaps between "surface" and deeper meaning. Twain claims that he had the good sense to know he was in the presence of a real master, even if that master was a young slave. The original manuscript of "Corn-Pone Opinions" in Mark Twain's archives reveals that Twain initially wrote that he believed Jerry was "the greatest man in the United States." (In the version that was printed posthumously in *Europe and Elsewhere*, however, Jerry became simply "the greatest orator in the United States.") Jerry's impact on Twain must have indeed been momentous for Twain to remember him this way fifty years later.[50]

We do not know whether Twain ever read Thomas Jefferson's assertion that Jefferson had never heard "that a black had uttered a thought above the level of plain narration." But if he had, Twain certainly would have scoffed at the idea. Daniel Quarles had taught Twain lessons about how to tell a story that he would return to all his life. Jerry had modeled for Twain the potential of satire as a tool of social criticism, still vividly brilliant after half a century. And Mary Ann Cord's demonstration of the possibilities of the vernacular in the service of literary art, and her evocation of Black grief, would indelibly shape Twain's entire subsequent career as a creative writer.

In addition to examples of Black literary and rhetorical brilliance, Twain would also have reason to scoff at Jefferson's claim that he had never encountered in a Black person the slightest talent for painting or sculpture. Twain had the good fortune to become a friend and patron of a Black Hartford painter named Charles Ethan Porter in the late 1870s or early 1880s. The renowned painter Frederic Edwin Church, who bought some of Porter's paintings, remarked in 1879 that Porter "had no superior as a colorist in the United States."[51] Another contemporary observed that same year that "being a colored man, Mr. Porter has found shameful obstacles placed in his path, but is manfully fighting them with a love of art and an enthusiasm that must conquer."[52] Twain bought Porter's work and encouraged others to do so. Believing that Porter would benefit from studying art in Paris, he helped make it possible for Porter to go there, providing him with a letter of introduction to Karl Gerhardt, a white sculptor from Hartford whom Twain knew, to assist his entry into the Paris art world. Porter's exposure to the new styles of Paris revolutionized his art. The apprenticeship that Twain facilitated allowed Porter to grow and develop as an artist and helped him launch his career.[53]

In sum, at a time when the reigning racial ideology of the day maintained that Blacks were mentally inferior, Mark Twain knew personally a number of very smart and gifted individuals whose very existence undermined that attitude. These included the urbane Black guide in Venice whose knowledge, taste, and judgment allowed him to run circles around all the other guides; the perceptive George Griffin in Hartford, whose astute insights into politics and human behavior let him gather information from Twain's well-placed political friends that enabled him to turn political bets he collected in the Black community into a tidy nest egg; and the quick-thinking John Lewis in Elmira, who instantly sized up a life-threatening situation and acted quickly enough to save several members of Twain's family from certain death. Twain's friendship with these three men, as well as with the remarkable Frederick Douglass, offered him clear evidence against the myths and stereotypes of Black capability that pervaded his world. At a time when a leading reference book asserted that "negroes were relatively insensible to pain," hearing Mary Ann Cord's eloquent evocation of her grief at being separated from her children stood as a powerful antidote, as did examples from Twain's reading and personal memory. And at a time when the culture largely dismissed Black creativity as inconsequential, Twain's personal memories of Daniel Quarles, an unmatched storyteller, and Jerry, an impressive satirist—as well as his acquaintance with Charles Ethan Porter, a stellar painter—acted as a counterweight.

It is important to note that while Twain has had good reason to recognize these myths for what they are, Huck, the narrator of his novel, does not: Huck the character, unlike Twain the writer, is a child. Huck is clearly familiar with the myths and stereotypes about Black people outlined here and buys into each of them to some extent (as Twain himself did when he was a child). Only over the course of the book does he learn to question some of them.

Take the myth of Black stupidity. For much of the novel, Huck views Jim as a childlike, laughable comic figure, a handy victim for practical jokes; for that reason Huck is flummoxed when the Black man he assumes to be mentally inferior to himself bests him in an argument. When Jim's logic trumps his own in their debate about why a Frenchman can't "talk like a man," Huck gives up, saying, "I see it warn't no use wasting words—you can't learn a nigger to argue. So I quit." Time and time again, Jim's intelligence catches him by surprise: "Well, he was right," Huck says, "he was most always right, he had an uncommon level head, for a nigger."

Or take the myth of Blacks being relatively insensible to pain: "their griefs are transient." Huck is genuinely surprised to see Jim's deep distress at his separation from his family. Huck says, when he finds Jim "moaning and mourning to himself," that "he was thinking about his wife and his children, away up yonder," and cared about his own family as much as white folks did for theirs. "It don't seem natural," Huck reflected, "but I reckon it's so." Huck witnesses the depth of Jim's grief and comes to think more of him for it: "He was often moaning and mourning, that way, nights, when he judged I was asleep, and saying 'Po' little 'Liza-beth! po' little Johnny! it mighty hard; I spec' I ain't ever gwyne to see you no mo', no mo'!' He was a mighty good nigger, Jim was."

Finally, what about the myth about Blacks lacking creativity? Huck never quite gets beyond that one. Jim invents a wildly imaginative story about the devil and being chased by witches; he concocts a tale he attributes to the magical hair ball about what the future holds for Huck; and he offers an extravagant "interpretation" of a dream he never had to teach the child a lesson—but despite all of these examples, Huck never believes Jim capable of offering anything more than what Jefferson called "plain narration." He takes Jim's stories at face value, assuming that Jim believes they are true. He is incapable of seeing Jim as a man with an imagination who knows how to use it.

Since Huck is the narrator of the book that bears his name, readers see Jim only through Huck's eyes. Huck buys into these myths, as noted above. But Twain does not. At least one astute critic saw exactly this when the book came out. A reviewer in the *San Francisco Chronicle* in 1885 shortly after the novel was published noted that "running all through the book is the sharpest satire on the ante-bellum estimate of the slave."[54] Alas, the *Chronicle* writer's savvy understanding of the book was an outlier. Most—but not all—reviewers over the century after the novel came out and beyond have tended to confuse the perspective of the book's narrator with that of its author and assumed that Twain, as well as Huck, bought into the stereotypes outlined here. Why haven't more critics appreciated that Twain was trying to undermine these racist assumptions rather than embrace them? As Jocelyn Chadwick asks in *The Jim Dilemma*, why haven't critics been able to distinguish Jim's "richly positive and generous humanity from the confusing crosscurrents of prejudice that obscure it"?[55]

Twain himself provides a possible answer in a little-known story he published five months before his death called "A Fable." It begins like this: "Once upon a time an artist who had painted a small and very beautiful picture placed it so that he could see it in the mirror. He said, 'This doubles the distance and softens it, and it is twice as lovely as it was before.'" The animals out in the woods hear about the picture from the housecat, who spoke of its great beauty. The ass decides to investigate but doesn't know where to stand. "And so, through error, he stood between the picture and the mirror. The result was that the picture had no chance, and didn't show up." He returned home and reported that the picture "was a handsome ass, and friendly, but just an ass, and nothing more." The bear decides to check it out and insists that "there was nothing in the hole but a bear." The cow found nothing in the hole but a cow. The tiger found nothing in it but a tiger. The lion found a lion. The leopard a leopard. The camel found a camel. Finally, the elephant "said that anybody but a near-sighted fool could see that there was nothing in the hole but an elephant." The piece closes with a "MORAL, BY THE CAT: You can find in a text whatever you bring, if you will stand between it and the mirror of your imagination." Might critics have been seeing in *Huckleberry Finn* reflections of themselves rather than the luminous work of art Twain created?[56]

Let's try this thought experiment: Imagine that Mark Twain saw Jim as intelligent, responsible, quick thinking, and mature—as someone as smart and resourceful as, say, George Griffin or John Lewis. Now imagine that Mark Twain saw Jim as a parent who cared about his children as much as Mary Ann Cord cared about hers and was as pained as she was when she was forced to be separated from them. And imagine that Twain saw Jim as a creative storyteller as talented as Uncle Daniel or Jerry.

What would Jim's story look like if we assumed that Mark Twain saw him as smart and resourceful, as a man with intelligence and agency, as a creative storyteller, and as a caring father weighed down with guilt about his own children who deals with that guilt by protecting two children who are not his own?

I suspect that it would look an awful lot like the book Twain actually wrote.

CHAPTER 3

———

The Debates

H OW IS THE READER meant to understand who Jim is, and why Twain crafted him the way he did? From the moment the book appeared critics disagreed about whether Jim embodied stereotypes or subverted them; about whether his role was to provide comic relief or something more; about the roots of his beliefs, his speech, and his behavior; even about what his name was. Did Twain see Jim as a stock figure with roots in minstrelsy whose role in the book was to make us laugh? Or did a different, more complex vision animate his creation of the central Black character in the novel? These debates are the subject of this chapter.

What's in a Name?

What do we call him? Mark Twain introduces Jim in chapter 2 of *Huckleberry Finn* as "Miss Watson's big nigger, named Jim." Throughout the rest of the book, he is simply referred to as "Jim." So when did Jim's name become attached to an offensive racial epithet? The first use of it in print seems to have been a *New York Sun* review of Mark Twain's reading at Chickering Hall in New York in November 1884, shortly before the book was published. The *Sun* did not quote Twain directly in this portion of the review but rather summarized the context for the "Sollermun" exchange that Twain read, writing, "It was in the Mississippi valley. Huck Finn, a white boy, and Nigger Jim [sic] ran away from the plantation and camped out, and they got to talking about kings one evening."[1] Throughout December 1884 this story was reprinted widely in cities as far-flung as Hamilton, Ontario; Madison, Wisconsin; Seattle, Washington; Newark, Ohio; Cheyenne, Wyoming; Fremont, Nebraska; Lima, Ohio; Davenport, Iowa; and Topeka, Kansas, planting the idea around the country that Twain had called his character by this name in the book, which he had not.[2]

After *Huckleberry Finn* was published in the United States on February 18, 1885, some papers reprised the *New York Sun*'s decision to treat the offensive slur as part of Jim's name. For example, the *Buffalo Evening Telegraph* in May 1885 wrote that "Huck and Nigger Jim sat in a cave's mouth" before describing the thunderstorm they witnessed. The *Larned Chronoscope* in Kansas and the *Crawford Avalanche* of Grayling, Michigan, ran headlines on their front pages in March and April 1885, respectively, that read "Nigger Jim's Story," before reprinting the story Jim tells about discovering that his little daughter is deaf. A number of papers around the country, including the *Parsons Palladium* in Kansas, the *Placer Herald* of Rocklin, California, and the *Santa Maria Times* in California ran the same excerpt under a subheading that read "Nigger Jim's Little Deaf and Dumb Daughter—How He Punished Her and Why He Couldn't Forgive Himself—a Pathetic Story" (preceded by the headline "Didn't Shut the Door").[3] Mark Twain may have first introduced Jim to the world during his lecture tour with fellow novelist George Washington Cable that included the comic conversation between Huck and Jim about King Solomon. But it is interesting that one of the most commonly reprinted postpublication excerpts from the book was the poignant story of Jim's remorse over his treatment of his daughter, a story that usually appeared under a headline calling Jim by a name that was not his. The distasteful nickname became hard to shake.[4]

In the twentieth century, the decision of Twain's first biographer, Albert Bigelow Paine, to attach the offensive epithet to Jim's name in the authoritative biography that he published in 1912 (as well as in his *Boys' Life of Mark Twain* in 1916) had much to do with its staying power. The error was reprised in a visible and often-quoted comment by Ernest Hemingway in *Green Hills of Africa* (1935) and was repeated even by Twain's great champion, the erudite Bernard DeVoto, in *Mark Twain's America* (1932), as well as by later critics ranging from Norman Mailer to Leslie Ficdler, from C. Vann Woodward to Mel Watkins.[5] We should add to this list novelists Malcolm Bradbury and Josef Škvorecký; historians Perry Miller and Edward Ayers; journalists Hilton Als, Russell Baker, and Michiko Kakutani; film scholar Donald Bogle; and comic Louis C.K.[6] It was also repeated by Twain scholars (who should have known better), including Harold Beaver, Gladys Bellamy, Kenneth Lynn, Leo Marx, Arthur G. Pettit, Tom Quirk, and Dixon Wecter.[7] Nor should we forget the director of the American Library Association's Office for Intellectual Freedom, who reiterated the canard about Jim's name while trying to defend the novel against would-be censors. Even Ralph Ellison, usually an astute and careful reader, made this mistake.[8] Seeing this racial slur attached to Jim's very name time and time again—with the implication that Twain gave him this name—may well have helped distort generations of readers' understanding of Jim's character.

How Did Early Reviewers View Jim?

If critics have had different views about what to call Jim, they diverge even more on how they understand his character. From the start, some were hostile to his presence in the book. Joe Fulton suggests that Jim was at the root of the decision by the Concord

Library in Massachusetts to remove the novel from their shelves when it first came out: "Huck was banned in Boston for fraternizing with Jim," he writes.[9]

Early reviewers assumed they were presenting Jim in a positive light when they referred to him as "a simple-minded, bighearted darky," as the *New York Sun* did in 1885.[10] But comments such as these mark the start of associating Jim with demeaning racial stereotypes familiar to readers of books and periodicals in the 1880s, a time when the plantation tradition dominated the portrayal of the South in fiction in magazines and books. The plantation tradition glorified the South before the war, presenting slavery as a benignly paternalistic institution that provided for the care of happy, artless slaves who couldn't look after themselves. Most early reviewers tended to describe Jim as comically simple-minded and gullible—an appropriate object of ridicule.

A different view of Jim appeared in 1937 when the eminent Black writer and critic Sterling Brown wrote that far from being "simple-minded," Jim had clear and sensible goals and desires involving his wife and children, as well as a poignant sense of guilt about his treatment of his daughter, Elizabeth.[11] Brown's respectful view of Jim would prefigure the poet T. S. Eliot's comment in 1950 that Huck and Jim "are equal in dignity."[12] But these positive views of Jim got relatively little traction.

When Did the Association of Jim with the "Stage-Negro" of Minstrel Shows Begin?

The earliest critic to refer to Jim as a figure from a minstrel show was Leo Marx, who, in an article from 1953 that would become one of the most reprinted and anthologized pieces of criticism on *Huck Finn* for the past seventy years, wrote that in the closing part of the book, Jim "ceases to be a man. . . . This creature who bleeds ink and feels no pain is something less than human. He has been made over in the image of a flat stereotype: the submissive stage-Negro."[13] What led Marx to raise this point at this time, and what made him think his readers would understand it?

It may be more than a coincidence that 1953 also saw the debut of the *Amos 'n' Andy* show on national television. The show grew out of the longest-running radio show of the same name, one that John Strausbaugh has described as "aural blackface."[14] Although the title roles in the radio show had been played by two white actors whose performances were shaped by their familiarity with blackface minstrelsy, in 1953 Black actors performed the roles on television; indeed, it was the first television sitcom to portray Black people. However, the actors were told to keep their performances as close as possible to that of the white actors who had originated the roles in a minstrel-show mold, complete with their exaggerated dialect and comic ignorance.[15] But if 1953 marked the first TV broadcast of *Amos 'n' Andy*, the year also marked significant rumblings of the early Civil Rights Movement, with a large eight-day-long protest against bus segregation in Baton Rouge, Louisiana. The Baton Rouge bus boycott made national headlines ("Bus Boycott Effective" read the headline in the *New York Times*) and developed strategies that would be important two years later in the better-known Montgomery, Alabama, bus boycott.[16] With exchanges redolent of minstrel shows being broadcast on the national airwaves and with the new assertiveness of the nascent Civil Rights Movement capturing headlines across the country, it is perhaps not surprising that Marx, who would become a supporter of the Civil Rights Movement, felt compelled to call out and criticize what he saw as residues of minstrel shows in Twain's portrayal of Jim in *Huckleberry Finn*.

Five years later in 1958, Ralph Ellison famously observed, "Writing at a time when the blackfaced minstrel was still popular, and shortly after a war which left even the abolitionists weary of those problems associated with the Negro, Twain fitted Jim into the outlines of the minstrel tradition, and it is from behind this stereotype mask that we see Jim's dignity and human capacity—and Twain's complexity—emerge."[17] Unfortunately, critics often focus only on the first half of Ellison's comment, ignoring the crucial larger point Ellison was making about "Jim's dignity and human capacity—and Twain's complexity."

As Eric Lott has shown, blackface minstrel shows were a theatrical practice that embodied a contradictory blend of "love and theft" from Black culture by white working-class Americans. Born in the 1830s, these shows became the most popular entertainment form in nineteenth-century America. A genre based in the formulaic, these shows were revues featuring short burlesque skits, sentimental songs, and raucous dancing. The actors were most often white men, their faces "blacked" with burnt cork, portraying ludicrous Blacks who were bumptious and boastful, fatuous fools who deserved to be objects of derision but who were also able to make fun of the upper classes in ways that working-class audiences found appealing.[18] Although early minstrel shows sometimes featured subtle instances of antislavery sentiment, by the time Mark Twain saw his first minstrel shows in Hannibal, St. Louis, New York, San Francisco, and elsewhere, they had come to be undergirded by the pretense "that slavery was amusing, right, and natural."[19] Minstrel shows often trafficked in the myths and stereotypes about Black people reviewed in the last chapter, and the Black characters they created were variously stupid, proud, gullible, ignorant, confident, passive, lazy, and impervious to pain.

After the Civil War, most minstrel shows featured a deep nostalgia for the bygone plantation era, celebrating it in story and song.[20] Although vaudeville, radio, and television all supplanted minstrel shows in America in the twentieth century, images and tropes derived from minstrel shows, as well minstrel shows them-

selves, would remain a visible part of the cultural landscape, re-
taining their power to inflict shame and pain on new generations
of Black Americans. The tradition of the minstrel show was sus-
tained largely by amateur productions reprising some of the earlier scripts and tropes. Well into the 1960s, for example, in Bedford,
Pennsylvania, the volunteer fire department mounted an annual
minstrel show in the local high school auditorium.[21]

Minstrel shows—along with ubiquitous post–Civil War fiction
that treated the vanished antebellum world as Edenic—helped
white Americans forget the brutality inflicted on slaves and ignore
the continuing injustices and indignities imposed on Black Americans in the present. Twain himself had fond memories of the
minstrel shows he saw in his youth in Hannibal, San Francisco,
New York, and St. Louis.[22] They even drew Black audiences, and
after the Civil War a number of Black actors formed their own
minstrel troupes to capitalize on the theatrical craze.

But what does this have to do with Jim?

Stereotype or Complex Hero?

The argument that Jim's character is fundamentally based on
racial stereotypes goes like this: Minstrel shows demeaned Black
people. Mark Twain liked minstrel shows. Therefore, Mark Twain
crafted Jim in the demeaning image of the stage Negro of the
minstrel show. Many critics since the 1950s have viewed Jim pri-
marily through the lens of minstrelsy, claiming to identify echoes
of minstrel-show dialogues, minstrel-show humor, and minstrel-
show language in episodes involving Jim in *Huckleberry Finn*.

But we have to remember that Twain recognized that what
minstrel shows presented had little to do with reality. "The so-
called 'negro minstrels' simply mis-represent the thing," he wrote
in 1873. "I do not think they ever saw a plantation."[23] Twain found
the shows "delightfully and satisfyingly funny," as did many of his

peers, both Black and white; but decades later, while still recalling minstrel shows with pleasure, Twain referred to the language minstrels used as "a very broad negro dialect."[24] Although Twain enjoyed minstrel shows, he viewed them as artificial concoctions created as a stylized form of entertainment.[25]

If "the so-called 'negro minstrels' simply misrepresent" the world of antebellum slavery, as Twain said they did, why would Twain base the book's central Black character on the foolish clowns of the minstrel stage when he had a plethora of authentic real-life models on whom he could draw—the smart, strong, creative, active, and admirable individuals described in chapter 2 of this book? Why would Twain use this meretricious form of popular entertainment so shot through with nostalgia for the slave South as a key source for a book that mounted a devastating critique of that world? And why would Twain draw on the minstrels' "very broad negro dialect" in a book in which he tells us that he crafted the "Missouri negro dialect" and the other dialects not "in a hap-hazard fashion, or by guess-work; but pains-takingly, and with the trustworthy guidance and support of personal familiarity with these several forms of speech"?[26] The "racial counterfeit" that was the minstrel show—with its premise of Black stupidity, its nostalgia for the world of slavery, and its speech as exaggerated and broad as its over-the-top costumes and makeup—was not the key source for Jim that many have claimed it was.[27]

First of all, think of how much we have to ignore or deny about Jim's character if we are to view him as descended from the stereotypical flat, passive, fatuous "stage Negro" of the minstrel show. Seeing Jim as a figure rooted in minstrelsy requires that we overlook the many occasions when he demonstrates knowledge, skill, agency, empathy, intellect, and understanding—as well as an awareness of the extent to which he can openly show these qualities to white people. As I will show, every example cited to demonstrate that Jim embodies stereotypes drawn from minstrelsy may alternatively be seen to highlight Jim's perceptive strategies for self-preservation and self-empowerment.

Second, there is a problem when it comes to cultural and literary sources: scenes involving Jim that critics claim to be derived from minstrelsy turn out to come from completely different sources—from African spiritual traditions, from the works of William Shakespeare, and from a book that Twain's friend William Wright (who wrote under the pen name Dan De Quille) composed in part in Twain's home. Meanwhile, a section involving the white king and duke, as it turns out, probably does have roots in minstrelsy. So while minstrelsy was one likely source that shaped aspects of the book, it was not necessarily the key source for scenes involving Jim or for the creation of his character.

Third, there is the problem of Jim's language. As I will show, Twain went to great pains to distinguish Jim's "Missouri Negro dialect" from what we might call minstrelese—the kind of talk found in minstrel shows. Twain listened with care to Black speakers (as we know from his listening to Mary Ann Cord in "A True Story") and carefully tried to capture key characteristics of their speech on the page. ("I amend dialect stuff by talking & *talking* it till it sounds right," he had written.)[28] But as we'll see, whether we focus on the lexicon, grammar, or orthography of Jim's speech, Twain wanted to make sure that Jim most definitely did not sound like someone in a minstrel show. His many corrections in the manuscript—even his marginal instructions to the copy editor— all bear this out.

The assumption that minstrel shows were the most significant influence shaping Twain's creation of the main Black character in the novel is both facile and misleading. Sterling Brown understood this. In *The Negro in American Fiction* (1937), Brown called Jim "the best example in nineteenth century fiction of the average

Negro slave. . . . And he is completely believable."²⁹ This comment is all the more significant given that Brown was widely known to be "bluntly honest and unhesitant to confront racists insult for insult," as David L. Smith reminds us.³⁰ Some thirty years after Brown wrote these words, they would be echoed by Langston Hughes, Milton Meltzer, and Charles Eric Lincoln in their *Pictorial History of the Negro in America*: "The character of Jim in *Huckleberry Finn*," they wrote, "is considered one of the best portraits in American fiction of an unlettered slave clinging to the hope of freedom."³¹

The inadequacy of the minstrel-show paradigm to describe Jim becomes clear when we attend to dimensions of Jim's character that challenge minstrel stereotypes; when we probe alternative cultural, literary, and real-life sources for episodes involving Jim; and when we focus on the care with which Twain differentiated Jim's speech from the speech of minstrel-show characters. Critics' obsession with viewing Jim through the lens of the minstrel show reveals their own limitations rather than Twain's.

Jim's Character and Behavior

Eight sections of the book in which critics have found resonances of minstrelsy turn out to be occasions where Jim shows agency, intelligence, and rationality that would be out of place in a minstrel show.

Let's start with the scene in which we meet Jim, in chapter 2. One night, Huck and Tom decide to steal some candles from the Widow's kitchen. They find Jim sitting outside under some trees near the kitchen door; they don't answer when he asks who's there, and are sure he hasn't spotted them. When he starts to snore, they assume he is asleep. They sneak by, steal three candles, and leave a nickel on the kitchen table for them. Then Tom decides to play a prank on Jim by hanging his hat from a tree limb.

When the boys leave, Jim palms the nickel. Afterward, Jim tells a wild, over-the-top story claiming that witches had bewitched him, put him into a trance, and ridden him all over the state before setting him down under the trees again and hanging "his hat on a limb to show who done it. And the next time Jim told it he said they rode him down to New Orleans, and after that, every time he told it he spread it out more and more, till by the end he said they rode him all over the world, and tired him most to death." Jim hung the five-cent piece around his neck and claimed that it was "a charm the devil give to him with his own hands and told him he could cure anybody with it and fetch witches whenever he wanted to." Slaves would come from all over and give Jim gifts just to get a glimpse of that charm and hear him tell the story of how he got it.[32]

Chadwick Hansen wrote in 1963 that "the Jim of this first episode is a recognizable type-character, the comic stage Negro, a type who has trod the less reputable boards of the American theatre almost from its beginnings. . . . His ignorance protects him from the mental pain of humiliation. . . . Since he does not suffer we are free to laugh at the incongruity between his account of the event and the reality. We are free to laugh at him, that is, because his ignorance is so sub-human that he cannot feel mental pain."[33] In a similar vein, Fredrick Woodard and Donnarae MacCann wrote in 1985 that "the swaggering buffoonery of the minstrel clown is represented early in the novel when Jim awakes and finds his hat in a tree (one of Tom's tricks), and then concocts a tale about witches and the devil. . . . Jim and the other slaves have the superstition-steeped minds that give the whole scene a minstrel flavor."[34] Echoing this perspective, Andrew Silver wrote in 2006 that "the first words Jim utters—'Whar is you? Dog my cats ef I didn' hear sumf'n' . . . —mirror the language and metaphorical expression of minstrelsy."[35] But we get a very different reading of this scene from Ralph Wiley, David L. Smith, Carl Wieck, and Robert Paul Lamb.

Wiley's reading comes across in a remarkable blend of criticism and creative writing: his screenplay *Spike Lee's Huckleberry Finn*, written in 1997.[36] Wiley, a brilliant Black satirist and sportswriter who coauthored all of Spike Lee's books with him, wrote this screenplay in the hopes of persuading his friend Lee to produce it and his friend Denzel Washington to star in it. The film was never made, although Lee did consider the project seriously and spent a day in his studio in New York discussing it with Wiley and me. Wiley allowed me to publish scenes from the screenplay for classroom use, and these scenes have been performed in American classrooms now for more than two decades. In his screenplay, Huck tells the story, as he does in the book, and the voiceover narrator speaks Huck's words—but the camera shows us the scene as Jim sees it. In this first scene with Jim, in Wiley's screenplay (as in the novel) the boys fail to be quiet as they sneak up on Jim: "I fell over a root and made a noise," Huck tells us.[37] Wiley notes in the stage directions, "Only a fool would not have seen the boys. So Jim pretends to be one."

What would we do if we heard a noise in the dark that we couldn't identify? Most of us would keep listening in silence until we heard it again, not announce, "Well, I know what I's gwyne to do: I's gwyne to set down here and listen tell I hears it agin." The latter behavior—announcing that you're going to listen—is the kind of thing one would say to humor children who think they've managed to hide from you when you know perfectly well where they are. Wiley assumes that Jim is not actually asleep, that he is aware of what's going on around him.[38] Why else would Twain have Huck tell us that "I fell over a root and made a noise" as they're sneaking up on Jim? Or why, the next moment, would he have Huck struggle with not being able to scratch an itch, and narrate it to us? ("Seemed like I'd die if I couldn't scratch.") The boys are making a racket, and Jim has heard them. Moreover, Huck reports that Jim "come tip-toeing down and stood right between us," announcing, "Whar is you?" before sitting down between the boys with his back against a tree. Rather than being the gullible victim of a hoax, he is an adult who has let some children think they've fooled him in order to make them happy.

After the boys leave, Jim retrieves his hat from the branch where Tom left it and is glad to claim the nickel Tom left for the candles. But now he has a problem: how does he account for having the money? Slaves with nickels are not common, so he comes up with a wild, over-the-top tale about being ridden by witches and having seen the devil. The story he tells over and over for the delight of his audiences makes him "most ruined, for a servant, because he got so stuck up on account of having seen the devil and been rode by witches." David L. Smith observes that "Jim clearly benefits from becoming more a celebrity and less a 'servant.' It is his owner, not Jim, who suffers when Jim reduces the amount of his uncompensated labor."[39] Noting that "the incident has often been interpreted as an example of risible Negro gullibility and ignorance as exemplified by blackface minstrelsy," Smith finds such an account wanting.

> If not for the final sentence, such an account might seem wholly satisfactory, but the information that Jim becomes, through his own story telling, unsuited for life as a slave introduces unexpected complications. Is it likely that Jim has been deceived by his own creative prevarications—especially given what we learn about his character subsequently? Or has he cleverly exploited the conventions of "Negro superstition" in order to turn a silly boy's prank to his own advantage?
>
> Regardless of whether we credit Jim with forethought in

this matter, it is undeniable that he turns Tom's attempt to humiliate him into a major personal triumph. . . . It is also obvious that he does so by exercising remarkable skills as a rhetorician. By constructing a fictitious narrative of his own experience, Jim elevates himself above his prescribed station in life. By becoming, in effect, an author, Jim writes himself a new destiny. . . . It is intelligence, not stupidity, that facilitates Jim's triumph.[40]

Smith adds that "forethought, creativity, and shrewdness" are qualities that racial discourse of the time "denied to 'the Negro.'" He writes that "Jim's darky performance here subverts the fundamental definition of 'darky.' For 'the Negro' is defined as an object, not a subject." But, Smith asks, "does an object construct its own narrative?"[41] As Carl F. Wieck puts it, Jim "shows a good head for the capitalist system and develops a small business on the basis of a story he makes up to explain the mysterious disappearance of the coin. . . . The talent of the black man in this instance far outshines the action of the white boys."[42]

Like Wiley, Robert Paul Lamb believes that Jim was only pretending to be asleep. Huck, on the other hand, "assumes that Jim fell for the prank, which clearly he did not, and that Jim's story reveals him as gullible, superstitious, dishonest, and lazy," traits that "are consistent with white stereotypes." The tall tale Jim invents, Lamb writes, "gains him authority and status within the slave community, he receives presents for telling his story, he appropriates and wears Tom's five-cent piece around his neck as an advertisement to prospective auditors and a conversation starter, and he now has an excuse for getting out of work."[43] Huck does not see Jim's creative achievement here for what it is—much as he has trouble seeing Jim for who he really is. When Huck sees Jim sitting in the doorway at the start of this scene, he says that "we could see him pretty clear, because there was a light behind him." As Lamb observes, "Since Jim is backlit and a silhouette, Huck obviously means that they can see his shape in the doorway. But Twain is subtly presenting a key to reading the novel. . . . When Huck 'sees' Jim, he apprehends only the blackness his culture has trained him to notice, which prevents him from seeing anything else."[44] A number of critics, sadly, have had the same problem.

Or take the hair ball episode in chapter 4. When Huck sees signs that pap has returned to town he is justly worried. He asks Jim to tell him what pap is going to do by consulting the hair ball from the stomach of an ox that Jim uses to tell predict the future. Hansen writes that Jim "is still the stage negro" who "is often the butt of low comedy . . . when Huck asks Jim to have the hair-ball tell his fortune."[45] But once again, Smith suggests a different way of reading this scene, interpreting the exchange between Huck and Jim as "an exercise in wily and understated bartering. In essence, Jim wants to be paid for his services, while Huck wants free advice." Huck comes up with a counterfeit quarter and Jim accepts it, explaining that he knows how to fix the coin so that "anybody in town would take it in a minute, let alone a hair-ball." The episode, in Smith's view, "shows Jim self-consciously subverting the prescribed definition of 'the Negro,' even as he performs within the limitations of that role." Jim appears to "be passive and subservient to the desires of Huck and the hair ball," but in fact, he has been serving his own interests, becoming twenty-five cents richer in the process. "Such resourcefulness," Smith writes, "is hardly consistent with the familiar, one-dimensional concept of 'the superstitious Negro.'"[46]

In a similar vein, Forrest Robinson calls Jim "shrewdly resourceful," noting that at the same time he "contrives to deceive," Jim knows that he must also appear "incorrigibly gullible."[47] Carl F. Wieck cites this scene as one bit of evidence (among many) of Jim's "ability to make a profit from exploiting the superstitions of others, including whites," noting that Jim makes up "some double-talk about white and black angels and light and dark girls, in order to extract payment of a counterfeit quarter from Huck."[48] Victor A. Doyno suggests that Jim's goals here are not simply self-serving. He writes that the predictions Jim offers may be more than "double-talk." Rather, the encounter "can be taken as a quite positive interaction"; the "long-term prediction" of an "enviable future" complete with "great wealth" is the "kind of positive, long-term prediction [that] could encourage an intelligent, rootless boy to avoid undue risk, to stay alive."[49]

When Huck surprises Jim on Jackson's Island in chapter 8, after Jim has run away, Jim thinks Huck, whom he believes to have been recently murdered, is a ghost. Genuinely scared, Jim says, "Doan' hurt me—don't! I hain't ever done no harm to a ghos'. I awluz liked dead people, en done all I could for 'em"—a comment that Woodard and MacCann call "addle-brained," supporting their view that Jim remains "forever frozen within the convention of the minstrel darky."[50] Elaine Mensh and Harry Mensh similarly refer to Jim's behavior on this occasion as "minstrel-like."[51]

But note that Tom Sawyer has the same reaction when he unexpectedly runs into Huck on his way to the Phelps's farm from the steamboat landing. Huck writes:

> So I started for town in the wagon, and when I was half way I see a wagon coming, and sure enough it was Tom Sawyer, and I stopped and waited till he come along. I says "Hold on!" and it stopped alongside, and his mouth opened up like a trunk, and staid so; and he swallowed two or three times, like a person that's got a dry throat, and then says:
> "I hain't ever done you no harm. You know that. So then, what you want to come back and ha'nt *me*, for?"

I says:

"I hain't come back—I hain't been *gone.*"

When he heard my voice, it righted him up, some, but he warn't quite satisfied, yet. He says:

"Don't you play nothing on me, because I wouldn't on you. Honest injun, now, you ain't a ghost?"

"Honest injun, I ain't," I says.[52]

Even though Tom's reaction to seeing Huck for the first time since his "murder" is virtually identical to Jim's reaction, Woodard and MacCann do not refer to Tom Sawyer's remark as "addle-brained," nor do they contend that this scene shows Tom as a "minstrel show darky."

In addition, Jim's response to seeing Huck's ghost—his insistence that he always did all he could for dead people—may be less "addle-brained" than Woodard and MacCann think it is. It is likely a statement of fact: in African spiritual traditions that clearly helped shape Jim, one is, indeed, expected to "do things" for dead people. The continuum that was thought to exist between the dead and the living in these traditions required that the living address the "needs" of the dead. Sterling Stuckey writes that slaves acknowledged a "continuous interplay between the living and the dead—a reciprocity of spirit enhanced through an observance of a whole range of African burial practices." He notes that "being on good terms with the ancestral spirits was an overarching conceptual concern for Africans everywhere in slavery."[53] Langston Hughes and Arna Bontemps observe this phenomenon as well: "The Ewe-speaking peoples of the west coast of Africa all make offerings of food and drink—particularly libations of palm wine and banana beer upon the graves of the ancestors. It is to be noted that in America the spirit is always given a good pint of whisky."[54] Jim comes from a spiritual tradition in which one does do things for dead people, and if one hasn't treated the dead properly, they come back as ghosts to complain about it. Twain's broad exposure to people of African descent in his youth makes it likely that he was aware of this tradition. (As I noted in *Was Huck Black? Mark Twain and African American Voices*, the fact that whites may have found this behavior "comical" may speak more to the limits imposed by their own ethnocentrism than to anything inherently "addled" about the tradition itself.) The point is that Jim may have made this comment in the novel not because Twain heard a comment like this in a minstrel show, but because African Americans in his past had spoken of such things within his hearing.

Later in chapter 8 we find the conversation often referred to as "Jim's Bank." Here Jim tells Huck that he was "rich" once, but then lost the money in a series of comically unfortunate speculations including the failure of the "bank" (run by a fellow slave) in which he had put the money. But the section culminates in a realization on Jim's part: "I's rich now, come to look at it. I owns mysef, en I's wuth eight hund'd dollars." Some critics see this dialogue as pure minstrelsy.[55] But when, in a minstrel show, would one ever find a slave making the bold assertion that he is rich because he owns himself? Carl F. Wieck observes that "Jim does not close the discussion foolishly or in humiliation, but with a piercing perception of his value as a human being," an implicit critique, in Andrew Silver's view, "of a nation that has valued African-American men and women only as property, commodifying their bodies, and denying them fair pay for labor."[56]

Donald B. Gibson writes that in the first chapters of the book, "Jim is presented as lacking dignity, as superstitious, ignorant, and comical." He adds, "Indeed, a slave such as Jim might well in fact have been undignified, superstitious, ignorant, and comical, but the problem is that he is presented as being *nothing but* these things."[57] But interpretations of these first chapters by Wiley,

Smith, Lamb, Robinson, Wieck, and Silver suggest how wrong Gibson was.

Like these three scenes from the book's first chapters, three scenes involving Jim in the middle portion of *Huckleberry Finn* are often seen as derived from minstrelsy: the conversations Huck and Jim have about Solomon and about Frenchmen, and the time when Huck and Jim get separated in the fog.

In chapter 14 of *Huckleberry Finn,* Huck and Jim go through the items they've taken from the wreck, and Huck, in reading to Jim about "kings, and dukes, and earls and such," brings up King Solomon. Jim responds with skepticism to the idea of a wise man's choosing to spend time in a harem, where, according to Huck, he kept "about a million wives." Why would Solomon want to subject himself to all those "rackety times in de nussery" if he were really wise, Jim asks.

> En I reck'n de wives quarrels considable; en dat 'crease de racket. Yit dey say Sollermun de wises' man dat ever live'. I doan' take no stock in dat. Bekase why: would a wise man want to live in de mids' er sich a blimblammin' all de time? No— 'deed he wouldn't. A wise man 'ud take en buil' a biler-factry; en den he could shet *down* de biler-factry when he want to res'.

Jim imagines the scene with clarity and logic within the confines of his own experience.

Huck insists that Solomon "*was* the wisest man, anyway; because the widow she told me so, her own self." Jim stands his ground and argues with Huck:

> "I doan k'yer what de widder say, he *warn't* no wise man, nuther. He had some er de dad-fetchedes' ways I ever see. Does you know 'bout dat chile dat he 'uz gwyne to chop in two?"

"Yes; the widow told me all about it."

"*Well,* den! Warn' dat de beatenes' notion in de worl'? You jis' take en look at it a minute. Dah's de stump, dah—dat's one er de women; heah's you—dat's de yuther one; I's Sollermun; en dish-yer dollar bill's de chile. Bofe un you claims it. What does I do? Does I shin aroun' mongs' de neighbors en fine out which un you de bill *do* b'long to, en han' it over to de right one, all safe en soun', de way dat anybody dat had any gumption would? No—I take en whack de bill in *two,* en give half un it to you, en de yuther half to de yuther woman. Dat's de way Sollermun was gwyne to do wid de chile. Now I want to ast you: what's de use er dat half a bill?—can't buy noth'n wid it. En what use is a half a chile? I wouldn' give a dern for a million un um."

"But hang it, Jim, you've clean missed the point—blame it, you've missed it a thousand mile."

"Who? me? Go 'long. Doan' talk to *me* 'bout yo' pints. I reck'n I knows sense when I sees it; en dey ain' no sense in sich doin's as dat. De 'spute warn't 'bout a half a chile, de 'spute was 'bout a whole chile; en de man dat think he kin settle a 'spute 'bout a whole chile wid a half a chile, doan' know enough to come in out'n de rain. Doan' talk to me 'bout Sollermun, Huck, I knows him by de back."

"But I tell you you don't get the point."

"Blame' de pint! I reck'n I knows what I knows. En mine you, de *real* pint is down furder—it's down deeper. It lays in de way Sollermun was raised. You take a man dat's got on'y one or two chillen: is dat man gwyne to be waseful o' chillen? No, he ain't; he can't 'ford it. *He* know how to value 'em. But you take a man dat's got 'bout five million chillen runnin' roun' de house, en it's diffunt. *He* as soon chop a chile in two as a cat. Dey's plenty mo'. A chile er two, mo' er less, warn't no consekens to Sollermun, dad fetch him!"

Huck's response? "I never see such a nigger. If he got a notion in his head once, there warn't no getting it out again. He was the most down on Solomon of any nigger I ever see. So I went to talking about other kings, and let Solomon slide."[58]

Fredrick Woodard and Donnarae MacCann refer to this exchange as "minstrel-like repartee," while Anthony J. Berret notes that "like the best comic dialogues of the minstrel shows, this passage both parodies and celebrates a display of social superiority."[59] But Neil Schmitz observes that "Jim has instinctively recognized in Solomon the figure of the slave holder, the white Southerner, who regards the Negro as chattel. He speaks from the depths of his own experience about the 'chile er two' that 'warn't no consekens to Solermun,'" recalling "his own children—all the black families, dismembered on the block."[60] Even Elaine Mensh and Harry Mensh, who tend to see the novel as shot through with echoes of minstrelsy, acknowledge that when Jim rejects the widow's view of Solomon, "he engages in an open denial of white authority."[61] The fact that Twain inserted the Solomon argument late in the writing process, not long before the book was published, suggests how important it was to him to include Jim's challenge to white authority here—a challenge, as Wieck suggests, that implicitly "signals a threat to the southern system of slavery by a man who dares, as did Frederick Douglass, to think for himself."[62]

Indeed, Frederick Douglass himself heard Twain give a reading of the "Sollermun" dialogue in the Congregational Church in Washington, DC, on November 24, 1885, and came backstage to say hello and chat afterward.[63] Would Douglass, who deplored minstrel shows and all they stood for, have embraced Twain's performance with the enthusiasm he did if the key number in it involving Jim had struck him as redolent of a minstrel show? There is humor in this section, to be sure, as there is in most of the book, but it is not humor at Jim's expense. Jim's reasoning and the intensity of his emotional response to the story are both compelling and understandable. Jim is unlettered and ignorant, but he is still smart, and his unexpected response to Huck's tale of Solomon's "wisdom" makes us like and respect him, not ridicule him.

Jim's conversation with Huck about Frenchmen and language has also been described as coming out of minstrelsy.

"Why, Huck, doan de French people talk de same way we does?"

"No, Jim; you couldn't understand a word they said—not a single word."

"Well, now, I be ding-busted! How do dat come?"

"*I* don't know; but it's so. I got some of their jabber out of a book. Spose a man was to come to you and say *Polly-voo-franzy*—what would you think?"

"I wouldn' think nuff'n; I'd take en bust him over de head. Dat is, ef he warn't white. I wouldn't 'low no nigger to call me dat."

"Shucks, it ain't calling you anything. It's only saying, do you know how to talk French."

"Well, den, why couldn't he *say* it?"

"Why, he *is* a-saying it. That's a Frenchman's *way* of saying it."

"Well, it's a blame' ridicklous way, en I doan want to hear no mo' 'bout it. Dey ain' no sense in it."

"Looky here, Jim, does a cat talk like we do?"

"No, a cat don't."

"Well, does a cow?"

"No, a cow don't, nuther."

"Does a cat talk like a cow, or a cow talk like a cat?"

"No, dey don't."

"It's natural and right for 'em to talk different from each other, ain't it?"

"'Course."

"And ain't it natural and right for a cat and a cow to talk different from *us?*"

"Why, mos' sholy it is."

"Well, then, why ain't it natural and right for a *Frenchman* to talk different from us?—you answer me that."

"Is a cat a man, Huck?"

"No."

"Well, den, dey ain't no sense in a cat talkin' like a man. Is a cow a man?—er is a cow a cat?"

"No, she ain't either of them."

"Well, den, she ain' got no business to talk like either one er the yuther of 'em. Is a Frenchman a man?"

"Yes."

"*Well,* den! Dad blame it, why doan' he *talk* like a man?— you answer me *dat!*"

I see it warn't no use wasting words—you can't learn a nigger to argue. So I quit.[64]

Berret writes that this conversation "may be viewed as a typical minstrel dialogue."[65] Woodard and MacCann agree, writing that because, in their view, "Jim has the information base of a child," believing English to be the only language in the world, this conversation "'plays' like the dialogue of a minstrel show."[66]

Sterling Brown, however, rejects this view, as David L. Smith reminds us. Suspecting that the real complaint of some who malign Twain's characterization of Jim through scenes like this— particularly Black critics—"is not that Jim is inaccurately rendered but rather that uneducated Negroes like Jim are embarrassments to the race who should not be depicted at all," Brown "by contrast, advocates an unflinching honesty in the representation of black history, social behavior, and culture. He therefore applauds the manifestations of such honesty in the work of Mark Twain," finding Jim's ignorant notions regarding Frenchmen as "amusingly realistic and not as embarrassments to the race."[67]

Jim may also be making a larger point here that Huck has failed to understand about the common humanity that all men share, an abstract idea that Jim implicitly grasps, but that Huck does not.[68] Steven Mailloux, David L. Smith, Arthur G. Pettit, and Jocelyn Chadwick similarly give Jim credit for the mental acuity he demonstrates here. Although he is ignorant about cultural diversity, his argument is superior to Huck's. As Pettit suggests, while the scene is indeed comic, "Jim's ignorance is credible and compassionate and carries no tones of inferiority or humiliation." Huck has, indeed, been "out-argued." Chadwick calls "Huck's ad hominem shift" at the end "a marker for his defeat and frustration as well as a reminder to the reader of the racist premises on which [Huck's] regard for Jim has been based."[69]

The scene in chapter 15 in which Huck and Jim become separated in the fog is another section in which some scholars find echoes of minstrelsy. Jim falls asleep on the raft in despair when he believes Huck's disappearance portends his death.

When Jim wakes after the fog and sees Huck next to him, he greets him with joy since he assumed he was dead. But Huck decides to play a trick on Jim and insists that he must have been dreaming. Jim "'terprets" the alleged dream, but when Huck points to the trash that has washed up on the raft during what was clearly an actual storm, Jim rebukes him sternly, leading Huck to apologize. Like many critics, Betty Jones see "the gullible and trusting Jim of chapter 15" as a "sadly comic victim" who is completely fooled by Huck's prank.[70] M. J. Sidnell similarly calls out Jim's "gullibility" and "credulity," while Woodard and MacCann

"Asleep on the Raft." Original illustration by E. W. Kemble in *Adventures of Huckleberry Finn*, 1885. Although most of Kemble's images in the original edition of *Huckleberry Finn* portray Jim as a stereotypical, comic figure, this image of him asleep on the raft after calling for Huck all night in the fog is respectful and serious, evoking the despair he felt at their separation. Impress/Alamy Stock Photo.

write that if Jim may appear "momentarily wise" in this scene (when he chides Huck), then "it comes off as an accident because he is simultaneously the head-scratching darky."[71]

But *is* Jim fooled by Huck's prank? Ralph Wiley thinks not. When Huck doesn't budge from his story and insists it was all a "dream," Wiley believes that Jim—frustrated by Huck's refusal to admit the truth—decides to give him what he's asking for: a clownish, over-the-top, stereotypical performance. In Wiley's screenplay, the stage directions tell Jim to affect a stronger dialect at this point, hamming it up as he pretends to be the easily manipulated dupe that Huck wants him to be. This idea is not Wiley's invention: it is Twain's. Twain has Jim call Huck "Boss," a name he hasn't used before, but that would be at home in a minstrel show: "Well, looky here, Boss," he says. Jim calls Huck "Boss" twice in this scene but nowhere else in the book.[72]

In Wiley's view, Jim behaves in this scene as any parent would who wants to lead a child to admit he's lying: he carefully reconstructs what happened during the night, step by step, giving Huck the chance, many times, to admit that he's trying to fool him. First he says (these lines are from the book, not Wiley's screenplay): "Huck—Huck Finn, you look me in de eye; look me in de eye. *Hain't* you ben gone away?" Then he asks, "Didn't you tote out de line in de canoe, fer to make fas' to de tow-head?" After that, he asks, "You hain't seen no tow-head? Looky-here—didn't de line pull loose en de raf' go a hummin' down de river, en leave you en de canoe behine in de fog?" Then he asks, "En didn't you whoop, en didn't I whoop, tell we got mix' up in de islands en one un us got los' en t'other one was jis' as good as los', 'kase he didn' know whah he wuz? En didn't I bust up agin a lot er dem islands en have a turrible time en mos' git drownded?"[73] Even after Jim has given him multiple chances to admit his prank, Huck insists it was all a dream. Jim is then silent for five minutes as he weighs how to teach this stubborn, insensitive child what was wrong with his behavior. The child needed to be taught a lesson, but he was a white child, after all, and it wasn't clear how Jim might go about doing that. In Wiley's screenplay, as in the novel, Jim's response to Huck's refusal to admit that he's trying to play a trick on him is to pause and then to start "affecting a slightly stronger dialect." In Wiley's screenplay, when Huck drops the deceit and points to the trash on the raft, Jim drops the heavier dialect and "points to detritus on the raft, speaks calmly, clearly." (Jim also drops the "Looky here, Boss" mode of speaking at this point in the book.)

> You was los' en I didn' k'yer no mo' what become er me en d'raf'. En when I wake up en fine you back agin, all safe en soun' . . . en all you wuz thinkin' 'bout wuz how you could make a fool uv ole Jim wid a lie. (*points to detritus on the raft, speaks calmly, clearly*). . . . **Dat truck dah is trash; en trash is what people is dat puts dirt on de head er dey fren's en makes 'em ashamed.**

The combination of Jim's affecting a heavier dialect to play the fool that Huck wants to make of him and the long pause he takes before he chastises Huck conveys how self-aware and perceptive Jim actually is during this scene. Wiley's stage directions unpack Jim's disappointment:

61A. INT. WIGWAM. NIGHT. — *Jim sits, pensively. It seems Huck is no different from the "witches and devils" that have ridden him in his days of bondage. Huck enters wigwam. Jim recoils, but holds it in. Huck gets on his haunches, looks at Jim, looks down. Looks up.*

HUCK

Jim, I . . . (*inhales, exhales deeply*) I'm sorry, Jim.

And with that, a crack in Jim's soul is patched. Huck looks down again as Jim regards him with slightly knitted brows. His face softens. He reaches out with the flat palm of his hand—hesitates, then rubs the boy's bowed head. Huck looks up, so thankfully, his eyes shining wet.

Wiley, to his credit, shows Jim in this scene acting as a father of an adolescent boy; it may have helped that he, himself *was*, in fact, the father of an adolescent boy at the time he wrote the screenplay. He sees Jim as a parent giving Huck the tutelage he desperately needs but has never had. I find his interpretation—and his method for conveying it—both persuasive and original.[74]

Other critics, as well, recognize the significance of Jim's response in this scene. Stephen Railton, for example, writes, "'Dignity' is too abstract a word for Huck's vocabulary, but Jim's answer is as authentically noble as any speech in Shakespeare." "What Jim insists upon here," Railton continues, "what Huck is made to see as the darkness brightens, is simply [Jim's] manhood. Because he is black, no one else in the novel even suspects it exists."[75] And Huck does learn the lesson. He states that Jim's words "made me feel so mean I could almost kissed *his* foot to get him to take it back." After he apologizes, Huck concludes the chapter, "I didn't do him no more mean tricks"—and he doesn't— "and I wouldn't done that one if I'd a knowed it would make him feel that way."[76]

In the final portion of the novel, Tom Sawyer surprises Huck and Jim by turning up at the Phelps farm (where Jim is imprisoned) and pledging to help free Jim—without revealing the fact that he knows Jim has actually been freed by Miss Watson in her will. Tom insists on modeling Jim's escape on escapes he has read about in novels, requiring Jim to complete a complicated series of absurd tasks as a result. Andrew Silver writes that Tom's entrance in the final portion of the book "allows Twain to return the text to minstrelsy once more," and E. L. Doctorow concludes that at this point Twain "portrays Jim in minstrelese, as a gullible black child-man led by white children."[77] Referring to the "sport" that Tom makes of Jim's misery in the closing section of the novel, Leo Marx writes, "It should be added at once that Jim doesn't mind too much."[78] Others have reiterated the idea that Jim has become "a flat cheap type" and have agreed with the idea that "Jim doesn't mind too much." Arthur Pettit avers, for example, that what is "most disturbing" is that Jim must put up with all these indignities passively."[79]

But is it true that "Jim doesn't mind too much," that he puts up with "all these indignities passively," that he becomes in the last portion of the novel "a flat stereotype: the submissive stage-Negro"?

Jim is more active, smart, and assertive in this portion of the book than he is often given credit for. Indeed, the first thing he does when he is taken to the Phelps farm is to blow the whistle on the king and the duke: Silas Phelps reports that "the runaway niggcr told Burton and me all about that scandalous show, and Burton said he would tell the people; so I reckon they've drove the owdacious loafers out of town."[80] Indeed, the two con men are soon tarred and feathered as a result of Jim's decision to finger them.

Jim's second action in the section of the book known as the Evasion (chapter 32 to the end) is to deny that he has ever seen Huck and Tom before, having grasped quickly that pretending he doesn't know them will be to his advantage. Even before he has a clue about what they are up to, he surmises that they want him to keep mum about knowing them.

> "Did you sing out?"
> "No, sah," says Jim, "I hain't said nothing, sah."
> "Not a word?"
> "No, sah, I hain't said a word."
> "Did you ever see us before?"
> "No, sah; not as I knows on."

Jim soon learns that the boys are working to free him. When anyone other than Huck and Jim are around, Tom does his best to impersonate the kind of person who'd punish a runaway like Jim with hanging. When Nate, the slave charged with bringing food to Jim, is within hearing, Tom asks, "I wonder if uncle Silas is going to hang this nigger. If I was to catch a nigger that was ungrateful enough to run away, *I* wouldn't give him up, I'd hang him." But as soon as Nate steps beyond hearing range, Tom "whispers to Jim" and makes a comment that earns Jim's trust: "Don't ever let on to know us. And if you hear any digging going on, nights, it's us: we're going to set you free." Huck adds, "Jim only had time to grab us by the hand and squeeze it" before they were no longer alone.[81]

Jim believes Tom and Huck are genuinely working to free him. He has reason to believe their good intentions on this point, even if the particulars of how they plan to free him are not yet clear. After all, Huck has helped him evade capture several times, and Tom has just asserted that the two of them would both be working to set Jim free. When the boys wake him up the next night to post him on how the plot to free him is going, "He was so glad to see us he most cried; and called us honey, and all the pet names he could think of; and was for having us hunt up a cold chisel to cut the chain off of his leg with, right away, and clearing out without losing any time." Tom rejects Jim's practical suggestion but reassures him that the alternative plan he proposes is safe and clearly designed to succeed: "But Tom he showed him how unregular it would be, and set down and told him all about our plans, and how we could alter them in a minute any time there was an alarm; and not to be the least afraid, because we would see he got away, *sure.*"[82]

Tom's guarantee—that emphatic *sure*—combined with the fact that Huck seems down with the plan, puts Jim's mind at ease: "So Jim he said it was all right, and we set there and talked over old times a while." As Tom spins out the plan, Huck tells us that "Jim he couldn't see no sense in the most of it, but he allowed we was white folks and knowed better than him; so he was satisfied and said he would do it all just as Tom said." Jim recognizes that he has no other option: if Tom is not having fun, he might get bored with the escape and either have nothing more to do with it or, worse, possibly even tell Aunt Sally and Uncle Silas that Jim is a runaway. He does know how much Huck looks up to and respects Tom, so he must at least mimic that respect at the risk of alienating Huck, the one white person he knows for sure is committed to freeing him. (Jim is not present when Tom remarks that it would be ideal if they could "leave Jim to our children to get out," stringing out the escape "to as much as eighty year.")[83]

Despite Leo Marx's assertion that "Jim doesn't mind too much" when Tom demands that he engage in a series of irritating, exhausting, and pointless actions, Jim does mind. He objects at various points to Tom's plans, refuses to go along with them, and sometimes prompts Tom to change them. For example, when Tom comes up with a four-part inscription for Jim to scratch into a log, Jim objects that "it would take him a year to scrabble such a lot of truck onto the logs with a nail, and he didn't know how to make letters, besides." When Tom decides Jim should scratch the inscriptions into a rock instead, Jim "said it would take him such a pison long time to dig them into a rock, he wouldn't ever get out," prompting Tom to say he would let Huck help him do it. When Tom asks if Jim has any spiders in the shack, and Jim jokes that he'd just as soon have rattlesnakes around, Jim is appalled when Tom takes him seriously and offers to get him a rattlesnake: "Why, if dey was a rattlesnake to come in heah, I'd take en bust right out thoo dat log wall, I would, wid my head." Jim objects violently to the idea of a rattlesnake in the shack, even when Tom tries to mollify him by telling him how much "glory" he'd gain if he let one in: "Why, mars Tom, I doan' *want* no sich glory. Snake take 'n bite Jim's chin off, den *whah* is de glory? No, sah, I doan' want no sich doin's." Tom doesn't give up. Jim responds once again with more logic than Tom is willing to entertain, noting that "de trouble all *done*" if the snake bites him while he's trying to train him. "Mars Tom," Jim continues, "I's willin' to tackle mos' anything 'at ain't onreasonable, but ef you en Huck fetches a rattlesnake in heah for me to tame, I's gwyne to *leave,* dat's *shore.*" Chadwick notes that "Jim says what he must, when he must. But he also realizes that the equation has changed with Tom Sawyer in it. Tom, a representative of the (un)reconstructed South, barely sees or hears Jim as a real person. Jim can afford to say only so much in front him." Tom finally relents: "Well, then, let it go, let it go, if you're so bull-headed about it. We can get you some garter-snakes, and you can tie some buttons on their tails, and let on they're rattlesnakes, and I reckon that'll have to do." Jim was likely persuaded that the boy was mad, but since Jim knew that his fate was still in the hands of these two white boys, one of whom, at least, was his friend, he did his best to go along.[84]

Peaches Henry claims that Jim in the final section of the novel is a "stereotypical, superstitious 'darky' that Twain's white audience would have expected and in which they would have delighted. . . . [Jim climbs] back into the minstrel costume. His self-respect and manly pursuit of freedom bow subserviently before the childish pranks of an adolescent white boy."[85] But Chadwick argues, to the contrary, that "Jim must maintain his mask for self-preservation. . . . When Jim assesses his situation and sees that Huck is acting in concert with Tom Sawyer, he shifts his language. Terms of subserviency—'Mars Tom,' 'Misto Tom,' and 'sah'—are suddenly prominent." She reminds us that Jim speaks out often to Huck and Tom, "as the situation warrants." But he never forgets "that he is still in the South" and "has been captured as a runaway."[86]

When Tom says he'll bring Jim some rats and insists that he

make pets of them and play music to them on his jew's harp, Jim protests. Tom says the rats, snakes, and spiders all like music and "will just fairly swarm over you, and have a noble good time." Jim responds by saying, "Yes, *dey* will, I reck'n, mars Tom, but what kine er time is *Jim* havin'? Blest if I kin see de pint." Jim objects so vociferously to all the crazy things Tom asks him to do that Tom becomes exasperated. When Tom says he'll put an onion in Jim's coffeepot to help him cry, so that he can water a flower with his tears, Jim "found so much fault with it, and with the work and bother of raising the mullen, and jewsharping the rats, and petting and flattering up the snakes and spiders and things, on top of all the other work he had to do on pens, and inscriptions, and journals, and things, which made it more trouble and worry and responsibility to be a prisoner than anything he ever undertook, that Tom most lost all patience with him."[87] Far from being a passive "stage-negro" quietly doing all the insane tasks Tom demands of him, Jim objects at nearly every point. In the end, however, Jim decides to go along with Tom's deranged scheme, exhausting and pointless as it is, since getting away from the shack and reaching freedom still depends on the protection and goodwill of these two white boys, however bizarre their plans may seem.

Tom gets shot in the leg during the misguided "escape" the boys have engineered. Jim is now faced with a terrible choice: throw away what he sees as his last chance at freedom by staying with the wounded child until a doctor comes, or leave and have the child's likely death on his conscience for the rest of his life. He decides to stay even though he knows it means giving up freedom. When his behavior can make the difference between life and death for a child, he acts with agency and insight, demonstrating a parent's sense of responsibility—even if that child has been a trial and a burden, as Tom has been to Jim. With that decision, Jim cements his status as the most admirable character in the entire book. That status is only enhanced when Jim refuses to "let on to know" Huck even when he is reimprisoned, this time with both his hands and legs chained. Jim's decision to stay with Tom is also shrewd. He knows that his chances of escaping to freedom on his own are virtually impossible and that, should a white child die as a result of his escape, he could be lynched despite being worth eight hundred dollars to his owner. By staying to help the doctor whom Huck sends to help, he chooses to play the faithful slave, and this turns out to his benefit. When Jim is captured, returned to the Phelpses, and roughly treated by the posse, the doctor speaks up for him, and this earns him credit with those who had been abusing him: "they all agreed that Jim had acted very well, and was deserving to have some notice took of it, and reward."[88]

While "up to this point, we have been able to admire Jim's good sense and to respond sentimentally to his good character," David L. Smith writes, "this is the first time that we see him making a significant (and wholly admirable) moral decision."

> His act sets him apart from everyone else in the novel except Huck. And modestly (if not disingenuously), he claims to be behaving just as Tom Sawyer would. Always conscious of his role as a "Negro," Jim knows better than to claim personal credit for his good deed. Yet the contrast between Jim's behavior and Tom's is unmistakable. Huck declares that Jim is "white inside" (chap. 40). He apparently intends this as a compliment, but Tom is fortunate that Jim does not behave like most of the whites in the novel.[89]

"Twain also contrasts Jim's self-sacrificing compassion with the cruel and mean-spirited behavior of his captors," Smith writes. His captors "abuse Jim, verbally and physically, and some want to lynch him as an example to other slaves." And "as if these enforcers of white supremacy did not appear contemptible enough already," even after the doctor attests to Jim's having risked his freedom to faithfully nurse Tom, and after "these vigilantes do admit that Jim deserves to be rewarded," all they do is agree to stop punching and cursing him: they don't remove his shackles.[90]

Scholars are increasingly viewing the final portion of the book as a satire on how the nation botched the enterprise of freeing the slaves: the convict lease system, sharecropping, lynchings, and violence directed at freedmen who tried to exercise rights they had been granted all effectively reenslaved the freed slaves, much as Tom effectively reenslaved Jim despite knowing that he was already free. Matthew Seybold writes that "the assumption (sometimes called the Holbrook Thesis because Hal Holbrook articulates it so convincingly in Ken Burns's *Mark Twain*) is that the continued degradation of formerly enslaved people which Twain witnessed during his first trip to the region since the outset of the Civil War . . . convinced him that a novel focused on the blinding hypocrisy, dehumanization, absurdity, and ritualized violence of the antebellum period was still relevant."[91] A steady chorus of scholars has voiced variations on the idea that the last portion of the novel is a commentary on race relations in the 1880s.[92] As Lamb describes it, "The Phelps episode is indeed a burlesque, but of postwar racial accommodations: one in which Jim receives forty dollars from Tom rather than the forty acres and a mule that the freedmen required to make their 'liberty' meaningful. In addition, it symbolizes the post-Reconstruction sell-out of former slaves after the 1877 compromise—in which Tom's class was allowed to decide the fate of the freedmen."[93] Perhaps Toni Morrison put it best when she wrote that during this period, "the nation, as well as Tom Sawyer, was deferring Jim's freedom in agonizing play."[94]

The Minstrel Mask

Several critics suggest that we may see Jim perform stereotypes drawn from minstrelsy when it is clearly to his advantage to do so. Forrest G. Robinson writes, "Almost from the moment of Jim's first appearance in the novel we are witness to hints and glancing suggestions that there may be an artful and self-interested deceiver at work behind the face of the gullible 'darky' that Jim presents to the world."[95] Robinson, James Cox, Lamb, and others have understood Jim as someone self-aware enough throughout the book to perform a version of himself that white people around him expect to see.[96] Robinson cites Frederick Douglass's observation that since "the masters had persuaded themselves, against overwhelming evidence to the contrary, that slavery was a benign and morally defensible institution," a "sadly ironic consequence of this delusion" was that "slaves were cruelly punished for the open expression of their feelings about their condition. The dark truth was too much for the master to bear. Thus the slave was obliged, for his or her survival, to retreat behind the mask of a docile, gullible, pliant 'darky' who suffers all manner of indignity with silence and a simpleminded smile."[97]

Critics who, unlike Ralph Ellison, fail to look behind the minstrel mask cannot see the larger point Twain is making with his characterization of Jim. The minstrel mask, Toni Morrison writes, fits Jim "like an ill-made clown suit that cannot hide the man within."[98]

In a book in which the basest scoundrels and most insensitive murderers are all white, Jim stands out as a paragon of virtue. As early as 1948 Dixon Wecter suggested that Jim was the "real hero" of the book.[99] In the decades that followed, many scholars embraced this view.[100] Chadwick enumerates Jim's virtues like this: "his sense of honor, ethics, loyalty, indomitable faith in the nuclear family (a faith that extends into guardianship of Huck Finn), masterful ability to manipulate language, sturdy sense of duty, grasp of the deep meaning of friendship, clear perception of himself as a man, unintimidating wisdom, desire to be self-reliant, and conscious awareness of taking risks. These traits are the marks of a hero."[101] The larger point Twain is making, as David L. Smith puts it, is this: "As an intelligent, sensitive, wily, and considerate individual, Jim demonstrates that race provides no useful index of character."[102] A number of critics—including Sterling Brown, Jocelyn Chadwick, Ralph Ellison, Lawrence Howe, Robert Paul Lamb, Forrest G. Robinson, David L. Smith, Ralph Wiley, and myself—all argue that Jim's and Mark Twain's complexity emerges from behind what on the surface might appear to be behavior inflected by stereotypes of minstrelsy.[103] As Lamb puts it, Jim "wears the minstrel mask so effectively that he deceives the novel's white characters, and, for a century, has deceived white readers and critics as well."[104]

While the idea of Jim as a character in a minstrel show has been the subject of debates about the eight portions of the book discussed here, Jim also demonstrates intelligence, agency, and empathy in order to control events and his own fate in at least two other scenes, as well. One such scene takes place in chapter 9, when Jim decides to keep pap's death to himself, and another occurs in chapter 16, when Jim manages to get Huck to change his mind about turning him over to some slave catchers. Hilton Obenzinger, James Cox, Forrest Robinson, Neil Schmitz, and Robert Paul Lamb all see Jim exercising agency as a deft manipulator of information in the first case, and of sentiment in the second—in both cases to his own advantage.

Why does Jim cover up pap's body and not tell Huck about his death until the end of the book? Many argue that the threat of pap's coming back into his life is what keeps Huck on the run.

They maintain that Jim knows this, and that he knows as well that the success of his own journey depends on Huck's being with him, able to claim that he owns him, to protect him from those seeking a reward for returning him to slavery. Jim also knows that in a society that prohibits men like him from testifying in court, producing a living, breathing Huck is the only way he can beat the charge that he is a murderer. Hilton Obenzinger makes the first of these points when he argues that Jim "had purposely hidden the truth in order to keep the white boy on the raft as his protective cover."[105] Robinson makes the second point, noting that Jim keeps pap's death to himself as long as possible in part because "Huck is the living proof that Jim is not a murderer. . . . The boy is Jim's best chance for survival."[106] So long as Jim keeps pap's death to himself, Robinson tells us, he "retains a substantial measure of control over Huck."[107] One might also argue (as I do, implicitly, in "Jim's Version") that Jim wants to protect Huck from seeing the degrading setting in which his father died, protecting him from the shame of knowing that his father died in such filthy surroundings—in a floating brothel, shot in the back by drunken miscreants who robbed, gambled, scrawled on the walls, and may have put an infant at risk in the process. Or he may have acted this way for a combination of these motives, as Toni Morrison suggests.[108]

Another key scene showing Jim's agency and intelligence occurs in chapter 16, when he manages to get Huck to change his mind about turning him over to some slave catchers. As Huck shoves off in the canoe supposedly to see whether they've passed Cairo, but—as Jim suspects—actually to turn Jim in, Jim calls out to him: "Pooty soon I'll be a-shout'n for joy, en I'll say, it's all on accounts o' Huck; I's a free man, en I couldn't ever ben free ef it hadn' ben for Huck; Huck done it. Jim won't ever forgit you, Huck; you's de bes' fren' Jim's ever had; en you's de *only* fren' ole Jim's got, now." Huck "was paddling off, all in a sweat to tell on him," but tells us that when he heard Jim say this, "it seemed to kind of take the tuck all out of me." When Huck is fifty yards from the raft, Jim shouts to him, "Dah you goes, de ole true Huck; de on'y white genlman dat ever kep' his promise to ole Jim."[109] Lamb suggests that in addition to flattering Huck and "reminding him of both their friendship and his promise not to tell" Jim may be conveying a subtle but effective warning. "Beneath his seeming gratitude," Lamb writes, "Jim is threatening to reveal that Huck has helped a fugitive slave, and Huck grasps the threat, if not the conscious intention." As Jim "slyly [elevates] Huck from 'white trash' to 'white gentleman,'" while "reminding him of his earlier promise," his words "hit their mark, as Huck confesses, 'I just felt sick.'"[110]

Jim's appeal does just what Jim hopes it will do: instead of giving Jim up to the slave catchers, Huck lies that the man on the raft is white and has smallpox. Jim's skillful manipulation of Huck's feelings allows him to evade what up to that point is the greatest single threat to his freedom; it also nets the two of them two twenty-dollar gold pieces. Before Jim knows that his appeal has worked, however, he demonstrates sensible caution and suspicion: Lamb suggests that "when Huck returns to the raft, after deceiving the slave-hunters, Jim lavishes him with compliments and explains that he's in the water in case he had to make a quick escape; but in fact he heard Huck pause when asked by the men whether his companion was white or black, and he didn't trust Huck to lie to them."[111]

Since we are seeing Jim through Huck's eyes, some of those moments when Huck tells us that Jim is silent may be hard to decipher. But they may be significant, nonetheless. On Jackson's Island, for example, when Jim finds out that Huck isn't dead, we learn that Huck "talked along, but [Jim] only set there and looked at me; never said nothing." Victor A. Doyno suggests that "Jim's act of silent staring could mask intense, rapid calculation. Is Huck a danger to him? Should Huck be somehow immobilized or silenced? Could Jim dare to trust Huck?"[112] One might also imagine what is running through Jim's mind after Huck shows his stubborn determination to continue to pretend that the fog was just a dream. We are told that "Jim didn't say nothing for about five minutes, but set there studying over it." What was he thinking during those five minutes? Toni Morrison has written eloquently about the importance of Huck's moments of silence in the novel, but we must pay close attention to those times when Jim is silent, as well.[113] A similar dynamic to the one that Doyno flags in the earlier silence could be at work here: Jim's silence "could mask intense, rapid calculation." How could he have been so wrong about the boy? How could the trust the two of them had built up be squandered so? And could he ever trust this child again? After silently trying to puzzle out issues like these, Jim launches into an over-the-top performance of the role Huck seems to be requiring him to play, soon boring Huck in the process. Then, after Jim drops the minstrel mask and tells Huck how wrong his prank was, he is silent for five minutes—but quite a lot may be going on in his mind. On those occasions when Huck tells us that Jim "didn't say nothing for a minute" or "studied it over," Lamb writes, "Jim is thinking prior to manipulating Huck; but because Huck assumes that black people are incapable of complex thought, he never realizes that he's being played. And Jim's manipulations virtually emplot the novel."[114]

The fact that Jim manipulates Huck and others while wearing "his minstrel mask and reflecting back the racial stereotypes that whites believe in," can make it difficult to discern "Jim's intelligence, motivations, and real thoughts and feelings," Lamb writes. "But if the reader looks closely and asks, at critical junctures, what are Jim's best options, the real Jim, a highly intelligent, three-dimensional man wearing the minstrel mask rather than a simpleton straight out of a minstrel show, comes sharply into focus."[115]

Alternative Cultural, Literary, and Real-Life Sources

If Jim's behavior in scenes that allegedly resemble minstrel routines goes well beyond anything one might see on a minstrel stage, it turns out that the assumption that minstrel shows are the source for these scenes may be questionable as well. We need to consider some alternative cultural, literary, and real-life roots of these sections of the novel.

When it comes to both Jim and Tom seeing Huck's "ghost," Twain may be drawing on a tradition other than minstrel shows. Twain was obsessed with Shakespeare all his life. He saw his first production as a teenager during his work as an itinerant printer, and one of his first long comic sketches—published in 1856, under the pseudonym Thomas Jefferson Snodgrass—was a parody of how a country bumpkin might describe a St. Louis production of *Julius Caesar*.[116] During his cub pilot days in 1858, he steered for many months for a steamboat pilot named George Ealer who was "an idolater of Shakespeare." Twain writes that "quite uninvited he would read Shakespeare to me; not just casually, but by the hour, when it was his watch and I was steering."[117] During the years when he was writing *Huckleberry Finn*, Twain wrote both a play and a comic sketch featuring Shakespeare and his works. He explored the possibilities of writing a burlesque of *Hamlet* in 1873 and returned to the project in 1881, as Gary Scharnhorst tells us.[118] He made Shakespeare a key character in the bawdy send-up of Elizabethans that he wrote in 1876, the same summer he began writing *Huckleberry Finn* (*Date, 1601. Conversation, as it was by the Social Fireside in the Time of the Tudors*). It is not too much to say that Shakespeare haunted Twain: his preoccupation with Shakespeare would later drive him to write a book called *Is Shakespeare Dead?*

Whether one thinks of the ghost of the murdered Julius Caesar or the ghost of Hamlet's murdered father or any of the other ghosts that appear in Shakespeare's plays, the Bard often has ghosts of the murdered appearing to the living to avenge their deaths.[119] (Indeed, Twain made the ghost of Hamlet's father a key character in the burlesque *Hamlet* he wrote while working on *Huckleberry Finn.*)[120] As far as Jim and Tom know, Huck was murdered. It's quite plausible that Shakespeare figured in Twain's mind at least subliminally while he was writing these "ghost" scenes in *Huckleberry Finn.*[121]

There is also a problem with assuming that "Jim's Bank" has its origins in minstrel shows. The scene's roots probably lie in *History of the Big Bonanza,* a book about the Comstock Lode by Twain's friend Dan De Quille (the pen name of William Wright), who had been close to Twain when both worked on the *Territorial Enterprise* in Nevada during the heady days of the first major discovery of silver and gold there that brought a rush of prospectors, miners, and financiers to the region. De Quille wrote a large part of *Big Bonanza* when he was a guest in Twain's Hartford home the year before Twain began writing *Huckleberry Finn,* and indeed Twain gave De Quille the idea for the book, secured his publishing contract with Twain's own publisher, and was De Quille's main mentor and cheerleader while he worked on the volume. Hamlin Hill and Walter Blair suggested back in 1962 that the conversation about money in chapter 8 of *Huckleberry Finn* ("Jim's Bank") may have been influenced by chapter 38 of De Quille's book, which contains a conversation with a Paiute named Captain Juan who served as a guide for a group of white men.[122] But critics have largely ignored this suggestion, asserting repeatedly that "Jim's Bank" comes out of minstrelsy.

De Quille writes that one evening, "when we were all seated about our camp-fire, after a hearty supper, being in a talkative mood, [Captain Juan] said: 'I was pretty well off once, over in California—I had *fifty dollars*.' He named that amount with an emphasis which showed that he considered the announcement one of considerable importance." Juan is asked, "And what became of all this wealth?" When he replies, "Me burst all to smash!" he is asked whether he lost it in some kind of speculation. Juan asks what "speculation" is, and one of the white men answers, "Well, it's when you put your money into something that you expect to make plenty more money out of—like you plant wheat. You plant your money in some speculation to get more money."[123] Did he have one bad speculation? Juan is asked. Juan comically describes an especially bad one that he made when he married a Spanish woman who had designs on his money. The seeds of Jim's disquisition on speculation may well have been planted in Twain's mind via Juan's story in *Big Bonanza*, rather than via any minstrel show.

In addition, a bank going bust—an idea central to the story Jim tells—may have come to mind for Twain because of the Great Financial Panic of 1873 (three years before Twain began writing the novel). During this year, at least one hundred banks across the nation failed. The Freedman's Bank failed one year later: it cost its sixty-one thousand depositors nearly three million dollars, leaving them as bereft of funds as Jim was before he realized that he was rich because he owned himself, and he was worth eight hundred dollars.

Like these three scenes from the book's first chapters, another scene involving Jim—the prank to which he is subjected after his separation from Huck in the fog—may come from the same source as "Jim's Bank": De Quille's book about the Comstock Lode, as Blair and Hill suggest. In *Big Bonanza*, companions of a white man named Pike who know that he is afraid of being attacked by Indians decide to stage a fake attack that Pike thinks is a real one. The next day when Pike is describing "the dreadful affair of the previous night" to a crowd, the friends he assumed to have been killed all show up alive and well and insist that he dreamed the whole thing. Pike is "thunderstruck." One of his friends says, "Pike, you must have dreamt all this about Indians." Pike insists it was no dream. "But, Pike, look at us," his friend says. "You were dreaming and suddenly rose up shouting 'Injuns! Injuns' and before we could stop you, you ran down the cañon." Finally, Pike relents, saying, "Yes, it must have been a dream." The crowd cries, "Give us the dream!" And then Pike narrates what he experienced as if he had dreamed it all. "Oh, yes, it was a dream, sartain and sure," he concludes. "But what gits me was its bein' so astonishin' plain— jist the same as bein' wide awake." De Quille adds, "Pike continued to tell his dream for some years, constantly adding new matter, till at last it was a wonderful yarn. He enlarged greatly on the part he took in the fight."[124] (Unlike Jim, who, as I have argued, clearly understands the prank for what it was, Pike persists in believing that he really did have a remarkable dream.)

Pike's "dream" may have also influenced the scene in chapter 2 where Jim similarly keeps retelling the story of his being chased by witches, "constantly adding new matter," making it a "a wonderful yarn." It would not be the first time Twain took something that happened to a white man as the basis for incidents involving Jim in the book: his white coachman, Patrick McAleer, had a child who was made deaf by scarlet fever; Twain's recollection of this fact may lie behind the deafness of Jim's daughter.[125]

Jim's Speech

Another major subject of debate involving Jim is his language. Does Jim's speech have its roots in the exaggerated stage dialect of minstrelsy, designed to make the reader laugh at him? Or does his dialect show something else? In the "Explanatory" that opens the book Twain lists "the Missouri negro dialect" first in his list of dialects used in the book and says clearly that he crafted the speech of his characters "pains-takingly, and with the trustworthy guidance and support of personal familiarity with these several forms of speech." Reading Black dialect makes many readers uncomfortable, bringing with it, as it does, all the racist baggage of minstrelsy and caricature. But as we'll see, Twain did not see it that way: he saw it as part of his effort to convey the reality of a particular Black man's world with accuracy and nuance.

As Arthur G. Pettit notes, in his notebooks and letters Twain "was constantly practicing his skill with black vernacularisms—playing with alternative spellings and pronunciations, honing the sound and the nuance to the highest possible pitch of perfection."[126] In "A True Story, Repeated Word for Word as I Heard It," Twain went to great pains to evoke the Black vernacular speech with which Mary Ann Cord told the true story of her separation from her son on the auction block and her reunion with him after the war. The language in which she expressed that pain would find its way directly into the language in which Jim would express his own pain in *Huckleberry Finn,* foreshadowing Jim's poignant expressions of grief over his separation from his children.

Although most of Twain's white contemporaries who wrote Black dialect used it for comic purposes, Twain did not. Mary Ann Cord (as well as other Black speakers he knew) had taught him that Black dialect was as capable as any other dialect of conveying strong emotions. And he was also convinced that it was as capable as standard English of conveying important concrete information.

To prove this latter point (and to show off his own virtuosity), in 1882 Twain wrote his publisher, James R. Osgood, a letter detailing the length of a manuscript he was about to send and the kinds of editorial judgments he was willing to accept. The letter would be unremarkable were it not for the fact that Twain decided to write it entirely in what Osgood would have recognized as Black dialect:

Dear Osgood—

I's gwyne to sen' you de stuff jis' as she stan', now; an' you an' Misto Howls kin weed out enuff o' dem 93,000 words fer to crowd de book down to *one* book; or you kin shove in enuff er dat ole Contrib-Club truck fer to swell her up en bust her in two an' make *two* books outen her.

Dey ain't no use to buil' no index, ner plan out no 'rangement er de stuff ontwel you is decided what you gwyne to do.

I don't want none er dat rot what is in de small onvolups to go in, 'cepp'n jis' what Misto Howls *say* shel go in.

I don' see how I come to git sich a goddam sight er truck on han', nohow.

Yourn truly

S L Clemens[127]

While Twain was obviously having fun here, the letter also demonstrates his belief that the Black vernacular speech he was experimenting with was as efficient as any other for communicating complex subjects with precision.

Twain crafted Jim's speech with great care. In his notes for the novel, Twain had told himself, "Let Jim say putty for 'pretty' and nuvver for 'never.'"[128] But, as Victor A. Doyno observes, when Twain was revising the emotionally powerful scene in which Jim expresses his guilt over having hit his deaf daughter for not doing as she was told before he knew she was deaf, Twain first followed the rule he had come up with for Jim's speech, writing "de chile nuvver move!" but then crossed out "nuvver" and substituted "never"—a "highly unusual modification of dialect form to standard language," as Doyno notes. Twain writes "never" instead of "nuvver" a second time in this passage. After Jim describes yelling, *"pow! Jus as loud as I could yell,"* Twain has Jim say, *"She never budge!* Oh, Huck, I bust out a-cryin', en grab her up en my arms en say, 'Oh, de po' little thing! de Lord God Amighty fogive po' ole Jim, kaze he never gwyne to fogive hisseff as long as he live!' Oh, she was plumb deef en dumb, Huck, plum deef and dumb— en I'd ben a-treat'n her so!"*[129] In the left margin, near *"She never budge!,"* Twain had written, uncharacteristically, a note to the copy editor in pencil: "This expression shall not be changed."[130] Jim does not say *nuvver* at any point in the book. Twain always has him say *never.*

American linguists in the 1880s were recognizing the difficulties of accurately rendering dialects and accents. Writing in 1880, prominent literary critic Richard Grant White commented on "the variableness in the perceptions of sound, even among professed phonologists," noting that phonologists themselves "are even unable to record their own [speech] with satisfactory accuracy."[131] Given these challenges, it is all the more striking that Jim's speech throughout the book manifests with great precision a number of features described and validated by linguists as characteristic of what they refer to as African American Vernacular English (AAVE) today. These include systematic consonant replacement—omitting the final *g* in gerunds (*goin'* for *going*), replacing *th* at the start of words with *d* (*dey* for *they*), replacing *th* at the ends of words with *f* (*mouf* for *mouth*), and omitting the final *t* in words ending with *st* (*mos'* for *most*). They also note the characteristic use of double subjects, as in "De widder she try," and double negatives, such as "ain't no."[132]

Lisa Cohen Minnick undertook a systematic study of Jim's use of thirty-one specific features of AAVE to determine whether Jim's speech reflected Twain's efforts to evoke how real people spoke (using features identified by linguists today) or whether it was shaped by stereotypical representations in popular theater and fiction. She concluded that "Twain incorporated features that have been identified with African American speakers in the scholarship, and he did so in a way that reveals his understanding of how these features functioned in real speech," showing himself to be a "sensitive (if not flawless) interpreter of the phonology and grammar associated with black speech." In Minnick's view, "The evidence that Twain actually uses the depiction of Jim's speech to disparage him is simply not found in the text of the novel."[133]

Writing on the same topic six years after Minnick's book came out, Ann Ryan independently affirms Minnick's conclusion, suggesting the likelihood that "Twain portrayed Jim's dialect realistically and respectfully and did not intend to create racial controversy through the use of his dialect."[134] But both Twain and Jim seem to have fallen victim to a phenomenon Holger Kersten has observed, writing about nineteenth-century American literature: "Critics assume that the selection of dialect as a literary medium implies derogatory if not racist intentions."[135] Although that assumption may be correct in some cases, it is not remotely relevant here, as both Minnick and Ryan have argued.

Twain "pains-takingly" tries make sure that Jim's dialect does not resemble the exaggerated caricature of Black speech one finds in minstrel shows. Although many readers of his day tended to assume that Black dialect in a text signaled that something comic was transpiring, Twain rejects that idea, as we know from his treatment of Mary Ann Cord's speech in "A True Story." Instead, Black dialect was simply another vehicle for telling a riveting story filled with drama and emotion. Twain did not stigmatize speakers of Black dialect as so many of his peers routinely did. Rather, he viewed Black dialect as a mode of communication different from standard English but not inferior to it—and one that he was determined to get down on the page as accurately as he could.

Twain edited Jim's dialect meticulously, even writing a note to himself in pencil on the very first page of the manuscript right before the famous "Notice" to remind himself that his preferred dialect equivalents for the word *of* were *er* or *o'*.[136] Twain knew he needed this reminder, since he had written *of* by mistake twenty-seven times. He changed it to *er* twenty-two times and to *o'* five times with his pencil. These dialect choices were deliberate and required editorial vigilance, as the hundreds of corrections he made in the manuscript make clear. As Twain wrote in 1874 as he revised the story Mary Ann Cord had told him for publication, "I want to work at the proofs & get the dialect as nearly right as possible."[137] He devoted equal care to crafting Jim's dialect in *Huckleberry Finn*.

In minstrel shows Black characters nearly always replace the final *f* or *v* sound in words like *of* or *give* or *have* with *b*, rendering these words as *ob* or *gib* or *hab*—deformations that convey the characters' ignorance and help make them sound ridiculous. For example, in a minstrel routine called "The Pass-word," Julius says, "Somefin' ob dat meridian ob slatitude," while in "The Sham Doctor," Liver refers to "de toughness ob de wood—de sharpness ob de saw."[138] The minstrel show routine called "We'll All Make a Laugh" includes the line, "Gib 'em what dey want," while "Going a Journey" includes the line, "Aunty, gib my lub to Sam," and "Happy Uncle Tom" has a line that reads, "Oh, just gib me some ob dat."[139] A minstrel routine called "Sleepy Tom" includes the question, "What hab you got to say for yourself?" while "Spirit Rappings" has the line, "I hab seen such sights dat I cannot rest."[140]

But Jim never says *ob*, *gib*, or *hab*. Rather than *ob*, he says *uv*, or *o'* or *er*: "One uv 'em's light en t'other one is dark," "So dey didn' none uv us git no money," "Is dat man gwyne to be waseful o' chillen?" and "He's one er dem chuckleheads." Twain's renderings of the word *of* in Jim's dialect are much more readable and flowing than the pointedly ludicrous *ob* of the minstrel show. The latter is there to make the characters sound ignorant and absurd; the former is simply a serviceable way to evoke natural speech. Similarly, Jim never says *gib* but always says *give*—as in, "Whoever give to de po' len' to de Lord," or "I take en whack de bill in two, en give half un it to you," and "I wouldn' give a dern for a million un um." And he also never says *hab*. Jim always says *have*, as in, "You gwyne to have considable trouble in yo' life, en considable joy," or "Can't have no luck," or "I doan' have to ast 'm twice."

In minstrelese, *v* sounds in the middle of words such as *river*, *ever*, and *every* are rendered as *riber* (or *ribber*), *eber*, and *ebery*. In a routine called "Old Times Gone By," Bones says he would like to be rowing in a flat boat "up de Swanee Riber," while in "The Three Black Smiths," Joe refers to the "Salt Riber." "Ring, Ring de Banjo" includes the phrase, "while de ribber's running high," while "Oh! Susanna" contains a line that says the speaker "trabelled down de riber." Similarly, in "A Tough Boarding-House," Julius refers to "de biggest sugarcane rose you eber did see." In "Grasshoppers," Pompey asks, "Sam, was you eber at a swaree?" The minstrel song "Jenny, Put de Kettle On" contains the line, "An' ebery night when he come home, he hung his hat on his left cheek bone," while the song "Dandy Broadway Swell" includes a chorus with the line, "As ebery one can tell."[141]

Jim, however, never says *riber*, *eber*, or *ebery*. He always says *river*: "You go en git in de river agin," he tells Huck when he thinks he's a ghost. "I tuck out up de river road," he says when he describes his escape to Jackson's Island. "Didn't de line pull loose en de raf' go a-hummin' down de river?" he asks Huck after the fog. When he tells Huck about his father's death, Jim asks, "Doan' you 'member de house dat was float'n down de river en dey wuz a man in dah, kivered up . . . ?" As Doyno notes, the manuscript shows that Twain originally had Jim say *riber* but then decided to change it to *river* and kept the change throughout.[142] Similarly, Jim always says *ever* or *every*, rather than *eber* or *ebery*. When he thinks Huck has come back from the dead as a ghost, Jim declares, "I hain't ever done no harm to a ghos'." Mourning his separation from his children, Jim cries, "I spec' I ain't ever gwyne to see you no mo'." When he's reading Huck's fortune via the hair ball, Jim says, "Sometimes you gwyne to git sick; but every time you's gwyne to git well agin." And when he's describing his escape to Jackson's Island he says that " 'bout eight er nine every skift dat went 'long wuz talkin' 'bout how yo' pap come over to de town en say you's killed."

In minstrelese the words *thing, things,* and *think* are usually rendered as *ting, tings,* and *tink*. In "Electric Shocks," for example, Pompey refers to "the fust ting I sed." In "The Grand Burlesque Lecture on Phrenology!" a "Colored Gemmen" says, "De fust ting you know." In "Patent Safe," Pompey says, "It is seldom one can take tings from one side ob de grabe to de oder arter deaf." In "Suke ob Tenisee," one finds the line, "She went away I tink to de springs," while in "Slap Jack," Pompey says, "Gib me time to tink, den."[143]

But Jim always says *thing, things,* and *think*. Grieving over his treatment of his daughter, he says, "Oh, Huck, I bust out a-cryin' en grab her up in my arms, en say, 'Oh, de po' little thing." In speaking about the speculation he planned, Jim says, "I'd inves' de thirty-five dollars right off en keep things a-movin'." And in his condemnation of Solomon, Jim says, "En de man dat think he kin settle a 'spute 'bout a whole chile wid a half a chile." After the fog, he chastises Huck by saying, "En all you wuz thinkin' 'bout wuz how you could make a fool uv ole Jim wid a lie."

Minstrelese characteristically renders *other* as *oder*. In "Sleepy Tom," Pompey tells what took place "de oder mornin'." In "The Fall," Pompey refers to "de oder day." In "A Tough Boarding-House," Pete says that one of a man's boots "was bigger dan de oder."[144]

Jim, by way of contrast, says (interpreting the hair ball's fortune for Huck), "Dey's two gals flyin' 'bout you in yo' life. One uv 'em's light en t'other one is dark. One is rich en t'other is po'." Or, during the debate about the Frenchman, "It's natural and right for 'em to talk different from each other, ain't it?"

There are other differences between Jim's speech and minstrelese. John Russell Rickford and Russell John Rickford note in *Spoken Soul* that demeaning minstrel-show stereotypes of African Americans "as comical, childlike, gullible, lazy" were:

> conveyed in part by a highly conventionalized "Negro dialect" used by the minstrel performers, as in this example in which *am* is used instead of "is"—a peculiarity one didn't hear in black speech of the time, and doesn't hear today:
>
> END: Mr. Cleveland, a fellow was trying to stuff me dat when it am day here it am night in China.
> MID: Well, James, that is true.
> END: What makes it true?
> MID: It is caused by the earth rotating on its axis, but—
> END: What am an axis?[145]

Jim never substitutes *am* for *is*. (For example, he says "One is rich en t'other is po'," and "Is a cow a man?—er is a cow a cat?").

When minstrel numbers appeared in print, they were often filled with "eye dialect"—words misspelled to convey the speaker's ignorance, rather than because the misspelling changed the sound of the word. For example, minstrelese commonly renders the word *enough* as *enuff*. In "The Senator, or Atlantic Cable," for example, Pompey says, "De gentlem dat hab de charge ob it didn't hab self-'steam enuff to lay it in a horizontal present style." The minstrel song "I Can't Help Dat" included the line, "Sum folks dey am mad enuff to . . ."[146] Jim, however, always says *enough*, saying, "doan' know enough to come in out'n de rain." Another example of eye dialect appears in the minstrel show "Burlesque Political Stump Speech," which includes a reference to "de Prince ob Whales," of course meaning Wales.[147] But Twain eschews eye dialect when writing Jim's speech, using it only very rarely, such as *wuz* for *was*. The end result is that Jim's conversation is easy to read and poses no unnecessary obstacles for the reader.[148]

Also missing from Jim's speech are the pompous malapropisms and labored puns that were often present in minstrel shows to make the speakers look ridiculous. In a routine called "Electric Shocks," published in 1869, Pompey tries to show off his learning by referring to "de mineralogical stretchical ram's hornical twisted cornsistency ob de aqueous electrical cord at de bottom ob de sea."[149] In other sketches Pompey calls a conductor a "corn-doctor" and calls a seminary a "cemetery."[150] Twain does not have Jim speak like this. Comic circumlocutions like these are designed to allow the reader to look down on the speaker for being pretentious or inane or both. But Twain doesn't look down on Jim. Indeed, he takes pains to limit his portrayal of Jim's subservience: Victor A. Doyno observes that at one point in the manuscript, Twain originally had Huck giving Jim an order, but he changed the wording to make Huck address Jim as more of an equal.[151]

Gavin Jones reminds us that it was widely assumed that "the 'humorous' inability of the blackface caricature to command the full meaning of conventional English" stemmed from "racial difference and deficiency."[152] Even though there was a huge gap between the inauthentic, artificial, and caricatured stage dialect

I'm calling minstrelese and the realistic Black dialect that Twain did his best to write for Jim, these assumptions of "racial difference and deficiency" were often made about efforts to render Black speech accurately, as well. The frequent stigmatization of Black English itself contributes to the erroneous idea that Jim is being presented in a demeaning manner.

Although the Black educator Booker T. Washington is not widely regarded as a particularly astute reader, and although he garbles a plot summary of the novel, Washington gets it right when it comes to the regard Twain had for Jim: "I do not believe any one can read this story closely . . . without becoming aware of the deep sympathy of the author in 'Jim,'" he wrote. "In fact, before one gets through with the book, one cannot fail to observe that, in some way or other the author, without making any comment and without going out of his way, has somehow succeeded in making his readers feel a genuine respect for 'Jim,' in spite of the ignorance he displays."[153] But the respect that Washington rightly sensed seems to elude many readers in part because of the culture's negative associations with Black English. Despite the note in the "Explanatory" about "Missouri Negro dialect" being only one of a number of dialects used in the book, a constellation of prejudices hovers around the appearance of Black English on the page for many American readers.[154] As John McWhorter writes in *Talking Back, Talking Black*, prominent among this host of prejudices, held by "most Americans," including some Black Americans, is the idea that "Black English means error."[155]

For McWhorter, "Black English is like a clockwork or an engine, a system every bit as coherent as Latin or Chinese." He and others, such as John Russell Rickford, have written books on exactly how that linguistic system works. But the prejudice against it as error-riddled speech persists, even among African Americans. For example, McWhorter notes that James Meredith, the first

Black student at the University of Mississippi, was prone, later in his life, to hand out flyers before he lectured to young Black audiences that included this advice:

BLACK ENGLISH LANGUAGE

PROPER ENGLISH LANGUAGE

Which one do you use? Most people in this room use a lot of Black English and a little Proper English.

Anyone who wants to become an intellectual giant must learn and use a lot of Proper English and as little Black English as possible.

I am not going to argue with anyone about the matter. You can do what you want to do.

However, I will tell you that anyone who continues to use a lot of Black English will never become an intellectual giant.[156]

Indeed, the tendency of some to associate Black English with ignorance and error can even lead to miscarriages of justice, as Sharese King and John Russell Rickford suggest in their article "Language on Trial," from 2023. King and Rickford note that the Black English spoken by the prosecution's star witness to the killing of Trayvon Martin helped lead her testimony to be "ultimately disregarded" by the jurors, who ended up acquitting Martin's murderer.[157]

It is likely that Twain would agree with McWhorter's view that Black English was as capable of conveying complex information as Latin or Chinese. Twain may even have suspected that Black vernacular speech could be a salutary corrective to some of the obfuscating abstractions and incongruities of "standard" English. Indeed, in *Huckleberry Finn*, Jim's conversation often centers on issues of language and meaning, decentering and exposing the hollow conventions that pass themselves off as meaningful and authoritative in the dominant discourse of the culture.

Twain's skill at putting Black dialect on the page has long been praised by critics. Twain admired Joel Chandler Harris's dialect writing, but Twain's own dialect writing is infinitely easier to comprehend. As Kenneth Eble has observed, "The difference between the rendering of vernacular speech in the dialogue of Mark Twain and that of any of his contemporaries" is that "Mark Twain's dialect is readable while almost all other attempts to re-produce a dialect accurately were not." When dialect was used for humorous and demeaning effect, as it often was, its unreadability was compounded. Consider, for example, Joel Chandler Harris's Tar-Baby story: "'Youer stuck up, dat's w'at you is,' says Brer Rabbit, sezee, ''en I'm gwineter kyore you, dat's w'at I'm a gwineter do,' sezee."[158] While Eble believes Twain is better than Joel Chandler Harris at reproducing in print Black dialect that is clear and readable, James A. Miller suggests that Twain may also be "better at" Black dialect than Paul Laurence Dunbar, a Black writer celebrated for his use of dialect.[159]

The erroneous association of Black English with "error"—something books by McWhorter, Rickford, and others try to dispel—leads to a problem that continues to plague Jim. As Rickford and Rickford note in *Spoken Soul* (writing about the many Black journalists "who sounded off on Ebonics" during the flap over Black English in Oakland, California, in the 1990s), "whether liberal or conservative, Black English in their minds represented a dark side, a streak of backwardness that had to be shunned, purged, stripped away, or lopped off like an unsightly carbuncle in order for the race to advance."[160] Respondents to a poll at the time disparaged Black English as "incorrect and substandard," "nothing more than ignorance," "lazy English," "bastardized English," "the language of illiteracy," and "this utmost ridiculous made-up language."[161] As Vernon E. Jordan Jr. remarked when he was president of the Urban League, teachers "automatically assumed" that the use of Black English "signified inferior intellectual intelligence, inability to learn or other negative connotations."[162] For Black people, McWhorter writes, "it's because Black English is so often associated with stupidity that one can't help wanting to disidentify from it."[163]

Here I need to take issue with a position staked out by a critic who wrote in 1993 that "Jim's voice is, ultimately, a diminished voice, a voice cramped within boundaries as confining as his prison-shack. . . . It is not a voice with which any student, black or white, whose self-esteem is intact would choose to identify for very long."[164] Or, as the same critic put it in 1999, "Jim's voice, despite its special strengths, often remains cramped within conventions as confining as the prison shack" on the Phelps farm.[165] That critic was me. I strongly reject that position now and can't imagine why I wrote that. I now believe that Jim's voice is *not* a "diminished voice." Rather, it is our continuing prejudice against Black English that leads us to devalue and fail to appreciate its richness and vitality. When I wrote those words about Jim's voice three decades ago, I simply got it wrong.[166] I am now certain that Twain respected Jim enormously and that he wanted us to do the same. I am convinced that Jim speaks Black English because Twain respected Jim's reality—because he wanted to get as close as he could on the page to how Jim would have sounded in real life. I now believe that any student—Black or white—should welcome the chance to identify with the most admirable character in the novel. Indeed, many do.[167]

It is not surprising, perhaps, that it was Sterling Brown, a master of dialect himself, who did not allow negative associations with Black dialect to blind him to the power of the remarkable Black character Twain had created in *Huckleberry Finn*. Brown's use of dialect in *Southern Road* (1932) had prompted the influential Black poet, playwright, and critic James Weldon Johnson, who was generally hostile to dialect literature, to rethink his position and "reevaluate the place of 'the common, racy, living speech of the Negro.'"[168] Brown did not hear minstrelsy when Jim spoke, nor did he see the negative stereotypes so many others saw; instead, he saw a man who was "illiterate, superstitious, yet clinging to his hope for freedom, to his love for his own."[169] Brown in the early twentieth century, along with David Bradley, Jocelyn Chadwick, Robert Paul Lamb, Forrest G. Robinson, David L. Smith, Ralph Wiley, myself, and others in the decades that followed, shared Washington's view that Twain has "succeeded in making his readers feel a genuine respect for 'Jim.'"

Minstrel shows, along with literary traditions from southwestern humor; northeastern literary comedians; Shakespeare; the Bible; Sir Walter Scott; travel books; *One Thousand and One Nights*; books on prison life and escape by Casanova, Carlyle, Cellini, Dickens, and Dumas; Julia Moore's *Sentimental Song Book*; De Quille's *Big Bonanza*; slave narratives; African American speakers and rhetorical traditions; relationships with Black and white individuals Twain knew; and a range of personal experiences that Twain had all shaped aspects of *Huckleberry Finn*. Some critics, including Anthony J. Berret, Hilton Obenzinger, and Tracey E. Ryser, among others, have argued persuasively that the tripartite structure of minstrel shows may have shaped the very architecture of the novel.[170] Nevertheless, minstrel shows are not the key source of Jim's behavior, character, or language that critics have often assumed they were. Jim is a complex and resourceful enslaved man seeking his freedom in a world determined to keep him enslaved. He is a father bereft at his separation from his children, a husband torn from his wife, a self-possessed man who is loyal to his friends and who loves his family. He's someone who sizes up people and situations with clarity and insight, who performs roles he is expected to perform when he believes that doing so would help him reach his goal. He is a man who acts with enviable wisdom, tact, insight, and agency in the face of a society in which everything was rigged against him. Twain respected Jim. So should we.

CHAPTER 4

———

Jim's Version

An Interpretive Exercise

*H*UCKLEBERRY FINN is told through Huck's eyes. He is the narrator, and we see everything in the book from his perspective. Huck's point of view is not synonymous with Mark Twain's. Twain crafts Jim with a complexity that Huck does not see, as critics and writers including Sterling Brown, Ralph Ellison, David L. Smith, Jocelyn Chadwick, and Ralph Wiley understood. Huck does not have access to what Jim is thinking and feeling, beyond what Jim chooses to convey to him. What would the story look like if we viewed it through Jim's eyes, from his perspective? By peeling away the filter of Huck's narration, with all its limitations, might we catch a glimpse of who Jim really is?

This exercise is shaped not only by the work of critics and writers cited in the previous chapter but also by the insights of actors who embodied Jim on stage and screen and brought to the role their own understanding of why he behaved the way he did. For example, Archie Moore, who played Jim in 1960, wrote that a great deal of Jim's ignorance had been surmounted by native intelligence and resourcefulness.[1] "He is not an educated man," Moore told an AP reporter, "but he uses his head to accomplish what he needs."[2] Ron Richardson, who performed as Jim on Broadway in 1985, observed that "Jim has to have survival techniques—teaching Huck the lessons of life without letting him know he's being taught. And he has to be shrewd enough to realize his life is up to the whims of two boys."[3] "Jim is an incredible survivor," Richardson continued, "a very moral man with a mission, and that mission was to free his family." He also was sure that that Jim had "a genuine love for Huck."[4] The interpretations of these actors and others will be discussed in detail in chapter 5. In this chapter I have endeavored to retain Jim's characteristic manner of expression as Twain presents it, as it was important to Twain to render his speech with accuracy. I have tried to replicate Twain's choices.

I awluz liked dat chile—felt sorry fo' him. Growin' up wid dat no-good drunk uv a father whalin' on him all de time fo' no reason. Didn' feed him. Awluz hungry, dat chile. Jake tole me dat. Sometimes Huck 'ud come by de quarters of de neighbor-woman who owned Jake roun' suppertime en Jake 'ud give him some o' what he had. Could tell by how grateful he wuz dat de boy hadn' eaten in a while.

Den arter Huck en Tom Sawyer foun' de treasure in de cave, en arter Huck save de widder's life, de widder she tuck him in. By den her sister, Miss Watson, who owned me, moved in wid her too. So I got to see mo' uv' Huck dan I used to. Tom, too.

De two o' dem wuz awluz together. Tom wuz a little devil—awluz tryin' to git Huck to help him put one ovah on ole Jim. Seein' as I couldn' git 'way to see my little Johnny an' 'Lizebeth 'cept every couple o' weeks, I liked lettin' de boys think dey fooled me. Made 'em feel good, en didn' do me no harm. One time I saw em sneakin' up on me when dey thought I wuz asleep. What wid steppin' on twigs en dry leaves as dey wriggled roun' hidin' in de bushes, dey made such a racket dat on'y a fool wouldn' know dey wuz dah. But why spoil dere fun? So I played dat fool. P'tended I didn' hear or see nuthin'. Tom stole some candles en left a five-cent piece fo' 'em. My wages fo' playin' along, as I saw it.

I put a hole in dat nickel en hung it roun' my neck—protection fum evil spirits—en to keep it handy case I needed it. But what to say 'bout how I got it? B'fo' he run off wid de candles, Tom played one mo' trick on me: hung my hat fum de branch uv a tree above whah I slept. Dat give me an idea. I made up a story 'bout witches who rode me all ovah de state en den set me down under de tree ag'in en set my hat on a limb to show who done it. Next time I tole it, dey rode me down to N'Orleans. An' de time arter dat, dey rode me all ovah de worl'. Tole em dey tired me out to death en left saddleboils all ovah my back. I knowed everyone'd be too scared to ax to see de saddleboils. Tole 'em de Devil give me dat five-center charm wid his own han's. Folks 'ud come fum miles roun' en give me whatever dey had to hear me tell dat story. Dey'd do some o' my chores too. I 'member hopin' Tom 'ud play some mo' tricks like dat on me sence de wages wuz so good. But later on, when he did, I changed my mine 'bout de whole business.

Didn' mine de work aroun' de widder's. Haulin' things en helpin' wid de plantin' en mindin' de cows warn't hard, tho Ole Missus—dat's Miss Watson—she be peckin' on me all de time. But I sure did miss my little Johnny an' 'Lizabeth. Didn' like de idea uv dem growin' up widout me aroun'. Me, I had my pappy 'til he got sick en died. My granny too. Don' know 'zackly where I wuz born, but I know I *wuz* born, en dey awluz made me feel dey was glad I come into dis worl'. Huck ain' never had nobody glad he come into dis worl', po' chile. His mama wuz gone en dat no-good drunk uv a father uv his warn't no father to him at all.

Huck wuz real worried when he realized dat no-good drunk uv a father uv his wuz back in town. Had ben gone so long, he stopped thinkin' 'bout him. But seein' his tracks in de snow nearly scared de po' chile to death. He come to see me to git me to tell him what 'ud happen. I had dis hair-ball fum de stomach uv an ox dat I used to tell fortunes wid on de side. Tole folks what dey needed to hear—en ef I got a few cents when I did it, dat 'uz on'y fair. Chile 'uz white as a sheet when he showed up wantin' to know what dat no-good drunk uv a father uv his 'uz a-gwyne to do en how long he 'uz a-gwyne to stay. All he had on han' to pay me wuz an ole fake quarter, but I knowed I could make it pass fo' good ef I left it in a cut in a raw Irish potato ovahnight, so I tuck it.

Tole him de ole man didn' know what he wuz gwyne to do, but de bes' thing 'uz to let him take his own way. Figured dat 'uz de bes' way fo' de chile to avoid gettin' whaled. I cooked up a fortune dat had white en black angels en rich en po' gals flyin' 'bout en warnings en such. I tole him he a-gwyne to have considable trouble in his life en considable joy. Sometimes he gwyne to git hurt, en sometimes he gwyne to git sick; but every time he's gwyne to git well agin. Tole him he gwyne to be all right. Chile never had nobody tell him dat b'fo'. I knowed dat's what he needed to hear. Sure 'nough dat no-good drunk uv a father uv his come dat very night en carried him off to live wid him in his shack deep in de woods.

Ole Missus she pecks on me all de time, en treats me pooty rough, but she awluz say she wouldn' sell me down to N'Orleans. My pappy awluz tole me don' trust nuffn a white person say kase dey don' keep dere word when black folks is involved. Sure 'nough I noticed dey wuz a nigger trader hangin' 'roun' de place considable lately en I begin to git oneasy. Well, one night I creeps to de do' pooty late, en de do' warn't quite shet, en I hear Ole Missus tell de widder she a-gwyne to sell me down to N'Orleans. She didn' want to, but she could git eight hund'd dollars fo' me, en it 'uz sich a big stack o' money she couldn' resis'. De widder she try to git her to say she wouldn' do it, but I never waited to hear de res'. I lit out mighty quick. Knew I'd never see my 'Lizabeth or Johnny—

or my Jenny—agin' ef I let her sell me souf. No time to take nuffn but my pipe en a plug o' dog-leg en some matches dat I put in my hat. Can't b'lieve arter all I done fo' her, she'd do me a turn like dat. Turns out Ole Missus wuz a greedy ole buzzard, dad fetch her! En all dat time I b'lievcd her when she promised she woudn' sell me. I mos' sholy learned my lesson: doan' trus' nuffn no white folks say. Shoulda listened to my pappy.

I tuck out en shin down de hill, en 'spected to steal a skift 'long de sho' som'ers 'bove de town, but dey wuz people a-stirrin' yit, so I hid in de ole tumble-down cooper-shop on de bank to wait fo' everybody to go 'way. Well, I wuz dah all night. Dey wuz somebody roun' all de time. 'Long 'bout six in de mawnin' skifts begin to go by, en 'bout eight er nine every skift dat went 'long wuz talkin' 'bout how Huck's pap come ovah to de town en say he's killed. Des las' skifts wuz full o' ladies en genlmen a-goin' ovah fo' to see de place. Sometimes dey'd pull up at de sho' en take a res' b'fo' dey started acrost, so by de talk I got to know all 'bout de killin'. I uz powful sorry to hear Huck was killed. Po' chile never had no luck.

I laid dah under de shavin's all day. I 'uz hungry, but I warn't afeard kase I knowed Ole Missus en de widder wuz a-goin' to start to de camp-meet'n' right arter breakfas' en be gone all day, en dey knows I goes off wid de cattle 'bout daylight, so dey wouldn' 'spec to see me roun' de place, en so dey wouldn' miss me 'til arter dark in de evenin'. De yuther servants woudn' miss me, kase dey'd shin out en take holiday soon as de ole folks 'uz out'n de way. Had time to think 'bout po' Huck. En had time to listen to some mo' o' what folks wuz sayin' as dere skifts went by. Dey wuz all still buzzin' 'bout Huck's murder, but now dey wuz sayin' de murderer had to be me kase I run off de night he 'uz killed! Run'ways git thirty-nine lashes. Murderers git hung. I knowed I better disappear mighty quick.

Well, when it come dark I tuck out up de river road en went 'bout two mile er mo' to whah dey warn't no houses. I'd made up my mine 'bout what I's a-gwyne to do. You see, ef I kep' on tryin' to git 'way afoot, de dogs 'ud track me; ef I stole a skift to cross ovah, dey'd miss dat skift, you see, en dey'd know 'bout whah I'd lan' on de yuther side, en whah to pick up my track. So I says, a raff is what I's arter; it doan' *make* no track.

I see a light a-comin' roun' de p'int byemby, so I wade' in en shove' a log ahead o' me en swum mo' 'n half way acrost de river, en got in 'mongst de drift-wood, en kep' my head down low, en kinder swum agin de current tell de raff come along. Den I swum to de stern uv it en tuck a-holt. It clouded up en 'uz pooty dark fo' a little while. So I clumb up en laid down on de planks. De men 'uz all 'way yonder in de middle, whah de lantern wuz. De river wuz a-risin', en dey wuz a good current, so I reck'n'd 'at by fo' in de mawnin' I'd be twenty-five mile down de river, en den I'd slip in jis' b'fo' daylight en swim asho', en take to de woods on de Illinois side.

But I didn' have no luck. When we 'uz mos' down to de head er de islan' a man begin to come aft wid de lantern. I see it warn't no use fo' to wait, so I slid ovahboard en struck out fo' de islan'. Well, I had a notion I could lan' mos' anywhers, but I couldn'— bank too bluff. I 'uz mos' to de foot er de islan' b'fo' I foun' a good place. I went into de woods en jedged I wouldn' fool wid raffs no mo', long as dey move de lantern roun' so. I had my pipe en a plug er dog-leg, en some matches in my cap, en dey warn't wet, so I 'uz all right. 'Cept fo' strawbries bein' all I had to eat. Had no gun. Brought no food. Had to hide out 'til dark every day. Ef I never see another strawbry dat's fine wid me.

I wuz sleepin' by de campfire I built, head wrapped in a blanket to keep warm, when I wuz woke up by de ghos' of dat po' murdered chile. I'd awluz treated de dead right—leavin' things dey liked in life on dere graves like my granny taught me—so I couldn' see why dis ghos' should come a-hauntin' me. I tole him to git back in de river whah he b'long en leave ole Jim alone. But soon de ghos' made it clear dat he warn't no ghos' at all: it wuz Huck hissef, alive, in de flesh! He ha'n't ben murdered. I wuz mighty glad to hear dat. But ef he warn't killed, den who wuz? I ax him. He tole me all 'bout how he made it look as ef he ben killed. I tole him it 'uz smart, real smart. Tole him even Tom Sawyer couldn' a done it wid mo' style.

He ax me how I come to be dah. I didn' say nuffn. Den I says I better not tell. Just a couple o' days b'fo', I promised mysef not to trust white folks no mo', en here I wuz axin' mysef, could I trust him? Ef I didn' tell him, he'd figure it out anyway, smart as he wuz. En ef I did . . . I decided to resk it. Made him promise not to tell on me ef I did tell him, en he promised. So I tole him: I run off.

Chile wuz shocked. But den he says people'd call him a low-down ab'litionist en hate him fo' keepin' mum, but still he would'n' tell. 'Sides, he warn't goin' back dah anyway en didn' care what people thought. So I tole him de whole story—en I knowed he'd keep his word. Leastways I thought he would. Couldn' really be sure. I sure wuz glad to see dat chile! Ef I got caught, showin' dat he wuz alive wuz de on'y way to prove I didn' kill him. On'y way I could avoid gittin' hung.

I sure wuz glad to see he'd brought a gun. Now we could kill us some food. I wuz so hungry, I could eat a hoss. I started to build a fire in a grassy open space in de woods. We went ovah to whah de chile had tied up his canoe, en dog my cats ef he hadn't brought along a sack o' meal, a side o' bacon, coffee, a coffeepot en fryin' pan, en sugar en tin cups! I 'spected he'd jis' taken it fum dat no-good drunk uv a father uv his, but I joked dat he must've gotten it all thoo witchcraff. Bacon's de best catfish bait dah is. Chile baited his hook wid some en caught a real big one. I cleaned him wid my knife jis' like my granny taught me en fried him on de fire. Lordy, it wuz good!

Some young birds come along. Dey'd fly a yard or two at a time en den light on a branch. It wuz a sign dat rain wuz a-comin'—leastways it wuz when young chickens flew dat way. Chile want' to catch one of 'em, but I wouldn' let him. 'Minded me o' de time when my pappy lay mighty sick en some uv us caught some birds flyin' like dat. My granny tole me he'd die, en he did.

Chile wuz real interested in signs, so I tole him some. Some came fum granny, some fum white folks, some fum both. Tole him you mustn' count de things you's a-gwyne to cook fo' dinner, kase dat 'ud bring bad luck. Same ef you shook de table-cloth arter sundown. En dat ef a man owned a beehive en dat man died, ef you didn' tell de bees 'bout it b'fo' sun-up next mawnin', dey'd all weaken en quit work en die.

Chile want' to know why dah wuz no signs fo' good luck. What 'ud be de use, I ax? I could see some sense in a good luck sign 'bout some time far ahead: knowin' dat ef you had hairy arms en a hairy breas' you'd be rich some day might stop you fum gittin' discouraged en killin' yo'sef ef you had to be po' fo' a long time fust. But gen'rally, why 'ud you want to be warned 'bout good luck? Would you want to keep it off?

He ax me ef I 'uz rich, seein' as I had hairy arms en a hairy breas'. So I tole him 'bout how I ben rich wunst en gwyne to be rich agin. Wunst I had foteen dollars, but I tuck to specalat'n' en got busted out. Well, fust I tackled stock—live stock—cattle, you know. I put ten dollars in a cow. But I ain' a-gwyne to resk no mo' money in stock. De cow up en died on my han's. I didn' lose all. I- on'y los' 'bout nine o' it. I sole de hide en taller for a dollar en ten cents. Dat one-laigged nigger dat b'longs to ole Misto Bradish he sot up a bank, en say anybody dat put in a dollar would git fo' dollars mo' at de en' er de year. Well, all de niggers went in, but dey didn' have much. I wuz de on'y one dat had much. So I stuck out for mo' dan fo' dollars, en I says 'f I didn' git it I'd start a bank mysef. Well, o' course dat nigger want to keep me out er de business, bekase he says dey warn't business 'nough for two banks, so he say I could put in my five dollars en he pay me thirty-five at de en' er de year.

So I done it. Den I reck'n'd I'd inves' de thirty-five dollars right off en keep things a-movin'. Dey wuz a nigger name' Bob dat had ketched a wood-flat, en his marster didn' know it; en I bought it off'n him en tole him to take de thirty-five dollars when de en' er de year come. But somebody stole de wood-flat dat night, en nex day de one-laigged nigger say de bank's busted. So dey didn' none uv us git no money.

I 'uz gwyne to spen' de ten cents, but I had a dream, en de dream tole me to give it to a nigger name' Balum—Balum's Ass, dey call him for short; he's one er dem chuckleheads, you know. But he's lucky, dey say, en I see I warn't lucky. De dream say let Balum inves' de ten cents, en he'd make a raise for me. Well, Balum he tuck de money, en when he wuz in church he hear de preacher say dat whoever give to de po' len' to de Lord, en boun' to git yo' money back a hund'd times. So Balum he tuck en give de ten cents to de po', en laid low to see what wuz a-gwyne to come of it.

Nuffn' never come of it. I couldn' manage to k'leck dat money no way, en Balum he couldn'. I ain' a-gwyne to len no mo' money 'dout I see de security. Boun' to git yo' money back a hund'd times, de preacher says! Ef I could git de ten *cents* back, I'd call it squah, en be glad er de chanst.

But come to look at it, I's rich now. I owns mysef, en I's wuth eight hund'd dollars. I wisht I had de money, I wouldn' want no mo'.

Chile want' to show me a place he foun' in de middle o' de

island on de top of a long, steep ridge 'bout fo'ty feet high. Dah wuz a good big cavern in de rock—as big as two er three rooms en high enough fo' me to stan' up straight in it. I tole him what we had to do wuz move all de traps up into de cave to keep 'em dry. Huck didn' want to lug all de traps up de ridge, but I tole him dose little birds wuz a sign it wuz goin' to rain, en I ax, did he want all our things to git wet? I tole him ef we hid de canoe in a good place whah it couldn' be seen, en had all de traps in de cave, we could rush in dah ef anybody wuz to come to de island, cn dcy 'ud never find us widout dogs. So we went back en got de canoe, paddled to de cave, en lugged all de traps up dah. We foun' a place to hide de canoe nearby in some thick willows, tuck some fish off de lines, en set de lines agin. Den we got ready fo' dinner. De floor o' de cave stuck out a little bit by de door en 'uz flat—a good place to build a fire. We spread blankets out fo' a carpet en cooked dinner.

Den de sky got dark. Soon dah wuz bursts o' lightnin' bright as glory en thunder crashin' en wind en rain like I never see b'fo'. But we wuz warm en dry. I fried de fish we caught en made some corn-bread fum de meal we'd hauled up fum de canoe. Chile had seconds—en thirds. Tole me, Jim, dis is nice. I wouldn' want to be nowhere but heah. Pass me along another hunk o' fish en some hot corn-bread. Had to mine him dat he wouldn'a ben here ef it hadn' a ben fo' Jim. He'd a ben down dah in de woods widout no dinner, en gittn' mos' drownded too. Tole him chickens knows when it's a-gwyne to rain, en so do de birds.

River kep' risin' fo' ten or twelve days 'til de water wuz three or fo' feet deep in de low places on de islan' en on de Illinois side.

One night a little section o' lumber raf' floated by en we caught it—nice pine planks twelve feet wide en 'bout fifteen o' sixteen feet long. We tied it up en hid it in de willow grove. We didn' show ourselves in daylight.

Chile foun' a snakeskin on de top o' de ridge one day en showed it to me. Tole him touchin' a snakeskin wid yo' han's could bring de worst kine o' bad luck, but he didn' b'lieve me.

Another night jis' b'fo' daylight, when we wuz up at de head o' de island, a two-story frame-house come floatin' by, leanin' ovah, almos' on its side. We paddled out to it in de canoe, but it wuz too dark to see yet, so we tied up de canoe en sat in her to wait fo' daylight. When de sun rose we look in at de window. We could make out a bed, en a table, en two ole chairs, a mess uv ole whiskey bottles, black cloth masks, greasy cards scattered everywhere on de flo', en two ole dirty calico dresses en a sunbonnet en women's underthings hangin' 'gainst de wall. Look like a room whah gamblers en drunks en robbers en dere gals 'ud feel right at home, but whah no decent person 'ud set foot. En de smell!

Dey wuz sumf'n layin' on de flo' in de far corner dat look like a man. So I shout, Hello, you!

But he didn' budge. Tole de chile to stay put while I tuck a look: dat man warn't asleep—he wuz dead. Stark naked, too. I reck'n he'd ben dead two er three days. I turned him ovah. It wuz Huck's no-good drunk uv a father. De boy didn' need to see dat. De ole man wuz no good, but dat didn' mean his boy needed to know de shameful way he died—naked en shot in de back in a place like dis! I threw some rags ovah him en tole de chile to come in but not to look at his face—said it wuz too gashly. He didn' look. Ax'd me 'bout him de next day—how he'd come to be killed. But I tole him I didn' want to talk 'bout it. Ef he knew he didn' have to run from his pap no mo', would he jus' go back? P'tendin' to be a white chile's slave warn't de bes' way to not get turned in as a run'way, but it was my on'y way.

We put a lot o' stuff fum de house in de canoe—some o' de clothin', an ole tin lantern, a new Barlow knife, a lot o' tallow candles, a tin candlestick en tin cup, an ole bed quilt, a hatchet, some nails, some needles en pins en buttons en threads, en a thick fishline wid big hooks, a curry comb. We left a heap o' stuff we had no use fo'—a broken baby bottle, a butcher-knife widout a han'l, a dog collar, a ole fiddle bow, a wooden leg. Whoever killed his ole man lef' in a hurry.

We rummaged thoo de clothes we got en foun' eight dollars in silver sewed into de linin' of a ole ovahcoat. Tole de boy I reck'n'd de folks in de house stole de coat, kase ef dey'd knowed de money 'uz dah, dey wouldn' uv left it. Chile says he thought dey wuz de ones who killed dat man—but I didn' want to talk 'bout it. Tole him it 'ud fetch bad luck—dat a man dat warn't buried 'uz mo' likely to go hauntin' roun' dan one dat 'uz planted en comf'table. Chile says dat soun' pooty reasonable. Dat got him to stop axin' questions.

By den de sun 'uz up, so chile says I should lay down in de canoe kivered up wid a quilt kase ef I sat up people could see me fum a good ways off en might figure I wuz a run'way. Dat wuz smart.

A few nights later when I lay down on my blanket fo' de night, a big ole black rattlesnake bit me in de heel. Chile killed him wid a stick. But it hurt powful bad! I grab' de ole man's whiskey-jug en poured it into my mouf. Had de chile chop off its head, skin de body, en roast a piece uv it fo' me to eat—also had him take off de rattles en tie 'em roun' my wrist. Not sure ef dat helped, but de whiskey sure did. Jis' kep' drinkin' dat whiskey 'til I wuz near out'n my mine. Foot swelled up en leg swelled up, but I had so much to drink dat I jis' passed out. Tuck fo' days en fo' nights fo' de swellin' to go down—en fo' me to run thoo de whiskey. Tole de chile han'lin' dat snakeskin wuz bad luck so as to make sure he didn' fine no mo' to fool wid. He didn' think I knowed it wuz all his fault—dat our bad luck warn't fum de snakeskin he'd ben foolin' wid a few days earlier, but fum de dead snake he left on my blanket as a prank. Snake's mate showed up bitin' mad 'bout it. I was bitin' mad too, soon as de whiskey begin to wear off. Ef my Johnny a done dat I'd a whaled him sure. Knew I'd be a goner ef I did dat to a white boy en folks foun' out—so I didn'. But I sure did want to. Still hoppin' mad de whole nex' day. But den I tells mysef: he's on'y a chile. Couldn' stay mad fo' long.

River begun to go down between its banks agin. We baited one o' de big hooks wid a skinned rabbit en set it. Caught a catfish big as a man—mo' 'n six feet long en ovah two hund'd pounds. Biggest one I ever seen—maybe de biggest anyone ever caught in dem parts. We didn' try to reel him in—jis' watched him rip en tear roun' 'til he drowned. I cut him up en cleaned him en fried as much as we could eat. Meat white as snow, en tender—Lordy, it wuz good!

Next mawnin' Huck says he want' take de canoe up de Illinois shore en find out what wuz goin' on. Sound' like a good idea, but I tole him he had to wait till dark en look sharp. I looked ovah de ole things we got at de floatin' house. Could he dress up as a girl? I ax. I shortened one o' dem calico gowns fo' him en hitched it behine wid de hooks. It fit him good. He turned up his trouser legs, put on de sunbonnet, en spent de day practicin' how to git roun' in 'em. Did OK but couldn' git de hang o' walkin' like a girl. Tole him he had to quit pullin' up his gown to git to his britches pocket. He tried to 'member dat en did better. When nighttime come, he tuck de canoe en set out fo' de next town down de river.

Didn' know what he'd fine dah—or who. Could I trust him? Had to. He was all I got. On'y thing 'tween me en de noose dey had waitin' fo' me back in Hannibal fo' killin' him. Next thing I know de chile come bustin' in de cave en shakes me to wake me up, yellin' git up en hump yo'sef, Jim. Dah ain't a minute to lose. Dey're arter us! What'd he tell folks on de shore? No time to find out. I put out de campfire in de cave fust thing en de candles. Too scared to talk. Made as many trips as it tuck to load our traps en meal en bacon en pans en clothes onto de raf' as fas' as I could in de moonlight. Moved so fas' I could scasely catch my breath. Didn' say nuffn. Chile made a new campfire on de far end o' de island to throw 'em off en fool 'em into waitin' fo' when we'd come back. Dat wuz smart. When everythin' we had wuz loaded on de raf' we shove' off—still not sayin' a word.

Got below de islan' maybe roun' one in de mawnin'. Tied de raf' up to a tow-head in a big ben' on de Illinois side, en hacked off cottonwoods wid de hatchet to cover it up wid—made it look like dah'd ben a cave-in on de bank dah. Hid de raf' en canoe, good. We laid dah all day en watched de raffs en steamboats go down de Missouri shore, en watched up-bound steamboats fight de current in de middle o' de river. Chile tole me how dat woman on de shore tested him to see ef he 'uz sure nuff a girl—en how he flunked. Should've worked wid him on de catchin'-like-a-girl part—not jis' de walkin'-like-a-girl part. Didn' think of it.

She wuz a smart one, dat woman. Tole de chile I figured dat ef she wuz to start arter us herself she wouldn' set down en watch a fire—no sir, she'd fetch a dog. Chile ax why couldn' she tell her husban' to fetch a dog? I says I bet she did think of it. Dey must've gone to town to git a dog en so dey los' all dat time—time dat let us git to whah we wuz, some sixteen mile below de town.

When it wuz beginnin' to git dark we poked our heads out'n de cottonwoods en looked up en down en acrost; nuffn in sight. I knowed we couldn' use de raf' fo' travel 'til I fixed it up—needed to keep things dry in de rain en cool in de sun. En I needed some-where on it whah I could git out'n sight. So I tuck up some o' de top planks o' de raf' en built a wigwam in de middle dat 'ud keep us fum burnin' up in de blazin' heat, en dat 'ud keep all our things dry when it rained. I made a flo' fo' de wigwam en raised it a little ovah a foot above de level o' de raf', so now de waves fum passin' steamboats wouldn' git de blankets all wet. I showed de chile how a layer o' dirt 'bout five or six inches deep wid a frame roun' it to hol' it in place in de middle o' de wigwam 'ud be whah we could light a fire when it 'uz wet or chilly: de wigwam 'ud keep it fum bein' seen. I tole him we needed to make an extra steerin'-oar, too, kase one o' de ones we had might git broke on a snag or sumf'n. We fixed up a short forked stick to hang de ole lantern on, kase we must awluz light de lantern whenever we see a steamboat comin' down-stream, to keep fum gittin' run ovah.

De second night we run between seven en eight hours wid a pooty fast current. We caught fish en talked, en tuck a swim now en den to keep off sleepiness. It 'uz quiet en calm, driftin' down de big, still river, layin' on our backs lookin' up at de stars. Didn' ever feel like talkin' loud, en didn' laugh much neither—on'y a little kine uv a low chuckle. We had mighty good weather as a gen'l thing, en nuffn ever happened to us at all—dat night, or de next, or de next.

Every night we pass' towns, some o' dem 'way up on black hillsides, nuffn but jis' a shiny bed o' lights. De fifth night we pass' St. Louis, en it 'uz like de whole worl' lit up. But quiet—everybody wuz asleep.

Every night roun' ten o'clock chile used to slip ashore at some little village en buy ten o' fifteen cents' worth o' meal er bacon er other stuff to eat, en sometimes take a chicken. Mawnins b'fo' daylight he'd slip into cornfields en take a watermelon, or a mushmelon, or a pumpkin, or some new corn, or things o' dat kine. Chile tole me his ole man used to say dat all dat 'uz borrowin' ef you meant to pay 'em back some time, but de ole man never did pay no one back. Chile says de widder says it 'uz jis' a sof' name fo' stealin'. I tole him I reck'n de widder 'uz partly right en his ole man 'uz partly right. We decided de best way 'ud be fo' us to pick out two er three things fum de list en say we wouldn' borrow 'em no mo'—den we reck'n'd it wouldn' hurt none to borrow de others. So we talked it all ovah one night, driftin' 'long down de river, tryin' to make up our mines whether to drop de watermelons, or de cantelopes, or de mushmelons, or whatever. But towards daylight we got it all settled en decided to drop crabapples en p'simmons. P'simmons wouldn' be ripe fo' two or three months yet anyways. Every now en den we'd shoot a duck dat got up too early in de mawnin' or didn' go to bed early enough in de evenin'.

De fifth night below St. Louis we had a big storm arter midnight, wid a power o' thunder en lightnin', en de rain poured down in a solid sheet. We stayed in de wigwam I built, all snug en warm, en let de raf' take care uv itself. Den de chile shouted out dat he spotted a steamboat dat done killed hersef on a rock. We wuz driftin' straight down fo' her. She wuz leanin' ovah, wid part o' her upper deck 'bove water. De lightnin' show' her real clear when de flashes come.

Huck want' to lan' on dat wrack like any chile 'ud—awluz on de lookout fo' adventures. Well, I didn' want no mo' adventures en tole him so. We wuz doin' fine, I tole him. I want to keep it dat way. I don' want to go foolin' wid no wrack. Like as not, dah's a watchman dah, anyways.

Chile says dah wouldn' be no watchman kase all dah wuz to watch wuz a pilot-house en nobody 'ud resk dere life fo' dat on a night like dis, when de wrack 'ud surely break up. Well, I couldn' think o' nuffn to say fast enough, en de chile went on en on 'bout how steamboat captains wuz awluz rich en we might borrow sumf'n worth havin' out'n de captain's stateroom—like five-cent seegars. Huck couldn' res' widout givin' dat wrack a rummagin'. He ax me, do you reck'n Tom Sawyer would ever go by dis thing? Not fo' pie, he wouldn', he say. He'd call it an adventure en he'd land on dat wrack ef it was his last act, Huck said. En wouldn' he throw style into it?—wouldn' he spread hisself? Said he wish'd

Tom Sawyer wuz heah. I didn'. One chile bent on havin' adventures wuz bad enough.

Tole him I still thought it wuz too resky. But he kep' on pushin' en I had to give in. Tole him we mustn' talk no mo' 'n we had to, en den talk mighty low. De lightnin' lit up de wrack, en we headed to de deck dat 'uz high up ovah de water en felt our way down its slope slowly in de dark. We heard low voices comin' fum de back. When we got closer, we could see in de dim light uv a lantern a man tied han' en foot en another man pointin' a pistol at his head. I felt powful sick en grab' de chile, tole him to come along. He begun to head to de raf' wid me when we heard a voice wail out, Oh, please doan', boys; I swear I won' never tell!

Another voice says pooty loud: It's a lie, Jim Turner. You acted dis way b'fo'. You awluz want mo' 'n yo' share o' de truck, en you awluz got it too, kase you swore ef you didn' you'd tell. . . .

Stubborn chile had to stick roun' en find out what he wouldn' tell. I didn' wait to heah mo'—I headed fo' de raf'.

Made my way to whah we left it. When I saw it done broke loose en wuz gone I couldn' do nuffn but moan. Den I heah de chile at my elbow sayin', Quick, Jim, it ain't no time fo' foolin' roun' en moanin'; Dah's a gang o' murderers yonder, en ef we doan' hunt up dere boat en set 'er driftin' down de river so dese fellas can't git 'way fum de wrack, dah's one of 'em goin' to be in a bad fix. But ef we find dere boat we kin put all of 'em in a bad fix—fo' de sheriff 'll git 'em. Quick—hurry! You start at de raf', en—

Den I tole him. Dey ain' no raf' no mo'. She done broke loose en gone!—en heah we is!

Chile caught his breath en almos' fainted. Shut up on a wrack wid a gang o' killers! We had to fine dat boat now. Wuz so scared it tuck near all my strength to work down one side o' de wrack to de back, lookin' fo' dere skift, but it warn't dah. Somehow managed to prowl up de other side, en dah it wuz! In another second we'd o' ben aboard her, but jis' den de do' open. One o' de men stuck his head out on'y 'bout a couple o' foot fum me en flung a bag o' sumf'n into de boat, en den got in hisself en set down. En den another one come out en got in en says in a low voice: All ready—shove off!

But den one ax t'other—Did you go thoo him? En he answer, no. So he got his share o' de cash yet, de fust one say. Well, den come 'long; no use to take truck en leave de money, he say.

So dey got out'n de skift en went inside. In half a second chile en I wuz in de skift. Chile tuck out his knife en cut de rope, en 'way we went!

We didn' touch an oar, en we didn' speak or whisper, or hardly even breathe. We went glidin' along, dead silent, past de tip o' de paddle-box, en past de stern; den in a second er two mo' we wuz a hund'd yards below de wrack, en de darkness soaked her up, en we wuz safe, en we knowed it.

When we wuz three or fo' hund'd yards down-stream we saw de lantern show like a little spark fo' a second, en we knowed dem crooks had missed dere boat en wuz beginnin' to understan' dat dey wuz in jis' as much trouble now as Jim Turner wuz.

I manned de oars. Rain kep' pourin' as we made our way down de river lookin' fo' de raf'. Arter a long time, de rain let up, but de clouds stayed, en de lightnin', too, but byemby a flash showed us a black thing ahead, floatin', en we made fo' it.

It wuz de raf', en we wuz mighty glad to git onto it agin.

Chile had his heart set on rescuin' dat gang o' murderers fum de sinkin' wrack dey wuz on. I tole him to leave 'em be, but he says he might come to be a murderer hisself yet, en den how 'ud he like it? er some such thing. Chile awluz did have a good heart.

De skift 'uz half full o' plunder dat gang on de wrack done stole. We hustled it on to de raf' in a pile, en Huck tole me to float along down, en show a light when it looked like I had gone 'bout two mile, en keep it burnin' til he come. Den chile manned de oars en went fo' a light on a ferryboat. Later he tole me he rousted her owner en cooked up a story dat somehow made him want to rescue dat gang o' deadbeats—made him think he wuz rescuin' de niece o' de riches' man in town. Dat boy sure could weave a yarn when he got a mine to.

Arter a powful long time, Huck reach me in de skift. We struck fo' an islan', hid de raf', sunk de skift, en turned in en slep' like dead people.

Byemby, when we got up, we turned ovah de truck we got off o' de wrack en foun' boots, blankets, clothes, en all sorts o' other things. A lot o' books, en a spyglass, en three boxes o' seegars. We never ben dis rich b'fo'. We laid off in de woods talkin' en havin' a gen'l good time, while de chile read some o' de books. He tole me all 'bout what happened at de ferryboat, en says dese kines o' things wuz adventures. I says I didn' want no mo' adventures. Says when I crawled back to git on de raf' en found her gone, I nearly died, bekase I judged it 'uz all up wid me: fo' ef I didn' git saved, I 'ud git drowned; en ef I did git saved, whoever saved me 'ud send me back home to git de reward, en den Miss Watson 'ud sell me South, sure. Chile had to admit I wuz right. It awluz su'prised him when I talked sense. Caught him off guard when I wuz right. But I usually wuz.

Chile read to me considable fum de ole books we got. Read 'bout kings en dukes en earls en such, en how gaudy dey dressed, en how much style dey put on; how dey called each other yo' majesty, en yo' grace, en yo' lordship, en so on, 'stead o' mister. I didn' know dah was so many of 'em. Hadn't heard 'bout 'em b'fo'— 'cept fo' ole King Sollermun. I ax how much do a king git.

Chile says, Git? Why, dey git a thousan' dollars a month ef dey want it. Dey kin have jis' as much as dey want; everythin' belongs to 'em.

Dat sounded pooty gay to me. I ax him what dey have to do.

Dey doan' do nuffn, he says. Dey jis' set roun'—'cept, maybe, when dah's a war; den dey goes to de war. But other times dey jis' lazy roun'. Mostly dey hang round de harem. Round de which? I ax. Harem says Huck. I ax him what dat wuz. He tole me it wuz de place whah de king kep' his wives. Says Sollermun had 'bout a million wives. Den I 'member'd: a harem's a kine o' bo'd'n-house. Mos' likely dah wuz awluz rackety times in de nussery, en I reck'n de wives quarrel considable, en dat 'crease de racket. Yit dey say Sollermun wuz de wises' man dat ever live'. Tole him I doan' take no stock in dat. Why would a wise man want to live in sich a blim-blammin' all de time? No—'deed he wouldn'. A wise man 'ud take en buil' a biler-factry; en den he could shet *down* de biler-factry when he want to res'.

Chile kep' insistin' he wuz de wisest man, anyway—kase de widder she tole him so, her own self. I tole him I doan k'yer what de widder say, he *warn't* no wise man nuther. He had some er de dad-fetchedes' ways I ever see. I ax him do he know 'bout dat chile he 'uz gwyne to chop in two. He say, yes, de widder tole him all 'bout dat.

Well, den, I says, warn't dat de beatenes' notion in de worl'? I says, say dah's de stump, dah—dat's one er de women; heah's you—dat's de yuther one. I's Sollermun; en dish yer dollar bill's de chile. Bofe un you claims it. What does I do? Does I shin aroun' mongs' de neighbors en fine out which un you de bill do b'long to, en han' it ovah to de right one, all safe en soun', de way dat anybody dat had got any gumption would? No; I take en whack de bill en *two*, en give half un it to you en de yuther half to de yuther woman. Dat's de way Sollermun wuz gwyne' to do wid de chile. Now I want to ast you, what's de use er dat half a bill?—can't buy noth'n wid it! En what use is half a chile? I wouldn' give a dern for a million un um.

Chile says I clean miss de pint. Who? Me? says I. Go 'long. Doan' talk to *me* 'bout yo' pints. I reck'n I knows sense when I sees it; en dey ain' no sense in sich doin's as dat. De 'spute warn't 'bout a half a chile, de 'spute was 'bout a whole chile; en de man dat think he kin settle a 'spute 'bout a whole chile wid a half a chile doan' know enough to come in out'n de rain. Doan' talk to me 'bout Sollermun. I knows him by de back.

De *real* pint is down furder—it's down deeper, I tole him. It lays in de way Sollermun was raised. You take a man dat's got on'y one er two chillen: is dat man gwyne to be waseful o' chillen? No, he ain't; he can't 'ford it. *He* knows how to value 'em. But you take a man dat's got 'bout five million chillen runnin' roun' de house, en it's diffunt. *He* as soon chop a chile in two as a cat. Dey's plenty mo'. A chile er two, mo' er less, warn't no consekens to Sollermun, dad fetch him!

Chile didn' bring up Sollermun agin. Talked 'bout other kings—like Louis Sixteen dat got his head cut off in France a long time ago, en 'bout his little boy de dolphin dat 'ud have ben a king ef he hadn' ben taken en shut up in jail. Some say he died dah. Po' little chap. But den chile say some say he got 'way en come to America. I wuz mighty glad to hear dat. But den I thought 'bout how lonesome he'd be here—sence dah wuz no kings here. He couldn' git a situation. What 'ud he do?

Chile say some o' dem teach people how to talk French. I ax him, doan' de French people talk de same way we does? He tole me no. Says I couldn' understan' a word dey says. I ax how dat could be, en he say he doan know, but it's so—dat he got some o' dere jabber out uv a book.

He ax me, ef a man 'uz to come to me en say Polly-voo-franzy—what 'ud I think? Tole him I wouldn' think nuffn, but I'd bust him ovah de head—dat is, ef he warn't white. I wouldn't 'low no nigger to call me dat. Chile tried to say it warn't callin' me noth'n'—on'y axin' ef I know how to talk French. Well, den, why couldn' he *say* it? I ax. Chile says he *is* sayin' it. Says dat's a Frenchman's way o' sayin' it. Tole him it 'uz a blame ridicklous way en I didn' want to hear no mo' 'bout it. Dey ain' no sense in it. But he didn' let up.

Looky here, Jim, he says to me. Does a cat talk like we do? No, a cat don't, I says. Well, does a cow? he ax. I tell him no, a cow don't nuther. Does a cat talk like a cow, or a cow talk like a cat? he ax. No, dey don't says I. It's natural en right fo' 'em to talk diffunt fum each other, ain' it? Huck ax. I says, 'Course it is. En ain' it natural en right fo' a cat en a cow to talk diffunt fum *us*? he ax. I says, Why, mos' sholy it is. Well, den, Huck says, why ain't it natural en right fo' a *Frenchman* to talk diffunt fum us? You answer me dat.

Is a cat a man? I ax him. No, says Huck. Well, den, dey ain' no sense in a cat talkin' like a man, I says. "Is a cow a man? Er is a cow a cat?

"No, she ain't either o' dem, Huck says. Well, den, says I, she ain' got no business to talk like either one er de yuther of 'em. I ax him, is Frenchman a man? He says yes. *Well*, den, says I, dad blame it, why doan' he *talk* like a man?—You answer me *dat!*

I had him dah, so he quit.

We judged dat three nights mo' 'ud fetch us to Cairo, at de bottom o' Illinois, whah de Ohio River come in, en dat 'uz what we wuz arter. We 'ud sell de raf' en git on a steamboat en go way up de Ohio 'mongst de free states, en den be out'n trouble.

Well, de second night a fog begin to come on, en we made fo' a tow-head to tie to, fo' it wouldn' do to try to run in a fog; but when Huck paddled ahead in de canoe, wid de line to make fast, dah warn't nuffn but little saplins to tie to. Chile passed de line roun' one o' dem right on de edge o' de cut bank, but dah wuz a stiff current, en de raf' come boomin' down so fast she tore it out by de roots en 'way she went wid me on her. I saw de fog closin' down en got scared: you couldn' see twenty yards.

I whooped as loud as I could, hopin' de chile 'ud answer, but I ain' heard nuffn, en de current 'uz tearin' along fast. I called out till I wuz hoarse en kep' whoopin', but still nuffn. Dat chile wuz los', fo' sure. En it 'uz my fault—I could've found a better cotton-wood fo' tyin' up. I could've whooped louder. I could've—oh, what's de use. Chile wuz gone. En I wuz a goner. I set down en hung my head between my knees en wept. I 'uz bone tired. Couldn' fight off sleep no mo'.

Arter I slept a long while, de chile's voice woke me up.

Hello, Jim, Huck says, gapin' en stretchin' under my nose. Have I ben asleep? Why didn' you stir me up? he ax.

I couldn' b'lieve it! It wuz him! I wanted to hug him.

Goodness gracious, is dat you, chile? I shout. You ain' dead? You ain' drowned? You's back agin? I says it's too good for true, it's too good for true. O, de joy I felt seein' dat chile agin! Lemme look at you, chile, lemme feel you, I says. Huck 'uz back agin, alive en soun'—de same ole Huck, thanks to goodness!

En den he starts wid crazy talk.

What's de matter wid you, Jim? He ax me. You ben a-drinkin'? Drinkin'? I couldn' b'lieve he wuz axin' me dis. Has I ben drinkin'? Has I had a chance to be a-drinkin'? Well, den, what makes you talk so wild? he ax. How does I talk wild? I ax. Why, hain't you ben talkin' 'bout my comin' back, en all dat stuff, as ef I'd ben gone 'way? he ax me.

I tuck a deep breath en look at de chile. So he wuz bent on foolin' wid ole Jim arter my heart ben near broke at de thought dat he wuz dead. Dat warn't right. It jis' warn't right.

Huck, I says, Huck Finn, you look me in de eye. Look me in de eye. *Hain't* you ben gone away? I ax. He says, why, what in de nation do you mean? *I hain't ben gone nowhere.* Whah 'ud I go to?

Chile want' to make a fool o' me. I 'xpected mo'. Prob'bly shouldn' uv. Ef he want' to make a fool o' me dat bad, I'd play dat fool . . . I laid it on thick.

Call' him boss. Made like I wuz real confused 'bout who I wuz en whah I wuz—jis' like he want'.

Well, I think you's heah, plain enough, Huck says. Den he calls me a tangle-headed ole fool.

Made up my mine to give him one mo' chance to make things right.

Well, you answer me dis, says I. Didn' you tote out de line in de canoe to make fast to de tow-head? I ax.

No, I didn'. What tow-head? Huck says. I hain't seen no tow-head.

No tow-head? Didn't de line pull loose en de raf' go a-hummin' down de river, en leave you en de canoe behine in de fog? I ax. Huck says, What fog?

Lordy, dat 'uz one stubborn chile! Why, *de* fog! I say. De fog dat's ben roun' all night.

I ax him, didn' he whoop, en didn' I whoop, till l we got mix' up in de islands, en one un us got los' en t'other one was jis' as good as los', kase he didn' know whah he wuz? I ax him didn't I bust up agin a lot er dem islands en have a turrible time en mos' git drownded?

Chile jis' kep' up de mean joke.

Well, dis is too many fo' me, Jim, he says. I hain't seen no fog, en no islands, en no troubles, or nuffn. I ben settin' here talkin' wid you all night 'til you went to sleep 'bout ten minutes ago, en I reck'n I done de same. You couldn' a got drunk in dat time, so o' course you ben dreamin'.

Dad fetch it, how is I gwyne to dream all dat in ten minutes?

I ax. Well, hang it all, you did dream it, kase there didn't any of it happen. I know, kase I ben here all de time, he says.

I sat dah fo' a full five minutes studyin'. How could I uv ben so wrong 'bout de boy? I played along some mo' wid his stupid joke. Says I reck'n'd I did dream it, but it 'uz de mos' powful dream I ever had—never had a dream dat tired me like dis one.

Clearly he wuz enjoyin' dis. Tell me all 'bout it, Jim, he says. So I tole him. Made it wild—real wild—'terpreted every part uv it en den some.

I says it wuz sent fo' a warnin'—dat de fust tow-head stood fo' a man dat 'ud try to do us some good, but de current wuz another man dat 'ud git us 'way fum him. De whoops wuz warnins dat 'ud come to us every now en den, en ef we didn' try hard to understan' 'em dey'd jis' take us into bad luck, s'tead o' keepin' us out uv it. De lot o' tow-heads wuz troubles we wuz goin' to git into wid quarrelsome people en all kines o' mean folks, but ef we minded our business en didn' talk back en aggravate 'em, we'd pull thoo en git out'n de fog en into de big clear river, which 'uz de free states, en wouldn' have no mo' trouble.

Chile begin to yawn, bored.

Oh, well, dat's all 'terpreted well enough as far as it goes, Jim, he says, but what does *dese* things stan' fo'? He pints to de leaves en rubbish on de raf' en de smashed oar. I look at de trash en den back at him en den at de trash. I thought long en hard b'fo' I opened my mouf. Chile wuz wrong, as wrong as wrong can be— but he wuz also white—en I knowed dat ef it ever came out dat I tole off a white chile, I'd git thirty-nine lashes sure. But chile had to be taught what he did wuz *wrong*. En who wuz dere to teach him? I ax you dat. All right den, I thought, I'll *resk* dat lash.

I look at him steady, widout smilin', en tole him what dey stood fo'. Tole him when I got wore out wid work, en wid callin' fo' him, en went to sleep wid my heart mos' broke bekase he wuz los', I didn' k'yer no mo' what become er me en de raf'. En when I wake' up en fine him back agin, all safe en soun', de tears come en I could a got down on my knees en kiss' his foot, I's so thankful. En all he wuz thinkin' 'bout, wuz how he could make a fool out uv ole Jim wid a lie. I tole him dat truck dah is *trash*—en trash is what people is dat puts dirt on de head er dey fren's en makes 'em ashamed.

Den I got up slow en walked to de wigwam, widout sayin' nuffn else. Jis' sat in dat wigwam I'd made to keep us warm en dry, en wonder'd how I'd ben so wrong. I really thought he wuz diffunt. Made me sad. En mad. I jis' sat dah mullin' it all ovah.

Fifteen minutes later he shows up.

I'm sorry, Jim, he says. I won't do you no mo' mean tricks—en I wouldn' a done dat one ef I'd a knowed it 'ud make you feel so.

All my hard feelin's jis' melted 'way.

De river wuz wide—solid timber on both sides; you couldn' see a break in it hardly ever, or a light. We talked 'bout Cairo, how we'd know it when we got to it. Chile says likely we wouldn', kase he heard say dah warn't but a dozen houses dah, en ef dey didn' happen to have 'em lit up, how 'ud we know we wuz passin' a town? I says ef de two big rivers joined together dah, dat 'ud be de sign. But he says maybe we might think we wuz passin' de foot uv an island en 'ud be comin' into de same ole river agin. Dat made me oneasy.

So how do we figure out ef we've got to Cairo? Chile says he should paddle ashore de fust time a light showed en tell 'em pap 'uz behind, comin' 'long wid a tradin' scow, en wuz a green hand in de business, en want' to know how far it wuz to Cairo. I thought it wuz a good plan, so we tuck a smoke on it en waited.

I wuz sure I saw de lights o' Cairo lots o' times—but it warn't Cairo. It wuz jack-o'-lanterns, er lightnin' bugs, so I set down agin

Jim. Wood engraving from the Pennyroyal Press edition
of *Adventures of Huckleberry Finn*, 1984, by Barry Moser.

en went to watchin', same as b'fo'. Made me all ovah trembly en feverish to be so close to freedom.

I wuz so excited 'bout finally gittin' to Cairo dat I'd shout out en dance roun' every time I thought we wuz dah. Neither uv us could keep still. Both uv us started fidgitin' all ovah de raf'. Chile started actin' nervous-like. Almos' like he hadn't 'member'd it wuz freedom I wuz arter, en when he did 'member, he got to worryin' 'bout what 'ud happen to him fo' helpin' me git it.

Tole him de fust thing I'd do when I got to a free state, I'd save up my money en never spend a single cent, en when I got enough I'd buy my wife, who wuz owned on a farm close to whah Miss Watson lived; en den both uv us 'ud work to buy our two chillen. En ef dere master wouldn' sell 'em, we'd git an ab'litionist to go en steal 'em. Chile changed de way he look at me arter dat. Prob'bly shouldn' uv tole him de part 'bout havin' an ab'litionist steal 'em . . .

But den it wuz as ef whatever wuz weighin' him down suddenly lifted, en he look all cheerful agin as we look out fo' a light. Fust light dat showed, I couldn' help mysef—had to shout, We's safe, Huck! We's safe! I tole him to jump up en crack his heels kase dat 'uz de good ole Cairo at last. I jis' knowed it.

Chile says, I'll take de canoe en go en see, Jim. It mightn' be, you know.

Sumf'n 'bout de way he says it made me oneasy. I jumped up en got de canoe ready, en put my ole coat in de bottom fo' him to sit on, en gave him de paddle. Could it be he done fo'got his prom-ise? Wuz he 'bout to play de meanes' trick uv all on ole Jim by tellin' some slave catchers dat I run off? I figure it couldn' hurt to 'mine him dat he wuz my fren'. As he shoved off, I says dat pooty soon I'll be shoutin' fo' joy, a free man—en it 'uz all on account o' him. Tole him I couldn' ever have ben free ef it hadn't ben fo' him, en I'd never fo'git him—dat he wuz de best fren' I ever had, en de on'y fren' I had now. He ben paddlin' off fast, but when I says dat he slow down considable. When he wuz fifty yards off, I yell' dat he wuz de on'y white genlman dat ever kep' his promise to ole Jim.

Den a skift wid two men wid guns on it stopped, en de men start talkin' to de chile. I could jis' make out what dey wuz sayin'. What's dat yonder? dey ax. A piece uv a raf', Huck says. Do you b'long on it?

Yes, sir, he says. Any men on it? dey ax. On'y one, sir. Dey says dey wuz lookin' fo' five run'ways—all run off tonight above de head uv de ben'. Dey ax him, Is yo' man white or black?

He didn' answer up prompt. What wuz he gwyne to say? I wuz all a-tremblin' en afeard. Den he up en says, he's white.

But den dey say, I reck'n we'll go en see fo' ourselves. Lordy, I thought I wuz done fo'. By dis time I'd jumped off de raf' en 'uz in de river, wid nuffn but my eyes en nose showin' above de water. Den I heard de chile say: I wish you 'ud kase it's Pap dat's dah, en maybe you'd help me tow de raf' ashore whah de light is. He's sick—en so is mam en Mary Ann. Den one o' de men says, Oh, de devil! We's in a hurry, boy. But I s'pose we got to. Come, buckle to yo' paddle, en let's git along.

Chile start to paddle, en de men laid to dere oars. Arter a stroke or two, chile says:

Pap'll be much obleeged to you, I can tell you. Everybody goes 'way when I want 'em to help me tow de raf' ashore, en I can't do it by mysef.

Well, dat's infe'nal mean, says one o' de men. Odd too. Say, boy, what's de matter wid yo' daddy? he ax. Well, it ain' nuffn much, Huck says.

De men stop pullin'. It warn't but a mighty little ways to de raf' now. One says: Boy, dat's a lie. What is de matter wid yo' pap? Answer up square now, en it'll be de better fo' you.

I will, sir, I will, honest, says Huck. But don' leave us, please. Genlmen, ef you'll on'y pull ahead, en lemme heave you de head-line, you won't have to come a-near de raf'—please do.

Set 'er back, John, set 'er back! says one. Dey backed water. Keep 'way, boy—confound it, I jis' expec' de wind has blowed it to us. Yo' pap's got de small-pox, en you know it. Why didn' you come out en say so? Do you want to spread it all ovah? Well, says Huck, a-blubberin', I tole everybody b'fo', en dey jis' went 'way en left us.

Po' devil, dah's sumfn in dat, says one o' de men. We's right down sorry fo' you, but we—well, hang it, we doan' want de small-pox, you see. Look here, dey says, doan' you try to lan' by yo'self, er you'll smash everythin' to pieces. You float 'long down 'bout twenty mile, en you'll come to a town on de left-han side o' de river. It will be long arter sun-up den, en when you ax fo' help you tell 'em yo' folks is all down wid chills en fever. Doan' be a fool agin, en let people guess what is de matter. Now we's tryin' to do you a kindness; so you jis' put twenty mile between us, dat's a good boy. It wouldn' do no good to lan' yonder whah de light is—it's on'y a wood-yard. Say, I reck'n yo' daddy's po', en I'm bound to say he's in pooty hard luck. Here, I'll put a twenty-dollar gold piece on dis board, en you git it when it floats by. I feel mighty mean to leave you; but it won't do to fool wid small-pox.

Hol' on, Parker, says de other man, here's a twenty to put on de board fo' me. Good-bye, boy; you do as Mr. Parker tole you, en you'll be all right.

Dat so, my boy—good-bye, good-bye. Ef you see any run'ways, you git help en nab 'em, en you can make some money by it.

Good-bye, sir, says de chile. I won't let no run'ways git by me ef I can help it.

Chile paddle' back to de raf' lookin' kiner los' in thought. Look fo' me in de wigwam en saw I warn't dah. Call out my name.

Here I is, chile, I call back. Is dey out'n sight yit? I ax. I 'minded him not to talk loud. When he tole me dey wuz gone, I clumb out'n de water.

Tole him I'd ben listenin' to all de talk, en dat I slipped into de river en 'uz a-gwyne to shove fo' shore ef dey come aboard. Den I wuz a-gwyne to swim to de raf' agin when dey wuz gone. But Lordy, I tole him dat wuz de smartes' dodge! Tole him I 'pec it saved me—dat I ain't never gwyne to fo'git him.

Den we talk' 'bout de gold. It wuz a pooty good haul—twenty dollars apiece. I says we could take deck passage on a steamboat now, en de money'd las' us as far as we want' to go in de free states. I says twenty mile mo' warn't far fo' de raf' to go, but I wished we wuz already dere.

Towards daybreak we tied up, en I wuz mighty partic'lar 'bout hidin' de raf' well. Den I worked all day fixin' things in bundles en gittin' all ready to quit raffin' soon as we hit Cairo.

Dat night 'bout ten we saw de lights uv a town 'way down a left-han ben'.

Chile went off in de canoe to ax 'bout it. Foun' a man out in de river wid a skift, settin' a trot-line. Chile ax him: Mister, is dat town Cairo?

Cairo? No. You must be a blame' fool, he says.

What town is it, mister? chile ax.

Ef you want to know, go en find out. Ef you stay here botherin' roun' me fo' 'bout a half a minute longer, you'll git sumf'n you won't want.

Chile paddled to de raf'. I 'uz awful dis'ppointed, but chile says nemmine, Cairo'd be de nex' place, sure, he reck'n'd.

We pass' another town b'fo' daylight, en Chile wuz goin' out agin; but it wuz high groun', so he didn' go. I tole him dah wuz no high groun' 'bout Cairo. We laid up fo' de day on a tow-head tol'able close to de left-han' bank. Both uv us begin to 'spec de worst.

Chile says: Maybe we went by Cairo in de fog dat night.

I says I didn' want to talk 'bout it, dat po' niggers can't have no luck. Says I alwuz 'spected dat rattlesnake-skin warn't done wid its work.

Chile says he wisht he never seen dat snake-skin.

Tole him it warn't his fault. But I knowed it wuz. Tole him not to blame hisself 'bout it.

When it wuz daylight, we knew it wuz all up wid Cairo.

We talked it all ovah. It wouldn' do to take to de shore, kase we couldn' take de raf' up de stream. All we could do wuz wait fo' dark en start back in de canoe en take oah chances. So we slep' all day 'mongst de cottonwoods, en when we went back to de raf' 'bout dark, de canoe wuz gone!

We didn' say a word fo' a good while. Warn't nuffn to say.

Byemby we talked 'bout what we better do, en found dah wuz no way but jis' to go along down wid de raf' 'til we got a chance to buy a canoe to go back in. We warn't goin' to borrow it when dah warn't nobody roun', fo' dat might set people arter us.

So we shoved out arter dark on de raf'.

De place to buy canoes is off o' raffs layin' up at shore. But we didn' see no raffs layin' up, so we went 'long durin' three hours en mo'. Well, de night got gray en thick, which is de next meanest thing to fog. It got to be very late en still, en den along come a steamboat up de river. We lit de lantern en judged she'd see it. We could heah her poundin' along, but we didn' see her well 'til she wuz close. She aimed right fo' us. Often dey try to see how close dey can come widout touchin' en den de pilot sticks his head out en laughs en thinks he's smart. Well, here she come. She wuz a big 'un, en she wuz comin' in a hurry too. Dey wuz a yellin' at us en a jinglin' o' bells to stop de engines. Dey was a heap uv cussin' at us, too. En as I went overboard on one side en Huck on t'other, she come smashin' straight thoo de raf'.

I dived under water en swum as fast as I could 'way fum dat
thirty-foot wheel. Could hardly breathe when I finally come up
fo' air. De current 'uz strong, en dat boat started her engines agin
ten seconds arter she stopped 'em. Soon she 'uz out'n sight in de
thick weather—but I could heah her.

I swum along behind de chile fo' a long while but couldn' quite
catch up. Heard him yell out fo' me but didn' dare answer kase
I didn' want nobody to pick me up en make me a slave agin. De
current wuz driftin' towards de left-han' shore, so I went in dat
d'rection. Scraped my leg on a rock juttin' out fum de shore dat I
didn' see, en dat slowed me down considable. Next thing I know
I hear a passel o' dogs howlin' en barkin' like anythin', en I knowed
dat de chile wuz ashore. Soon it wuz all quiet agin, so I knowed
de chile wuz in dat big white house I could spot way up de shore.

I wuz afeard o' de dogs, so I hid in de woods 'til mawnin'. Early
in de mawnin' some er de niggers come along, a-gwyne to de
fields, en dey tuk me en showed me dis swamp whah de dogs can't
track me on accounts o' de water. Dey wuz a little flat piece o' lan'
big as a bedroom dat wuz dry en hid by thick trees en bushes en
vines. Says dey'd bring me truck to eat every night en tells me how
de chile's a-gitt'n along. Sure enough dat night dey come back wid
cole corn-pone, cole corn-beef, butter, en some buttermilk to
wash it all down. Tasted better'n anythin' I ever had. Must uv ben
'bout a hund'd uv 'em workin' diffunt jobs roun' de farm, some in
de fields, some in de house. Brought me anythin' I needed—didn'
have to ax twice. Dey wuz mighty good to me.

Tole me de chile had a little fren' his age—name o' Buck—en
wuz havin' a high ole time wid him. Dat wuz good, sence I needed
time fo' my leg to heal while I thought 'bout what we oughta do
next. My leg healed up, en dey kep' bringin' me good things to eat.
Boy called Jack who dey tole to do whatever de little stranger says
to do brought me reports on how Huck wuz doin' up at de house.

| 159 |

Tole me how he went huntin' en ridin' wid Buck en went to church wid de fambly. Sometimes a stack o' people 'ud come dah, on horseback, fum ten er fifteen mile roun'—quality, mainly—en stay five er six days en have big parties 'round 'bout en on de river, en dances, en picnics in de woods, daytimes, en balls at de house, nights. Chile went along en enjoy' hissef.

One evenin' when dey wuz bringin' me some corn-pone en buttermilk, I heard 'em talkin' 'bout a raf' dey found caught on a snag along de bank dat dey hid in a creek 'mongst de willows. En dey wuz so much jawin' 'bout which one uv 'um she b'long to de mos' dat I come to heah 'bout it pooty soon, so I ups en settles de trouble by tellin' 'um she doan' b'long to none uv um, but to de chile en me, en I ast 'em if dey gwyne to grab a young white genlman's propaty, en git a hid'n fo' it. I had coins I'd sewed into my trousers fum dat haul we tuck on de steamboat, en I gave 'em ten cents apiece fo' it, en dey wuz mighty well satisfied en wisht some mo' raffs 'ud come along en make 'm rich agin.

Dey got me a pot en pan en vittles—all dat we'd need when we tuck off agin. En nights I worked at patchin' up de raf'. One end wuz pooty tore up, but I wuz able to fix it. One day I ax Jack to figure out a way to get Huck to come see me. Heard him ax de chile ef he want' to see whole stack o' water-moccasins. Soon I see Huck comin'. Dat Jack's pooty smart: ef anyone ax him, He ain't mixed up wid no run'way. He can say he never saw us together, en it'll be de truth. Chile ax why didn' I send fo' Jack to fetch him sooner. Tole him dah wuz no use to 'sturb him 'til we could do sumf'n—but we wuz all right now. Tole him de raf' wuz fixed up good as new. Chile couldn' b'lieve it hadn' ben smashed all to flinders. Tole him we had a lot o' new stuff in place uv what wuz los', en now we could leave any time. He want' to spend a few mo' days wid his fren', Buck, so I says fine.

Every now en den you could hear shots echoin' thoo de woods.

Jack says it wuz on account o' Shepherdsons shootin' Granger-fords er Grangerfords shootin' Shepherdsons. Jack tole me no one could 'member how it all started, but everyone jis' want' to keep de body count even on both sides. One evenin' de whole woods seemed to explode wid shootin'. En next thing I know, Jack comes en tells me de chile 'uz shot.

I couldn' breathe. I felt as ef I'd ben shot—en I knew I ain't never a-gwyne to fo'give myseff fo' not figurin' some way to keep him from stoppin' one o' dem bullets.

But den, bless my soul, I hear de chile hissef shoutin' out fo' me. A chile *wuz* shot, but it warn't him. It wuz his little fren'.

Tole him to hush en not make a soun'. Chile raced along de bank en clumb on de raf', whah I hugged him harder'n I ever had b'fo'. Lordy, wuz I glad to git him back!

Chile says we better shove off. Dey won't find me, en dey'll think I've ben killed, en floated down de river—so doan' you lose no time, Jim, but jis' shove off fo' de big water as fast as you can, he says. Den he was real quiet. Just stared at the water fo' a real long time. Chile didn' want to talk 'bout all de shootin', en I didn' blame him. Watchin' his little fren' git killed fo' nuffn—dat had to be real hard. Couldn' get my head 'round it—but den I 'mem-bered dat rich white folks doan' need to give no 'scuse if dey wants to go 'roun' killin' people. I was jis' glad chile wuz back on de raf' 'way fum all dat. En I was glad dat it was all white folks killin' white folks—dat black folks like Jack who worked fo' 'em didn' count as no Grangerford, or like as not he'd be dead, too.

We finally felt easy when de raf' wuz two mile below dah en we wuz free en safe once mo'. Chile hadn't had a bite to eat sence yesterday, so I got out some corn-dodgers en buttermilk en pork en cabbage en greens en cooked 'em. Chile scarfed 'em down en says, Dah ain't nuffn in de worl' so good when it's cooked right. Gave him some mo' corn-dodgers en greens. I wuz glad to see de color come back to his face—he wuz white as de buttermilk when he clumb on de raf'.

We talked while we ate supper. I wuz glad he was able to talk agin—tho' he didn' want to say nuffn 'bout what happen' dat day. Chile wuz powful glad to git 'way fum all de shootin', en I wuz powful glad to git 'way fum de swamp.

We says dah warn't no home like a raf', arter all. Other places do seem so cramped up en smothery, but a raf' doan'. You feel mighty free en easy en comf'able on a raf'.

Two er three days en nights slid by so quiet en smooth. It wuz a monstrous big river down dah—sometimes a mile en a half wide; we run nights en laid up en hid daytimes. Soon as night wuz mos' gone we stopped en tied up—nearly awluz in de dead water under a tow-head—en den we cut young cottonwoods en willows, en hid de raf' wid 'em. Den we set out de lines. Next we slid into de river en had a swim, so as to freshen up en cool off; den we set down on de sandy bottom whah de water wuz 'bout knee deep en watch' de daylight come. Not a sound anywheres—jis' like de whole worl' wuz asleep, on'y sometimes de bullfrogs callin' out fo' what sure sounded like a jug-o-rum—tho' I never seen a bull-frog drink nuffn.

Sun begin to come up, you couldn' make nuffn else out but a kine o' line dat wuz de woods on de other side way ovah de water; den you could see little dark spots driftin' along far 'way—tradin' scows en such things—raffs. Byemby you could make out a log-cabin 'way on t'other side o' de river. En next you got de full day, en everythin' smilin' in de sun, en de song-birds—Lordy, how dey sing!

A little smoke couldn' be noticed now, so we 'ud take some fish off de lines en cook up a hot breakfas'. En arterwards we'd watch de river real quiet, en kine o' lazy along, en byemby lazy off to sleep. Sumf'n 'ud wake us up byemby, en we'd look to see what done it, en maybe see a steamboat comin' along up-stream; den fo' 'bout an hour dah 'ud be nuffn to heah or see. Dat's how we'd put in de day, lazyin' roun', listenin' to de stillness. Once dah wuz a thick fog, en de raffs en things dat went by wuz beatin' tin pans so de steamboats wouldn' run ovah dem. 'Minded me o' dat dern fog we'd ben thoo ourselves, en de time I had to teach de chile a lesson. A scow or a raf' 'ud go by so close we could hear 'em talkin' en cussin' en laughin'—heard 'em plain; but we couldn' see 'em. I says I b'lieved it wuz spirits carryin' on dat way in de air. But chile says: No; spirits wouldn' say, dern de dern fog.

Soon as it wuz night out we shoved. When we got her out to 'bout de middle we let her alone en let 'er float wherever de current want' her to; den we lit de pipes, en dangled our legs in de water, en talked 'bout all kines o' things. We wuz awluz naked, day en night—whenever de mosquitoes would let us. De new clothes Buck's folks made fo' de chile wuz too good to be comf'able. He didn' put much stock in clothes, nohow.

Sometimes we'd have dat whole river all to ourselves fo' de longes' time. You could see a candle in a cabin window on de shore; en sometimes on de water you could see a spark er two on a raf' or a scow; en maybe you could hear a fiddle or a song comin' ovah fum one uv 'em. Sure is nice to live on a raf'.

We had de sky up dah, all speckled wid stars, en we used to lay on our backs en look up at 'em, en talk 'bout whether dey wuz made er on'y jis' happened. I allowed dey wuz made, but de chile thought dey happened. Chile judged it'd uv took too long to make so many. I says de moon could've laid 'em. Well, dat look kine o' reasonable, so chile didn' say nuffn agin it, kase he'd seen a frog lay mos' as many, so o' course it could be done. We used to watch de stars dat fell too en see 'em streak down. I allowed dey'd got spoiled en wuz hove out'n de nest.

Once er twice a night we'd see a steamboat slippin' along in de dark, en now en den she'd belch a whole worl' o' sparks up out'n her chimbleys; den she'd turn a corner en leave de river still agin. En byemby her waves 'ud git to us, a long time arter she wuz gone, en joggle de raf' a bit. Arter midnight de people on de shore went to bed, en den fo' two er three hours de shore wuz black. When de fust spark showed in de winder uv a cabin on de shore, it meant mawnin' wuz comin', so we hunted a place to hide en tie up right 'way.

One mawnin' 'bout daybreak chile foun' a canoe en crossed ovah to de main shore en paddled 'bout a mile up a crick to see ef he could git some berries. Next thing I know, he comes back wid a couple o' men on de run fum some dogs en some folks on shore who wuz chasin' 'em. Made demselves right comf'able en at home. Made no diff'ence no one had invited 'em.

One wuz 'bout seventy or upwards en had a bald head en gray whiskers. He had a battered-up slouch hat on en a greasy blue wool shirt en ragged ole blue jeans britches stuffed into his boot-tops. He had an ole long-tail' blue jeans coat wid brass buttons flung ovah his arm, en both uv 'em had big, fat carpet-bags.

De other one wuz 'bout thirty. Arter breakfas' we all laid off en talked, en de fust thing dat come out wuz dat dese two didn' know each another.

What got you into trouble? baldhead ax de younger one.

De younger one says he' ben sellin' an article to take de tartar off de teeth—dat worked too—but dat tuck de enamel off along wid it. De ole one says he ben runnin' a temp'rance revival en takin' as much as five er six dollars a night, wid de business growin' all de time when word got roun' last night dat he ben sneakin' off wid a private jug on de sly. A boy tole him dat dey'd tar en feather him ef dey caught him. He left widout breakfas'. De young un says dey might work together, en de ole one says sure. Says he wuz a printer by trade, who also did a little in patent medicines. Wuz also

Never Saying a Word. Wood engraving from the Pennyroyal Press
edition of *Adventures of Huckleberry Finn,* 1984, by Barry Moser.

a actor on de stage. De young one says he' done considable doctorin'. Also did a fair 'mount o' preachin'—workin' camp meetin's en such.

I didn' like havin' all dis company on de raf'. Warn't safe. But I didn' know how to ditch 'em nuther.

Nobody says nuffn fo' a while; den de young un give a sigh en says: Alas! What 're you alassin' 'bout? ax de baldhead. De young un begun to wipe de corner o' his eye wid a rag. Says—like he wuz tellin' a big secret—he wuz really a duke. Pooty strange havin' a duke lan' on our raf' jis' like dat. Says he wuz de rightful Duke o' Bilgewater, tuck down fum his high place en forced to hang wid de likes uv us on a raf'.

Spun quite a tale. Want' to pass it off as de truth. I didn' b'lieve mo' 'n dat he want' us to think he wuz high-born so we'd wait on him, en serve him supper b'fo' we ate ourselves. But I couldn' resk lettin' him know I saw thoo him. So I played along.

De duke says we should bow when we speak to him, en say Yo' Grace, o' My Lord, o' Yo' Lordship. En one uv us was to wait on him at dinner, en do any little thing fo' him he want' done.

Well, dat wuz all easy, so we done it.

Warn't hard to bring him some bacon en greens en say, Will yo' Grace have some o' dis er some o' dat? En so on. A body could see it wuz mighty pleasin' to him.

But de ole man got pooty silent en byemby he tells de young un dat he warn't de on'y person dat's ben snaked down wrongly out'n a high place. En den he begin to cry. De young un ax him what he means, en de ole man ax ef he can trust him, still sort o' sobbin'. De young un says yes, en den de ole man tell him dat he wuz de dolphin—dat very chile Huck wuz tellin' me 'bout, on'y all growed up. He says we wuz all lookin' at de po' disappeared Looy de Seventeen, son o' Looy de Sixteen en Marry Antonette. De young un warn't havin' none uv it, kase de dolphin 'uz too ole, but de ole man says trouble made him gray en bald. Says he wuz de wanderin' en sufferin' rightful king o' France.

Well, he cried en laid it on real thick. Dem two frauds meant trouble. Now de ole one want' us to treat him like a king en call him Yo' Majesty en wait on him fust at meals, en stay stan'in 'til he tole us to set down. Dis made him cheerful en comf'able. But den de young un didn' look a bit satisfied wid de way things wuz goin'. Byemby de ole one says, like as not we got to be together a blame' long time on dis raf', so why doan' we make de best o' things? So dey shook han's, en Huck en me wuz glad to see it—kase what you want on a raf' is fo' everybody to be satisfied en feel right en kine towards de others.

I knowed dese liars warn't real kings er dukes at all, but jis' low-down humbugs. But I never let on. Didn' want no trouble. Ef dey want' us to call 'em kings en dukes, fine wid me. Huck thought dey'd fooled me. Left it dat way. Didn' want to say dey warn't who dey says dey wuz, or pooty soon dey might decide I warn't who chile says I wuz. So I let it slide.

I wuz glad I did kase dey wuz all full o' questions—want' to know what we kivered up de raf' dat way fo' en laid by in de daytime 'stead o' runnin'. Dey ax, wuz I a run'way?

Huck says, Goodness sakes! Would a run'way nigger run south?

Dat wuz smart. So wuz de story he made up fo' why it's jis' him en me on de raf' en why we doan' run durin' de day. Can't beat dat chile fo' stretchers! He says we wuz livin' in Pike County, in Missouri, whah he wuz born, en everybody died off but him en Pa en his baby brother. Says his pa want' to go down en live wid a uncle wid a little place on de river b'low N'Orleans. Says Pa wuz pooty po' en had some debts, so when he'd squared up, de on'y propaty dey had left wuz sixteen dollars en me. Says dat warn't enough to take us down de river deck passage or any other way, but when de river rise, we caught dis piece o' raf' en fixed to take it down to N'Orleans. Says a steamboat run ovah de raf' one night, en we all went ovahboar' en I came up all right, but Pa wuz drunk, en his brother wuz on'y fo' years ole, so dey never come up agin. Says dat we had considable trouble, bekase people wuz awluz comin' out in skifts en tryin' to take me 'way fum him, sayin' dey b'lieved I wuz a run'way en want' de reward. Tole 'em we don' run daytimes no mo' now; nights dey doan' bother us. Duke says he want' to fix things so we kin run in de daytime ef we want to.

Duke tuck my bed—corn-shuck tick. King tuck Huck's—straw tick wid no corn cobs pokin' you. We got 'way soon as it 'uz good en dark. 'Bout ten o'clock it begun to rain en blow en thunder en lightnin' like anythin', so de king tole us to both stay on watch 'til de weather got better. Den him en de duke dey crawl' into de wigwam en turn'd in fo' de night. Lordy, it wuz a big storm! How dat wind did scream! De waves mos' washed me off de raf', but I ha'nt no clothes on en didn' mine.

Chile had de middle watch, but he wuz pooty sleepy by dat time, so I says I' stan' de fust half uv it fo' him. De king en duke spread out so in de wigwam dah warn't room fo' de chile, so he lay outside in de warm rain. De waves warn't runnin' so high now. 'Bout two dey come up agin, en I 'uz goin' to call de chile, but I change' my mine: I reck'n' dey warn't high enough yet to do me no harm. But pooty soon all uv a sudden along comes a reglar ripper en wash' de chile ovahboard. He warn't hurt—jis' soaked thoo—en su'prised. I mos' died laughin'.

I lay down en got some sleep when Huck tuck de watch. Byemby de storm let up. Chile rousted me out b'fo' daylight, en we slid de raf' into hidin' fo' de day.

Dem two ole frauds played some cards en den begun figurin' out how to separate folks on shore fum dere money. Dey warn't thieves—flat-out thieves, dat is. Dey tuck people's money, but dey got 'em to give it to 'em thoo no end o' schemes en such. Duke tole de king dey should hire a hall en put on a play. King says he knowed nuffn 'bout plays, but dat didn' matter. Neither did de duke, when you git down to it—or de folks in town dey want' to sell tickets to.

So dey spent de day prancin' 'bout de raf' en spoutin' nonsense. De king wuz dressed up in a night-gown en ruffled nightcap dat on'y partly kivered his bald head, en de duke kep' callin' him Juliet en tole him to learn his lines by heart.

Dere wuz a little one-horse town 'bout three mile down de ben', en arter dinner de duke says he had an idea 'bout how to run in daylight widout it bein' dangersome fo' me, so he allowed he'd go down to de town en fix dat thing. De king allowed he'd go too en see ef he couldn' strike sumf'n. We wuz out'n coffee, so I says Huck better go 'long wid' 'em in de canoe en git some.

While dey wuz gone, I kep' tryin' to come up wid ways we could rid ourselves o' dem two rascals, but I couldn' think uv any. A few hours later de three o' dem come back to de raf'. De king had worked a camp meet'n' tellin' folks some lies 'bout his bein' a pirate dat went en got reformed en dat made 'em give him dere money. Counted it when he got back to de raf' en found he had taken in eighty-seven dollars en seventy-five cents. En a three-gallon jug o' whiskey too dat he found under a wagon when he wuz startin' home thoo de woods. De king says, take it all roun', it laid ovah any day he ever put in in de missionaryin' line. Duke wuz thinkin' he'd ben doin' pooty well 'til de king show up, but arter dat he didn' think dat so much. He had set up en printed off two little jobs fo' farmers in dat printin'-office—horse bills—en tuck de money, fo' dollars. Sole some stuff dat warn't his en tuck in five en a half dollars mo'.

Den he showed us another little job he'd printed en hadn't charged fo', bekase it 'uz fo' us. It had a picture uv a run'way wid a bundle on a stick ovah his shoulder, en $200 reward under it. It tole all 'bout somebody s'posed to be me—says I run 'way fum St. Jacques' plantation, forty mile belo' N'Orleans, last winter, en likely went north, en whoever 'ud catch me en send me back he could have de reward en expenses.

Now, says de duke, arter to-night we kin run in de daytime ef we want to. Says ef dey sees anybody comin' dey kin tie me han en foot wid a rope, en lay me in de wigwam en show dis hanbill en say dey captured me up de river en wuz too po' to travel on a steamboat, so dey got dis little raf' on credit fum some fren's en are goin' down to git de reward. Dey says han'cuffs en chains 'ud look better on me, but it wouldn' go well wid de story uv us bein' so po'. Too much like jew'lry. I never thought hancuffs en chains look like jew'lry, but I wuz glad dey settled on ropes.

We all says de duke wuz pooty smart, en dah couldn' be no trouble 'bout runnin' daytimes now.

When I called Huck to take de watch at fo' in de mawnin', I ax him ef he reck'n'd we wuz goin' to run acrost any mo' kings on dis trip. He says no, en dat wuz good. I doan' mine one er two kings—but dat's enough. Dis one's powful drunk, en de duke ain' much better.

Arter sun-up next day, we went right on en didn' tie up. De king en de duke turned out byemby lookin' pooty rusty; but arter dey jumped ovahboard en tuck a swim, dey perked up a good deal. I tried to git de king to talk French so I could hear what it wuz like. Says he'd ben in dis country so long en had so much trouble, he' fo'got it.

Arter breakfas' de king he tuck a seat on de corner o' de raf', en pulled off his boots en rolled up his britches, en let his legs dangle in de water, so as to be comf'able, en lit his pipe, en went to gittin' his part in de play by heart. When he got it down pooty good, he en de duke begun to practice it together. De duke had to learn him ovah en ovah agin how to say every speech. Tole him

not to bellow out Romeo! like a bull—says he had to say it sof'
kase Juliet's jis' a sweet chile, en she don' bray like a jackass.

Well, next dey got out a couple o' long swords dat de duke
made out uv a couple uv pieces uv oak, en dey begun to practice
de sword fight—de duke called hisself Richard de Third. Lordy,
how dey laid on en pranced roun' de raf'! But byemby de king
tripped en fell ovahboard, en dat give me a chuckle. En arter dat
dey tuck a res' en talked 'bout other scams dey'd pulled along de
river.

Duke says dey had to add a little mo'—sumf'n 'bout oncores—
extra stuff you did arter de show to keep de crowd happy. Says
he'd do a sailor's dance en dat de king should do de speech dat
Hamlet done give dat awluz fetches de house.

Duke marched up en down de raf' tryin' to 'member what he
'sposed to say, frownin' horrible every now en den, hoistin' up his
eyebrows, squeezin' his han on his forehead en staggerin' back
wid a kine o' moan, en den a sigh, en a tear. Byemby he got it. He
tole us to listen up. Den wid his head tilted back, lookin' up at de
sky, he begin to rip en rave. Speech 'uz filled wid a lot o' fancy
words I didn' know. Made no sense, but he sure said it pooty. King
liked de speech, en pooty soon he could say it all by hissef.

Fust chance he got, de duke had some show bills printed. Arter
dat, fo' two er three days as we floated along, de raf' wuz an uncommon lively place—nuffn but sword-fightin' en practicin' goin'
on all de time.

One mawnin', when we wuz pooty well down de state uv Arkansas, we saw a little town, en dem two rascals tuck de canoe en
went dah to see ef dah wuz any chanst in dat place fo' dere show.
When dey come back dey says dey struck it mighty lucky; dah wuz
goin' to be a circus dah dat arternoon, en de country folks wuz
already beginnin' to come in. De circus 'ud leave b'fo' night, so de
show 'ud have a pooty good chanst. De duke he hired de court-

house en had de chile help de two o' dem stick up de bills roun' town. Huck got to see de circus en 'uz all excited 'bout it. Arterwards, de king en de duke pick up dere git-ups en swords en head out to de courthouse. Dey come back late dat night wid de tuck all tuck out'n dem: said on'y twelve people come, en dey laughed all de time, 'cept fo' one boy who 'uz asleep. Duke says de show 'uz too high-falutin' fo' dis Arkansas crowd. But he knowed jis' what dey'd like. He boughta bunch o' cans o' paint, diffunt colors, en printed new hanbills. Wrote at de bottom o' de bill sumpn 'bout not lettin' in no ladies er chillen. Duke says, ef dat line don' fetch 'em, he don' know Arkansas.

It 'uz pooty quiet on de raf' while de three o' dem wuz in town gittin' ready fo' dat show. Had a chanst to think 'bout what my fambly might be doin' right now. Jenny 'uz prob'ly shellin' peas er peelin' potatoes. Maybe Johnny wuz takin' de pods en peels out to de hogs. Or maybe haulin' in firewood fum de woodpile—not de really big pieces, on'y little ones. I could see little 'Lizabeth playin' wid dat doll I made fo' her out uv an ole corn cob, wid yellow corn silk fo' de hair. She sure love' dat doll. Or maybe dey had her sweepin' up wid de little short-han'led broom I cut fo' her. Awluz happy to do sumf'n useful, dat chile. Sunset come, en I thought uv 'em lookin' out de winder en watchin' de way de sky change' colors ovah de trees. I hope' dey warn't too worried 'bout me. I'd tell 'em everythin' dat happened some day when we wuz all together agin.

I doan' know how dis new show went, but when dey come back arterwards 'bout midnight, dey made me en Huck back de raf' out en float her down de middle o' de river, 'bout two mile below town, en hide her dah. Never tole me why. Nex de king en de duke fairly laughed dere bones loose ovah de way dey'd served dem people. Seems dey played some mean trick on de folks who come de fust two nights en knowed dey'd let de res' uv de town git roped in too. Dey knowed dey'd lay fo' dem de third night, thinkin' it wuz dere turn now. De king says dey could take all dem rotten apples en tomatoes dey brought to throw at 'em en have a picnic. Dem rascals tuck in fo' hund'ed en sixty-five dollars in three nights. I never saw money hauled in by de wagon-load like dat befo'. Byemby, when dey wuz asleep en snorin', I ax Huck ef he warn't su'prised de way dem two carried on.

No, Huck says. Why not? I ax him. Says it's in de breed—reck'n'd dey wuz all alike. Chile says kings is kings, en you got to make allowances. Take 'em all roun', dey're a mighty ornery lot. It's de way dey're raised. I knowed dat. Jis' look at dat king Sollermun who wuz raised to think chillen is so plentiful it wuz fine to cut one en two ef he'd a mine to! Kings may be kings, I tole him, but dis one sure do smell. Smell like de nation. Huck tole me dey all do. Say we can't help de way a king smells. I says de duke 'uz a tolable likely man in some ways. Chile says dukes wuz diffunt but not very diffunt—en when he's drunk dah's no man dat could tell him fum a king.

I tole de chile I didn' hanker fo' no mo' uv 'em. Dese wuz all I could stan'. Chile say dat's de way he feels too. But we got 'em on our han's, en we got to 'member what dey are, en make 'lowances. I could tell he thought I didn' know dat dese two warn't a real king en duke. I let him think dat. Didn' hurt any en made him feel smart.

Chile went to sleep. I didn' awluz call him when it wuz his turn. I kine o' liked de quiet at night, when I wuz alone stan'ing watch. Give me time to 'member my wife en chillen—dere faces, dere hugs, dere laughs. Lordy, I missed 'em. Never ben dis far 'way fum dem fo' dis long. But den I thought 'bout how, ef I'd stayed, Miss Watson coulda sent me far 'way fum dem forever, wid me not even knowin' whah I wuz, to send word. We wuz apart now—but on'y to find a way to be t'gether later. I kep' dat thought in mine as I 'membered how much I missed 'em. How much I missed feelin' Jenny's sweet breath on my cheek nights, b'fo' Miss Watson made me move to de widder Douglas'; how soft she felt, how good she smelled. How much I missed Johnny awluz hidin' when bedtime come, en little 'Lizabeth awluz wantin' to be in my lap. Po' little 'Lizabeth! Po' little Johnny! it's mighty hard; I spec' I ain't ever gwyne to see you no mo'! Den I'd fall to thinkin' 'bout how far 'way I wuz, en what a mess I got us into . . . .

Jis' when Huck wake up, I hear sumfn ovah yonder on de bank like a whack, er a slam, en all I could do 'uz give a low moan—not loud enough to wake 'em—but a moan kase I was so mis'able. Huck ax me what wuz up. I tole him dat sound on de shore 'minded me uv de time I treated my little 'Lizabeth so ornery.

She warn't on'y 'bout fo' year ole, en she tuck de sk'yarlet fever en had a powful rough spell; but she got well, en one day she was a-stannin' aroun', en I says to her, I says:

Shet de do'.

She never done it; jis' stood dah, kiner smilin' up at me. It make me mad en I says agin, mighty loud, I says:

Doan' you hear me? Shet de do'!

She jis stood de same way, kiner smilin' up. I was a-bilin'! I says:

I lay I *make* you mine!

En wid dat I fetch' her a slap side de head dat sont her a-sprawlin'. Den I went into de yuther room en 'uz gone 'bout ten minutes, en when I come back dah was dat do' a-stannin' open yit, en dat chile stannin' mos' right in it, a-lookin' down and mournin', en de tears runnin' down. My, but I wuz mad! I was a-gwyne fo' de chile, but jis' den—it was a do' dat open innerds—jis' den, 'long come de wind en slam it to, behine de chile, ker-*blam!*—en my lan', de chile never move'! My breff mos' hop outer me, en I feel so—so—I doan' know how I feel. I crope out, all a-tremblin', en crope aroun' en open de do' easy en slow, en poke my head in behine de chile, sof' en still, en all uv a sudden I says POW! jis' as loud as I could yell. *She never budge!*

Oh, Huck, I sez, I bust out a-cryin' en grab her up in my arms, en say, Oh, de po' little thing! De Lord God Amighty fogive po' ole Jim, kaze he never a-gwyne to fogive hisself as long's he live! Oh, she was plumb deef en dumb, Huck, plumb deef en dumb—en I'd ben a-treat'n her so!

Nex day I tole de duke how mighty heavy en tiresome to me it wuz to have to lay all day in de wigwam tied wid de rope so as not to look like a run'way. Duke says he'd fine some way to git roun' it. He wuz a smart man, dat duke, en he soon struck it. He dressed me up in a long curtain-calico gown en a white horse-hair wig en whiskers, en den he tuck his paint fum de show en painted my face en han's en ears en neck all ovah a dead, dull, solid blue, like a man dat's ben drownded nine days. Chile said I wuz de horriblest lookin' thing he ever see. Den de duke tuk a shingle en wrote on it dat I wuz a sick A-rab but wouldn' do no one no harm—when I warn't out'n my head. Nailed dat shingle to a board en stood it up fo' er five foot in front o' de wigwam. I says it wuz a sight better dan lyin' tied a couple o' years every day en tremblin' all ovah every time dah wuz a soun'. De duke tole me to make myself free en easy, en ef anybody come meddlin' roun', I must hop out'n de wigwam en carry on some, en fetch a howl er two like a wild beas'. He reck'n'd dey 'ud light out en leave me 'lone arter dat. Which 'uz sound enough judgmen'; but you take de average man, en he wouldn' wait fo' me to howl. Chile said I look like I ben dead a year.

Huck en de two rascals got some store-bought clothes. I clean'd up de canoe. King said he was gwyne to git on a big steamboat layin' at de shore up under de pint, 'bout three mile 'bove de town takin' on freight. King said seein' how he wuz dressed, he better arrive down fum St. Louis er Cincinnati, er some other big place. Tole Huck to go fo' de steamboat, sayin' dey'd come down to de village on her. I saw de king en de chile take de canoe to shore en pick up a country boy carryin' some carpet-bags en head to de steamboat, talkin' to him de whole time. Couldn' hear what dey wuz sayin'. Arter a while dey come back fo' de duke. Dey set down en tole him dey wuz goin' to trick some fambly on shore dat had jis' los' a loved one out'n dere money. De duke wuz goin' to have to p'tend to be deef en dumb. Den dey waited fo' a steamboat. King said he'd talk 'em into carryin' 'em fo' or five mile down river en puttin' 'em down in a yawl by tellin' 'em dey'd make a dollar a mile. At las' dah wuz a big 'un, en dey hailed her. I couldn' see 'em arter de boat tuck 'em on.

I stayed hid on de raf' fo' a few days. Good thing we had plenty o' provisions. It wuz nice en peaceful widout dem rascals aboard. I wuz kine o' likin' having nuffn to do but fish en swim en think 'bout what I'd do when I got to a free state. I'd find some job dat paid me en save up my money en den buy my wife en chillen en set up house up North. Yessir, we'd have our own little place—bigger'n de shack whah 'Lizabeth en Johnny wuz born. En I'd plant veg'tables out back—peas en corn en tomatoes—so we'd awluz have fresh things to eat on han'.

Den one day I see de chile racin' to me in a canoe. He jumps aboard en sings out, Set her loose, Jim! Glory be to goodness, we's shut uv 'em! I wuz burstin' wid joy! I come out'n de wigwam en head fo' de chile wid both arms spread. Fo'got dat I wuz painted blue—scared de livin' daylights out uv him! Chile went ovahboard backwards. I fished him out en wuz goin' to give him a big hug, I wuz so glad he wuz back—en so glad to be shut o' dem two rascals. But chile says, not now; save it fo' breakfas'! Cut loose en let 'er slide! So in two seconds 'way we went a-slidin' down de river, en it did seem so good to be free agin en all by ourselves on de big river, en nobody to bother us. Chile begun to skip roun' a bit en jump up en crack his heels. But 'bout de third crack he notice' a sound dat he knowed mighty well, en held his breath en listened en waited; en sure enough, when de next flash busted out ovah de water, here dey come!—en jis' a-layin' to dere oars en making dere skift hum! It wuz de king en de duke.

Chile wilted right down to de planks en it wuz all he could do to keep fum cryin'. When dey got aboard de king went fo' de chile en shook him by de collar fo' tryin' to give dem the slip. Chile said we warn't a-gwyne to do that. P'tended he ben afeard de king en de duke wuz kilt en wuz awful sorry, en so wuz I—en we wuz awful glad when we seen dem comin'. I says it wuz so. But de king tole Huck to shut up. Den dey tuck to carpin' at each other 'bout whah things went wrong, en who wuz mos' to blame. Den dey started accusin' each other uv hidin' some money in a coffin so dey could dig it up en steal it. Dey kep' at it fo' a while, gittin' hotter en hotter de whole time. Den each one tuck to his bottle en b'fo' long dey went off a-snorin' en each other's arms. En when dey got to snorin' Huck tole me everythin'.

We didn' dare stop agin at no town fo' days en days; kep' right along down de river. We wuz down souf in de warm weather now, en a mighty long ways fum home. So now dem frauds reck'n'd dey wuz out'n danger, en dey begun to work de villages agin.

Fust dey done a lecture on temp'rance, but dey didn' make enough fo' 'em both to git drunk on. Den in another place dey started a dancin' school, but dey didn' know no mo' how to dance dan a hog do, so de fust prance dey made de gen'l public jumped in en pranced 'em out'n town. Another time dey tried to go at yellocution, but dey didn' yellocute long 'til de people got up en give 'em a solid good cussin' en made 'em skip out. Dey tackled a little o' everythin', but didn' have no luck. So at last dey got jis' 'bout dead broke en laid roun' de raf' as she floated along, thinkin' en thinkin', en never sayin' nuffn.

Den dey begun to lay dere heads together in de wigwam en talk real low two or three hours at a time. Chile en me begun to git oneasy. We judged dey wuz studyin' up some kine o' mischief worse dan ever. Early one mawnin' we hid de raf' in a good, safe place 'bout two mile below a town name' Pikesville, en de king he went ashorc en tole us all to stay hid while he smelt 'roun' to see ef anybody dere got wind o' de Royal One Such yet. En he says ef he warn't back by midday, den de duke en de chile'd know it wuz all right, en dey wuz to come along.

So we stayed whah we wuz. De duke he fretted en sweated roun'. He scold' us fo' everythin', en we couldn' seem to do nuffn right. Sumfn 'uz a-brewin', sure. When mid-day come en no king, Huck en de duke went up to de town, to hunt roun' dah fo' de king. But soon as dey wuz gone de king come back to de raf', tied my han's with ropes, en pulled me onto de shore. Farmer come by en said his name wuz Phelps. King flashed dat reward notice he printed up, give him some fool talk 'bout how he had to go up river en couldn' wait for no reward, en he sole me to dat man fo' forty dollars.

Arter all I'd done fo' him, dat weasel—to do me a turn like dat! Farmer tuck hol' o' de rope en made me walk behind him 'til we got to his house, whah he tuck me to a little shack he had in de back, chained me to de bed, en locked de do'. 'Fore he lef', I tole him 'bout de Royal One Such show. Least I made sure dem cheats 'ud git run out'n town ef dey tried to do it agin.

But den I 'membered dat soon as de farmer found dah warn't no reward fo' me, he'd sell me down river fo' sure, en I'd be jis' as bad off as ef I let Miss Watson sell me. I cried. What else wuz dah to do? It warn't de thought o' bein' worked to death on one o' dem plantations down souf—it wuz de thought o' never seein' my wife or little Johnny or 'Lizabeth agin.

To keep fum cryin' mo', I tried to 'member everythin' I could 'bout 'em fum when we all wuz together, b'fo' Miss Watson tuck me to live at de widder Douglas'. How it felt in de winter to be snug next to my Jenny under de quilt she made, feelin' her close to me, reachin' out fo' me in de dark, me pullin' her close, so warm en soft. Hearin' de chillen breathin', sleepin' so peaceful on dere pallets on de flo'. How de wind shook de walls, en de do'—but I didn' pay it no mine, wid de room still hot fum de fire I made. Mawnin's roustin' de little ones . . . 'Lizabeth awluz liked to sleep in. I could call out to Johnny, but I had to tap 'Lizabeth's shoulder real gentle-like when it wuz time to git up—arter de sk'yarlet fever en she couldn' hear no mo'. How fust thing she'd do when she wake up wuz race to look out de do' to see ef de sun wuz out yet. How she love to watch dat sun rise! Her whole little face 'ud break into a big smile as daylight come. I hope Johnny 'members what I awluz tole him 'bout watchin' out fo' his little sister—dat he gotta 'member to make sure nobody hurt her or make her feel bad. She need him to protect her. But den I thought 'bout how he could be sole 'way fum her, en both uv 'em could be sole 'way fum dere mother, en dah'd be nuffn I could do, tied to some rusty ole bed in some part o' de country I had no idea whah. En den all I could do wuz hang my head. Po' little 'Lizabeth! Po' little Johnny! Chances are I'd never see 'em agin. Maybe dat ole snakeskin wuz still workin' its bad luck: I sure had no luck sence dem two rascals tuck ovah our raf'. En den I thought o' Huck. No way he would know whah I wuz, ef he wuz uv a mine to rescue me. No, dis look like de end o' de line. Nobody wuz comin' to git me out'n de mess I wuz in now.

It warn't all bad: Nat, who b'longed to de farmer en his wife, brought me a plate arter supper—wid good food, too—watermelon, corn-pone, meat, en greens—same food de white folks ate on'y what wuz left arter dey wuz done. Nat had a good heart en laughed easy. He had his hair all tied up in little bunches wid thread to keep de witches off. He says de witches wuz pesterin' him awful dese nights, en makin' him see all kine o' strange things, en hear all kine' o' strange noises, en he didn' b'lieve he 'uz ever witched so long b'fo' in his life.

Next mawnin' when it 'uz still dark outside, Nat opens de do' to bring my tin plate o' food, en I nearly jumped out'n my skin: it 'uz Huck en Tom! I shouted out dere names, I 'uz so shocked to see 'em. But soon as I did, I knew dat was a bad idea. Nat 'uz real su'prised en ax me do I know dese genlmen? But Tom look at Nat, steady en kine o' wonderin', en ax, do who know us? Why, dis-yer run'way nigger, says Nat. I doan' reck'n he does, says Tom, but what put dat into yo' head, he ax. Didn' he jis' dis minute sing out like he knowed you? Nat says. Tom says, in a puzzled-up kine o' way: Well, dat's mighty curious. Who sung out? When did he sing out? What did he sing out? En turns to Huck, perfec'ly calm, en says, Did you hear nobody sing out? Huck says: No, I ain't heard nobody say nuffn.

Well, I picked up on what dey wuz up to, so when Tom turns to me en looks me ovah like he never seen me b'fo', en ax did I sing out? I says, no, sah, I hain't said nuffn, sah.

Not a word?, he ax. No, sah, I hain't said a word, I says. Did you ever see us b'fo'? he ax.

No, sah, not as I knows on, I says. So Tom turns to Nat, who wuz lookin' wild, en ax, kine o' severe: What do you reck'n's de matter wid you, anyways? What made you think somebody sung out?

Nat says it's de dad-blame' witches en dat he wisht he wuz dead. Says dey's awluz at it, en dey do mos' kill me, dey sk'yers me so. Nat says please doan' tell nobody 'bout it, er ole Mars Silas he'll scol' me kase he say dey ain't no witches. I jis' wish to goodness he 'uz heah now—I jis' bet he couldn' fine no way to git aroun' it dis time.

Tom give him a dime en tell him to buy some mo' thread to tie up his wool wid, en den Tom he look at me en says I wonder ef dis run'way's gwyne' to be hanged. En while Nat steps to de do' to look at de dime en bite it to see ef it's good, Tom tells me in a real sof' voice, doan' ever let on to know us. En ef you hear any diggin' goin' on nights, it's us; we's goin' to set you free.

I on'y had time to grab Huck by de han en squeeze it; den Nat come back, en de boys say dey'd come agin some time ef Nat wants em to. Nat he says he would, mo' particular ef it 'uz dark, kase de witches went fo' him mostly in de dark, en it wuz good to have folks roun' den.

Arter dey left, I wuz so happy I could burst. One minute, I wuz all alone wid no hope uv anybody comin' to rescue me, en de next dah wuz dese two white boys sayin' dey wuz goin' to dig me out en set me free! Lordy, de thought o' bein' free when I'd los' all hope made me wan' to jump fo' joy—en I would have ef de chains warn't so heavy.

Next night I could hear some diggin' goin' on near de bottom log o' de shack. Thought it must be de boys, but I but I didn' make no noise sence I couldn' be sure who 'uz dah. Diggin' seem to last several hours. Had time to try to git my head roun' de puzzle o' why Tom Sawyer 'uz helpin' to set me free. Huck, I could understan'. But Tom Sawyer 'uz too respect'ble to be doin' sumfn dis resky. Maybe I wuz wrong 'bout dat snakeskin. Maybe my luck had changed. All I knowed wuz dese two white boys wuz de on'y hope I had uv evah seein' my wife en chillen agin, so you bet I wuz glad dey wuz dah.

Next night, arter I wuz asleep, de boys wake me up en wuz stan'in' ovah me wid a lit candle. Nat warn't roun' now, so I didn' have to p'tend I didn' know 'em. I tole Huck he wuz de bes' fren'

I ever had—en tole Mars Tom he wuz a good fren' too. Tole 'em both how glad I wuz to see 'em en ax whether dey could hunt up a chisel to cut de chain off'n my leg so we could clear out right 'way. Den Tom tole me dat warn't de way it wuz done. Seemed to have some pooty strong ideas 'bout de right way to set me free en de wrong way, en he wuz set on doin' things de right way. I never heard o' no right way or wrong way—jis' knowed dah wuz ways dat worked en ways dat didn'. Tom sat down en tole me a bunch o' things dat made no sense, but de main thing he says dat did make sense wuz dat dey'd change de plans right 'way ef dah wuz any danger, en dat I shouldn' be de least afeard, kase dey'd see to it dat I got 'way, sure. So I says it wuz all right. Tom ax a lot o' questions, en when I tole him de farmer comes in every day or two to pray wid me, en his wife comes in to see ef I 'uz comf'able en had enough to eat, en both o' dem wuz kine as dey could be, Tom says, now he knew how to fix it: he'd git me things thoo dem. Huck says, Doan' do nuffn o' de kine; said it was a jackass idea. But Tom never paid him no mine en went right on. I never seen such a stubborn chile when he got his plans set.

Tom tole me how dey'd have to smuggle in de rope-ladder pie en other large things by Nat, en I must be on de lookout, en not be su'prised, en not let Nat see me pull de ladder out'n de pie. I ax why on earth did I need a rope-ladder, but he ignored me en jis' kep' talkin'. Says dey'd put small things in de farmer's coat-pockets, en I must steal 'em out; en dey'd tie things to his wife's apron-strings or put 'em in her apron-pocket, ef dey got a chanst; en tole me what dey'd be en what dey wuz fo'. En tole me to write on a shirt wid my blood. I couldn' see no sense in none uv it en tole 'em. Also tole 'em I couldn' write nohow. I hated to think dat right now dese two boys wid dere blame' fool 'structions wuz my on'y hope. But dey wuz white folks, arter all. Dey could go any-wheres dey want' on dat farm en knowed whah things stood, so I says I'd do it all jis' as Tom says, en dey wuz satisfied. I had plenty o' corn-cob pipes en tobacco. De boys sat down wid me, en we had a good time, talkin' ovah ole times. Den dey crawled out thoo de hole dey dug.

Next day Nat come wid a pan o' corn-pone fo' me. I near mashed my teeth when I bit into it: boys hid a piece o' brass candlestick inside. Dah wuz no sense in none o' de things dey did de next few days. Never bit nuffn agin widout jabbing my fork in three er fo' places fust.

Next thing I know, ten or 'leven hounds come pilin' into de shack—de boys lef' de lean-to do' open—en po' Nat thought witches wuz arter him agin en keeled ovah on de flo', groanin' like he wuz dyin'. Tom flings out a piece o' my meat, en de dogs went fo' it—but I wisht I coulda eaten it myse'f. Den Tom comes back en tries to talk Nat into thinkin' he wuz imaginin' things agin. Oh—en another thing; he kep' callin' Huck Tom en Tom Mars Sid en I doan' know why.

Nat says, Dad fetch it, I jis' wisht I could git my han's on one er dem witches jis' wunst—on'y jis' wunst—it's all I'd ast. But mos'ly I wisht dey'd lemme 'lone, I does. Po' Nat. I figured Tom wouldn' want me to tell him dah warn't no witches. Seemed part o' de plan fo' him to think dah wuz.

Tom says: what makes 'em come here jist at breakfast-time? It's kase dey're hungry; dats de reason. You make 'em a witch pie; that's de thing fo' you to do. Nat tole him he didn' know how to make no witch pie. So Tom says he gonna make it hisself. Nat was so happy to hear dat he said he'd wusshup de groun' under his feet ef he does dat.

Tom tole Nat he'd do it, seein' as he ben good to 'em and showed 'em de run'way nigger. But he tole Nat he gotta be mighty careful. Tole him to turn his back and not let on he seen dem put nothin' in de pan. And he shouldn' look when I unloads de pan, or touch de witch things or sumf'n bad might happen. He didn' say what. Nat said he wouldn' touch no witch things fo' ten hund'd thousan' billion dollars. So Tom figured we wuz safe.

I didn' know what dey wuz plannin' on gittin' me dat dey wuz callin' witch-things, but Nat sure warn't 'bout to mess wid 'em. When Nat brought me my pan dat night, dah wuz three tins in de bottom under de vittles. En when I wuz by myself, I busted into de pie en sure 'nough dah wuz de rope-ladder dey tole me 'bout. I needed a rope-ladder like a hound needs a Bible, but dey said I got to have it, so I hid it inside o' my straw tick, jis' like de boys said I should. En I scratched some marks on a tin plate en threw it out'n de window-hole, jis' like dey said. But it made no sense at all. Had to keep 'mindin' myself dat dem boys' bein' willin' to bust me out'n dah wuz de on'y way I'd git out. So I tried to 'member all dere dern fool instructions en do what dey said.

Makin' pens out'n de broken candlestick wuz hard. Boys worked at it dat night fo' quite some time, en I pitched in, too. It wuz even harder to make all dem marks on dat shirt dey brought me. But de roughest part wuz makin' what dey called my 'scription on de wall. Tom said I got to do my 'scription en coat o' arms. I tole him I didn' have no coat o' arms—I on'y had dis ole shirt dat he'd tole me to keep writin' on. Tom said I didn' understan'.

Huck tried to take my part. Said Jim's right, anyways, when he says he ain't got no coat o' arms, kase he ain't. Tom said he reck'n'd he knowed dat but dat I'd have one b'fo' I got out. Said I wuz goin' out right en dat dah warn't goin' to be no flaw in my record. I didn' know what record he 'uz talkin' 'bout, but I jis' kep' doin' like he says to be on de safe side.

Huck en I filed 'way at de pens. I made mine out'n de piece o' de brass candlestick, en Huck made his out out'n de spoon dey'd smouched. Tom set to work to think out de thing he called my coat o' arms. Didn' look like a coat, en had no arms on it, but he seemed satisfied arter a while when he thought up de picture he want' me to copy on de wall.

Huck didn' git it either en ax what it mean', but Tom said we didn' have time to bother ovah dat. He jis' kep' writin' stuff fo' me to copy, en it wuz dern hard work to scratch it on pans en walls en such. Den Tom says he'd fetch a rock fo' me to scratch it on. I tole him de rock 'ud be worse than de logs; I says it 'ud take me such a long time to dig 'em into a rock I wouldn' ever git out. But Tom says he en Huck 'ud help me do it. Den he tuck a look to see how Huck en I wuz gittin' along wid de pens. It 'uz darn hard work en slow, en made my han's sore. We didn' seem to make any headway hardly, so Tom says he's gonna fetch a grindstone, which 'ud be better, en we could scratch de marks on dat.

Dey went out fo' a while en den came back, slid my chain off de bed-leg en wrapped it roun' my neck. Den we crawled thoo de hole dey dug under de shack, en I thought we wuz finally goin' to run fo' it. But Tom jis' kep' orderin' us 'roun'. Tole us to push de grindstone thoo de hole, but de hole warn't big enough, so I tuck de pick en made it big enough. Den Tom marked out dem scratch marks on it wid de nail en set me to work on 'em, wid de nail fo' a chisel en an iron bolt fo' a hammer, en tole me to work 'til de res' o' his candle quit on me en den I could go to bed. En I should hide de grindstone under my straw tick en sleep on it. Den dey fixed my chain back on de bed-leg.

B'fo' he left, Tom ax me, you got any spiders in here, Jim? I tole him thanks to goodness no, en he says, All right, we'll git you some. I tole him I didn' want none! Dat I wuz afeard uv 'em, en I'd jis' as soon have rattlesnakes 'roun'. Wouldn' you know dat arter a minute er two, Tom says, It's a good idea. Yes, it's a prime good idea. Whah could you keep it? He meant de rattlesnake! I tole him ef a rattlesnake wuz to come in here, I'd bust right out thoo dat log wall wid my head. Fool chile says I wouldn' be afeard uv it arter a little while—dat I could tame it. Tame it!

Clear as day, de chile 'uz plumb crazy. Says every animal likes kindness en pettin' en is grateful fo' it, en you kin git him so dat he'll love you, en sleep wid you, en let you wrap him round yo' neck en put his head in yo' mouf. I tole him it 'ud be a powful long time b'fo' I ax any snake to lemme shove his head in my mouf. En dat I didn' want any snake to sleep wid me!

Tom says, Jim, doan' act so foolish. A prisoner's got to have some kine o' a dumb pet, en ef a rattlesnake hain't ever ben tried, why, dah's mo' glory to be gained in yo' bein' de fust to ever try it dan any other way you could ever think o' to save yo' life.

I tole him I didn' want no glory. Says de snake 'ud bite my chin off, en whah's de glory den? Crazy chile wouldn' let up. Says, blame it, cain't you try? I on'y want you to try—you needn' keep it up ef it doan' work. I tole him I 'uz willin' to tackle most anythin' dat warn't onreasonable, but dat ef he en Huck fetched a rattlesnake in here fo' me to tame, I 'uz goin' to leave, *sure!*

Tom says, Well, den, let it go. Ef you's so bull-headed 'bout it. We kin git you some garter-snakes, en you kin tie some buttons on dere tails en let on dey're rattlesnakes, en I reck'n dat 'll have to do.

I tole him dat I kin stan 'em, but blame' ef I couldn' git along widout 'em. I never knowed b'fo' it 'uz so much bother en trouble to be a prisoner.

Tom says, well, it awluz is when it's done right.

I tole him I didn' want no glory—I jis' want' to be sprung out'n dis shack en have Huck git us tickets on some steamboat dat 'ud take us up North, playin' like he owned me en all jis' like we planned. But ever sence Tom Sawyer come back, Huck went along wid what he said.

Ef I could on'y git Huck alone, when Tom warn't 'roun', I 'uz sure we could straighten it all out en go back to de plan. But I couldn' never git Huck alone.

Tom ax me, You got any rats roun' here? I tole him no. He says dey'd git me some. I tole him I didn' want no rats! Dey're de dad-blamedes' creatures to disturb a body—dey rustle roun' ovah you en bite yo' feet when you's tryin' to sleep. No sir, I says, give me garter-snakes ef I got to have sumf'n, but no rats. Tom insisted I got to have rats. Wuz clearly out'n his mine. Tole me all prisoners have rats—dat dey train 'em, en pet 'em, en teach 'em tricks, en dey git to be as sociable as flies. But he says I got to play music to 'em en ax me ef I had sumf'n to play on. I tole him dat I had nuffn but a coarse comb en piece o' paper I could play, en a juice-harp, but I reck'n'd dey'd take no stock in a juice-harp. Tom says rats doan' care what kine o' music it is, en a juice-harp 'ud be jis' fine. Says all animals like music—'specially in prison. Painful music. It'll interes' dem, en dey'd come out to see what's de matter wid you.

Like I says, de chile wuz plumb crazy. Tole me to set on my bed nights b'fo' I went to sleep en I should play some sad song on my juice-harp; said when I played 'bout two minutes I'd see all de rats, en de snakes, en spiders, en things begin to feel worried 'bout me en come. En dey'll jis' swarm ovah me en have a good time.

I tole him, yes, dey will, I reck'n. But, I ax, what kine o' time is Jim havin'?

He didn' pay me no mine. Blame ef I could see de point. But I'd do it ef I got to. I couldn' see why we had to have spiders en snakes en rats en music. It 'uz jis' one big ornery mess o' trouble. But I couldn' git Huck alone to ax when he en I wuz goin' to give Tom de slip en make fo' de river. So I did as Tom said.

Dat Tom wuz tetched in de head, fo' sure. He ax me could I raise a flower here. I tole him I had no use fo' a flower, en besides,

it wuz so dark in heah, dat it'd be a powful sight o' trouble. Boy
jis' wouldn' let up. Tole me to try it anyway. Some other prisoners
done it. What does I care what other prisoners done? I jis' want
to git home to my wife en my 'Lizabeth en my Johnny. But all ways
out'n my chains seemed to lead right thoo dis doggone crazy chile
who want' me to raise a flower. Tole him maybe I could raise one
o' dem big mullen stalks dat looks like cat-tails. But I reck'n'd she
wouldn' be wuth half de trouble she'd cause.

Tom says dey'd fetch me a little one, en I had to plant it in de
corner ovah dah en raise it. En says I should water it wid my tears.
I tole him I had plenty o' spring water. Dad fetch it, de boy jis' dug
in, sayin' you doan' want spring water; you want to water it wid
yo' tears. It's de way dey awluz do. Tole him I could raise one o'
dem mullen stalks twice wid spring water while another man's jis'
startin' one wid tears. Fool says I got to do it wid tears. Tole him
she'd die on my han's kase I doan scasely ever cry—but dat warn't
de truth. I did cry. All de time. But blame' ef I'd use de tears I shed
ovah my wife en chillen waterin' some dern mullen stalk. Fool
says he'd bring me an onion so as I could make mo' tears. Says
he'd drop one in my coffeepot next day. Tole him I'd jis' as soon
have tobacco in my coffee, but he didn' pay me no mine. I says I
never heard no fool plan like dis one fo' gittin' someone free—
loadin' 'em up wid de work en de bother o' raisin' de mullen en
juice-harpin' de rats en pettin' de snakes en spiders—all on top
uv all de other work I had to do makin' pens out'n candlesticks
en writin' 'scriptions on grindstones en on tin plates. Tole him
dat it wuz mo' trouble en work en care dan anythin' I ever had to
do b'fo', en enough wuz enough!

Tom wuz hoppin' mad. Said he'd given me mo' chances dan a
prisoner ever had in de worl' to make a name fo' hisself, en yet I
didn' know enough to appreciate 'em, en dey wuz wasted on me.
I want' to tell him I didn' care to make no name fo' myself, jis'

want' to git out'n here. But den I 'minded myseff dat all roads out ran thoo dis crazy chile—so I jis' said I wuz sorry instead.

I kep' wantin' to git Huck by hisself en talk some sense into de boy, but Tom wuz awluz at his side. Couple o' days later dey show up wid bags full o' spiders. Day arter dat bags full o' snakes en rats. I didn' like de spiders, en de spiders didn' like me; so dey'd lay fo' me en make it mighty warm fo' me. Between de rats en de snakes en de grindstone dah 'uz no room in bed fo' me, skasely; en when dah wuz, a body couldn' sleep, it 'uz so lively. It 'uz awluz lively kase dey never all slep' at one time, but tuck turns, so when de snakes wuz asleep, de rats wuz on deck, en when de rats turned in, de snakes come on watch. I awluz had one gang under me, in my way, en t'other gang havin' a circus ovah me. En ef I got up to hunt a new place, de spiders 'ud take a chanst at me as I crossed ovah. Every time a rat bit me, I had to scribble things on de shirt usin' my blood. En I had to keep carvin' things on de grindstone, which 'uz no slouch uv a job. Tole 'em ef I ever got out dis time I wouldn' never be a prisoner agin, not fo' a salary.

I got so worn out, what wid de entertainin' de snakes en spiders en rats wid de juice-harp en writin' wid my blood en carvin' dat grindstone dat I jis' sat en stared at 'em, not even a little curious 'bout what fool job dey'd come up wid nex'.

I knowed dem boys wuz both crazy when dey sawed de bed-leg in two en et up all de sawdust. Dey wuz su'prised by de stomach-aches dey got. Warn't no su'prise to me. Dey thought dey wuz gonna die. Had to be fools to swallow dat much sawdust fo' no good reason!

I liked to think Huck wuz tryin' to talk some sense into his fren' en git him to stop all dis foolishness en clear out wid me, but I couldn' be sure. Dey didn' come 'round much de next few days.

But den, all uv a sudden, a few nights later, Tom sneaks into de cabin wid a calico dress ovah his clothes. Takes it off en tells me to change into it—says sumf'n 'bout personatin' my mother, but dat don't make no mo' sense than anythin' else he's ax me to do—so I done it. Den he tuck my own clothes en stuffed 'em full o' straw en put 'em in de bed. Huck sneaks in too. I figger'd dey're finally gonna git me out now, sure.

But den we heard de tramp uv a bunch o' men comin' to de door en begin to mess wid de pad-lock. One uv 'em tole de others to go in de cabin en lay fo' dem in de dark en kill 'em when dey come. I didn' know who all dey wuz spectin', but I shook so I could barely git under de bed wid de boys, en den out en thoo de hole—fas' but quiet—me fust, den Huck den Tom last, jis' like Tom order' us. Now we wuz in de lean-to en heard trampin' close-by outside.

Tom stopped us dah en put his eye to de crack but couldn' make nuffn out, it wuz so dark; we listen'd fo' de steps to git fu'ther 'way. Tom says I mus' glide out fust en him last. So he set his ear to de crack en listen'd, en listen'd, en listen'd, de steps a-scrapin' roun' out dah all de time; en at last he give us a nudge, en we slid out, not breathin', en not makin' de leas' noise, en slipped real quiet toward de fence Injun file, en got to it all right, en Huck en I got ovah it; but Tom's britches caught on a splinter on de top rail, en den he hear de steps comin', so he had to pull loose. He snapped de splinter en made a noise, en somebody sing out:

Who's dat? Answer, er I'll shoot!

But we didn' answer; we jis' ran as fast as we could. De bullets whizzed roun' us! We heard 'em sing out: Here dey are! Dey broke fo' de river! Arter 'em, boys, en turn loose de dogs!

We could hear 'em kase dey wore boots en yelled, but we didn' wear no boots en didn' yell, so dey couldn' hear us. We wuz in de path to de mill, en when dey got pooty close to us we dodged into de bush en let 'em go by en den dropped in behind 'em. Dey brought dogs, but dey wuz ouah dogs, so we stopped in ouah tracks 'til dey caught up. When dey saw it warn't nobody but us, dey on'y jis' says howdy en tore right ahead towards de shoutin' en clatterin'. Den we headed up-stream agin, 'til we wuz nearly to de mill en den struck up thoo de bush to whah Huck had tied de canoe en hopped in en pulled fo' dear life toward de middle o' de river, not makin' no mo' noise dan we had to. Den we struck out, easy en comf'able, fo' de island whah Huck stashed de raf'. We could hear 'em yellin' en barkin' at each other all up en down de bank, 'til we wuz so far 'way de sounds got dim en died out. En when we stepped on to de raf' Huck says: Now, ole Jim, you's a free man agin, en I bet you won't never be a slave no mo'.

I want' to jump up en crack my heels a few times, I wuz so happy! All I knowed wuz dat all dat craziness somehow worked. I ben mad 'bout spiders en snakes en rats but warn't mad no mo'. Dey got me out. I wuz free. Free!

I tole Huck it wuz a mighty good job too. Tole him it wuz planned beautiful, en it 'uz done beautiful, en dah ain't nobody dat kin git up a plan dat's mo' mixed up en splendid dan dat one wuz.

We wuz all glad as we could be, but when I saw dat Tom he had a bullet in de calf o' his leg, it kine o' tuck de tuck right out'n me. It 'uz hurtin' de chile consid'able, en he wuz bleedin' a lot, so we laid him in de wigwam en tore up one o' de duke's shirts to bandage him. Tom says gimme de rags; I kin do it myself. Doan' stop now. Doan' fool roun' here, he says, en set her loose!

But Huck en I wuz consultin'. I thought 'bout how I'd feel ef I made my way to freedom en left dis chile here to die—dis po' tetched chile playin' make-b'lieve roun' men wid guns who knowed how to shoot 'em. I knowed I couldn' leave.

I says, It looks to me like dis: ef it wuz Tom dat 'uz bein' sot free, en one er de boys wuz to git shot, would he say, Go on en save me, nemmine 'bout a doctor f'r to save dis one? Is dat like mars Tom Sawyer? Would he say dat?

I kine o' thought he might, but dat's not what I tole Huck. I 'spected dat his gettin' shot had sumf'n to do wid all de mischief he'd ben up to roun' de house en all de fool stuff he had me doin', but wuz I goin' to make de chile feel worse dan he did already, wid his leg kivered wid blood en de pain startin' in bad? No sir. I says. I wouldn' budge a step out'n dis place widout a doctor, not ef it's forty year!

Huck tole Tom he 'uz goin' fo' a doctor. Tom raised a considable row 'bout it, want' to crawl out en set de raf' loose hisself, but we wouldn' let him. Den he give us a piece o' his mine, but it didn' do no good.

So when he sees Huck gettin' de canoe ready, he says: Well, ef you's bound to here's what you do when you git to de village. Shut de do' en blindfole de doctor tight en make him swear to say nuffn en put a purse full o' gol' in his han', en den fetch him here in de canoe, in a round 'bout way. . . .

Huck says he would en left, en I 'uz to hide in de woods when I see de doctor comin' en stay dah 'til he 'uz gone agin.

I washed de chile's leg en tore up some mo' o' de king's shirts fo' bandages. Tried to make 'em tight as I could to stop de bleedin'. Meanwhile chile uz gettin' feverish. I gave him water to drink en sponged him down wid cool water to help bring de fever down. My, didn' we do things up fine, Jim? he ax me. En den started talkin' excited-like 'bout de spiders en snakes en rats en de grindstone en all dat he'd had me do fo' Lord knows why. I jis' agreed wid him. Tried to git him to calm down. Kep' spongin' him off wid cool water. Changed de bandage when it got soaked thoo.

Byemby de ole doctor come by in our canoe. I crawled out fum de bushes en says I was dere to help. He sure wuz su'prised to see me. Figured out I must be de run'way. Couldn' figure out why I stayed close by 'stead o' runnin'. I showed him de boy's leg, en he tuck a close look at him. All de res' o' de day en all night de doctor worked on cuttin' dat bullet out en cleanin' de wound. Fever kep' up, en Tom 'uz shoutin' all kines o' nonsense, but I kep' spongin' him to cool him off, strokin' his brow to calm him down. Finally, he wore hisself out wid all dat shoutin' en fell asleep.

Arter we loaded Tom into de canoe, de doctor says he had to tie my han's—but kine o' apologized as he says it. He says ef I hadn' took such good care o' de chile, he'd uv died b'fo' he got dah. I'd already figured dat out. I thought 'bout how I'd want someone to act ef it wuz my Johnny who'd ben shot, en I wuz glad I'd stayed. Den I thought 'bout how now I'd never see Johnny agin, en I hung my head.

I musta ben quite a sight in dat stolen calico dress kivered wid blood, han's tied behine me, followin' de doctor en de men who helped him carry Tom up fum de river on a mattress. Farmer's wife she flung herself at Tom, cryin' he's dead! I know he's dead!

Tom he turned his head a little en said sumf'n er other, which showed he warn't in his right mine—but warn't dead nuther, en den she flung up her han's, en says: He's alive, thank God! En dat's enough! En she snatched a kiss o' him en flew fo' de house to git de bed ready, givin' everybody orders, fast as her tongue could go.

De farmer en de ole doctor followed arter Tom into de house wid de men who'd ben carryin' Tom. Huck wuz dah, too. You bet I wuz glad to see dat chile! But I didn' let on to know him. Some o' de men want' to hang me as an example so others wouldn' be tryin' to run 'way like I did, makin' such a raf' o' trouble, en keepin' a whole family scared mos' to death fo' so many days en nights. But de others say, doan' do it: he doan' b'long to us, en his owner 'ud turn up en make us pay fo' him, sure. So dat cooled 'em down a little.

Dey cussed me considable, en give me a cuff er two side de head once in a while, but I never says nuffn. Dey tuck me to de same cabin, en put my own clothes on me, en chained me agin, en not to any bed-leg dis time, but to a big staple driven into de bottom log. Dey chained my han's, too, en both legs, en says I warn't to have nuffn but bread en water to eat arter dis 'til my owner come, or 'til I 'uz sole at auction ef he didn' come arter a certain length o' time. Dey filled up our hole en said a couple o' farmers wid guns must stan' watch roun' 'bout de cabin every night, en a bulldog must be tied to de door in de daytime. 'Bout dis time dey wuz thoo wid de job en wuz taperin' off wid a kine o' gen'l good-bye cussin'. Den de ole doctor come en takes a look en tole 'em to be no rougher on me than dey had to be.

He says when he got to whah he foun' de boy, he saw he couldn' cut de bullet out widout some help, en de boy warn't in any condition fo' him to leave to go en git help. Said de boy got a little worse en a little worse, en arter a long time he went out'n his head, en wouldn' let him come near him no mo'. He saw he couldn' do nuffn at all wid him, so he says, I got to have help somehow; en de minute he says it, out I crawled fum somewhere en says I'd help—en I done it too, en done it very well. O' course he judged I must be a run'way, he said, but he wuz in a real fix. He had a couple o' patients wid de chills en want' to run up to town en see 'em but dare not kase I might git 'way, en den he'd be to blame. No skift come close enough fo' him to hail, so he had to stay dah till daylight dis mawnin'. De doctor he says he had everything he needed, en de boy 'uz doin' as well as he would a done at home—better, maybe, kase it 'uz so quiet.

De doctor he says finally, 'bout dawn dis mawnin' some men in a skift come by. He says I 'uz settin' by de pallet wid my head propped on my knees soun' asleep; so he motioned 'em in quiet, en dey slipped up on me en grabbed me en tied me b'fo' I knowed

it. En de boy bein' in a kine o' a flighty sleep, dey muffled de oars
en hitched de raf' on, en towed her ovah nice en quiet. He says I
never made de least row en didn' say a word fum de start.
De doctor he says he never saw a better nuss or a mo' faithful
one, yet I wuz reskin' my freedom to do it. He says I wuz all tired
out too, en he could see plain enough dat I'd ben worked main
hard lately—which sure wuz de truth. He liked me fo' dat. Says
I 'uz worth a thousan' dollars—en kine treatment, too.
    Den de others softened up a little too. Dey all agreed dat I'd
acted very well, en wuz deservin' to have some notice taken uv it,
en reward. So every one uv 'em promised, right out en hearty, dat
dey wouldn' cuss me no mo'. Den dey locked me up again.
    I thought 'bout dat little cabin I used to have on de Watson's
farm b'fo' Miss Watson tuk me 'way. How we'd set down to dinner
wid de chillen en say grace b'fo' we ate. How I'd never see any o'
dem ever agin. En den I looked roun' de shack I wuz in now, wid
all dem crazy things scratched on de grindstone en on de walls,
en a bunch o' spiders en rats en snakes comin' up to me to say
hello arter my havin' ben 'way fo' a stretch—en I jis' start' to cry.
But I warn't sorry. A chile 'uz alive who'd uv ben dead ef I hadn'
stayed.
    But den—Lordy, I hardly know whah to begin!
    All uv a sudden Huck en Tom come bustin' into de cabin wid
a bunch o' other folks en cut off my chains! Dey tell me Tom say
dat Ole Miss Watson died two months ago, en she wuz ashamed
she wuz ever gwyne to sell me down de river, en says so—en she
set me free in her will!!!!!
    I smile' my make b'lieve happy smile—kase dat's what I
knowed dey 'pected. But deep down was I hoppin' mad. How dare
dat lyin', thievin' Tom Sawyer, dat tetched-in-de-head white boy,
make me do all dem plumb crazy things when he knowed I wuz
free all along! I doan' think Huck knew I wuz free, but Tom sure

did. En I ain't never gwyne to fo'give dat boy as long as I live! I wuz almos' sorry I stayed wid him 'stead of takin' off when I had de chanst when he got shot. Almos' sorry but not quite: didn' want no guilt on my head fo' lettin' dat chile die. Even a mean en ornery en lowdown chile like Tom still deserve' to live.

Dey made a heap o' a fuss ovah me, en fixed me up prime wid new clothes, en set me up in a bedroom in de house wid real sheets en pillows, en give me all I want' to eat. I went up to de sick room en had a good talk wid de boys. Dey explained why Huck want' to be taken fo' Tom en why Tom had to be taken fo' Sid en how all dem fool things dey made me do wuz things Tom read in a book somewheres. Tom give me forty dollars fo' bein' prisoner fo' 'em so patient, en doin' it up so good. I wouldn' never be a prisoner agin fo' ten times dat, it 'uz such hard work. I still say dat Tom wuz teched-in-de-head. Crazy and mean. But I couldn' 'ford to get on his bad side. I didn' have no free papers, no way to prove I warn't no slave; Tom he was de on'y one dat knew me thoo en thoo en also wuz known en 'spect'd in St. Petersburg. His word could get me my free papers back home. Dat boy needed killin' sure. But it wouldn' be by me. I still needed him.

I ax Huck ef he 'membered how on Jackson's Island I tole him I had a hairy breas' en dat it wuz a sign I wuz goin' to be rich. I tole him I ben rich wunst en wuz a-gwyne to be rich agin, en now it's come true. I never had dat much money in my life! But it sure wuz hard work to git it. Dat doan' matter now.

Tom en Huck started to make some plans 'bout goin' out to Injun Territory. Want' me to come too. I didn' tell 'em right 'way dat I warn't goin' wid 'em—dat I had other things on my mine.

Den Huck says he prob'ly didn' have any money fo' adventures sence it's likely Pap had gotten all his money 'way fum Judge Thatcher en drunk it up. Tom says dat all de six thousan' dollars en mo' wuz still dah when he lef' St. Petersburg.

Jim Alone. Wood engraving from the Pennyroyal Press
edition of *Adventures of Huckleberry Finn,* 1984, by Barry Moser.

I knowed den I had to tell Huck 'bout his pap. So I tole him.
Says he warn't comin' back no mo'. Chile ax why. I says nemmine,
he ain't comin' back. Chile wouldn' stop axin' 'bout it. So at last I
ax do he 'member de house dat wuz floatin' down de river, en how

dey wuz a man in dah, kivered up, en how I went in en unkivered him en didn' let him come in. Well, den, I tole him: You kin git yo' money when you wants it, kase dat wuz him.

Chile didn' react at all. Dat filthy place where de ole man wuz shot in de back had prob'bly faded fum his mine arter all dis time, en dat wuz good. De main thing wuz, now he knowed de ole man couldn' hurt him no mo'.

Dis is my version o' de story he tole in his book, en his story ends here, so mine will too. I wuz free. Chile wuz safe, en so wuz his tetched fren', God bless him. Mos' important: I got to see my wife en my Johnny en my 'Lizabeth—en now dey're safe too. But dat's another story fo' another time.

CHAPTER 5

———

Afterlives

Jim on Stage and Screen

EW OF THE many versions of *Huckleberry Finn* on screen or on the stage over the last century do justice to the novel; scenes that Twain wrote are often cut, scenes that he didn't write are often added, and both the letter and spirit of the book are often violated. That being said, the many Black actors who have portrayed Jim in these productions have tried valiantly to embody the Black character at the center of this complex and challenging work of fiction. Jim has been portrayed in film, television, and on the stage by actors born in Baltimore, Boston, and Burgaw, North Carolina; in Cairo, Illinois, and Lincoln, Nebraska; in Macon, Georgia, Philadelphia, and Ouagadougou, Burkina Faso. Jim has been played in films by a world light heavyweight champion from Benoit, Mississippi, a geology student from Lagos, Nigeria, and a body builder from Anse-Bertrand, Guadeloupe.[1] Jim has traveled on a raft down the Dnieper River in Soviet Ukraine; the Danube River in Romania; and the Sacramento, Ohio, and Mississippi Rivers in the United States. Some of these actors developed and deepened our understanding of Jim and his world. Others distorted and diminished him as a character—but rarely due to failures on the part of the actor.

Although our response to the version of Jim that we see on stage or screen is shaped by an actor's physical appearance, voice, accent, facial expressions, body language, and delivery, it is shaped as well as by a host of factors beyond the actor himself. The script, the director, the goals of the producers, and the audience's expectations all influence what an actor does with the role, as does the context provided by the plot, title cards, and mise-en-scène. In addition, the social, political, and cultural conversations that the film enters when it appears—about racism, about slavery, about Mark Twain, about Black masculinity, and so on—affect the Jim that the audience encounters. Portrayals of Jim are also influenced, as we will see, by national ideologies—ideologies involving the Russian revolution and socialism, for example, or the Cold War. Within these constraints, each actor embodies the character as he sees him, bringing his own background, experience, talents, and insights to bear on his understanding of the role. We'll explore these factors by looking at how thirteen actors brought Jim to life in movies, on television, or on stage from 1920 to 2012.

Whitewashing Slavery in the Silent Film Era and Early Sound Era: George Reed (1920) and Clarence Muse (1931) Negotiate Stereotypes

When images of slavery were presented on screen during the silent film era and early sound era, the cruelty and injustice the institution entailed were omitted, replaced by images of benign slaveholders and happy slaves, echoing the plantation tradition in popular literature at the time. In the nation's first blockbuster film, *The Birth of a Nation* (1915), in which major Black roles were played by white actors in blackface, slavery was shown in this positive light and enslaved people were presented as well cared for and contented. The first Black actor to play Jim in *Huckleberry Finn* was George Reed in the silent film *Huckleberry Finn* (1920), directed by William Desmond Taylor. It was Reed's first major role, and "probably the most important role of his career."[2]

The film was credited with being "impressively faithful to the novel," and veteran screen writer Julia Crawford Ivers was praised for her "extensive use of Clemens' own words."[3] But when it came to Jim, Ivers's scenario departed from both the words and the spirit of the text, adding scenes and lines Twain never wrote that reduced Jim to a flat stock character in a minstrel show.

The stage directions for the scene in which Jim is introduced features three of Widow Douglas's servants in the backyard "patting Juba."[4] "In front of them," Ivers writes, "Nigger Jim [sic] is dancing breakdown, singing joyfully." Next, Ivers calls for a close-up of Jim "dancing and singing at the same time—evidently having a joyful time."[5] No such scene exists anywhere in the novel.

In another early scene, after the boys have played the trick on Jim by hanging his hat from a tree branch when he's asleep, Ivers presents him as a superstitious fool who speaks full-blown "minstrelese":

65 Ext. back door of Widow's house—night—Closeup Jim—his eyes rolling wildly—

He says:

ST [subtitle] "I'se bewitched, Missis. De debble hab got me sure!"[6]

Director Taylor seems to have relied on E. W. Kemble's original illustrations for the novel as he brought the story to the screen, most of which involved hackneyed racist stereotypes derived from minstrelsy, and Ivers's scenario generally had Jim behaving in a formulaic, comic manner. Although George Reed is viewed as a pioneer for being one of the first Black actors to play a Black man in a Hollywood film—indeed, a Black man playing a fugitive slave—his performance as Jim is constrained by the script's demand that he conform to the stereotypes that dominated Hollywood's treatment of race in 1920.

Clarence Muse, the second Black actor to play Jim in a Hollywood film, appeared in the Paramount version of *Huckleberry Finn* (1931), directed by Norman Taurog, the first adaptation to use sound. A founder of Harlem's Lafayette Theatre in 1913, the first major American theater to desegregate, Muse also helped found the Lafayette Players, a Black stock company, two years later. He relocated to Los Angeles in 1920 and appeared in *Hearts in Dixie* (1929), one of the first big-studio sound films to feature a mainly Black cast.[7]

Muse's experience had a gravitas that was often out of sync with the comic or subservient roles in which Hollywood cast him. Film scholar Donald Bogle writes that "what was most intriguing" about Muse's portrayal of Jim in 1931 was that he

> seemed miscast because his slave was too intelligent. His dialect was obviously faked and forced and during excruciatingly harsh close-ups used solely for laughs, audiences must have felt pained to see such a dignified and decent presence demeaned so. No other Black performer of the period ever had quite such an effect, perhaps because most were able to forget themselves and become lost in the part. Muse always seemed to be standing at great distance looking on with his large questioning eyes and sadly shaking his head.[8]

Following the success of its film version of *Tom Sawyer* in 1930, Paramount assigned the same screenwriters to write *Huckleberry Finn* and requested a film in a similar mold.[9] As a result, adolescent romance takes center stage, and Huck's crush on Mary Jane Wilks gets much more screen time than the relationship between Huck and Jim.

At one point, Jim's anger at hearing pap beating Huck leads him to talk about wanting to take "Ol' man Finn by the neck"— but Tom remonstrates, "You can't do that, Jim. You know what'll happen to you if you put hands on a white man." Jim is horrified at the reminder of the punishment such an act would incur—a rare gesture to the plight of a Black man in the South at the time. When Huck and Tom decide to take a raft down the river to "be pirates," Jim decides to go with them. When he is reminded that he'd be a "runaway slave" if he did that, he consults his hair ball in a scene in which he is portrayed as stereotypically superstitious: the hair ball says he should go, so he does. It would be hard to imagine a weaker motive for flight. That is the only discussion of slavery in the film, and this arbitrary motive is the only one given for Jim's presence on the journey. There is no mention of his family and no threat of being sold.

In a twist on Twain's plot, instead of Jim being dependent on Huck and Tom to free him when he is held captive on the Phelps farm, here Jim saves *them* when they're violently set upon by the duke and king. When the king and the duke physically attack Huck and Tom in the apple cellar of the Wilks home after realizing that the boys are foiling their plot to steal the girls' money, Jim calls for help loudly and repeatedly while he bombards the two conmen with apples. A crowd rushes to the scene, more apples are thrown, and the boys are saved. Jim's quick thinking and his actions in effect make him the hero of the film.

In a pamphlet titled "The Dilemma of the Negro Actor" that Muse published the year after he appeared in *Huckleberry Finn*, Muse complained that "customs and tradition of the white stage and white audiences have demanded, principally, entertainers or

'Uncle Tom' characterizations from the Negro actor."[10] Given Hollywood's commercial imperatives of catering to a white audience, he writes, "the Negro is invariably a stereotype."[11] Muse would occasionally be cast in nonstereotypical roles, such as playing a renegade slave whose fiery speech helped spark a slave revolt in King Vidor's Civil War drama *So Red the Rose*.[12] Such roles, however, were relatively rare. As Bogle has observed, "Clarence Muse is best remembered today as an actor who repeatedly sought to invest his servant roles of the 1930s with a semblance of dignity and a degree of seriousness," playing "those figures with [a] great intelligence and thoughtfulness" that "has often been overlooked."[13]

Unmasking Slavery with Power and Pride: Rex Ingram (1939) and Archie Moore (1960) Portray Jim with Strength and Courage

It would take two professional boxers to knock these reductive images of Jim off the silver screen. Rex Ingram, who worked as a boxer to support himself between films, was cast as Jim in MGM's film version of *Huckleberry Finn* in 1939.[14] Archie Moore held the title of world light heavyweight champion at the time he undertook the role of Jim in 1960 in the second film version of *Huckleberry Finn* made by MGM.[15] Both men brought strength and courage to the screen, allowing audiences to see a self-possessed Jim who chafed under the constraints of slavery and was determined to secure a better life for himself and his family.

Ingram, a handsome man over six feet tall who exuded a natural dignity, had not planned to become an actor. But after graduating from medical school at Northwestern University (where he was the first Black man elected to Phi Beta Kappa), he was approached while walking down a California street one day and invited to take an uncredited role in a silent screen version of

Edgar Rice Burroughs's *Tarzan of the Apes* in 1918. For the next eight years, he later told a reporter, "I did everything from porters to butlers to natives. I got a lot of work because of my size."[16]

Ingram's confidence as an actor grew after he played the lead part ("De Lawd") in the film version of *Green Pastures* in 1936, the same year he became a charter director of the recently founded Negro Actors' Guild.[17] He no longer had patience for the menial bit parts he had generally been given, and made a decision: "I decided to help our cause to the best of my ability. I wouldn't take parts which didn't at least do us justice." As a result, he was out of work for two years and was forced to declare bankruptcy.[18]

In 1938 he was cast as the Black nationalist hero Henri Christophe in *Haiti: A Drama of the Black Napoleon*, a play about the successful Haitian slave revolution of 1791 at Harlem's Negro Theatre Unit (part of the New Deal–era Federal Theatre Project). At one point in the play, Christophe, a ferocious leader, menaces the enemy holding a gun in each hand.[19] Playing the powerful "Lawd" in *Green Pastures,* and the fearless Christophe in *Haiti* helped confirm Ingram's commitment to give up playing butlers and only take parts that truly mattered—even if poverty was the result.

His desperate need for employment was not the only reason Ingram was delighted the following year when he was offered the role of Jim in MGM's film version of *Huckleberry Finn* (1939). Ingram's father had been a fireman on the steamer *Robert E. Lee,* and Ingram had worked alongside him before heading to college. And although genealogical records suggest that he may have been born in Corsicana, Texas, Ingram himself always claimed to have been born on a boat on the Mississippi, near Cairo, Illinois, his mother having gone into labor while returning from a visit to relatives in Natchez.[20] "My life ran almost parallel with that of Huck and Jim," Ingram wrote in *Ebony.* "I was born on a houseboat on the Mississippi in 1895, near Cairo, Ill. The river was in my blood as it was in Huck and Jim's. When I finished the work on *Huckleberry Finn* I felt that I had done a meaningful thing and had spelled out in theatrical terms the powerful message of human brotherhood. The job paid well in money, but it paid off, too, in terms of principles and ideals." "My best and most important role," Ingram told *Ebony*, "was Jim in MGM's *Huckleberry Finn*, based on Mark Twain's great novel."[21]

From the start, Ingram's Jim is shown to love his wife and son: in an early scene, when Huck and Jim are relaxing together in the yard, Jim asks Huck to read again a loving letter he has received from his wife, Jenny. Later, on Jackson's Island, explaining why he ran off, Jim tells Huck that he'd heard the Widow Douglas talking to a slave trader about selling him to raise the ransom pap has demanded after kidnapping Huck: "If one o' them slave traders got me, I never *would* get to that free state. I never would see my wife, or little Joey," Jim explains.

The brutality of the world that surrounds Jim is evoked clearly as a backdrop to the choices he makes. When Huck visits Mrs. Judith Loftus to learn about responses to his "death," he discovers that Jim is believed to have murdered him. He asks, "Will they put him in jail when they find him?" Her husband responds, "We don't put that kind in jail." In the next scene, the first of two lynch mobs in the film appears, running down the street with torches, hunting for Jim.

Ingram's Jim is resourceful and intelligent. In scenes such as the debate over language and Frenchmen, he shows himself to be independent and self-assured.

When the king and the duke show up, Ingram's Jim indicates, through subtle facial expressions, that he is not fooled but just playing along to keep the peace. When Huck is bitten by a rattlesnake while he and Jim flee a mob, Jim, acting like the father he

Rex Ingram as Jim with Mickey Rooney as Huck in MGM's film version
of *Huckleberry Finn* (1939). Cinematic/Alamy Stock Photo © MGM.

has become to Huck, insists on carrying him to a doctor even
though doing so will cost him his freedom. A local steamboat
captain sees a poster indicating that Jim is wanted for having
murdered Huck and sends him back to St. Petersburg, where he
is thrown in jail awaiting trial. Huck, who has recovered from the
snakebite, knows he is Jim's alibi—the proof that Jim did not
commit murder. He manages to get back to St. Petersburg as fast

as he can on a steamboat. Meanwhile a lynch mob in St. Petersburg comes to the jail for Jim but fails to gain entry. Huck arrives in time to disrupt the trial, and the Widow Douglas agrees to free Jim if Huck agrees to live with the Widow, go to school, stop smoking, and wear shoes. Before the film ends, Huck demonstrates more of a change in consciousness than he shows in the novel, asserting that he's learned that "a human being doesn't have the right to own another human being." The film ends with Jim riding a steamboat heading out to be reunited with his family.

There was nothing servile about Ingram, as Donald Bogle has observed. As he "projected an inner sense of his own worth," Ingram embodied "a new definition of Black masculinity" characterized by "a gentleness" and "an overriding interest and sympathy in all of mankind."[22] "Physically robust, athletic-looking," Bogle writes, Ingram "exuded in his films of the 1930s and 1940s an air of unbridled confidence and heroic vigor. Blessed with a resonant baritone voice, Ingram always spoke like a man in charge. ... For black audiences of that time, he was clearly an emblem of pride and assertion."[23] Bogle tells us that Rex Ingram's Jim "was a heroic guide leading Huck to manhood. And with his large chest and thick biceps Ingram seemed so powerful that audiences knew there were no chains strong enough to hold him down."[24] The year after he played Jim in *Huckleberry Finn*, Ingram played the Genie of the Lamp in a British film, *The Thief of Bagdad* (1940). In this latter role, when the previously enslaved Genie is finally freed after hundreds of years of being trapped in a bottle, his shout of "I'm free!" reverberated powerfully for Black audiences who saw the film.[25]

It is worth remembering that the film in which Rex Ingram played Jim appeared the same year as *Gone with the Wind*. The latter probably did more than any other film—with the exception of *The Birth of a Nation*—to lay down the tracks for a whitewashed version of slavery on the screen. Enslaved people such as Mammy in *Gone with the Wind* live only to serve their mistress and have no family of their own or even a life of their own, while enslaved people such as Prissy in the same film are simply ignorant and silly—proper objects of ridicule. The film embodies the plantation tradition, in which slavery is presented as a benign institution rather than one that terrorized any American with Black skin. The film won eight Academy Awards, one of which went to the Black actress Hattie McDaniel for her portrayal of Mammy, a first in academy history, but that didn't change its retrograde nature. (At the awards ceremony, McDaniel was seated at a separate table some distance from her white fellow nominees at Los Angeles' Ambassador Hotel. Indeed, producer David O. Selznick had to call in a special favor to get McDaniel admitted to the building.)[26]

Unlike the stereotypical Black characters in *Gone with the Wind*, Rex Ingram's Jim is a loving, self-assured husband, father, and friend and a resourceful, intelligent, enslaved man desperate to be free; yet he is subjected to unjust imprisonment, threatened with permanent separation from his family, chased by dogs, and threatened by two lynch mobs. Ingram's portrayal of Jim implicitly undermined the air-brushed, false views of slavery and the South that Hollywood was celebrating when it bestowed honors on *Gone with the Wind*. Indeed, it did more than bring Twain's most famous Black character alive: in subtle ways Ingram used his own forceful acting style to broaden the range of roles offered to Black actors in Hollywood in the future.[27]

The film got mixed reviews from the critics. But even commentators who complained about virtually everyone else in the film except Mickey Rooney (as Huck) gave Ingram consistently high marks.[28] Interestingly, according to at least one scholar's estimates, this film version of the novel is the most popular worldwide. Rex Ingram's Jim, then, has probably been seen by more viewers globally than all other portrayals combined.[29]

In 1959, when Archie Moore was contacted by Samuel Goldwyn Jr. about playing the role of Jim in an MGM film version of *Huckleberry Finn*, he had been the reigning world light heavyweight champion for seven years.[30] He had been named "Fighter of the Year" the previous year and was renowned for a boxing style that was powerful, precise, strategic, shrewd, and focused—qualities that earned him the nickname "The Mongoose." But he had never acted in a film or play. And he wasn't sure about the wisdom of playing a slave.

His wife wasn't sure about that, either. "It's apt to bring a lot of criticism down on you," she warned. "You know how all of us feel about handkerchief head parts," she said, referring to what Moore himself called "the 'Yassuh, Boss' type role."[31] Nonetheless, Moore was intrigued. He spent nearly two months studying the script and found nothing in it that he viewed as detrimental to his race.[32]

But his wife was right. Critics came down hard on him. When one journalist heard he had been tapped for the role, she urged him to reconsider the "senseless move." Noting that Moore's name was "known around the world" and that he had proven time and time again that he was "a real champion," she wrote that "he doesn't have to stoop to portraying a slave to see his name in lights." "In a few minutes on the screen" appearing as a slave, she opined, Moore could "erase forever the image of greatness" that he had "worked so hard for years to create. Once you slip from your pedestal (in the public's subconscious mind)," she warned, "you remain a fallen idol."[33]

The headline in *Jet* on October 15, 1959, read, "Will 'Uncle Tom' Role Hurt Archie Moore?"[34] But Moore had become increasingly convinced that Jim was no "Uncle Tom."[35] The role was no "handkerchief head" or "'Yassuh, Boss' type role." Jim was not subservient. "I didn't want to play an 'Uncle Tom' role," Moore told the producer and director, and they agreed with him.[36] In Moore's view, Jim was smart and capable and determined to free himself and his family. Jim, he had come to believe, was a warm and clever man of superior intelligence and great charm. "He is not an educated man," he told an AP reporter, "but he uses his head to accomplish what he needs."[37]

While deliberating for two months about whether to accept the part, Moore consulted his brother-in-law, actor Sidney Poitier, who told him that he could "play the role really easily, and even offered to give [him] some pointers on how to handle some of the more delicate lines."[38] Then, as Moore writes in *Ebony*,

> One day, without telling Sidney that that I was merely acting, I cited to him the lines of one sequence in the film. In this sequence, Jim breaks down, confessing to Huck that once he slapped his little daughter for disobeying an order before discovering that she could not have heard his order because she was deaf from scarlet fever. Since I substituted my real daughter's name for Elizabeth, the name in the script, Sidney thought that I was actually confessing to something I had done in real life, and began to cry.

When Moore told him he had been doing his lines from the show, Poitier "laughed through his tears, [and] said: '[M]y God, Archie, don't ever do that again.'"[39]

Moore learned his lines and then flew to Los Angeles for his screen test. He knew that "most other fighters who were wooed by Hollywood played tough guys or prize-fighting roles. Here I had a chance to play a slave in a film based on an American classic. I felt more tension that night than I have ever felt before an important fight."[40]

When asked how he got the part, Moore, who was born in Benoit, Mississippi, in 1913 and grew up in poverty in St. Louis, where he was raised by an aunt and uncle from age three, sometimes said, "I was lucky. You see, I have one big advantage. I can talk the Missouri dialect and the Mississippi dialect. I got 'em down cold."[41] But he was being modest. He got the part because of his screen test.

He learned his lines and arrived at the studio two hours early to walk through the scene by himself. Finally, "'Places!' was called and I was on." He performed the scene he had performed for his brother-in-law. "I did the scene and it was like a fight," Moore says. "I heard the first word just as you feel the first punch and the next thing was the bell ending the round, the voice of [director] Mike Curtiz saying, 'That's it—cut!'"[42]

Moore recalls that "the boy playing Huckleberry Finn in the scene was crying. The technician and other members of the crew were crying and yelling and applauding. Curtiz and Goldwyn were beaming. I was in. I had made it. I was later told that a reaction like this was rare indeed. It was one of the happiest days of my life."[43] Curtiz's biographer writes that Moore's test of that scene "blew everyone away. Curtiz was observed wiping away tears and the professionals on the set—electricians, stage hands and the like—broke into spontaneous applause. Curtiz told Goldwyn, 'This is the man to do the part.'" According to MGM officials, "Moore's screen test was one of the best in studio history."[44]

The longest-reigning light heavyweight champion of all time was still at the peak of his career as a fighter when he decided to take on this role. Moore published an essay in *Ebony* entitled, "Why I Played Jim, the Slave Role in Huck Finn Movie; Might Help, Rather than Hurt, Negroes, Says World Champ." After studying the script, he had come to the conclusion that "a great deal of Jim's ignorance had been surmounted by native intelligence and resourcefulness."[45] In addition, he had come to believe that "as light heavyweight champion of the world, I could perhaps strike out some of the lines in the picture that I felt might be offensive to Negroes."[46] "My main objection," he wrote, "was the constant use of the word 'nigger.' It was a common word in those days, too common, but I felt it was unnecessary to use it as often as they did."[47] He demanded some changes in the script before he said yes, and got them: at Moore's insistence, the director cut all but two of the offensive racial epithets in the picture. Moore felt that a young actor in his position might have been hesitant to try to do that. Having succeeded in getting unnecessary racial slurs cut from the script, Moore wrote that he "found nothing in it to disturb or embarrass Negroes."[48] On the contrary: he thought it could do some good. Jim was admirable, resourceful, and caring—a man to whom Moore could relate.

This is the first film version of *Huckleberry Finn* to include the poignant story about Jim's little girl, the scene Moore read for his screen test. Moore's own two young daughters, Reena Marie and J'Marie, would occasionally visit him in the studio with his wife while he was working on the film.[49] It was easy for Moore to relate to a father who felt anguished over having punished his little girl in error. "I really feel this character," he told a reporter.[50]

Although the plot included a number of scenes that were faithful to the book, there were some rather preposterous additions, as well—such as an invented sequence in which Huck and Jim join a circus, with Huck presenting himself as the World's

During some free time between scenes, Archie Moore nuzzles his
seven-month-old daughter, J'Marie, who was brought to the studio
by his wife (right). Moore found it easy to relate to a father who felt
anguished over having punished his little girl in error. "I really feel
this character," he told an AP reporter (*Life*, June 27, 1960, 113).
Grey Villet/The LIFE Picture Collection/Shutterstock.

Youngest Lion Tamer and Jim as the Emperor of Patagonia. Huck
sabotages efforts of the king and the duke to capture Jim for the
reward (and gets the two of them locked up instead by persuading the sheriff that they're "abolitionists"). He helps Jim elude the
sheriff and his bloodhounds—assistance that is crucial, since Jim's
ankles are bleeding from the tight shackles he was forced to wear.
Huck and Jim manage to escape across a creek to free territory,
and at the film's end Jim's plan is to work in a store and buy his
family out of slavery, while Huck plans to take a steamboat to New
Orleans—maybe to South America. Jim is not subject to any *deus
ex machina* deathbed manumission. Rather, as Donald Ingram
Ulin notes, "Unlike the novel, this film ends with both Huck and
Jim poised to claim their own versions of freedom against the

dictates and laws of their society."[51] (The fact that Jim's freedom across the river is precarious, given the ubiquity of slave catchers, doesn't come up.)

Moore was pleased with the picture that resulted. "I am anxious for all my friends to see this picture so they can see for themselves that I wasn't put in as a freak attraction to sell tickets," he wrote. "I honestly think I turned in a performance and not an appearance."[52]

Contemporary critics damned the film as a whole with faint praise, but everyone had good things to say about Moore's portrayal of Jim.[53] Moore was called the "most surprising star discovery of the year" in publications as far from Hollywood as Wellington, New Zealand.[54] In the decades that followed, scholars and critics would continue to pay tribute to Moore's portrayal of Jim. In 1985 Perry Frank noted the "warmth, humanity and courage" that Moore brought to the role, while in 2005 R. Kent Rasmussen and Mark Dawidziak praised Moore for having projected "the strength and dignity of Twain's character."[55]

Moore's comments in *Ebony* make clear that he had thought long and hard about the issue at the center of the novel. "Above all, I accepted the role," Moore told *Ebony*, "because the story deals with two human beings' struggle for freedom. Huckleberry Finn, the white boy, wants to be free so he can go to sleep, go out and fish, or roam the countryside whenever he wants to, and Jim wants to be free from bondage, servitude and his chains."[56] By the end of the book, in Moore's view, "each finds his freedom. Huck finds freedom of the road, the rivers and wood, and Jim finds the freedom to get a new start in life, to become a real human being." That freedom, Moore wrote, is "something, I feel, every Negro is looking for even today. In taking this role, I felt that, perhaps, Negroes would again be made aware of the necessity to continue their fight for freedom."[57]

Jim on the Dnieper: Wayland Rudd (1936) and Feliks Imokuede (1973) Enact the Soviet Critique of American Racism

When Jim next appears on screen five years later, he is speaking Russian, and the Dnieper River in Ukraine serves as the Mississippi. The Dnieper would be the setting of two Soviet versions of *Huckleberry Finn*, one in 1936 and another in 1973. Both films use the novel as a vehicle to criticize America and to champion socialist ideals of interracial proletarian solidarity.

Twain's works were tremendously popular in Russia from the moment they appeared in translation. *Huckleberry Finn* first appeared in Russian in 1885, the same year it came out in the United States, and *Tom Sawyer* made its Russian debut in 1877, one year after its publication in the United States. Margarita Marinova notes that "the prerevolutionary fascination with Twain and the Russian admiration for his satirical talents (he was often compared to Gogol in the press), only intensified after the emergence of the Soviet State, as his critical stance towards the realities of American life, his antiracist position, and his disdain for organized religion made him extremely palatable to the new socialist government." "After the Soviets came to power in 1917," Marinova writes, Twain was "deemed to be ideologically relevant by the new political leadership. While his immense talents as a humorist were still acknowledged and enjoyed by reviewers and readers alike, now he was predominantly celebrated as a critic of American capitalism and the Western way of life in general."[58]

Tom Sawyer dominated the market, but *Huck Finn* was quite popular as well. Both were widely used in English-language classes in schools and were often staged by children's theaters around the country. Marinova tells us that "the Soviet critical insistence upon the importance of Jim—not as an individual, but as a representative of a disenfranchised class—was so great that a 1926 edition of the novel came out under the title *Приключения Геккельберри Финна и беглого негра Джима* (*Adventures of Huckleberry Finn and the Runaway Negro Jim*)." According to Marinova, "Not only is [Jim] allowed to share the spotlight with Huck in the title, but he is also presented as fully capable of taking charge of his fate (as the title suggests, he has dared to escape from slavery and live a life of adventure alongside Huck Finn)." Indeed a prominent Soviet critic would assert that while Tom Sawyer and Huck Finn "are favorite heroes of Soviet boys," it is Jim who "holds their inalienable affection."[59]

The film produced in 1936 by the Kyiv branch of Ukrainfilm, the main studio in Soviet Ukraine, places Jim front and center, along with the theme of racism.[60] Nebraska-born Wayland Rudd, who portrays Jim in this Soviet film, broke new ground as the first Black man to play Othello in the United States, and by the early 1930s his performances on and off Broadway were earning praise from theater critics in New York. Nonetheless, he knew that options for Black actors in the United States were severely limited, and when the opportunity arose for him to hone his acting skills in the Soviet Union, a country that condemned American racism and trumpeted its own egalitarianism, Rudd was intrigued.[61]

Between 1928 and 1937, the Soviet Union made the promotion of antiracism a priority policy, aware of the propaganda value at home to be gained by calling out racism in the United States. Extensive coverage in the Soviet press of the Scottsboro trial in Alabama in 1931, in which two white women falsely accused nine young Black men of rape, exposed Soviet citizens to the oppressions of the Jim Crow South. As Cassio de Oliveira reminds us, the trial put a host of "articles, photographs, and illustrations depicting American racism" before the Soviet public. Official Soviet policy during this period challenged ideas of white supremacy prevalent in the United States and considered African Americans as potentially helpful in disputing America's claim to be "the world's beacon of democracy and freedom." In the spring of 1932, the Black press in New York and Chicago buzzed with reports about a new film to be called *Black and White* (*Chernyi i belyi*), that would counter racist stereotypes and present "Negroes on screen as humans, for the first time," in the words of the film's screenwriter.[62]

Rudd was a member of the delegation of twenty-two young African Americans heading to Moscow to make the film, led by Langston Hughes, who was to serve as script consultant. The film was to be produced by Mezhrabpom, the main production house for international films, and directed by Carl Junghans.[63]

As Arnold Rampersad writes in his biography of Langston Hughes, "As visiting Blacks, in fact, the twenty-two Americans were instant celebrities. Lines retreated impulsively before them, seats emptied as they approached. . . . Muscovites loved most foreigners, but the Scottsboro case gave American Blacks an instant prestige."[64] Much to the actors' frustration, however, *Black and White* was never made. The government aborted the project when, in an unofficial protest, an American leading the construction of a major dam in Ukraine objected to the film, warning that making it might delay US diplomatic recognition of the Soviet Union. Disappointed and angry, most of the delegation went home. But Rudd decided to stay, fascinated by what he saw on the Soviet stage during the months he'd been waiting for *Black and White* to begin shooting.[65] In 1936, after a brief sojourn back in the United States, Rudd found himself cast as Jim in a Soviet adaptation of *Huckleberry Finn*.[66]

Despite its title—*Tom Soier*—the film released by Ukrainfilm in 1936 is actually an amalgam of *Tom Sawyer* and *Huck Finn* in which Jim figures significantly.[67] As Cassio de Oliveira writes, *Tom Soier*—a "potpourri of plot elements from Twain's Mississippi novels, with a generous heaping of Soviet revolutionary spirit to go with it"—was intended mainly for the domestic market and especially for young audiences. The film was designed to exploit the immense popularity of Mark Twain's novel "in order to propagate its antiracist message."[68]

The film establishes the trauma inflicted by slavery in its opening scene, which features a fugitive slave named George—played by the American actor Lloyd Patterson—being chased, captured, attacked by vicious dogs, and then, with bound hands, led abjectly behind the horse of a man who turns out to be the town's pastor, and forced to drink water out of a trough alongside a horse.

Jim's owner, Dr. Robinson, has told him that he is setting him free and put that intention in writing, making Jim supremely happy. But Pap Finn, who has long hated Dr. Robinson, kills him and frames Jim for the murder. Jim is jailed.

The "Star-Spangled Banner" plays at the start of the trial. Judge Thatcher, flanked by two large American flags, announces that the physical and moral crime of killing a white man demands the gallows.

Tom and Huck show up as witnesses in his defense, freeing him from the murder charge. But Dr. Robinson's brother denies that his brother intended to set Jim free and plans to sell Jim himself, making him a slave again. When the boys help Jim escape and set out on a raft, a lynch mob chases them on horseback along the shore while Judge Thatcher, in a small sternwheeler, chases them on the water. The judge hits George, the former runaway who is now an enslaved member of the crew on his boat, for not stoking the boiler fast enough. When the judge boards the raft to recapture Jim, George hits the judge over the head, and Huck,

Wayland Rudd as Jim at his trial for having "murdered" Huck Finn in
Том Сойер—romanized as *Tom Soier*—released by Ukrainefilm in 1936.

Tom, and Jim tie him up, spread tar on his face (in effect putting
him in blackface), place him in the wigwam, and put up a sign indicating that he has smallpox. The two boys and the two slaves
commandeer the little sternwheeler (named "The Missouri River")
and sail off, heading for free territory. As de Oliveira notes, "In
featuring so prominently the question of slavery—and, by exten-
sion, of racial inequality in America—*Tom Soier* follows a perva-
sive trend in Soviet culture of the time," of consistently alluding
to America's racial travails.[69]

Wayland Rudd's Jim is clearly a man who cares about his family, fervently dreams of freedom, and justly fears the brutal treatment runaway slaves can expect; but he also conforms to some
familiar racial stereotypes as a fairly docile subject who expresses
both sadness and joy by breaking into song. The closing image of
the progressive white boys and the slaves thwarting the efforts
of the evil judge to return Jim to slavery is emblematic of the

Soviet ideal of an alliance between Black and white to challenge the corruption of the religious and civil powers-that-be.

In the decades that followed, Rudd would become the most visible Black actor in the USSR, cast almost exclusively as uneducated, oppressed Black American characters (although he would eventually achieve his dream of playing Othello in Russian). Rudd had been attracted to the Soviet Union "by the Soviet state's unapologetic attack on US white supremacy and its propaganda's insistence—on a world scale—that Black lives matter," as Meredith Roman writes.[70] His role in later films was principally to win the audience's sympathy and mobilize them against racism.

When Feliks Imokuede arrived in Moscow in the late 1960s to study petroleum engineering and geology at Patrice Lumumba University, he expected some of the challenges his fellow Nigerian students had encountered there in recent years. He was warned about the cold—his first week at Lumumba (named for the pro-Soviet first prime minister of the Congo, an African nationalist who was executed in 1961), he was taken to the GUM department store on Red Square, where a coat, boots, and warm clothing were purchased for him (the new clothing couldn't fully counter the frigid temperatures). He knew that learning Russian would be hard. He wasn't surprised by the lack of privacy in the overcrowded dorm rooms and the fact that one could bathe only on Wednesdays from five to eleven in the evening (the only time hot water was available); nor was he surprised by the dull and monotonous food and the general drabness of life all around him. He had been told not to be shocked by questions like "Do you have houses in Africa?" He had been warned that taxi drivers called Patrice Lumumba University "the zoo" and ordinary Soviet citizens were prone to call African students "monkeys." Nigerian students who had arrived in Moscow shortly before him told him about the dis-

Feliks Imokuede with costar eleven-year-old Roman Sergeevitsch Madyanov in *Совсем пропащий*—romanized as *Sovsem propashchiy* (*Hopelessly Lost*, 1973).

crimination and racial abuse that he could expect even in the supposedly antiracist land of socialist brotherhood. The frequent racist attacks from Soviet youngsters on African students were well known, and he had been advised to carry a knife for protection. He had heard about the incident, a few years earlier, of the Nigerian student sleeping in his dorm room who was attacked with a chisel by a drunken Russian incensed by the success that he had been having with Russian girls. No, he was not surprised by how hard it was to learn Russian, how cold it was, how tasteless the food was, how uncomfortable the dorms were, how racist ordinary Russians could be, and how ignorant they were about Africa.[71]

But he never dreamt that he would be cast in a major role in a film that would be nominated for best picture at the Cannes Film Festival in 1974.

Feliks Imokuede would play Jim in *Совсем пропащий* (romanized as *Sovsem propashchiy*), translated as *Hopelessly Lost* in English and *The Lost Boy* in French.[72] A joint effort by the celebrated Georgian director Georgiy Daneliya and acclaimed cinematographer Vadim Yusov, the film was produced in 1973 by Mosfilm, the Soviet Union's largest film studio, known for movies that would appeal to a broad public and could compete with foreign productions.[73] It was applauded by Soviet audiences and critics alike.[74] Imokuede may have been cast as Jim not because of his acting skills but because he physically conformed to many Soviet ideas of what a Black slave should look like. But the Nigerian-accented mix of Russian and English that he spoke was a problem. Daneliya decided that he had to be dubbed. So in the film, although Imokuede does not *look* Russian, he definitely sounds Russian, speaking the same standardized Russian as all the other characters.[75]

Soviet leaders at the time seized every chance they had to underline the hypocrisy of racism in the nation that claimed the mantle of leader of the "free world."[76] In the film, the king and the duke represent the rapacious materialism the Soviets associated with American capitalism, while Huck and Jim become "a metaphor for interracial working-class alliance fighting against capitalist bullies embodied by the pair of conmen onscreen."[77] Daria Goncharova tells us that the film fit into a Soviet tradition of "reclaiming Twain as a socialist rather than as a national writer and Huck as an anti-imperialist rebel embodying Soviet values of comradery and interracial solidarity."[78] Committed to ideals of "colorblind internationalism and proletarian solidarity," Goncharova writes, the film "prioritizes scenes that draw attention to the social ills that, in the Soviet interpretation, constituted the foundation of a capitalist regime: racial exploitation and mindless pursuit of wealth."[79] Greed is a motivating factor for the film's villains: Miss Watson can't resist the eight hundred dollars she can get for Jim, and the king and the duke avidly count the gold they've taken in through their scams without distributing shares to Huck and Jim, who have been integral to their success. Implicitly, the money-hungry king and duke and Miss Watson are emblems of capitalism, while Huck and Jim are emblems of what "comradery and interracial solidarity" can accomplish. (The film also includes some other social criticism implicit in the novel, such as the critique of mindless gun violence in the Grangerford-Shepherdson feud.) The film foregrounds the racial violence that lay just beneath the surface in the American South. This is conveyed not only by showing Jim's ankles bleeding from the shackles he is forced to wear when the king sells him but also by Huck's referencing lynchings as a reason why he and Jim should stick with the two conmen.

There are, as always, some major departures from the book—including the elimination of Tom Sawyer. Nonetheless, *Hopelessly Lost* is a film that lovingly honors Twain's original. The scenes—despite being truncated—remain remarkably faithful to Twain's text, often verbatim. In addition, Vadim Yusov's wonderfully luminous cinematography makes the Dnieper River shimmer in the moonlight and glisten in the sunlight in ways that evoke Huck's lyrical descriptions of the Mississippi. The replication of Twain's words combined with the incandescent shots of the river make *Hopelessly Lost* seem closer in spirit to the original than most other films based on the novel.

Although Black characters in Russian literature and art were portrayed stereotypically as servile, Imokuede's Jim is constantly showing agency, intelligence, and empathy in the face of the many obstacles thrown his way—a daunting task, given that he is in nearly every scene (with a few exceptions, such as scenes in pap's cabin or in the Wilks home or those involving Colonel Sherburn). His acting is always adequate and sometimes pitch-perfect. He plays Jim with confidence and aplomb.

Imokuede portrays Jim as a father who cares deeply about both his own children and Huck. Jim's wife and daughter appear briefly near the start of the film and are invoked along the journey as the motive for his flight. In the hair ball scene, he reassures Huck and tells him not to worry in a fatherly way. Jim calls Huck "son" and always behaves in a paternal manner, treating and calming him when he is bitten by a poisonous snake, reprimanding him when he deserves it. One of Imokuede's most compelling scenes takes place when he wakes and finds that Huck is back after their separation in the fog. Imokuede's Jim is overwhelmed with emotion—his very real tears visible—but he is still the parent, demanding truth from the lying child.

Imokuede's Jim is resourceful, self-assured, and smart. He steals a canoe when he realizes he is likely to be sold. When Jim tells Huck why he ran off—explaining that Miss Watson couldn't resist the eight hundred dollars a slave trader offered her—he observes that a Black man can't last more than two years if he is sold South. The raft is Jim's idea, not Huck's. Jim has caught a raft and provisioned it with cooking utensils and other supplies. The Frenchman debate is presented just as it is in the book. Huck's response to Jim's "winning" the argument is to spit and say, "Dammit."

But Jim's most significant demonstration of agency comes in the film's final scenes. Even though the king and the duke have sold Jim back into slavery and have been abusive to him, Jim makes a split-second decision when he sees the two men—tarred and feathered—swimming toward the raft as a mob chases them. The camera closes in on Jim's eyes. Then, still shackled, with his ankles bleeding, Jim decides to save their lives by steering the raft toward them and letting them get on board once again. The moral turpitude of the king is underlined when, after Jim has saved his life, the disgusting-looking, tarred and feathered man has the gall to still demand that Jim address him with deference, insisting that he rise when talking to the "king of France"!

In Soviet culture, as Goncharova observes, "Jim's decision to extend his hand to his oppressors would indicate his moral superiority, and, with it, the superiority of the oppressed races. Indeed, since the King and Duke have previously been established onscreen as metaphors for everything that is wrong with contemporary America, their pitiful state at the end of the film—tarred-and-feathered, kneeling by Huck and Jim's feet—indicates the deficiencies of the American way of life. In contrast, Huck and Jim are shown to stand by each other as equals . . . representing the Soviets' anti-racist image."[80]

The courage with which Jim stands up to the king when he is about to hit Huck for having tried to elude the two conmen is striking. Goncharova tells us that as Imokuede openly confronts the king saying, "'Не троньте мальчишку' [Don't you touch the boy]. This defiance on the part of the slave causes the still panting King to stop dead in his tracks." In outraged disbelief, the king spots an ax nearby, reaches for it, and lunges at Jim with a dire threat: "'Убью! Раб!' [I'll kill you! Slave!]" But Huck quickly jumps in front of Jim screaming at the top of his lungs, "'Не убивайте его! Это мой негр!' [Don't kill him! This is my Negro!]" "Although Huck's speech evokes the mentality of white masters," Goncharova writes, by this point the viewer knows "that Huck's appropriation of racist discourse is just a performance, a tactic, showcasing his code-switching skills."[81]

In the film's final scene, Huck tells Jim that he will bend over backward to help him be a free man. Jim smiles broadly. Although Jim is not free yet at the end of the film, and although he and Huck may be floating down the river, "hopelessly lost" on a raft with two scoundrels, he knows he has a true friend and ally. Their bond is strong, and it gives Jim optimism and strength.

By making *Hopelessly Lost* the Soviet nominee for best picture at Cannes, jumping it ahead of a film that had been championed earlier, the Soviets wanted to demonstrate that they could make a film that was faithful to the spirit of this great American novel while also being an impressive achievement in Soviet filmmaking. They also wanted to stake out their claim to Twain as a kindred spirit, someone who spoke to Soviet ideals of proletarian egalitarianism and racial harmony.

Foreign students were not allowed to stay in the country after their terms of study ended. But Imokuede was allowed to remain in Moscow for a year after graduation in order to make the film, returning home to Nigeria after it was completed.[82] The first Nigerian to be featured in a film nominated for best picture at Cannes, Imokuede must have been gratified when a street in Lagos was named in his honor.[83]

Jim at One Hundred: Meshach Taylor, Ron Richardson, and Samm-Art Williams Defend Jim's Power and Twain's Satire around the *Huckleberry Finn* Centennial (1985)

The year 1985, the one-hundredth anniversary of the publication of *Adventures of Huckleberry Finn* in the United States, brought a spate of new efforts to challenge the book in the classroom, in libraries, and on stage. But it also gave three stellar actors—Meshach Taylor, Ron Richardson, and Samm-Art Williams—the opportunity to play Jim in three acclaimed, award-winning stage and screen productions. In 1985, Meshach Taylor brought Jim alive in a play developed by the Organic Theater Company and the Goodman Theatre in Chicago, which won an Emmy when it was broadcast on WTTV, an Indianapolis-based CBS affiliate. Ron Richardson starred in a Broadway musical that garnered seven Tony awards. And Samm-Art Williams stood out in a Peabody Award–winning four-part original PBS television series that is widely recognized by critics as the most successful film adaptation of the novel (produced in 1985, it was not broadcast until

February 1986). The centennial focused intense national attention on each of these productions, and all three actors rose to the occasion, portraying Jim with impressive insight, notable craft, and an awareness that on some level they might just be making history.

Moments after the final curtain was met with thunderous applause on opening night of the Organic Theater Company's production of *Huckleberry Finn* at Chicago's Goodman Theatre on February 4, 1985, Meshach Taylor, who starred as Jim, raced to the studio of a local ABC affiliate to appear on *Nightline*. The show opened with a brief background report by ABC's Jeff Greenfield in which a Black Chicago educator named Dr. John Wallace opined that *Huckleberry Finn* "is the most grotesque example of racist trash ever written."[84] Wallace, Greenfield said, "has traveled across America attacking the book. He says the frequent references to Nigger Jim [*sic*], Huck's companion on his adventures, and the use of rural Black dialect, portrays Blacks in demeaning, insulting terms." Wallace told Greenfield that "100% of the Black young people whom I spoke to are humiliated and embarrassed when they've had to sit in the classroom and read this kind of filth."[85]

Greenfield then quoted Chicago drama critic Lenny Kleinfeld's comments at a symposium on "Racism, Censorship and *Huckleberry Finn*" that the Goodman had held a week earlier: "Bigotry was in fact Mark Twain's target," Kleinfeld said, "The book is set up to embarrass white people into seeing how poisoned their minds are, and their attitudes towards Black people are. The assertions about Black people's inadequacies are being made in this book by a bunch of white murderers and white thieves and white con men and white homicidal maniacs, who are the southern aristocracy."[86]

After announcing that Wallace and Taylor (along with Waukegan, Illinois, alderman Robert Evans Jr. and civil libertarian Nat Hentoff) were joining the program live from the ABC studio in Chicago, host Ted Koppel addressed Taylor: "You must've gone through a little bit of soul-searching, I suspect, Mr. Taylor, given all this controversy about whether indeed you should even be in the production. Did you, and if so, why did you decide to do it?"[87]

"Initially I did," Taylor said. When he'd first considered appearing in a dramatic adaptation of the book ten years earlier, the director had insisted that he read Twain's novel, and Taylor took his advice. "I felt it was one of the best indictments against racism in the United States that I ever read," Taylor said. John Wallace met this comment with a glare.

Koppel continued, "And you do not feel that it enhances bigotry when words like 'nigger' are used on the stage—that this somehow gives the bigots out there perhaps a feeling that it's all right?" Taylor responded, "No. First of all, let me say that I feel that the word 'nigger' is an offensive word. I do feel that slavery was offensive as well." He paused for a moment to let the remark sink in, and then continued: "I think that if we're going to be true to the time, however, that we must speak the way the people spoke during that time. And I think it's important for people to understand exactly what the history of racism in this country is." The character of Jim had appealed to him, Taylor said, because he "felt that an individual who speaks with a dialect is . . . an individual who may be uneducated but not stupid."[88]

Taylor spoke with a sense of conviction that infuriated Wallace but that was well earned. Taylor had first played Jim a decade earlier. In 1975, after finishing a stint as part of the touring company of *Hair*, twenty-seven-year-old Taylor was offered the role of Jim in an adaptation of Twain's novel by Stewart Gordon at the Organic Theater Company in Chicago. Gordon's creative adaptation of Twain's novel was stunningly faithful to the original, with virtually all of the dialogue being words Twain had written.[89] "The gimmick of the production is that there are no gimmicks," Gordon said, "We can cut, but we can't rewrite."[90] This devotion to the source required a production that was longer than usual: it took two nights to perform parts 1 and 2 in their entirety. Gordon recalls that when he first offered Taylor the chance to play Jim, "he was reluctant to accept the role because he was worried about being accused of playing an 'Uncle Tom' character," but after he read the book and heard Gordon's "assurances that Jim would be the moral center of the play as he is in the original Twain," he accepted the role.[91]

Calling the production "triumphant" (despite its unusual length), the influential Chicago theater critic Richard Christiansen singled out for special praise the moment when Jim chastises Huck for having tried to fool him after the fog. Taylor handled the scene "so beautifully that I found myself weeping uncontrollably at its conclusion," he wrote in the *Chicago Daily News.*[92] Earl Calloway, arts critic for the *Chicago Defender,* one of the nation's leading Black newspapers, recalled Taylor's Jim as "a profound and wonderful interpretation of a man who was [surviving] under the shackles of slavery."[93] The play went on a statewide tour, and a six-week tour of Europe followed. "Taylor is a wonderful Jim," a reviewer in the Bloomington, Illinois, *Pantagraph* wrote, "ignorant and yet keen in perceiving human nature." His performance earned Taylor a nomination for a Joseph Jefferson Award for best actor.[94]

When the play was revived at the Goodman a decade later, Taylor, now thirty-seven, was the obvious choice to play Jim. His career in television and film in Los Angeles had just gotten off to a promising start when he was invited back to Chicago to play the role he had performed on stage to such acclaim a decade earlier. In the 1985 version—a collaboration of the Organic Theater that had originated it and Chicago's Goodman Theater—substantial cuts were made in order to perform it in one evening instead of two.[95] Something else in addition to the cuts made this new production different: some local civil rights leaders and educators were threatening to picket the production and close it down. About fifty miles away, in the Chicago suburb of Waukegan, after some Black parents had complained to Alderman Evans that the book represented a "gross injustice" to Black students in the city, which was 50 percent Black, Evans led the drive to get the book banned from required reading lists in the city's high schools.[96] Now Wallace and Evans planned to organize protests to picket the Goodman during the run of the play.

For most of the play, the stage is bare except for a single chair. Props are minimal, too: little more than a jug and a basket of yarn. But the audience forgets the lack of scenery or props due to the brilliantly choreographed body movements and flawless sound effects. With grace and skill, Meshach Taylor's Jim pantomimes propelling the raft through the water; the chaotic filth of the "floating house" where pap is killed is conveyed by the sound of Jim's climbing over empty liquor bottles. A perfectly deployed fog machine makes the separation of Huck and Jim in the fog terrifyingly real.

Taylor's Jim speaks in an easy and natural southern accent that Taylor had the chance to hone during a childhood spent in part in New Orleans. He plays Jim as confident and self-assured when debating the nature of King Solomon with Huck or discussing why a Frenchman can't talk like a man. He holds his own in these discussions, showing none of the timidity or deference that might be expected of a slave when talking to a white person. Throughout the play, Taylor's Jim clearly embraces his role as Huck's key tutor in emotional intelligence, as his guide to understanding the meaning of friendship, trust, reciprocity, and respon-

Meshach Taylor as Jim and John Cameron Mitchell as Huck
during rehearsal for the Goodman Theatre's production of
Adventures of Huckleberry Finn, adapted by the Organic Theater Company,
directed by Stuart Gordon, and presented January 23–March 5, 1985,
at the Goodman Theatre, Chicago. Photo by Keith Swinden.

sibility. He brings out the best in him through his love. The doctor's speech extolling the selflessness of Jim's decision to put Tom's well-being before his own freedom when Tom is shot is included in full, something that had never happened in any of the film adaptations of the novel.

Earl Calloway of the *Chicago Defender*, who had called Taylor's earlier performance of Jim "profound and wonderful," felt that Taylor portrayed Jim with an even greater depth and texture ten years later: "Now a more seasoned actor, Taylor, in his role of Jim, provides us with a character that is really a shrewd and witty man. He projects Jim as a man of dignity, an individual with a stirring temperament and one with a fighting intensity. He was a compelling human being as Mr. Taylor portrayed him filled with beguiling charm, . . . unerring in his evaluation of life. The actor also provided us with a vivid imagination of the man's humor and articulated his personality with a masterful radiance."[97]

As for the objections that some local residents had raised to the presence of an offensive racial slur in the play, in Calloway's view the offensive term, while unacceptable today, was part of the world in which the novel was set, and it was used in service of the novelist's—and playwright's—laudable larger ends. The bottom line for Calloway, as he noted in the long review he published in the *Defender*, was that Meshach Taylor—and Twain—had created Jim as a "tremendous person" whom Huck and the audience learn to "love and respect."[98]

And then there was *Nightline*. After an opening night that was exhilarating in every way, Taylor found himself defending Jim—and Twain—on national television, interrupted constantly by a doggedly adversarial John Wallace, who refused to believe that the book contained any irony and who wanted the play shut down.

The adventure set in motion for me personally by that broadcast could not have been more unexpected. My husband woke me up and said I had to watch the show. He knew that I'd be incensed by Wallace's refusal to recognize the book and the play as satire despite Taylor's and Hentoff's insistence. In my first book I'd told the story of how, as a young reporter in San Francisco, Mark Twain had tried to write up an incident he had witnessed in which racist hoodlums abused a Chinese man while the police stood by and laughed. His editor and publisher refused to publish the story, caring more for the prejudices of their subscribers (who shared the police's prejudice) than for the truth. In order to get into print at all on the subject of racism in San Francisco, Twain had to turn the piece into a satire—something he could sell to the paper that had formerly employed him in Nevada. He continued to publish satires about racism toward the Chinese—and one about racism toward African Americans—in the 1860s and early 1870s.[99] These satires of racism turned out to be rehearsals for the novel Twain would publish in 1885. How ironic, then, that after having had to turn to satire to get into print at all on the subject of racism, now Twain was being censored as "racist" by people unable to recognize his satire for what it was. I stayed up all night crafting an op-ed that laid this out. I sent it off cold the next day to the *New York Times*. To my astonishment and delight, the *Times* accepted it and ran it two weeks later, on February 18, 1985, the exact hundredth anniversary of the publication of *Huck Finn* in the United States.[100]

The day my op-ed ran, I was awakened at 6:30 a.m. by a phone call from an antiques dealer in Hamden, Connecticut. "You don't know me," Nancy Stiner said, "but I just read your piece in the *New York Times*, and I've got to see you right away. I have a letter Mark Twain wrote that nobody knows about yet, and after reading your column, I know you'll know what to do with it. Here's what it says." She read it to me over the phone.

December 24, 1885

Dear Sir,

Do you know him? And is he worthy? I do not believe I would very cheerfully help a white student who would ask a benevolence of a stranger, but I do not feel so about the other color. We have ground the manhood out of them, & the shame is ours, not theirs, & we should pay for it.

If this young man lives as economically as it is & should be the pride of one to do who is straitened, I would like to know what the cost is, so that I may send 6, 12, or 24 months' board, as the size of the bill may determine.

You see he refers to you, or I would not venture to intrude. Truly yours, S. L. Clemens[101]

A chill went through me as I realized the significance of what I had just heard. The letter contained the most direct, nonironic condemnation of racism that we had from Twain himself during this period—and it was written in Hartford on Christmas Eve, 1885, the same year *Huckleberry Finn* was published. Stiner had found it in an old desk. She lived fifteen minutes from Yale, where my husband and I then lived and worked. I dressed and drove out to her house. She and her husband let me borrow the letter to compare it with other Twain letters in Yale's Beinecke Library, many of which were written from Hartford around the same time, allowing me to confirm its authenticity. But to whom was it sent? Who was the Black student who was the subject of the letter? And what, if anything, happened as a result?

The reply to Twain's letter—which was in his papers at the Bancroft Library at UC Berkeley—and an article by literary scholar Philip Butcher made it clear that the addressee was Francis Wayland, dean of Yale Law School, and that the "young man" to whom Twain referred was Warner T. McGuinn.[102] But McGuinn himself was still largely a mystery. A scrapbook McGuinn kept that someone had sent to the Yale Library after his death, and his obituary in 1937 in the *Baltimore Afro-American* began to reveal the contours of a career as distinguished as it was obscure. Born near Richmond, Virginia, in 1862, McGuinn attended Lincoln University and then read law in Washington, DC, with Richard Greener, the first Black graduate of Harvard. In 1885 McGuinn was admitted to study law at Yale. He supported himself as a waiter, accountant, and bill collector during his first year in New Haven. The one extracurricular activity for which he managed to find time was the Kent Club, a student organization that debated political and social questions of the day. Two warring factions vied for the presidency of the club in the fall of 1885, and McGuinn ended up being selected as a compromise. His main duty was meeting the club's guest speakers at the railroad station and introducing them before their lectures. The first speaker that year was Mark Twain.

Twain must have been impressed by the young law student and by the introduction he gave. Back in Hartford, Twain wrote Dean Wayland on Christmas Eve, inquiring about McGuinn's circumstances and asking whether it was a good idea for him to offer to pay his board. Wayland responded positively, and Twain ended up paying McGuinn's board for the next year and a half (the remainder of McGuinn's time at Yale). Once freed of the need to juggle his three part-time jobs, McGuinn excelled, winning a top prize at graduation and going on to edit a newspaper in Kansas. He then settled in Baltimore, where he had a major civil rights victory in federal court that was key to the eventual desegregation of American cities. He also helped found the local branch of the NAACP and served as counsel to the *Afro-American*. In addition (when I learned this, my jaw dropped), McGuinn became the key mentor for a young attorney he brought under his wing named Thurgood Marshall.[103]

Contacted by Yale's news bureau, the *New York Times* expressed interest in running the story, but their reporter, Edwin McDowell, wanted to reach Supreme Court Justice Thurgood Marshall first. Justice Marshall was somewhat unclear about why the *Times* was eager to talk with him, but when he finally understood that the subject was Warner McGuinn, McDowell got his quote: "He was one of the greatest lawyers who ever lived. . . . If he had been white, he'd have been a judge." I was stunned on the morning of March 14, 1985, to see McDowell's story occupying nearly the entire lower-left quadrant of page 1.[104]

Twain's condemnation of racism in the 1880s was not news to scholars, who had long been familiar with his private, unpublished jibes at it from the late 1860s on. Nor was it news to careful readers of *Huckleberry Finn*, who could not help grasping the antiracist thrust of the book's satire. But Twain's irony was hard for some to recognize, and the book was filled with a racial epithet that retained its power to inflict pain. Many ordinary readers simply believed John Wallace when he charged that Mark Twain and his book were racist, pure and simple. The letter provided Twain's defenders with some welcome ammunition.

"It's the smoking gun. The man was not a racist," Henry Louis Gates Jr. told news anchor Peter Jennings on the *ABC Evening News*. I gave interviews to the *Today Show*, the *ABC Evening News*, a dozen radio stations across the country, a newspaper in Australia, a radio station in Canada, and a literary publication in Moscow. I also debated John Wallace on CNN's *Freeman Reports* that night, as well as the next morning on the *CBS Morning News*.

The letter clearly made Wallace unhappy. He repeated the charges he had made on *Nightline*—that the book was racist, its author was racist, and *Huck Finn* had no place in America's classrooms. I didn't doubt that Twain's novel had been poorly taught in the school Wallace attended and that it had caused him pain and discomfort as a result. But it seemed to me that the solution was to help those who wanted to teach the book learn how to teach it more successfully by framing the discussion in the context of the history of racism in the United States and by helping their students recognize irony, rather than forcing them to remove it from their reading lists and libraries. During the call-in portion of our hourlong debate on CNN, a Black high school student accused Wallace of insulting her and all Black high school students by suggesting they were incapable of understanding Mark Twain's irony. "Mr. Wallace," she said, "are you saying I'm not smart enough to read this book?" I felt like giving her a hug.

I called my father after the show. "How was I?" I asked. He paused and then said, "Too ladylike." He was right. Wallace had interrupted and harangued me at every turn—much as he had interrupted Meshach Taylor and Nat Hentoff on *Nightline*. And I had let him.

I knew I'd have a rematch, albeit a brief one, on the next morning's *CBS Morning News*. I woke up two hours earlier than I had to just to get psyched. Before the broadcast, Wallace and I chatted casually over coffee. We got along fine when we weren't talking about Mark Twain. He seemed relaxed when we entered the set: he had me pegged, having debated me the previous evening. Only the "me" who turned up that morning wasn't quite the same "me" of the night before. His "ladylike" opponent was gone, and in her place was someone who ignored his interruptions and finished her sentences against all odds.

When the show was over, a Black cameraman who had been shooting us came up to me. He said he had never read the book by Mark Twain that we had been arguing about—but now he really wanted to. One thing that puzzled him, though, was why a white woman was defending it and a Black man was attacking it, because as far as he could see from what we'd been saying, the book made whites look pretty bad.[105]

From that point on, journalists referred to Twain's condemnation of racism in the McGuinn letter whenever they covered debates about the alleged racism of the book or its author. As I've said, the letter shouldn't have been necessary to prove what the novel is and does—and it certainly does not absolve Twain of all charges of racism (a charge that could be leveled against virtually any white American, given our nation's past). But it seemed to be useful to Twain's defenders to be able to invoke it. It came to light at exactly the right moment to be helpful.

The Broadway musical *Big River,* based on *Huck Finn,* was slated to open on April 25, 1985, one month after the front-page *New York Times* story about my research. The producers had monitored with concern the protests facing the Goodman Theatre production of *Huckleberry Finn* and had worried that they would face pickets and protests themselves. But they faced no protests; it was all clear sailing. They believed my research was the reason. Someone from *Big River*'s production team got in touch with me to thank me. Would I like to come to the show?

"When I am playing Jim, I am playing my grandfather," actor Ron Richardson told the *New York Times* shortly after the Broadway opening of *Big River*, which featured Richardson as Jim.[106] His grandfather, he said, "was born a free man, but his father and mother were slaves. He was very strong, and very majestic."[107] His grandfather the Reverend Wade Ellison, a farmer and Methodist minister, had died four months earlier at ninety-two, and Richardson dedicated his performance to him. "I look like him and he had a special influence on my life." In Richardson's view, Jim, like his grandfather, was a heroic figure who was "strong and full of life's pain, and its despair."[108]

Although *Big River* received some mixed reviews, Richardson himself got nothing but raves.[109] Critics often used the word he had used to describe his grandfather to characterize his performance: "majestic." They also used "compelling" and "thrilling" to describe the voice and presence that the thirty-three year-old actor brought to the role of Jim.[110] Richardson appreciated Twain's efforts to depict the South as it was a century and a half before, making it "blatantly clear that slavery was condoned by the church, the Government, [and] the educational system" and how wrong that was.[111] Nonetheless, Richardson braced himself for the flak he expected to get for having agreed to take the role. "It doesn't bother me," he said. "I have to live with myself, and Jim is a proud, dignified and noble character."[112] He saw him as a role model.

When he agreed to take the part, Richardson had no idea that he would win a Tony for his first Broadway appearance—"best supporting actor in a musical"—as well as a Drama Desk Award. And it certainly had never occurred to him that within three years he would be credited with heralding a new era in *Japanese* theater, but that's exactly what happened when he performed the role of Jim—"proud, dignified and noble"—in Tokyo *in Japanese.*[113]

Richardson's close extended family—mainly farmers and clergymen—had its roots in rural and small-town South Carolina, where his great-grandparents and other family members had been enslaved. Before being cast in *Big River,* he had performed in regional theater around Philadelphia, where he was raised. The first Black role in which he was cast was the character Sportin' Life in a Houston Grand Opera production of *Porgy and Bess* (a role written for a tenor that gave Richardson, a bass baritone, no end of trouble).[114] But he had never appeared on Broadway before. Now he was a star overnight.

The *New York Times* described "his powerful natural" baritone when he "pulled out all the stops" nightly at the Eugene O'Neill Theatre as being "as deep and dark as the Mississippi down which Huck and Jim are rafting."[115] *Variety* called his performance as Jim "near-operatic," noting that "he's got a booming baritone which fills the theater in his big songs 'Muddy Water' and 'River in the Rain' and a stirring spiritual, 'Free at Last.'"[116] He was praised for "the tragic resonance" of his "dynamic performance" and his "powerful singing," as well as for the "humor and high spirits" he brought to the role.[117]

John Wallace continued to fume that *Huckleberry Finn* reinforces stereotypes and is hurtful to Blacks, but he never managed to get anyone to picket the show. Meanwhile, the NAACP magazine *Crisis* affirmed the show's success in shining a light on a shameful chapter of America's past: "Stereotypes melt away" in

Big River, the *Crisis* wrote, "and the truth about one of this country's ugliest periods is exposed."[118]

Director Des McAnuff held four days of "intense seminars" when rehearsals began, a process that included sharing letters from former slaves and going over the attitudes and social mores that prevailed in the 1840s in the Mississippi River valley. He noted that many enslaved men and women "had been set free without knowing it"—as was the case with Jim. For some cast members, including Richardson, this was news.[119]

Richardson brought to the role astute insights into Jim's character. Among them was the idea that "Jim has to have survival techniques—teaching Huck the lessons of life without letting him know he's being taught. And he has to be shrewd enough to realize his life is up to the whims of two boys."[120] Richardson found a growing respect for Jim's strength and dignity as he worked on the role. "Jim is an incredible survivor," he said, "a very moral man with a mission, and that mission was to free his family. I think that there was a genuine love for Huck. It's very difficult not to love a child, especially when you can see the child is very naive and innocent about a society which you've seen the underbelly of—which Jim had seen the underbelly of."[121] He believed that the character was "not so far removed from [his] own life." His great grandfather had been enslaved, his father had been a sharecropper, and Richardson noted that he'd "dealt with racism" personally.[122]

Richardson initially had some qualms about the presence of the offensive racial epithet in the show. But he recognized the necessity of the word given that it was part and parcel of the dehumanization that slavery and the racism undergirding it required. "I grew up in the time of Martin Luther King, and Malcolm X, and I can't remember a time when someone called me 'nigger.' But, at that time, that was the word, that's what you were—chattel."[123]

Although some large sections of the book, such as the Grang-erford episodes, were cut in the interest of length and focus, Hauptman's script retained Twain's original words as much as it could. Any new lines Hauptman assigns Jim amplify dimensions of Jim's character that are implicit in the original. As in the orig-inal, Jim has good ideas (he suggests that Huck dress up like a girl when he goes ashore to get information), and he knows a lot of signs ("most every one there is"). As in the book, he tells Huck that he's going to have "considerable trouble and considerable joy" (except in the libretto the prediction applies to the two of them). Hauptman wrote Jim a lighter dialect than Twain had, and indeed, Richardson delivered his lines in an accent that was a blend of his Philadelphia and South Carolina roots.

The easy camaraderie between Dan Jenkins's Huck and Rich-ardson's Jim is evoked not just through their conversations, the food they eat together, and the tasks on the raft that they share but also through the harmonies of the three major duets they sing. One such duet—the lyrical "River in the Rain"—"is the peak of [Jim's] happiness," Richardson said.[124] In the song, Richardson's deep, mellow, and full-bodied baritone and Jenkins's reedy tenor alternate and finally harmonize in unison. The soft major chord on which the song ends is a lovely emblem of the bond that has grown between them. Although critics declared the duets "River in the Rain" and "Muddy Water" to be "show-stoppers," Richard-son's favorite among their duets is "Worlds Apart."[125] "It's such a tender moment," he told a reporter, "For me, he becomes my son at that moment, and if it were today, I could adopt such a boy."[126] Richardson then began to sing the lyrics for the reporter: "I see the same stars through my window, that you see through yours / But we're worlds apart, worlds apart." His signature song in the show was "Free at Last," a title that renowned country singer-songwriter Roger Miller said he borrowed from the words of Martin Luther King Jr.[127]

Roger Miller's inspired score interweaves Black and white musical traditions as artfully as Twain blended Black and white voices and rhetorical traditions.[128] His stunning contrapuntal montage of bluegrass and spirituals, country and gospel, fugues and rounds and calls and responses, succeeds to a large extent in capturing Twain's alchemy in the novel. Music also conveys important information in the show. At one point a flatboat passes Jim and Huck's raft, rowed by a crew of slaves in chains guarded by a white overseer with a gun. Jim tells Huck they are slaves who have run off like he did, but got caught, and are now crossing back. Huck can't figure out how Jim knew that. "I hears it in their singing," Jim tells him. The slaves convey their pain and disappointment in the melody and lyrics of the poignant song, "The Crossing"—a song whose meaning Jim (but not Huck) knows how to "read."

Hauptman changes the trick Huck plays on Jim. Instead of pretending that the fog was a dream, Huck impersonates some slave catchers when he's returning to the raft from the shore. "Ain't that a runaway?" Huck shouts, in a disguised voice, "I believe it is. Let's get him, boys." Jim then says, "(*Grabbing a stick and holding it high*) Don't come any closer, whoever you are! I'll knock your brains out!"[129] Huck then leaps up and callously makes fun of how Jim looks, dressed up by the duke and king to appear repulsive (the "Sick Arab" disguise in the book). Jim responds to Huck's prank with words Jim used in the fog episode in the book: "I was so thankful to see you I could have gotten down on my knees and kissed your foot. And all you were thinking about was making a fool of Jim. . . . Well, go on—get your face out of my sight."[130] Huck accuses Jim of "talking trash," but Jim angrily

Ron Richardson in a scene from the original Broadway production of the musical *Big River*, New York, 1985. Photo by Martha Swope © Billy Rose Theatre Division, The New York Public Library for the Performing Arts.

directs that term at Huck: "You're the one who's trash! Trash is people who puts dirt on the heads of their friends and makes 'em ashamed."[131] Huck's apology follows.

At the Phelps farm, Jim objects to Tom's shenanigans, as he did in the book. Because this section is so relatively truncated here, Jim's objections stand out more. Richardson's rendition of the moving song "Free at Last" beautifully conveys his emotional response to being free.[132] As R. Kent Rasmussen and Mark Dawidziak have observed, "Miller understood that songs—basically musical monologues—are ideal for expressing *Huckleberry Finn*'s strongest emotional moments."[133]

Richardson's Jim is firm in his decision not to abandon the

wounded Tom Sawyer and takes his role as Tom's protector so seriously that he grills the doctor about why he brought a flask of whiskey along. "What you got the bottle for?" Jim demands, grabbing the flask from the doctor. "We need a doctor, not a drunk." The doctor explains that he is going to pour whiskey on Tom's wound to clean it. Jim hands him back the flask and says, "See that's the only place you pour it."[134] After holding Tom while the doctor pours the whiskey on his wound and takes out his scalpel, Jim says, "(*Looking him in the eye evenly*) See you do your job—do it good."[135] In this scene Richardson's Jim is more assertive and bold in his interactions with a white character than Jim is in any other dramatization of the novel on stage or screen with the exception of the Soviet production, *Hopelessly Lost*, from 1973, in which Feliks Imokuede's Jim prevents the king from striking Huck, shouting, "'Не троньте мальчишку' [Don't you touch the boy]"—an act of defiance that nearly gets Jim killed by the king with a nearby ax. Hauptman also has Jim talk back to Tom Sawyer one last time when he learns that Tom has kept from him the fact that Miss Watson had freed him in her will—something many readers have longed for him to do. When Jim and Huck decide to go their separate ways at the end of the show, they part with affection before Jim exits "*slowly and proudly*" as the stage directions instruct.[136]

Big River won seven Tony Awards, including Best Actor (Richardson), Best Original Score (Miller), and the top prize as Best Musical. More than three decades after the show closed on Broadway, scholars are still extolling its distinctive strengths. In 2020 R. Kent Rasmussen called the show "arguably the best dramatization of *Huckleberry Finn* in any form."[137]

The year after *Big River* closed, Richardson went on a concert tour of the Soviet Union with a delegation of American musical artists as part of a cultural exchange. He performed his main songs from the show in Moscow, St. Petersburg, and Riga, Latvia. As his manager, Michael Bolanos, wrote in *Soviet Life*, the audiences were especially moved by the lyrics to "Worlds Apart"—"I see the friendship in your eyes that you see in mine. . . . But we're worlds apart." In Riga, Richardson's performance of "Free at Last" was backed up by Latvian music students. At the curtain call, Bolanos reports, "The audience wouldn't stop its unison clapping." Latvian television broadcast all the concerts on the tour.[138]

In 1988 Richardson was invited to reprise his role as Jim in Japan alongside a largely Japanese cast. He initially agreed to do the lines in Japanese "as a joke." "I was completely ignorant of how difficult it was going to be," Richardson said.[139] The only word in Japanese that he knew at that point was *sushi*. He embarked on more than four months of intensive study with Kyoko Hosaka, a coach from Tokyo.[140] Richardson sang his songs in English but learned his lines phonetically with the help of his Japanese coach and delivered all spoken dialogue in Japanese.[141] Richardson "learned which lines to stress and which to glide past, which ones were emotion-laden and which lighthearted." The biggest challenge after memorizing the lines, Richardson said, was getting past his "fear of speaking Japanese in front of Japanese people."[142] Although there were three other Americans in the twenty-nine-person cast, Richardson was the only one who had to make long speeches in Japanese.[143]

When the show debuted at the Aoyama Theater in Tokyo, it was believed to be the first time that a foreign actor had re-created a major role in Japan by phonetically reading his lines in Japanese.[144] "When I walk out onto the stage and deliver my first line I hear a loud, swift intake of breath," Richardson told the Associated Press. "The audience is surprised to see a Black man walk out onto the stage and speak in Japanese."[145] As the *New York Times* reported, "The audience was clearly impressed. This is, bear in mind, a country filled with people who explode in wonderment when a foreigner merely says hello in their language. So to have Mr. Richardson hold forth for an entire evening struck some Japanese as more peculiar than the notion of a well-made American car."[146] The *Times* went on to note that "there were a few giggles from the audience and exchanges of nervous glances when Mr. Richardson first opened his mouth. Afterward, some said they had trouble catching it all."[147] But "what made up for that drawback," one Japanese critic opined, "was Richardson's sincerity on stage and his splendid voice."[148] The loud clapping and foot-stomping that rocked the theater on opening night suggests that he made himself understood by most of the audience, which included Crown Prince Akihito and Crown Princess Michiko.[149] Richardson added enormously to the impact of the production: one headline, for example, asserted, "The Play Was Deepened by Black Actor."[150] After the two-month tour of Tokyo and Osaka ended, Akihiko Senda, one of Japan's leading theater critics, wrote that "language has always been a formidable barrier restricting the Japanese stage to Japanese actors." But, he argued, Richardson's performance in *Big River* showed that the barrier could be surmounted. That performance, he wrote, might well "herald a new era in Japanese theater."[151] Richardson, sadly, died of complications from AIDS in 1995 at age forty-three. As the *New York Times* noted in his obituary, for Richardson, *Big River* "was a life-changing experience, and it remained the high point of his career."[152]

During the *Huck Finn* centennial, a time when scholars and the public continued to charge Jim with embodying demeaning stereotypes derived from minstrelsy, playwright and actor Samm-Art Williams was asked by *USA Today* how he felt about playing Jim in an American Playhouse production of *Huckleberry Finn* airing on PBS. "Personally I look at the Jims of the world as heroes," Williams said. "The Jims ran for their lives so I wouldn't have to run for mine. I look at them from a sense of pride. I'm not ashamed of knowing that three generations ago my family were slaves."[153]

Williams had given minstrel shows and the stereotypes they projected a lot of thought: *Cork,* a new play he had written about minstrel shows and the Black actors who appeared in them, would be produced that same year off-Broadway.[154] Williams knew that Jim was no minstrel. He played him as a man who was serious, intelligent, firm, and self-possessed—devoted both to his actual family and to the abused child whose journey coalesced with his own. Williams had also given a lot of thought to the Uncle Tom stereotype—an image of servility that critics sometimes ascribed to Jim. Williams didn't believe anyone existed who embodied the Uncle Tom stereotype. In his view, "People did what they had to do to live, in order to get along."[155] The description applied to his own ancestors—and it applied to Jim.

By the time Williams undertook the role of Jim in 1985, he was an experienced actor who had played a range of roles in plays produced by New York's Negro Ensemble Company and in regional theaters; he was also a playwright who had written some half-dozen plays that had made it to the stage. And he had been deeply immersed in the history of slavery, both as a writer and as an actor who had been involved in a trilogy of productions centered on slavery that were broadcast on PBS shortly before he played Jim. One year before *Huckleberry Finn* was filmed, he had played the title role in *Denmark Vesey,* on public television, a drama about an important historical figure who had planned a major slave revolt in Charleston, South Carolina, and was executed in 1822. In 1985 before filming *Huckleberry Finn,* Williams coauthored and acted in *Solomon Northup's Odyssey,* a drama based on

Northup's slave narrative (in 2013 Williams would return to Northup's story as coauthor of the feature film *Twelve Years a Slave*). And he was also the author of *Charlotte Forten's Mission: Experiment in Freedom*, a docudrama about an important but largely unsung abolitionist, activist, and writer that also ran on public television. In short, he was a pro—confident, capable, and undaunted by the challenge of playing an enslaved man struggling to survive against all odds in a system that defined him as nonhuman and that required him to exhibit deference to people who were his moral inferiors.[156]

The four-hour film, which aired on the New York PBS station WNET in the American Playhouse series, directed by Peter H. Hunt from a teleplay by Guy Gallo, was distinctive for a number of reasons, including cameo appearances by Lillian Gish and Butterfly McQueen, both of whom had been memorable cast members of previous films that had offered pointedly whitewashed views of the antebellum South: Gish had appeared in *Birth of a Nation*, McQueen in *Gone with the Wind*. This new film adaptation of *Huckleberry Finn* whitewashed nothing: here, the racism, violence, and barbarity of the world in which Huck and Jim moved was front and center.[157]

In addition to being the longest film adaptation of the novel ever made, it was decidedly the darkest—literally as well as figuratively. The film claimed to be exploring "the darker, non-Hollywood aspects of the Mark Twain story."[158] The darkness of the story resonated with the darkness that enveloped award-winning Walter Lassally's striking cinematography. Here the sunlit world of boyhood that characterized so many of the earlier adaptations was replaced by a nightmarish world in which treacherous, terrifying human and natural forces lurked in the ever-present shadows. The darkness is not an invention of the filmmakers: it is central to the novel itself, as many scholars have recognized, even though it was usually neglected in film adaptations.

Toni Morrison has noted the darkness at the core of Huck's narrative: "References to death, looking at it or contemplating it, are numerous," she writes. "Huck yearns for death, runs from its certainty and feigns it," and "his deepest, uncomic feelings about his status as an outsider, someone 'dead' to society, are murmuring interludes of despair, soleness, isolation and unlove."[159] Robert Paul Lamb asks, "Why is Huck so morbid, depressed, guilt-ridden and lonely?" His answer is that "Huck's character is the product of Mark Twain's own lifelong depressiveness, loneliness, morbidity, and haunting sense of guilt.[160] Gary Scharnhorst tells us that "nightmares became part of a larger pattern of sleep disorders" the writer suffered his entire life."[161] Ron Powers reminds us that before his twelfth birthday, Sam Clemens had seen the bloody corpses of murder and manslaughter victims. He had seen a classmate drown, nearly drowned several times himself, watched a man burn to death, and seen another man killed by a lump of iron ore thrown at his head. Night in Hannibal gave cover to drunken sociopaths with revolvers. "Hannibal was 'a heavenly place for a boy,'" Powers writes, "and a hellish one as well."[162] The hellish nature of the world of the novel is on full display in this PBS adaptation, which is famous for being scrupulously faithful to the spirit of Twain's text. The reader knows that the world in which Huck and Jim live is a world marked by lynchings and gratuitous violence, one in which child abuse goes unpunished while runaway slaves are always punished. Huck may tell us in chapter 6 that "pap got too handy with his hick'ry, and I couldn't stand it. I was all over welts"; but in this film the viewer actually sees nine large, ugly red welts on Huck's back—as well as a lynching and at least two cold-blooded murders. The world in which Huck and Jim live is, in short, violent, cruel, and chaotic. This is the dimension of the book that appealed to the writer of this teleplay for this adaptation: "In adapting *Huckleberry Finn*," Gallo told the *New York Times*, "I was taken by its much darker side."[163]

Morrison points out that "nothing in society makes sense" to Huck. "Upper-class, churchgoing, elegantly housed families annihilate themselves in a psychotic feud, and Huck has to drag their corpses from the water . . . ; he sees the public slaughter of a drunk; he hears the vicious plans of murderers on a wrecked steamboat; he spends a large portion of the book in the company of . . . the fraudulent, thieving Duke and King who wield brutal power over him, just as his father did." At this point, Morrison asks, "If the emotional environment into which Twain places his protagonist is dangerous, then the leading question the novel poses for me is, What does Huck need to live without terror, melancholy and suicidal thoughts? The answer, of course, is Jim." Morrison writes, "It is in Jim's company that . . . even storms are beautiful and sublime, that real talk—comic, pointed, sad—takes place. Talk so free of lies it produces an aura of restfulness and peace unavailable anywhere else in the novel."[164]

Samm-Art Williams was on the same page as Morrison when he was asked by *Dial* magazine what appealed to him about playing the role of Jim. Williams replied, "The humanity. The relationship between Jim and Huck Finn at a time so bitter, at a time so inhumane. There was slavery, people were being hanged, but these two really cared for each other. It's really a love story."[165]

Both the *New York Times* and the *Hartford Courant* noted with approval Williams's portrayal of Jim as a surrogate father for Huck. The *Courant* wrote that "through the rite of passage on the river, Jim, and Huck eventually become much like father and son," while the *Times* described Williams's Jim as "a patient, loving father dealing with an imaginative, loveable son."[166] Williams takes seriously the task of guiding Huck, teaching him to be a better

Samm-Art Williams as Jim and Patrick Day as Huck in *Adventures of Huckleberry Finn* on PBS (1986). Movie-store Collection Ltd/ Alamy Stock Photo.

human being. The six-foot, six-inch actor is a tower of strength and reliability to the child who becomes his surrogate son. He is practical and competent, teaching Huck crucial survival skills during their journey (for example, it is Jim who collects branches to camouflage the raft, hiding it during the day). He is firmly resolute when he gives Huck multiple opportunities to admit that he is playing a childish trick on him after the fog. When he insists on staying with a wounded Tom Sawyer even if it means giving up his freedom, he is showing Huck what it means to be human being with a sense of responsibility for others. Williams's Jim communicates with Huck in speech that is clear and cogent, supportive and open, yet assertive. One critic wrote that his speech was "several cuts above the thick dialect Twain laboriously created for the novel's character."[167] I'd suggest, however, that Williams, who grew up in the small town of Burgaw, North Carolina, with a population of 1,700 and one stoplight, simply handled the dialect so deftly as to make viewers forget that he was speaking dialect at all.

The film foregrounds the violence and danger that Jim fears. Williams's Jim accurately gauges the peril he faces when he hears that people are saying he murdered Huck. "Lord have mercy!" he says, "Now I'm a runaway and a murderer, too. They'll string me up sure if they catch me." When Huck says he could cross the river to Illinois, he says, "Never thought about running to Illinois. Too many nigger hunters." Jim listens to slave hunters and their dogs on the shore with grim apprehension. He is understandably fearful when Huck goes ashore to trade some catfish he caught for store-bought goods like coffee: "Don't leave me here, Huck," he implores. Jim may love Huck as a son, but he also doesn't know how far he can trust him.

Against the backdrop of all of this violence and hypocrisy, the comfortable intimacy of Huck's quiet conversation with Jim about who made the stars is an interlude of caring, comfort, and calm. Clyde Haupt writes that "without question, this is the most beautiful scene in the film, and poetically beyond anything ever shown in any prior adaptation of Huck. . . . The harmony, peace, humor, and humanity of Huck and Jim on the raft together in a realistically credible mood, setting and atmosphere had never been done before."[168]

Critics noted, mainly with approval mixed with some surprise, the film's attentiveness to the rawness and barbarity of the world of the novel, as well as its overall fidelity to the book, a fidelity achieved, in part, by the producers' decision to seek the help of four eminent Twain scholars—Robert H. Hirst, Walter Blair, Hamlin Hill, and Justin Kaplan—and listen to their advice.[169] "Unlike other Huck adaptations," writes Haupt, "it has not been rarified into the stuff of story books, fairytales, children's fare, or even classic Hollywood movies."[170] Some complained that the film was too long and too slow. A critic for *People* magazine wrote that "the plot moves so slowly it doesn't appear to move at all."[171] But even critics who complained about the film's length or pacing had positive responses to Williams's portrayal of Jim. A writer for the Associated Press, for example, stated that "Williams manages to breathe humanity and dignity into the part" of Jim, while the *Hartford Courant* wrote that Williams's Jim is "a noble and heroic character."[172]

Nearly two decades after the series was made, it had still not been surpassed: in 2005 Mark Dawidziak and R. Kent Rasmussen, two of the most respected Twain scholars on the planet as well as experts on efforts to capture Twain's work on film and video, wrote, "If any screen version of *Huckleberry Finn* must be shown to students to help explain the novel, it should be this version— and only this version—until something finer comes along."[173] Williams can count among his many successes his sensitive portrayal of Jim in what is widely considered the best screen adaptation of *Huckleberry Finn* ever made.[174]

Jim fared well during the *Huck Finn* centennial. Meshach Taylor brought maturity and self-awareness to a role he had first played a decade earlier. The production in which he starred aspired to be scrupulously faithful to Mark Twain's words while enhancing their effectiveness through impressively creative choreographed movement and sound effects on a minimalist set. Eloquent and outspoken about the book's critique of racism, Taylor helped rescue Twain's novel from the jibes of critics who refused to recognize its satire. Taylor's personal connection to the slave past may have helped infuse his performance with sincerity and power: he was "the great great grandson of a man who was on the last slave ship to arrive in the country."[175] Ron Richardson's beautiful portrayal of Jim was also informed by Richardson's sense of connection to that past: Richardson's closeness to his grandfather, whose parents had been enslaved, made playing Jim intensely personal for him, helping him project his admiration for the character not only on Broadway but also in the Soviet Union and Japan. Samm-Art Williams's immersion in the slave past through previous acting and writing roles in dramas about slavery helped give him the confidence to play Jim with insight and grace. The fact that Williams had thought deeply about racist stereotypes as the author of a play about them helped reinforce his certainty about how little those demeaning images had to do with Jim. The performances of these three actors on stage and television deserved the accolades they received, along with the Emmy, Peabody, Tony, and Drama Desk awards that they earned. One hundred years after Mark Twain had introduced Jim to the world, these consummate professionals brought Jim alive with intelligence, sensitivity, and verve.

"Dignity Checks" and Three-Piece Suits: Courtney B. Vance (1993) and Charles Dumas (2001) Polish Jim's Image

Many talented actors had played Jim on stage and screen before Courtney Vance and Charles Dumas took on the challenge of doing so in 1993 and 2001, respectively. But no previous actors had the opportunity that Vance and Dumas had to shape the script from the inside: both of these highly educated and experienced actors were invited to share their visions of the role with their directors from the start, and both were empowered to change aspects of the production—even the words they spoke—if the ones they encountered in the script didn't fit their image of who Jim was and what he would say. In each production, both the actors and directors wanted to present Jim in a positive light; and in each case, this involved smoothing some of Jim's rough edges. . . .

Thirty-three-year-old Courtney Vance, who had earned a BA in history from Harvard and an MFA from the Yale School of Drama, was intrigued by the prospect of playing Jim in the Disney film *The Adventures of Huck Finn* (1993), written and directed by Stephen Sommers, in part to prove to himself and others that he could "convincingly portray an uneducated character" despite his background.[176] The Ivy League–educated, Tony-nominated actor had played a high school athlete, a New York conman, a Vietnam medic, and a range of Shakespearean characters—but he had never played a slave.

He quickly realized that playing Jim "was like walking through a minefield."[177] On the one hand, he had to be careful not to sound too refined, "You've got to recognize that he's an uneducated, unworldly character." But at the same time, he had to be careful not to sound ignorant or stupid: "It's 1993," he noted, and "having him talk in that field-hand dialect," Vance felt, had "very offensive connotations."[178] Vance himself seemed to buy into the contemporary mindset that registered heavy rural Black southern dialect as indicative of a lack of intelligence. He wanted to be true to the history that informed the story while portraying a Jim worthy of admiration and respect.

His concern during the filming, Vance said, was "how to protect Jim's dignity while preserving a sense of the time period we were working with." Vance was able to make Jim's "dignity" the lodestar of his interpretation of the role because director Stephen Sommers gave him more control over the script and the production as a whole than any director had previously given any actor. Vance even had a name for the process: "I'd analyze scenes, looking for ways to emphasize Jim's humanity and tone down the racial cliches. I called it 'making a dignity check.'"[179]

Sommers welcomed Vance's input: "The character of Jim has such dignity and humanity, and I was totally in synch with Courtney Vance on it. . . . I told Courtney, 'Anything you find offensive or worrisome, just tell me and we'll work it out.' We went over it scene by scene. We wanted it to be true to life but not offensive."[180] Vance's "dignity check" worked like this. Huck (played by twelve-year-old Elijah Wood) is enjoying his time at the Grangerfords and rejects Jim's entreaty that they leave, even though Jim (in this film) has been reenslaved there. Jim has just been whipped by an overseer. Huck, who hadn't realized what his self-indulgent decision meant for Jim, sees the multiple stripes on Jim's back and feels guilty about it. As Vance tells us, Huck "comes up to him and apologizes. As originally written, Jim is sitting on a stool, and he and Huck hug each other. But I suggested that the scene take place with Jim standing, because the difference in their heights reaffirms the idea that Huck is a boy and Jim is a man, but because he's white it's Huck who has all the rights. Also, having Jim stand makes him seem more assertive, less a victim."[181] Or take another case—an early scene on the raft in which Jim says, "Smell that, Huck? Smells like freedom. If it's Cairo I'm a free man." Vance tells us that the way Sommers "had blocked it in this scene was that we were building a wigwam on the raft together. And I said, 'That's not right, I should be whittling by myself or something.'" He and Sommers went back to their trailers, and about ten minutes later, Sommers knocked on Vance's door and said, "Courtney, you're right. This is the way to handle it."[182]

Producer Laurence Mark agreed with Vance and Sommers on these issues: "What we always kept in mind with Jim was one thing," he said. "No matter what indignities were going on around him, we tried to make certain that he would always retain his own dignity and stature as a human being."[183] Some changes in the plot help enhance Jim's characterization as autonomous and intelligent: for example, Allen Carey-Webb notes that in the film Jim runs away "with a plan and a map," exercising "planning and foresight."[184] Disney was gratified when previews of the film in predominantly Black neighborhoods got enthusiastic responses.

Jim in this film embodies an array of admirable qualities that include compassion, intelligence, agency, and an embrace of his quasi-parental role as Huck's guide in life. From the first time we meet him—in a scene in which he is acting as a fortune teller and seer—Vance's Jim is empathetic and caring as regards Huck, who has come to consult him about whether pap is about to return. "When your pap's around, he's always beatin' on you, ain't he?" he asks Huck, who winces silently. Jim tells him the "hairball thinks maybe you should skedaddle for a while, at least until your pap goes away again."

Vance's Jim is clearheaded and candid—if somewhat fatalistic—about the risks and dangers he faces himself. When Huck says he could be tarred and feathered for not turning Jim in, Jim says, "I could get lynched." In this film, Jim is clearly protecting himself rather than focused on Huck's well-being when he fails to tell Huck about pap's death. And Jim is attentive to what he needs to teach Huck about what's moral and right: when the two of them have a moment alone in the Wilks kitchen, Jim says to Huck, "And these are the girls we're letting those reptiles rob of their money!" In the book it is Huck who says these words to the reader. Giving Jim the line underscores his role as Huck's guide and mentor.

Tom Sawyer is eliminated from this production, and it is Huck

Courtney B. Vance as Jim and Elijah Wood as Huck in
The Adventures of Huckleberry Finn, 1993. Photo 12/Alamy Stock Photo.

alone who rescues Jim after the king and duke have sold him and
he has been jailed.

Huck steals the sheriff's keys to the jail and liberates Jim as a
heavily armed mob chases them both. As Huck and Jim are running to catch a steamboat, Huck gets shot. Jim insists on staying
with him, even as the steamboat captain calls out, "Last call for
Cairo and points north!" "Oh, my little friend," Jim says, lifting
Huck in his arms to carry him to safety, "I ain't goin' nowhere
without you. . . . I got to get you to a doctor." Huck protests,
"They'll catch you. They'll lynch you." "I don't care what happens
to me, Huck," Jim says. "I just want to get you well." As Carey-
Webb points out, "By making Huck (instead of Tom, as in the
novel) the injured boy that Jim must save, the climax of the film
becomes a reciprocating act of friendship, rather than a *deus ex
machina* revelation that Jim has all along been free."[185]

Running back toward the house with Huck, Jim runs right into the lynch mob, who angrily put a noose around his neck. Huck, distraught, says, "Don't kill him!" and tells Jim, "You're the best friend I ever had." Jim says, "You're the only friend I ever had." The lynch mob tightens the noose and has actually begun to hang him when Mary Jane Wilks arrives, shoots her gun in the air, and demands that the mob "let them both go—NOW!" The would-be lynchers cut Jim down. He and Huck exchange relieved smiles for a moment before Huck passes out and Jim registers extreme alarm and concern over his condition. In a penultimate scene where Huck wakes up in his sickbed, Jim enters the room dressed in a gold and beige silk brocade vest, a white shirt, and a beige silk tie. Kneeling on the floor next to Huck's bed, he gently explains that Miss Watson died a few weeks ago, and "she was so ashamed that she was going to sell me away from my wife and my children that she set me free in her will." He can't quite believe it and announces with quiet intensity, "I'm a free man, Huck. I'm a free man." Huck puts his hand in Jim's. Huck, who has been given five hundred dollars by the Wilks family ("for my trouble and chivalrousness"), decides to give the money to Jim to buy his family. One of the Wilks brothers shakes Jim's hand as they part. They exchange a smile. Huck disappears as the Widow prepares to take him back to St. Petersburg. When Jim realizes that Huck has run off to have more adventures instead of heading back with the Widow, he breaks into a long and deep belly laugh that shakes his whole frame.

Although neither Vance nor Sommers said so in public, they had to be aware that a frequent complaint when people challenged *Huckleberry Finn* in schools was that nobody in the book actually condemns slavery. Presumably, in an effort to head off such a complaint about the film, Sommers's script includes two iterations of how wrong slavery is—one from Jim and one, in the end, from the Widow Douglas. When Huck expresses shock that Jim plans to steal his wife and children if their owner won't sell them, Jim says, "They're my wife and my children. It ain't right that they be bought and sold. Someone gonna do it, ought to be me." Huck responds, "Listen to yourself. You hear what you're sayin'?" And Jim answers, "Sellin' people an' usin' em for slaves ain't right, Huck. . . . Don't ya see that to be true? Slavery ain't right. All men should be free." When the Widow Douglas arrives at the Wilks home in a scene near the end of the film, Huck says she probably thinks he's "low down" for trying to set Jim free. "Do you hate me?" he asks her. "Not at all, child," the Widow says. "I'm right proud of you. Just because an idea is popular, like slavery, don't make it right." Huck responds, "That's what Jim told me." As Carey-Webb observes, "The film shuns the complexities of irony and satire that make understanding the novel difficult. All points of view are simply and directly argued; offending passages are cut away."[186]

Vance's "dignity check" seems to have accomplished its purpose: "dignity" becomes the go-to word for describing his performance. "'Huck' Player Brings Dignity to Slave Character," read the headline in the *Fort Worth Star Telegram*.[187] The *Kansas City Star* ran the headline, "'Huckleberry Finn' Actor Finds Dignity in Difficult Role."[188] The *Salt Lake Tribune* reported that Vance brought "a subtle dignity and innocence—and not an ounce of self-righteousness—to the search for freedom."[189] The *Greenville (SC) News* wrote, "Vance is superb as Jim; he brings a perfect restraint and dignity to the role," while Gannett News Service wrote, "Vance is solid as Jim, lending him both dignity and humanity." The words *noble* and *proud* were also used to describe Vance's portrayal.[190]

For some reviewers, however, all of these efforts to make the film less offensive and more edifying compromised and distorted the venture. The *Chicago Tribune*, for example, wrote that "Jim (a grave and dignified Courtney B. Vance) is far too didactically presented." "Most of the changes have been made in the interest of a didactic, unmistakably right-minded approach to Twain's racial politics," this reviewer continued. "Twain's deadly irony is gone, replaced by windy, finger-wagging speeches on the evils of racism. The intent is less to instruct and provoke the viewer than to ennoble the film and its makers."[191] *Newsweek* wrote that the director had reconceived the story "as a slam-bang action movie with an antislavery message."[192]

With his pitch-perfect sense of irony, Twain had written a novel in which no characters see the morally bankrupt society in which they live for what it is. Therein lies a good part of the book's brilliance and power—for Twain's irony forces readers to think for themselves, passing judgment on the glaring hypocrisies and failures of what passed for "civilization" in the slave South. Sommers seems to have made the film for a target audience incapable of grasping that vision. One reviewer concluded that it was "aimed at the preteen crowd with its cuddly hero and proud Black companion."[193] In place of Twain's caustic satire, Sommers offers unobjectionable, flat-footed platitudes. But even reviews expressing lukewarm or negative reactions to the film as a whole usually had good things to say about Vance's performance. His "dignity check" seems to have worked. In some reviewers' eyes, it may have worked *too* well.

A one-time high school dropout from the South Side of Chicago, Charles Dumas's first real career was working for the Civil Rights Movement in the 1960s, first with the Congress for Racial Equality and then as Student Nonviolent Coordinating Committee project director in Leland, Mississippi, during the Mississippi Freedom Summer. Realizing that "we needed more lawyers in the

Charles Dumas as OLD JIM with Jim Baker as OLD HUCK standing next
to a trunk that belonged to Mark Twain in Edward Morgan's *Sounding
the River (Huckleberry Finn Revisited)* (2001) at the Milwaukee Rep.
Production photo by Jay Westhauser.

movement," Dumas went back to school, got his GED, and bachelor's, and earned a juris doctor degree from Yale Law School—before he found out that his real passion was for both social justice and the theater. Dumas, the first African American to receive tenure in the Penn State University School of Theatre, was teaching and directing at Penn State when writer and director Edward Morgan offered him the opportunity to play "OLD JIM" in the world debut of a postmodern adaptation of *Huckleberry Finn* at the Milwaukee Repertory Theater in 2001 called *Sounding the River (Huck Finn Revisited)*.[194] It would be the first Jim ever played in a three-piece suit.

In this distinctive production, there were two Jims—YOUNG JIM, played by a young actor from New York, Raphael Peacock, and

OLD JIM, played by Dumas. Morgan, then associate artistic director of the Milwaukee Rep, recalls that he began with a "simple idea": "If we retold the story with an OLD HUCK and OLD JIM watching the events as they occur, then we could 'editorialize' where necessary, we could emphasize modern parallels, and most importantly, we could try to bring an African-American point of view to the story. Jim, in effect, could speak much more for himself."[195]

A sloppy, disheveled, and shaggy old white man, OLD HUCK steals a trunk that belonged to Mark Twain and finds an antique oil lamp in it by whose light Twain wrote *Huckleberry Finn*. To his surprise, OLD JIM, wearing an old-fashioned three-piece suit, appears next to him, chiding, "I thought I told you conjurin' ain't for white folks." OLD HUCK had invited OLD JIM, now a success in life, to "relive our days of glory," and he had turned him down. But then OLD JIM decided that OLD HUCK would ruin his hard-earned reputation if he didn't come, so he changed his mind. In the years since their original story ended, Jim has gotten an education and is a family man with a successful career; Huck has largely remained the unkempt improviser he always was. OLD HUCK decides to light the magic lamp, and "a river of shadowy figures emerges from the void"—including HUCK and JIM, their younger selves. At that point, the original story that Twain wrote unfolds onstage, as OLD HUCK and OLD JIM observe it, comment on it, and on occasion, intervene in it.

If Courtney Vance had deployed a "dignity check" to make sure his portrayal of Jim avoided demeaning stereotypes, Charles Dumas had the chance to shape all aspects of the script and direction of *Sounding the River (Huck Finn Revisited)* from the start. Dumas, Morgan told me, "was a scholar and an intellectual and so really engaged the ideas like a dramaturg as well as an actor."[196]

Dumas and Morgan discussed the script at length after Dumas

had been cast, before rehearsals began, as well as throughout the production. "It was very collaborative," Morgan recalls. "We wanted to find a balance with a tone that matched with Twain, was modern enough, was ironic/witty enough, but also real in responding to the ugliness of the history." Dumas "contributed ideas and even some lines that ended up in the script." Jim's voice in the show was amplified through the singing of baritone BLUES-MAN Cedric Turner, becoming "in many ways a kind of voice for Jim throughout the show." Morgan adds that "as young Huck and Jim are carried downstream, trusting, and relying on each other more and more," Black and white musical traditions, too, "began to flow together."[197]

OLD JIM and OLD HUCK voice very different perspectives as they comment on the scenes Twain crafted. When they watch a stern Miss Watson urging her sister to give Huck "another good hiding" as she tries to scare him about the "fiery furnace" that awaits sinners like himself, OLD HUCK calls her "a pillar of Pres-byterianism," while OLD JIM calls her "a right old Southern bitch." When OLD HUCK recalls praying, without success, for fishhooks, OLD JIM recalls that "I prayed for freedom and that pious old viper tried to sell me down river."[198]

OLD JIM has second thoughts about revisiting their adven-tures. "Seeing it all spring to life again; I swear it just makes my skin crawl. . . . Slavery days. And Miss Watson. And Jennie, wearin that house-mammy smile—*yes'm dis, yes'm dat.* I spent my whole life going forward—trying to get ahead; trying to provide for my family; to help my race—one struggle after the next and all the time pushing forward. So now a part of me just doesn't want to look back. Not this close." But when OLD HUCK conjures Mark Twain's "magic hat" and gives it to Jim, OLD JIM reconsiders. "You mean—we can mess around with this thing?" OLD JIM asks incredulously. "Why not?" OLD HUCK responds. "I conjured it, didn't I? I'm in charge here." He gives OLD JIM the hat and says he can be Judge Thatcher—and, indeed, OLD JIM does "become" Judge Thatcher at a key point in the plot.[199]

OLD JIM, as Judge Thatcher, lets Pap know that the court's unlikely to give him custody of Huck and access to his money: he tells Pap, "Considering your criminal record, your dementia, chronic alcoholism, and child abuse, not to mention your remarkably pungent stink, it's possible the court might be persuaded in [Miss Watson's] favor." OLD JIM, as Judge Thatcher, loses patience with Pap's rants and has him jailed. When OLD JIM is clearly unhappy about being called an offensive racial slur, OLD HUCK has an inspiration: "Hey, I got an idea. Let's just eliminate *that word.*" He waves a hand over the lamp intoning, "No more 'nigger'—the word does not exist." But OLD JIM tells him not to do that. "But it offends you, Jim," OLD HUCK says, "so maybe I can fix it. I mean, why the hell not?" OLD JIM replies, "I'll tell you why not. The word offends me because bigotry offends me, and bigotry's alive and well. But if we're going back to slavery days, then we're going back, and I don't want it prettied up."[200]

In one scene, Jim and his wife, Jennie, embrace and kiss, while the BLUESMAN plays guitar in the background." "Now this is more like it," says OLD JIM, as he watches them. When OLD HUCK says, "I don't recall this," OLD JIM responds, "Yeah, there's a lot you wouldn't recall, 'cause there's a lot you never noticed."[201]

Most of the scenes that OLD HUCK and OLD JIM witness transpire much as Twain wrote them in the novel, using his exact words—but with occasional changes that underline Jim's forethought and agency. For example, Jim shows up on Jackson's Island with a "crude map of the Mississippi and Ohio Rivers with Slave and Free States and Territories" as well as a clear plan to head to Cairo (much as Vance had in the Disney film). It is Jim who proposes that Huck go with him down the river ("We both got to keep low. We kin help each other out.") OLD HUCK and OLD JIM discuss why Jim kept Pap's death from Huck as they watch the scene in the floating house unfold. When OLD HUCK suggests it was "'cause I was your ticket to freedom," OLD JIM responds, "No, 'cause I was your guardian angel . . . I was the only one you had. Why do you think I stayed with you even when I knew you might turn me in?"²⁰²

Another example is an exchange between OLD JIM and OLD HUCK after Huck and Jim debate why a Frenchman "don't talk like a man." OLD HUCK says to OLD JIM, "How can you stand to see yourself so ignorant?" OLD JIM replies, "I won the argument." "OK, fine," OLD HUCK says after this exchange, "But sometimes [Mark Twain] made you seem kinda smart and sometimes just as dumb as an ox." OLD JIM responds, "That's right. He wrote the story *like you saw it*. And half the time you looked at me all you saw was a dumb ox." Scenes involving Jim that Huck described in the novel here take place before our eyes: for example, we see and hear Jim trying to get the king to speak French.²⁰³

The brutality of slavery is conveyed by a scene in which one of the slave catchers is seen "pulling several RUNAWAYS on a chain leash. Their wrists are bound, and they are bloody and shivering." It is also conveyed through a haunting song (whose words and music were both written by Morgan) called "Many Thousand Gone" (but not the folk song of that title). Sung slowly, with intense emotion by the BLUESMAN, the song is a poignant and moving reminder of the violence and trauma that lie behind everything the audience has seen on stage.²⁰⁴

Things begin to get increasingly wild and metafictional toward the end as all of a sudden, characters from the two separate time frames begin to interact. OLD JIM realizes that "somethin's wrong. We've lost control of this thing." SAM (Sam Clemens) arrives, and acknowledges that he's the one who set the whole plot in motion to begin with—although not before confessing that at that point, he's "not in control of this thing either." With SAM, OLD JIM plots a new ending and SAM compliments him on the way he figured out to end the play: "Well done, Jim. A graceful resolution and carried out with style." JIM gets to reunite with his family.[205]

During the process of creating the play with Morgan, Dumas "got into the community a lot," as Morgan recalls: "He went to churches and other gatherings and spoke about the show and really created interest in the play in the Black community. He really believed in the project and particularly wanted people of color to see it."[206] Morgan's ambitious goal had been to open "a fresh window on this great story."[207] Critics' positive responses suggest that he largely succeeded.[208]

Jim on the Danube: Serge Nubret (1968) and Jacky Ido (2012) Reflect Changing German Attitudes toward Race

When German production companies set out to film *Huckleberry Finn*, first in 1968 and then again in 2012, the Danube served as the Mississippi, and the filming was done in Romania. But as far as Jim is concerned, the two productions could not have been more different. In 1968, Serge Nubret's Jim was a stereotypical, attentive servant; in 2012, Jacky Ido's Jim was a fierce fighter who protected those he loved with combative physical strength. The distance between these two portrayals reflects, in part, changing German attitudes toward race. The film from 1968 was directed by a man whose career had thrived under the Nazis and who became adept, after the war, at remaking Nazi films with their political content removed. On this occasion he eliminated virtually all of the novel's antiracist critique.[209] Between 1968 and 2012, Germany witnessed from afar the rise of the Civil Rights and Black Power Movements, and the Black German community engaged in its own fight against racism, while German youth had become fascinated with hip-hop and rap and the boldness and confidence they entailed.[210] In addition, the film from 2012 was made after Barack Obama was elected president.[211] Serge Nubret may have been directed to play Jim as an acquiescent house servant in 1968, but once he got on the river with Huck, it would have been hard for any director to hide his strength and power: at the time he was cast in the film, Nubret held the title of the "World's Most Muscular Man." Despite Nubret's memorable physical presence on the screen, it would be Jacky Ido, a French rapper-turned-actor, who would finally give those who had longed for a truly assertive and aggressive Jim what they had been hoping for in 2012, when he played Jim in the only film version of the novel with a screenplay written by a writer of color.

Born in Anse-Bertrand, Guadeloupe, Serge Nubret had moved with his parents to Paris when he was twelve, returning to Guadeloupe in 1958 to avoid being drafted in the Algerian War, and it was there that he discovered bodybuilding, winning the title of Mr. Guadeloupe, and two years later, the title of the "World's Most Muscular Man." Nubret returned to Paris in the early 1960s and was cast in an Italian–West German spy film and two Italian sword-and-sandal films—adventure films set in classical antiquity that featured bodybuilders.[212]

It is likely that it was his fourth film, released in 1964, that caught the eye of German director Wolfgang Liebeneiner. *Un gosse de la butte* (also known as *Rue des cascades*), directed by Maurice Delbez and based on the novel *Alain et le nègre* by Robert Sabatier, was a love story involving a middle-aged white woman and a handsome younger Black jazz musician. It was also a story about the relationship between the musician and the woman's ten-year-old son, Alain. This film, which views racism through the eyes of a child and focuses on a friendship between a Black man and a white boy, may well have served as Nubret's audition for the role of Jim.[213]

The four-part miniseries featuring Nubret that aired on German television on consecutive Sundays in early 1968—called *Tom Sawyers und Huckleberry Finns Abenteuer*—denuded the story of its social critique and ignored the issue of racism almost entirely.[214] It turns out that removing social and political content was a familiar project for Liebeneiner. Although he had been a successful director of melodramatic fare under the Nazis, after the war he remade a number of films of the Nazi era that depoliticized the originals.[215] He was on familiar ground, then, eliminating virtually all of Twain's social criticism from the story. At the start of episode 4, the episode in which Jim figures prominently, Jim is a coachman who works for Miss Watson and the Widow Douglas, driving Huck to school in a carriage, waiting on table at home, and acting as Huck's valet. We don't learn that he is a slave, in fact, until Huck meets him on Jackson's Island, when he admits that he has run off because Miss Watson planned to sell him. He tells Huck he wants to get to a free state, work, and buy his family, and the two set off down the Danube together. The series had a rather disconcerting habit of taking a memorable exchange between Jim and Huck in the novel—such as the conversation about where stars come from—and turning it into a highly improbable conversation between Huck and Pap.

But whatever else one might say about this sloppily constructed mash-up of Twain's Mississippi writings, Nubret's Jim is the best-dressed Jim ever to appear on screen. Also the least dressed. When we first see him, costume designer Jacqueline Guyot has dressed him in vermillion coachman's livery with velvet trim and a top hat. When he is giving Huck a thorough scrubbing, he is wearing a dramatically patterned gold satin vest. In the

Serge Nubret, holder of the title "World's Most Muscular Man," as Jim with costar Marc di Napoli as Huck in the German TV miniseries *Tom Sawyers und Huckleberry Finns Abenteuer* (1968).

next scene—in which he is whisking dust off Huck's shoulders—he is wearing an elegant silver and gray vest with a cravat. However, from the moment he and Huck meet on Jackson's Island, Jim is bare-chested, wearing only a red scarf and khaki-colored pants—a state of undress that does full justice to his stunning physique, which dominates the screen during much of the final section of the series.

The inoffensive and pedestrian broadcast got good reviews from Germany's weekly television magazine and received the Perla Television Prize in Milan. Frustratingly mediocre as it was, it was so successful that it was rebroadcast on German TV "just a year later due to high demand, which was unusual at the time."[216]

Fast forward to German director Hermine Huntgeburth's very different adaptation, *Die Abenteuer des Huck Finn* (2012), with a

Jacky Ido as Jim watches with Huck (Leon Seidel) and Tom (Louis Hofmann) as slave traders unload a coffle of slaves at the St. Petersburg docks in *Die Abenteuer des Huck Finn* (2012). TCD/Prod.DB/Alamy Stock Photo.

screenplay by Sascha Arango.[217] When she wanted to find an actor who could portray Jim as powerful and assertive, she immediately thought of her favorite Masai warrior. Huntgeburth had cast Jacky Ido in a film she directed in 2005, *Die Weisse Massai* (*The White Masai*), in which a Swiss woman who goes to Kenya on vacation falls in love with a Masai warrior played by Ido.[218]

Although the film in which Ido plays Jim was produced for a young audience, the brutality of slavery is front and center. The violence inflicted on slaves is presented in all its harshness. At one point Huck is shocked to see the stripes on Jim's back: "They did this to you?" he asks incredulously. And the anguish of slave family separations is also presented clearly. In an early scene set on the St. Petersburg docks, Ido's Jim, a house servant in the home of the Widow Douglas and Miss Watson who has come to the docks to hunt for Huck, watches some slave traders unloading a coffle of slaves for auction.

He spots his wife with their child in her arms among the slaves about to be auctioned off. He screams her name, and she screams "Jim!" as she tries to escape the men who restrain her. Ido pushes through the crowd, shouting at her in an African language. As the slave traders try to keep him from his family, he picks up a ten-foot log from the dock in a rush of adrenalin and swings it at them, temporarily knocking them out. He fights ferociously but is outnumbered. The slave traders are outraged, but when Huck shows up and announces that Jim is *his* slave, they back off. Later in the film, even though his hands are chained, Jim will prevent Pap from recapturing Huck by throwing his full body weight against him, knocking him to the ground.

On those occasions when he is not aggressively trying to protect people he loves, Ido's Jim is surprisingly elegant: he eats his dinner in his room at a little table set with a crystal wine glass, a linen napkin, and a bottle of wine; indeed, he takes those items when he runs off and uses them when he's camped out on Jackson's Island. These accoutrements are a bit jarring, but perhaps their function was to show Jim as "civilized" to offset his violent outburst at the docks and prevent him from being associated with a different stereotype, that of the savage Black beast.

"Mark Twain is one of my heroes," Ido once told an interviewer. I love everything he did."[219] Ido, who was born in Ouagadougou, Burkina Faso, first made his mark as a rapper, slam poet, and musician in France, where he lives: under the pseudonym John Pucc'Chocolat, he appeared on French slam poet Grand Corps Malade's best-selling album *Midi 20* (2006) and played a sold-out stadium tour throughout France. As an actor, before performing as Jim, he was best known for having played the projectionist Marcel in Quentin Tarantino's *Inglourious Basterds* and the heartthrob lead in *Die Weisse Massai*. He also played an uncredited role in Tarantino's *Django Unchained* the same year he appeared in this German adaptation of *Huckleberry Finn.*[220]

Throughout the film, Ido's Jim is self-assured, confident, smart, and blunt: "I'm not being a slave any more. I'm an American like you," he asserts on Jackson's Island. When Huck and Jim are playing poker, Jim beats Huck's full house with his royal flush. It is Jim who plays a practical joke on Huck rather than the other way around: he pretends he doesn't know how to swim, lets Huck "teach" him, and then pretends to drown.

Jim is clear about his goals. When he tells Huck he plans to steal his children if the master won't sell them, and Huck says that would be breaking the law, Jim responds, "White man's law." After a *deus ex machina* ending that brings Twain himself into the story, a voiceover narrator tells us that Jim got to a free state, found work, and eventually bought his wife and son their freedom. Reviewers singled out Ido's performance for praise. Reviewers also made clear that the central theme of the film was slavery, a challenging topic that the filmmakers were credited with having addressed with sensitivity, helping to teach children important values.[221] The irony that is so central to the original is completely missing here: Jim is a hero of Twain' s novel in part because of, not despite, the fact that he is illiterate, constrained in word and action, and deeply aware of the precarity of his position. One can view Jacky Ido's confident, literate, and powerful Jim as perhaps the Jim that many critics of Twain's novel longed for and implicitly demanded.

Whether they were evoking Jim's intelligence, kindness, decency, paternal qualities, determination, strength, or resourcefulness, each of these thirteen actors found him to be an admirable human being.[222] They also defended and shaped his character according to the needs of Cold War politics and the roiling debates over the novel at its centennial. Most of all, and this needs to be stressed, these actors drew their interpretations from the source—the admirable character Mark Twain created in 1885.

CHAPTER 6

———

Afterlives

Jim in Translation

J IM CAN BE READ and heard conversing with Huck in at least sixty-seven languages: Afrikaans, Albanian, Alemannic, Arabic, Armenian, Assamese, Basque, Bengali, Bulgarian, Burmese, Catalan, Chinese, Chuvash, Croatian, Czech, Danish, Dutch-Flemish, English, Esperanto, Estonian, Finnish, French, Georgian, German, Greek, Gujarati, Hebrew, Hindi, Hungarian, Icelandic, Indonesian, Italian, Japanese, Kazakh, Kirghiz, Korean, Latvian, Lithuanian, Macedonian, Malay, Malayalam, Marathi, Moldavian, Norwegian, Oriya, Persian, Polish, Portuguese, Punjabi, Romanian, Russian, Serbo-Croatian, Sinhalese, Slovak, Slovenian, Spanish, Swedish, Tamil, Tatar, Telugu, Thai, Turkish, Turkmen, Ukrainian, Uzbek, Vietnamese, and Yiddish. In many of these languages, there are multiple translations: Selina Lai-Henderson, for example, has identified as many as ninety Chinese-language translations of the novel.[1]

But what does Jim say in these languages? How have translators around the world presented Jim's character and his role in the novel? How have they presented his speech? The choices translators make reflect their understanding of Twain's most famous Black character and of the mid-nineteenth-century "Missouri negro dialect" that he speaks. They also reflect the translators' grasp of the novel's satiric critique of racism, as well as the dynamics of race and marginalization in the translators' own countries.[2]

Translating the Plot, Losing Jim

Ronald Jenn has noted that "through his distinctive speech pattern, Jim sounds expectedly illiterate but his vibrant language allows him to be a full-blown character speaking from the margins of society, from which he contrives rhetorical survival strategies to cope with the hardships of bondage and the immediate dangers of flight."[3] But translators have often simply omitted much of what Jim says and does in the novel by cutting key passages or lines. Whether these omissions stem from state censorship, a translator's view of what is important and what is not, or the sheer difficulty of translating Jim's dialect and the complex wealth of cultural codes inscribed both in his words and in the novel, they significantly change the reader's understanding of who Jim is and what motivates him.

In the first Japanese translation of the novel, published by Kuni Sasaki in 1921, many scenes key to illuminating positive dimensions of Jim's character are eliminated.[4] For example, Sasaki simply omits the scene in which Jim rebukes Huck as "trash" for playing a practical joke on him after their separation in the fog, as well as the scene in which Jim recalls with shame the time he beat his little daughter for disobeying before realizing she was deaf. Both scenes are crucial to understanding the seriousness of Jim's parental role, not only to his own child but as a surrogate parent to Huck. The deletions significantly diminish Jim's complexity and his humanity. "The result of such deletions," Tsuyoshi Ishihara writes, "is that Sasaki failed to introduce Jim as a caring father who has both family and dignity, turning him into a merely obedient and somewhat foolish character."[5] Sasaki also mistranslates Jim's comments about buying his own children out of slavery, having Jim talk about buying "two children or so" after he is free, thereby turning a parent distraught at being separated from his children into a would-be slave owner!

These distortions and the disregard for Jim's role as a parent and surrogate parent that they reflect may have been shaped by several factors. One is a nationalist ideology of Japanese supremacy that fostered a Japanese propensity to disregard the humanity of imperial Japan's own marginalized racial and ethnic minorities during this period (including the indigenous Ainu people, Burakumins, and Koreans) and that also helped justify the country's harsh colonial rule over Korea at the time.[6] As Ishihara tells us, they may also reflect the fact that the Japanese at this time, who generally identified with white Americans, had absorbed white America's racism toward Blacks in the process, rejecting people whom white Americans scorned.[7] He notes that "even though Sasaki had a more liberal and democratic mind-set than most of his contemporaries, he probably shared some of their prejudices against blacks and therefore minimized the importance of Jim in *Huckleberry Finn*."[8] (It is fortunate that a much more accurate Japanese translation of *Huckleberry Finn* by Tameji Nakamura appeared in 1941. It was this inexpensive paperback edition from a prestigious Japanese publisher that a young boy named Kenzaburō Ōe read in a remote mountain village on the island of Shikoku. Ōe, who would go on to win the Nobel Prize in Literature, credits *Huckleberry Finn* with having inspired his first novel, *The Catch*, which is about two young boys charged with guarding a Black American airman who crashed on their island in World War II.)[9]

Sasaki is not alone in eliminating the fog scene or the scene involving Jim's daughter. The entire fog episode is missing in nineteen German translations of the novel published in between 1890 and 2010.[10] It is also missing in M. Teresa Monguió's Spanish translation (1957), which also cuts the scene in which Jim berates himself for having slapped his little daughter before he realized that she was deaf.[11] This latter scene is also missing from German translations by Henny Koch (1890), Ulrich Johannsen and Marie Schloss (1913), and Fred Wübben (1951), as well as the first French translation by William-Little Hughes (1886).[12] The importance of both of these scenes for understanding Jim's character cannot be overstated. The fog scene—the trick Huck plays on Jim, Jim's pointed rebuke, and the apology from Huck that ensues—shows Jim teaching Huck (as his real father never did) how to be a responsible human being who treats others with respect. It is a key moment of assertiveness and self-confidence on Jim's part and is a very rare incident in nineteenth-century American fiction in which an enslaved Black man reproaches a white person. The scene in which Jim is distraught to recall his treatment of his four-year-old daughter is equally significant. As Arthur Egon Kunst writes, "It is the point where Jim's humanity comes most fully alive."[13] Cutting this scene also eliminates Huck's surprise, in chapter 23, at the idea that Jim "cared just as much for his people as white folks does for theirn"—a key line central to the book's critique of slavery and racism. Although many factors may have shaped these omissions, it is worth noting that during the period when these translations were published, many European nations were pursuing colonialist agendas in Africa—agendas bolstered by ideologies of white supremacy that denied Africans their full humanity.

Other scenes important to Jim's character development are also cut from several of these translations: the hair ball scene is eliminated from Monguió's Spanish translation and Hughes's French translation; the scene in which Jim tells the story of being ridden by witches is cut from Hughes's French version as well as a Korean translation from 2008 by Kim Uk Dong. The debate about why a Frenchman can't talk like a man is cut in German translations by Wübben (1951) and Franz Geiger (1947), a Chinese translation by Ren Aoshuang (2003), and Kim's Korean translation, among others.[14] Jim's excitement about nearing Cairo was excised from Wolfram Gramowski's German translation (1954), as well as from Ren Aoshuang's Chinese translation and Olav Angell's Norwegian translation (2003); the conversation between Huck and Jim in the swamp where Jim has been hiding near the Grangerfords' home, where we see an example of slave cooperation between Jim and the Grangerfords' slave Jack and where Jim describes how he recovered and repaired the raft, was deleted from German translations by Koch, Geiger, Wübben, and Gramowski; a Spanish translation by Simón Santainé (1957); and a Russian version edited by Korneĭ Chukovsky (1933). And the discussion of Solomon is cut from German translations by Geiger and Wübben, as well as from Kim's Korean translation and from Arabic translations by Shawqi Alameer (1992), Kawthar Mahmoud Mohammad (2012), and Nasr Abdulrahman (2015).[15] Although each translator had his or her own reasons for eliminating these scenes, all of these instances show the translator's failure to appreciate the significance of Twain's inclusion of them in the first place and the nuanced aspects of Jim's character they illuminate.

The book's first French translator was Irish-born William-Little Hughes (who also wrote under the pen name of William O'Gorman). Hughes, a French government official who worked as chief clerk in the foreign press department of the Ministry of the Interior, translated the book as part of a series for young people— *Bibliothèque nouvelle de la jeunesse*—for the Paris-based publishing house Hennuyer. French laws passed in 1881 making school compulsory, free, and secular helped fuel a market for children's books in the late nineteenth century; in particular, there was a demand for prize and gift books given as awards to children who demonstrated good behavior and diligence.[16] With its handsome, full-color embossed cover, Hughes's translation, reviewed in the "gift book" section of *La Revue des Deux Mondes* when it came out in 1886, was clearly designed to be a book that could be awarded as a prize to students in recognition of their excellence.[17] But Hughes eliminated so many passages involving Jim—including the hair ball scene, Jim's narrative about being ridden by witches, and his story about his little daughter—that the result was Jim's misrepresentation in French as a stereotyped, one-dimensional figure.[18]

Arthur de Gobineau's infamous *Essay on the Inequality of Human Races*, whose impact on the United States was discussed in Chapter 2, originally appeared in France in 1853–55 and helped justify treating Black people there as inferior and relegating them to subservient positions (slavery had been abolished before its publication). Even in scenes that Hughes left in place, he cut comments of Jim's that did not make Jim look sufficiently deferential. Take, for example, the conversation that Jim has with Huck in the swamp at the Grangerfords in chapter 18. In addition to showing great practical sense and resourcefulness as he describes how he gained possession of, patched, and refurbished the raft, Jim also criticizes Huck as well as himself when he explains how the raft got away from them. In the original, Jim tells Huck, if "we warn't so sk'yerd, en ben sich punkin-heads, as de sayin' is, we'd a seed de raf'."[19] But the line does not fit Hughes's image of Jim as subservient, so he eliminates it. As Judith Lavoie points out, in Hughes's view, "Jim doit parler, penser et agir comme un serviteur, ou un serviteur ne critique pas son patron, il ne le traite pas d'imbécile" (Jim must speak, think, and act like a servant, but a servant doesn't criticize his boss or treat him like a fool). In the original, Jim tells Huck that he told the slaves who wanted their raft that "she don't b'long to none uv um, but to you en me."

Tellingly, Lavoie notes, Hughes changes Jim's line to "le radeau n'était à aucun d'eux, mais à vous" (the raft doesn't belong to any of them but to you). In the original, it is Jim who blows the whistle on the two con artists who unmasked him as a runaway and sold him back into slavery; in Hughes's version, Jim's role in apprehending the scammers is erased. In scene after scene, then, in subtle cuts like these, Hughes denies Jim agency, autonomy, and respect.[20]

Hughes robs Jim of his enterprise, intelligence, assertiveness, and commitment to justice, giving us instead, in Lavoie's view, a big, foolish child—a model of submission and stupidity. But that is not the Jim that Twain wrote. That Jim, Lavoie tells us in her groundbreaking study, *Mark Twain et la parole noire* (2002), is "intelligent, autonome, débrouillard, autoritaire, [et] sensible" (intelligent, autonomous, resourceful, authoritative, [and] sensitive).[21] The Jim that Mark Twain created would have to wait for Suzanne Nétillard's impressive translation of 1948 to be introduced to French readers with his humanity intact.[22]

In some translations, key scenes involving Jim, though not cut, are altered so drastically as to obscure the reason Twain included them in the first place. Such is the case with the scene where Huck returns to Jim after the fog in a Hindi translation by Omkar Sharad (2018).[23] Seema Sharma writes that Sharad depicts "Jim's joy at being reunited with [Huck], but misses the climactic moment of Jim's displeasure with Huck and the latter's apology to Jim for playing a trick on him."[24] Jim's crucial rebuke of Huck for having fooled with his emotions and the importance of this interaction to Huck's moral education are simply lost. (Missing are Huck's apology, Jim's rebuke, and Huck's pledge to himself, "I didn't do him no more mean tricks, and I wouldn't have done that one if I'd a knowed it would make him feel that way.")[25] Instead, as Sharma tells us, this translation "strikes an erroneous note by paraphrasing the scene as an uncomplicated reconciliation between the two: 'मुझे देखकर ईश्वर को धन्यवाद देने व प्रार्थना करने लगा। फरि हम लोगों ने नावों की सफाई की' (On seeing me Jim began to thank God and offer his prayers. Then we both cleaned the boat)."[26] Sharma adds that even though this translation "mentions Jim's excitement at the prospect of reaching Cairo," it glosses over "Jim's plans for freeing his family," something that is crucial in sensitizing readers in India "to what family life was for enslaved people and how slavery took away the natural rights of parents over their own children and turned them into the property of their white masters." This edition, as well as a second Hindi version Sharma has analyzed, simply omits "Jim's emotional journey—his longing for his family, his remorse at hitting his daughter, and other such incidents that humanize [him]."[27]

Some of the nuances of the novel's language seem to elude translators across the board. An example that Kunst provides from his examination of twenty-four translations in French, German, Portuguese, Russian, and Spanish is how translators deal with what Jim says as he tries to prevent Huck from revealing his presence to passing slave catchers. Jim delivers several "mortal thrusts to the softer part of Huck's conscience," Kunst reminds us, when he says, "'Jim won't ever forgit you, Huck; you's de bes' fren' Jim ever had, en you's de ony fren' Jim's got now.'" Kunst emphasizes that it will be "the memory of Huck that Jim treasures, not the memory of the service done him." In the translations that Kunst examined, only about half of the versions render the line the way Twain wrote it; the others change "won't ever forgit you" to "won't ever forget it." Kunst asks us to "witness the difference in emotiveness" between the Spanish "Jim no olvidará este servicio" (Jim will not forget this service) and "Jim jamás te olvidará, Huck" (Jim will never forget you, Huck), or between the French "Jim ne l'oubliera pas, Huck" (I will never forget it, Huck) and "Jim ne t'oubliera jamais, Huck!" (I will never forget you, Huck).[28]

Winston Kelley observes that when the fog scene *is* included in German translations, all translators fail to convey the full significance of the name Jim calls Huck: "trash." Jim, in effect, calls Huck "white trash" for his shameful behavior. But, as Kelley points out, "in Germany, where the dominating ideology until the end of World War II had identified white citizens as a 'master race,' no concept corresponding to 'poor white trash' evolved." For that reason, perhaps, the twenty-two German translations between 1890 and 2010 that Kelley examined translate the word as various kinds of debris but don't convey Jim's powerful challenge to Huck's entitled and arrogant efforts to toy with his very real emotions.[29]

In Jim's story of why he ran off, the first Chinese translation (by Zhang Duosheng and Guo Zhen) omits Jim's reference to a slave trader hanging around, thus obscuring the rationale for his flight.[30] Kim Uk Dong's Korean translation includes Jim's story about his financial setbacks, but it inexplicably omits his important declaration that "I's rich now, come to look at it. I owns mysef, en I's wuth eight hund'd dollars."[31] That omission manages to turn a complex and memorable scene into a mere shaggy dog story.

By way of contrast, most Soviet translations leave Jim's line in the text as "I am my own master" or "Jim now is his own master" or "I belong to myself," according to Cassio de Oliveira's back translation (translation back into English, allowing us to compare it with the words Twain wrote.)[32] Given the Russian fascination with Jim (even giving him dual billing in the title alongside Huck in an early translation) and given the Soviet interest in using the novel as a vehicle for criticizing racism in the United States, it is not surprising that Russian translators were attentive to the significance of this important line.

Another key scene involving Jim—his debate with Huck about King Solomon—proved problematic for translators in Francisco Franco's fascist Spain, where the "filtering mechanism of state censorship . . . functioned to keep out the ideas that the regime deemed undesirable for its moral education," according to Julia Lin.[33] In an ingenious thesis that makes use of the templates state censors used to assess translations, Lin shows that in 1968, when censors were asked to approve for classroom use a reprint edition of Monguió's previously approved translation from 1957, they objected so strongly to Jim's criticisms of Solomon that they disqualified the translation from use in schools and deemed it appropriate only for adult readers. Lin also observes that due to the Franco regime's resistance to anything that would lead young people to be skeptical of religion, the censor objected to many of Huck's comments on the Bible, demanding that "the publisher omit Huck's comment on not caring about Moses, since he had been dead for a long time" and also Huck's "remark that hogs prefer going to church more than people do."[34] As it turns out, a later censor reviewed the work of this censor and opined that "the negative depictions of religion in the narrative are so exaggerated that the readers are unlikely to perceive these as realities, let alone to imitate them," and he reauthorized Monguió's translation for use in schools.[35]

Jim's comments on King Solomon were controversial in Egypt in 1958 for different reasons, as Mariam Abdulmalik tells us. In this section, where Jim and Huck are debating the lifestyles of kings, Jim wonders whether the biblical King Solomon was as wise as he was reputed to be, since he lived with a harem of all his wives and children. Abdulmalik tells us that Mahir Naseem, in his translation from 1958, translated "Solomon had [a harem]" as "Kings had 'harem.'"[36] Abdulmalik writes that Naseem "changed the image from . . . King Solomon into an unidentified king . . . for religious reasons, since it is unacceptable and disgraceful to talk about prophets and religious figures as [Twain does in his] satire and criticism."[37] As a result, the later discussion of Solomon had to go as well. (The Solomon discussion—naming names—was restored to a new Arabic translation produced by Nasr Abdulraman that came out in 2015.)[38] Religious sensibilities shaped other changes related to Jim made by Arabic translators. For example, as Abdulmalik tells us, when Jim is in severe pain from the rattlesnake bite, he does not consume whiskey in two of three Arabic translations she examined due to the prohibition on drinking alcohol in Islam. Shawqi Alameer, for example, translates *whiskey* as *the drink*. And Jim does not eat bacon in any of the Arabic translations due to Islam's prohibition on pork: he eats "leg meat" or meat.[39] Hamada Kassam notes that even though the period in which Naseem worked was viewed as the "golden age of literary translation" in Egypt, state censorship forced Naseem to omit all ideas that had religious or political meanings or implications.[40] Naseem didn't need censors to tell him to cut the sign Jim was forced to wear by the duke that read "Sick Arab—but harmless when not out of his head." That offensive sentence—or at least the word *Arab*—is eliminated from Arabic translations of the book.

While translators often omitted several of Jim's scenes and lines, some of them added lines and phrases of their own. But rather than adding features that emphasized Jim's significance, translators tended to add lines that demeaned him and diminished his importance. Such was the case in two early German translations, as Raphael Berthele observes: lines were added "mainly to generate an effect of simplemindedness."[41] "In a clear example of racist attribution of stupidity to Jim," Berthele writes, translator

Henny Koch (1892) "has Jim think that African-American people are not seen at night (Jim refers to himself in the 3rd person): '*Ero denken, Nacht sein schwarz, Jim sein auch schwarz, werden also nix gesehen.*' . . . [He think, night be black, Jim be black, too, will not be seen]."[42] And in a German translation from 1913, translators Ulrich Johannsen and Marie Schloss have Jim express the self-evident fact that he "usually walks with his feet."[43]

These additions to German translations from 1892 and 1913 reflect the anti-Black racism that developed in connection with Germany's colonial exploits in Africa during the period when these books were published, a phenomenon that Robert W. Kestling has examined. Kestling notes that between 1885 and 1918, anti-Black racism developed among Germans who colonized German South West Africa, Togo, the Cameroons, and German East Africa.[44] Much as the idea of Black inferiority was embraced by slaveholders in the United States (including Thomas Jefferson) as part of their justification for slavery, the idea undergirded the behavior of many European colonizers in Africa, including the Germans, who engaged in widespread human rights abuses with impunity. Kestling tells us that in 1908, Dr. Eugen Fischer, a professor of medicine, anthropology, and eugenics, took a field expedition to the German colony of South West Africa to study the offspring of Boers and Africans. In his published research report, he stated flatly that "Negroes . . . are inferior." However, Fischer advocated protecting them "because they were useful as slaves."[45] In addition to being exposed to the views of returning German colonial administrators who "brought their anti-black racism with them," upper- and middle-class Germans learned anti-Black racism from scholars such as the French aristocrat Gobineau, a leading proponent of the idea of Aryan superiority.[46]

Sometimes translators added lines to *Huckleberry Finn* that emasculate Jim. William-Little Hughes inserts a line found nowhere in the original when he has Huck say: "Jim, comme beau-coup de nègres, savait coudre" (Jim, like many negroes, knew how to sew).[47] Translators Carlos Peyrera and Fernando de la Milla added the same line in their Spanish translation of 1923: "Jim tenia habilidad para la costura, como muchos negros" (Jim was accustomed to sewing, as many negroes are).[48] (The repeated line suggests the possibility that the translation by Peyrera and de la Milla was shaped at least in part by Hughes's earlier French translation—a common practice among Spanish translators.) On other occasions translators added lines that contribute to an image of Jim as subservient. For example, Cassiano Teixeira de Freitas Fagundes tells us that in the Evasion section, when Jim complains to Tom Sawyer about the absurd and taxing tasks he is being asked to perform, Monteiro Lobato adds to the Portuguese trans-lation he published in Brazil in 1957 that Jim "protestava humilde-mente" (humbly protested).[49] (Jim does protest in the book, as I noted in chapter 3, but nowhere does Twain suggest that he did it "humbly.")

Although, as Judith Lavoie points out, the original text portrays Jim as a "character who is resolute and independent," Hughes adds a completely invented early scene in the book that presents him as a "docile servant."[50] Hughes also emphasizes Jim's sub-servience by having him call Huck "Massa Huck," while in the original Jim simply calls him Huck—never "Mister, Misto Huck, or Master, Mars Huck"—as he does in Hughes's version. Calling Huck by these names, Lavoie notes, emphasizes his subservient role.[51] Lavoie observes that Hughes also casts Jim as a devoted servant in the Evasion section: instead of heroically offering to give up his freedom to stay with a wounded Tom Sawyer, Jim simply complies with Tom's request that he carry him on his back, a request invented by Hughes.[52]

Hughes also adds lines that are designed to whitewash slavery. Lavoie tells us that when Huck learns that Jim has run off from Miss Watson's, Hughes has him say, "*Jim, je ne me serais jamais attendu a ça ta part.*' . . . [Jim, I would never have thought that you could do such a thing]. This line is not in the original text. And Jim replies: '*Je n'aurais pas mieux demandé que de rester.*' . . . [I would have liked nothing better than to stay there], another line which is not to be found in the original novel."[53] As Lavoie notes, these lines invented by Hughes suggest that "when slaves are treated well, they do not want to free themselves," blunting the novel's critique of slavery and racism in the process.[54]

The marketing and presentation of Hughes's translation when it came out in 1886 suggest that it reflected the values that mainstream French society at the time wanted the school system to transmit. Indeed, the cultural conversation that it entered when it appeared was rife with the attitudes conveyed by Hughes's cuts and additions. As William B. Cohen notes, during the last decades of the nineteenth century, Black people in French literature generally "were depicted as loyal servants, desiring nothing but to serve their white masters." "As one looks back at the history of French-black relations through the ages," Cohen writes, "one is struck by the hardy life that the belief in black inferiority has enjoyed," a belief that had first surfaced with the "French establishment of a slave society in the Caribbean." "Wishing to justify slavery and observing the degraded condition of the black slaves," Cohen tells us, "Frenchmen posited the idea of black inferiority." The phenomenon was not unique to France but was experienced by "all European slave owning societies."[55] Hughes's editorial decisions, then, which resonate with choices made by translators in other colonial powers, reflected ideas about the hierarchy of the races that were widely accepted in Europe at the time and that were difficult to dislodge. But even in nations that were not colonizers themselves, ideas of Black inferiority seeped deep into the culture and shaped the way translators dealt with Jim.

Janko Trupej tells us, for example, that Pavel Holeček, who translated the novel into Slovenian in 1948 under the title *Pustolovščine Huckleberryja Finna* three years after a socialist government was established in Yugoslavia, adds a number of racist lines about Jim that he assigns to both Huck and Tom.[56] In the original, when Huck and Jim become separated during the fog, Huck says, "I did wish the fool would think to beat a tin pan, and beat it all the time, but he never did."[57] In Holeček's translation, Trupej writes, instead of "he never did," Huck adds: "but this was too much for his black brains" (in Slovenian, "ali to je bilo za njegovo črno pamet že preveč").[58] Tom Sawyer also displays more racism in Holeček's translation, as Trupej notes, "twice reducing Jim to the level of an animal." Instead of saying that "the glorious chances given to Jim to escape from captivity were 'wasted on him,'" Tom calls Jim a "stupid animal"—"neumna žival." Tom also gratuitously refers to Jim as a "rotten black dog"—"pokvarjeni črni pes." These additions, Trupej tells us, make it much harder for the Slovenian reader to "appreciate the affection between Huck and Jim, and the latter's role in the former's moral growth."[59]

Even more significant, in Trupej's view, is the translator's decision on three occasions to have Jim call himself variations on "poor, silly nigger"—"ubog, bebast zamorec"—something not based on anything in the book.[60] Trupej writes that these and other choices make "Jim's frequent displays of good reasoning skills and intelligence seem less believable, as is also the case with Huck's expressions of admiration for Jim."[61] In Holeček's translation, according to Trubej, Jim refers to himself in negative terms that portray him as "a passive, helpless, unintelligent person" who "is consequently perceived as such by the other characters."[62]

A new Slovenian translation, *Prigode Huckleberryja Finna*, was published by the highly respected Slovenian translator Janez Gradišnik in 1962, one year after the formation of the Non-Aligned Movement, in which countries sought greater independence from the influence of the United States and Soviet Union during the Cold War.[63] In this new translation much of the racism in Holeček's earlier version was softened, and Trupej suggests that shifting international relations may account for the change. The first translation was published at a time when the young socialist nation of Yugoslavia was closely allied with the Soviet Union. The United States was perceived as "an ideological adversary to any socialist government," and Slovenian periodicals often ran anti-American articles at the time about "the injustices committed by US-American capitalists against their workers." The second translation appeared "after Yugoslavia had distanced itself from the Soviet Union, and its relations with the United States were significantly better than at the time of the first translation." Trubej believes that this shift may help account for the toning down of descriptions of American racism in the first translation.[64]

Lines added by translators are often demeaning to Jim, but not always. In the Hindi translation by Omkar Sharad (2018), Sharma tells us, "after Jim is discovered to be a free man and his role in helping the injured Tom is revealed, he is freed from chains and also 'he is given respect' (उसकी इज़्ज़त करने लगे)."[65] It would be nice, of course, if that had transpired, but it didn't. (Huck hoped that he'd be treated better, but that didn't happen either.) Sharma writes that "such a mistranslation overturns the satire intended by the original, of the way the political gains made by freed Black people after the abolition of slavery were reversed by subsequent Supreme Court decisions, the passing of Jim Crow laws, and the rise of lynching." In Sharma's view, the well-meaning added line "He is given respect" ties everything up too neatly and makes it impossible for readers to grasp the messy and tragic history of American race relations after the story ends.[66]

Translating Jim's Dialect

The choices translators make about how to represent Jim's speech, like their decisions to omit certain passages and invent others, reflect their understanding of Twain's most famous Black character and their own racial attitudes. Many experiment with a range of ways to differentiate Jim's speech from that of other characters. Raphael Berthele divides these experiments into those that present the African American Vernacular English that Jim speaks as "deficient" and those that present it as simply "different." Berthele distinguishes choices involving grammar, spelling, and diction that "represent Jim as socially, linguistically, [and] even cognitively deficient" from those that show him as speaking in a distinctive but not necessarily inferior manner.[67] Berthele's "deficit" versus "difference" categories are useful to understand translators' practice not only in the forty German texts he examines but also, more broadly, across other languages.

Though it is clear from the novel that Twain viewed Jim as illiterate but not unintelligent, translators who adopt the "deficit" model come up with a range of strategies for letting Jim's speech mark him as comically stupid. (This practice may have been adopted most broadly in countries that maintained colonies in Africa or the Caribbean, but it can also be found in countries that did not, such as China. Not until the 1960s, as the Civil Rights Movement came into its own, did translators generally begin to abandon this practice—although some did a few years earlier, as a discussion below of the Chinese translation by Zhang Yousong and Zhang Zhenxian from 1955 makes clear.) As Berthele observes, in some early German translations, translators "render Jim's (but not Huck's) speech as a pidgin-like learner's English, even though in the English original, both Jim's and Huck Finn's speech deviate systematically from standard grammar." Since neither the translators nor the original book suggests that Jim speaks any language other than English, "these translations represent Jim as fundamentally deficient: as unable to speak *any* language properly."[68]

Many early German translators have Jim speak in infinitives—a grammatical mistake, Berthele tells us, that "portrays him either as foreign, uneducated, or simpleminded. A Jim who speaks this way was an object of ridicule for both translators and readers in the first half of the twentieth century—both from a cognitive and linguistic point of view he is presented as deficient."[69] "This type of 'infinitive language,'" Berthele writes, is widely used in German literature for the speech of idiots and savages, as well as language learners.[70] An Italian translation by Gabriele Musumarra from 1964 also uses this technique. As Iain Halliday tells us, "rendering a character's verbs in the infinitive" is "a classic, stereotypical approach to the rendition of immigrants' speech in Italian."[71] Other devices German translators used to mark Jim's speech as deficient include wrong word order and missing articles—errors that similarly "have a very strong connotation as features produced by beginning German language-learners."[72] A related strategy was used by some Chinese translators as well, who have Jim "speak with a false Chinese tone in some of the words to highlight his dialect and illiteracy."[73] In the view of the book's most recent translator into Chinese, An-chi Wang, these translations "end up turning Jim into a monster talking gibberish nonsense, which has certainly insulted his intelligence. Jim is merely uneducated, but his intelligence is above average."[74]

Ronald Jenn has suggested that "strategies that foreground a lack of linguistic competence in Jim actually reflect the translators' own difficulties understanding African American voices."[75]

Persian scholars Masoud Sharififar and Seyed A. Enjavi Nejad agree with this view, as Jenn notes, having argued that "at a time when African American voices were rarely heard, let alone studied in the US, some translators on foreign shores were baffled. They failed to construe Jim's speech as a coherent whole, a 'self-contained variety of language,' and read its specificities as grammatical errors."[76] Translators' lack of familiarity with and respect for African American Vernacular English, as well as their failure to recognize the racism underlying colonialism and their countries' treatment of immigrants and minorities, all conspired to lead many of them to portray Jim as foolish, inane, and, sometimes, mute.

In Swedish, Danish, and Norwegian translations, B. J. Epstein notes, the white characters "speak standard Swedish, Danish, or Norwegian, while Jim's Swedish, Danish, or Norwegian is not quite standard and not quite a dialect; it is marked as 'wrong' or 'off.' So Jim speaks brokenly rather than in dialect." While "white characters had their words standardised," Epstein writes, the speech of Jim and other Black characters was "translated in a way that suggested they were deficient and intellectually incapable of learning language." Epstein sees echoes of colonialism in this method of portraying the speech of Black characters, "where the natives are seen as child-like and less intelligent and as people who need to be taken care of, while the (white) colonisers are smart adults with power." Epstein suggests that "larger racist ideologies in the society at large" may have shaped the pattern in Scandinavian translations of having white characters "speak Scandinavian languages well and black ones speak brokenly."[77] She is also troubled by the decision of some translators simply to cut dialect-heavy passages of Jim's, such as the one in which he expresses his joy at approaching Cairo, a passage that disappears in Olav Angell's Norwegian translation. "Given that some of these translations are quite recent," Epstein adds, "new generations of readers—including young people who may be the target audience of this book—are being exposed to the idea that blacks, and perhaps other minorities, are either deficient or should remain voiceless."[78] Berthele makes a similar point when he notes that instead of quoting what Jim says, some German translators instead summarize Jim's speech with the effect of giving Jim "no 'direct' voice at all."[79]

By the 1960s and 1970s, in the wake of the Civil Rights Movement in the United States and its global reverberations, translators in Germany began to move from the "deficit" model of representing Jim's speech to the "difference" model, to use Berthele's helpful framework (the first German version to abandon the "deficit" model, Berthele tells us, was Lore Krüger's from 1963).[80] There were also changes in the prefaces and afterwords that accompanied these translations: in the preface to a translation by Sybil Countess Schönfeldt from 1978, the editor "explicitly informs the reader that this novel is to be read as an 'appeal against slavery and disdain for African-American people.'"[81] Berthele notes that the reissue in 1979 of a translation by Lore Krüger features a similar comment.[82]

While before the 1960s most translation strategies "downgrade Jim's linguistic and cognitive faculties, depicting his speech as a grammatically simplified pidgin," Berthele writes, contemporary translations tend to "opt for devices that depict Jim in colloquial and spoken language that does not carry the same amount of sociolinguistic stigma."[83] Interestingly, Berthele asserts that despite the varied views of Jim's intelligence that characterize the thirteen German translations he studied in depth, all of the translators share the assumption that "Jim is the only moral grown-up in the novel" and "are faithful in their representation of Jim's moral worth."[84] Translators who were open to discarding the "deficit" model in translating Jim's speech found support for that effort at a workshop in 1983 sponsored by the European translation committee whose focus was explicitly on "Black American English." This workshop led to the production of a glossary of African American Vernacular English phrases and paraphrases in standard English—a document emphasizing AAVE as an example of "difference" rather than "deficit."[85]

From the earliest translations in the 1880s to the present, many other translators have opted to dispense with dialect entirely in the book, having Jim, along with all the other characters, speak a standardized version of the target language. This was the case with many Arabic, Assamese, Chinese, Czech, Danish, French, German, Italian, Japanese, Korean, Norwegian, Russian, Spanish, Swedish, Urdu, Vietnamese, Yiddish, and other translations.[86] Sometimes, this was because translators simply found the dialect too hard to translate. Epstein notes that in the preface to his Norwegian translation, Olav Angell wrote: "Denne nyanserikdommen er selvfølgelig uråd å få til på norsk. Det ville ta en menneskealder å få til noe lignende. Så god tid hadde jeg ikke. Mea culpa." Translated, this reads: "This richness of nuance is of course difficult to express in Norwegian. It would take ages to get something similar. I didn't have so much time. Mea culpa."[87]

The perceived limitations of the target language were often cited as the rationale for standardizing all speech in the book. Margarita Marinova tells us that Korneĭ Chukovsky, a famous poet, children's author, and theorist of translation studies in Russia, believed that Twain's Explanatory enumerating the dialects in the book "is written as if to terrify" his Russian translators and for this reason most simply leave it out. "However talented one may be," Chukovsky wrote, "one will never manage to reproduce a single one of these seven colorful dialects in translation, because the Russian language has not the slightest lexical means for the implementation of tasks like this."[88] This is why all speech in the most prominent Soviet translations is presented in the standard "blandscript" (*gladkopis'*).

Sometimes the standardization was the result of national publishing norms or government policies, particularly when publications were designed for use in schools. Tsuyoshi Ishihara notes that Japan had a strict policy of standardizing the language used in children's literature and education, a policy enforced by the Japanese Ministry of Education. "For example, in schools in the Okinawa area in the early twentieth century," he tells us, "students who used Okinawa vernacular in class were forced to wear heavy 'dialect boards' from their necks for punishment."[89]

Miguel Sanz Jiménez notes that "given publishing conventions in Spain that discourage departures from standard spelling and diction, translators there had little leeway and have only timidly pushed beyond those norms." Four of the six twenty-first-century Spanish editions he examined "utilize Standard Spanish throughout, largely ignoring the linguistic variety of the original." The impact of this choice, Sanz Jiménez writes, is that Jim sounds as literate and educated as Miss Watson.[90]

An Arabic translation published by Mahir Naseem in Cairo in 1958 also suggested Jim's literacy and education: as Mariam Abdulmalik tells us, the translator "polished the slave's dialect into Classical Arabic."[91] When Jim is prophesying Huck's future with the aid of the hair ball, he says, "Dey's two angels hoverin' roun' 'bout him. One uv 'em is white en shiny en t'other one is black. De white one gits him to go right, a little while, den de black one sail in en bust it all up."[92] Naseem translates this passage like this:

"إن هناك ملاكين يحومان حوله، أحدهما أبيض متألق والآخر أسود اللون، أما الملاك الأبيض فيحاول أن يهديه إلى السبيل السوي، ولكن الملاك الأسود لا يلبث أن يتدخل في الأمر ويفسد كل شيء." Here is Abdulmalik's back translation: "There are two angels hovering around him, one is a shiny white and the other is black, the white angel tries *to guide him onto right path,* but the black angel presently intervenes and busts everything up." Abdulmalik notes that the Arabic translation here echoes the language of the Quran, Naseem having Jim using such Quranic terms as "يهديه إلى السبيل السوي," meaning "guides him to the right path"; Hamada Kassam suggests that "guides him to the righteous path" is a more accurate translation.[93]

Translations that don't make Jim's speech a hodgepodge of demeaning mistakes often standardize his speech in a manner identical to that of the other characters but have him use a handful of distinctive phrases. That was the choice made by František Gel in the Czech translation he published in 1953, in which Jim "mostly speaks standard Czech with some expressive words and a few colloquial expressions."[94] Twain had ended his Explanatory note about all the dialects in the book with this comment: "I make this explanation for the reason that without it many would suppose that all these characters were trying to talk alike and not succeeding." Tereza Šedivá quips that in Gel's translation, Twain's characters are "trying to talk alike" and "succeeding."[95]

Standardizing Jim's language, as Nina Daruzes does in her translation, does have one advantage, in Margarita Marinova's view: "As both Huck and Jim now could speak perfectly correct Russian, there was no risk that their ideas would not be taken seriously. Soviet children may not have known much about the real experiences of an enslaved American, but they never doubted their own abilities to understand his language."[96]

Nonetheless, the practice of standardizing Jim's speech is problematic. Marinova writes that "Jim's speech, in particular, embodies the troubled history of racial relations in America, and helps reveal his intelligence and evolving emotional connection to Huck. The forced standardization of his language, therefore, leads to a kind of monologism that robs him of his individuality."[97]

Scholars working in other languages, such as Slovenian, have noted in a similar vein that Jim's humanity comes across in part through the way he articulates himself in the original; standardizing his speech flattens his complexity.[98]

For José Manuel Rodríguez Herrera, the practice of standardizing Jim's speech, as most Spanish translations do, is regrettable: he writes that when Twain carefully marked Jim's speech with a host of specific features of Black English it was because he wanted readers to see Jim as different, but not in a pejorative sense. In addition, Rodríguez Herrera suggests, "Twain found in the vernacular an effective way of satirizing entrenched attitudes of racism in his country (despite his poor diction, Jim's reasoning proves to be excellent)."[99] In standardized versions such as J. A. de Larrinaga's Spanish translation of 1974—an example of what Rodríguez Herrera calls "neutered versions"—there are no markers, "no signs at all of an uncultured status." As a result, "the intrinsic value of Jim's superior reasoning vanishes into thin air."[100] For Rodríguez Herrera, Twain clearly wants the reader to recognize that Jim's illiteracy and lack of schooling are no impediment to his making cogent, winning arguments.

But there is a middle ground between having Jim speak a deformed language and having him speak an undifferentiated, standardized one. A number of translators have come up with a range of nonpejorative, creative strategies to convey Jim's speech as "different" but not "deficient."

Selina Lai-Henderson notes, for example, that the translation produced by Zhang Yousong and Zhang Zhenxian in 1955

vividly grasps Jim's use of vernacular and lack of education. They turned "pecks on me all de time" into "老找我的碴儿" "laozhao wode cha er," which is a very colloquial expression meaning "constantly nitpicks at me," and is clearly spoken among non-elites. For "roun' de place considable," the translators focused on the word "round" and came up with "在这带地方轉" "zhai zhe dai defang zhuan," which literally means "to keep wandering around that place." And "creeps to de do'" is an informal way of describing walking to the door quietly, so the translators wrote that as "悄悄儿溜到門口" "qiaoqiao er liudao menkou" (slipping to the door unnoticeably).[101]

This translation renders Jim's speech as colloquial but not distorted. As Lai-Henderson points out, it appeared the same year as the Bandung Conference, which brought representatives from twenty-nine nonaligned Asian and African nations together to explore shared interests and concerns. She suggests that "China's strong involvement in the Conference and continued effort in fostering an Afro-Asian alliance might be a reason for the translators being more aware of African and African American histories, cultures, and literatures overall" and therefore treating Jim with more respect.[102]

Lai-Henderson tells us that two more recent and innovative attempts at translating Jim's dialect were undertaken by Cheng Shi (1989) and Xu Ruzhi (1995).[103] These translators are widely studied at Chinese universities because of the nuances they brought to their translation of Jim's language. Cheng acknowledges that "the dialects used by Twain are basically untranslatable," but Lai-Henderson writes that despite Cheng's "awareness of the potential inadequacies in his work," his selective use of malapropism "is highly inventive and deserves applause."[104] (Lai-Henderson herself deserves applause for her valiant effort to back translate Cheng's Chinese malapropisms to give English readers a sense of how they work. For example, rendering "how it went" as "howl it went" or "pretty rough" as "petty rough.")[105] Cheng signaled Jim's lack of education by writing incorrect characters in the text with the correct ones next to them in parentheses.[106]

Six years after Cheng's translation appeared, Xu Ruzhi deployed creative punctuation to differentiate Jim's speech. Although Xu's language is "at times still rather formal," Lai-Henderson writes, "he does a good job of showing Jim's illiteracy through the use of punctuation, with frequent dashes and commas between sentences to imply the lack of structure and pauses in his speech."[107]

In her Czech translation from 2007, Jana Mertinová abandoned the earlier strategy of František Gel, who had Jim speak "standard, neutral Czech" with almost "no grammatical irregularities."[108] Although in Mertinová's translation both Huck and Jim use informal, colloquial Czech filled with idiomatic expressions, Jim uses more adjectives with nonstandard endings, as well as more idiosyncratic spellings, sound loss, regional vocabulary, and the occasional malapropism. All of these mark his speech as "different" but not "deficient."[109]

Ronald Jenn and Véronique Channaut outline the relatively successful efforts of recent French translators Bernard Hoepffner and Freddy Michalski to evoke Jim's speech. Hoepffner and Michalski were both professional translators from multilingual backgrounds that equipped them to tackle the nuances of Twain's dialects. Noting that the loss of the final *r* that Twain uses in rendering Jim's speech "is commonly used in French as well as to characterize Black speech," Jenn and Channaut tell us that "Hoepffner and Michalski make repetitive use of it." Strategies such as this, along with grammatical, syntactic, and phonological markers suggesting Jim's illiteracy, allow them to "elicit a sense of difference when Jim speaks even as the reading process remains smooth and accessible." Syntactic markers include "truncated negations (French negation usually requires two elements 'ne' and 'pas'), along with . . . faulty subject-verb agreement that sounds grammatically incorrect but also has overtones of dialect (for example, 'je vas' for 'I'm going' instead of 'je vais')."[110]

Several translators have tried to come up with dialects within their own languages that present Jim's speech as "different" without being "deficient." In her Spanish translation from 1976, Cristina Cerezales, for example, experimented with having Jim speak Andalusian Spanish, a dialect spoken in southern Spain that allows Jim's speech to deviate from standard pronunciation and that would remind Spanish readers of the speech heard in regions such as Seville. But, as Rodríguez Herrera observes, the experiment doesn't work since "no one in Spain would reasonably make the least remote connection here with African-American English." Since in Cerezales's translation, "Jim ceases to have credibility as a black slave from Missouri," Rodríguez Herrera deems the experiment a failure.[111] In a Portuguese translation published in Brazil in 2011 that received positive critical attention, Rosaura Eichenberg had Jim (but not white characters) speak like a "hick in the interior of the state of São Paulo."[112]

Hamada Kassam is currently completing a translation of the novel into vernacular Arabic, something that has never been done before (previous translations were in Modern Standard Arabic, with a sprinkling of Classical Arabic mixed in). In Kassam's translation, Huck and Jim will both use the colloquial Syrian dialect spoken in Damascus and the countryside surrounding the Syrian capital. Although, as Kassam notes, each Arab country "speaks a uniquely accented Arabic and hosts a variety of colloquial regional dialects that are deemed almost impenetrable and incomprehensible by Arabs in other Arabic-speaking countries," the Damascene dialect Kassam has selected for his translation is widely understood, he tells us, because of "the impressive success that Syrian drama has earned in all twenty-two Arab countries

over the past three decades," as well as the fact that it is the dialect of choice for dubbing the increasingly popular Turkish dramas broadcast throughout the Arab world.[113]

Kassam plans to translate the book fully and accurately in its
entirety, "producing cultural equivalents in vernacular Arabic
that would consequently enable Arab readers to understand and
enjoy Twain's implicit and subtle social, historical, and political
messages and nuances of meaning."[114] In this translation, Jim
speaks in the "voice of a simple, uneducated, and unpretentious
countryman who uses natural and superstitious idioms and
phrases in the Damascene dialect." While Jim and Huck speak the
same dialect in his translation, Kassam says he is trying to highlight Jim's "spontaneity, his goodness/kindheartedness, his occasional selflessness, his belief in superstitions, his countryside
background, and his lack of formal education, and the fact that
he is stripped of all social pretensions."[115]

Kassam introduces his translation with a "Notice from the
Translator" that echoes in purpose, style, and tone the "Explanatory" that Twain inserts at the start of the novel. "I am trying
to convince my readers that my . . . employment of a vernacular
dialect—to use Twain's words in his 'Explanatory'—has not been
done in a hap-hazard fashion, or by guesswork, but painstakingly,"
Kassam writes. Twain uses formal English only in his "Notice"
and "Explanatory." Similarly, Kassam uses Modern Standard Arabic only on these same two occasions in his translation.[116]

Sometimes translators are reticent to experiment with dialects in their own language because the dialect spoken in one
region of a country is incomprehensible to residents of other regions. In the case of India, however, Seema Sharma believes there
are as yet untapped opportunities to re-create the uses to which
Twain puts dialect. "Indian languages have several dialects which
are comprehensible to the speakers of the standard language of

that region," Sharma writes, much as African American English is understandable to speakers of "standard English" in the United States. She tells us that "Hindi has more than fifty dialects spoken in the Hindi-speaking belt of Northern India. *Awadhi, Brajbhasha, Garhwali, Khari Boli, Rajasthani, Bhojpuri,* [and] *Haryanvi* are some of the popular dialects. Indian literary tradition also offers a way out with its precedent of vernacular storytelling. . . . The Hindi translations of *Huckleberry Finn* can retain the flavor and intent of the original by having Huck and Jim speak in differing peasant dialects to reflect Huck's colloquial style and Jim's Black vernacular."[117]

Occasionally, a translator has come up with a creative alternative to at least a part of the dialect issue. Although Andrés M. Mateo's Spanish translation of *Huckleberry Finn* published in Mexico in 1967 has Huck speak standard Spanish, Jessica Harris demonstrates that Mateo has Jim and several of the other black characters in the book speak a variant of Spanish that is markedly different from the Spanish that Huck speaks.[118] Harris argues persuasively that Mateo's translation of Jim's speech is based in reality on an actual, observable Mexican dialect of Spanish inflected by African linguistic features documented by a Mexican anthropologist. In his book *Cuijla: Esbozo etnográfico de un pueblo negro* (1958), anthropologist Gonzalo Aguirre Beltrán described his study of a community in Oaxaca of descendants of African slaves brought by the Spanish conquistadors to what is now Mexico. He devoted significant attention to their speech.[119]

Beltrán describes in detail the speech patterns he documented in this "Africano-Mexicano" town of Cuijla, noting the ways in which they differ from standard Spanish. Cuijleños, he tells us, for example, frequently eliminate the final syllable in words: "Se dice: pa por para; ca por casa; pue por puede; mu por muy."[120] Mateo's Jim says *despué* for *después, mejo* for *mejor, po fin* for *por fin, verdá* for *verdád, cruzá* for *cruzar, la mitá* for *la mitad, tién* for *tienen,* and *seño* for *señor.*[121] One can see a similar pattern in Twain's representation of the Black English that Jim speaks. Jim says *didn'* for *didn't, mos'* for *most, doan'* for *don't,* and *buil'* for *build.*[122] Other distinctive traits include eliminating some internal syllables. For example, Beltrán writes that Cuijleños might say *onde'stá* and *on'stá* for *donde está.*[123] Indeed, Mateo's Jim says *tú ties* for *tu tienes;* he says *la señita* for *la señorita* and *tu quiés* for *tu quieres.*[124] In Mateo's translation, Jim says *tuavía* for *todavia*—much as Jim eliminates an internal syllable when he says *considable* instead of *considerable* or *strawbries* instead of *strawberries* or *ridicklous* for *ridiculous.*[125] Other comparable examples in Jim's speech include *mo' er less* for *more or less* and *t'other one* for *the other one.*

In Harris's view, "Jim's dialectal Spanish as written by Andrés Mateo exhibits too many of the features of Spanish dialect described in *Cuijla* for the similarity to be coincidental," and I agree. Harris believes that Mateo consciously chose "a dialect spoken by Africano-Mexicanos" for Jim in his efforts to retain "some of Twain's original vernacular energy." His decision to use a dialect spoken by "the descendants of former African slaves" would allow readers to recognize Mateo's Jim "as belonging to a formerly subjugated and persecuted class of people."[126]

Francisco José Tenreiro made an equally creative choice when crafting the speech of Black characters in his Portuguese translation of *Huckleberry Finn* published in Lisbon in 1972. Tenreiro, who was born in São Tomé, the capital of the African nation of São Tomé and Principe, where he was a respected poet (as well as a geographer), was inspired by Francophone poet Aimé Césaire as well as by Langston Hughes. Tenreiro is credited with having introduced Césaire's concept of *négritude* to Afro-Portuguese poetry. In his translation of *Huckleberry Finn,* Jim and other Black characters speak in a Cape Verde dialect.[127] The Portuguese-based creole he deploys in the book is the oldest creole still spoken globally and is used as a second language in the Cape Verde diaspora.[128] Examples of Tenreiro's use of features of Cape Verde creole include the double negative—*não tem mais nada* instead of the Portuguese *tem mais nada* (for "there's nothing left") and the elimination of consonants at the end of words as in *fazê* instead of *fazer* ("Pra quê fazê fogueira?" instead of "Para que fazer uma fogueira?").[129] The respect Tenreiro enjoys in the country of his birth is indicated by the fact that his face appears on the paper currency of São Tomé and Principe.

It is interesting that both Mateo's and Tenreiro's intriguing experiments, as Jenn has observed, "were enabled by the shared history of contact between African and European languages and cultures through the transatlantic slave trade."[130] But as we have seen, that shared contact was no guarantee that Jim's African-inflected language—or Jim himself—would be treated with the respect that these twentieth-century Mexican and Portuguese translators accord him.

Language and Power

Whether translators are experimenting with dialects or sticking to standard syntax and diction, there is a choice they need to make in languages that feature formal and informal forms of *you*: Do Huck and Jim address each other using the same form of *you*, or is there asymmetry, with Jim using a more formal and deferential term when he addresses Huck (and other white people as well)? In short, do their forms of address for each other evoke equality or racial hierarchy?

In the Portuguese translation Ricardo A. Fernandes published in Lisbon in 1956, Jim addresses Huck with terms "reminiscent of the bondage of slavery," according to Kunst. Jim uses the terms *senhor* (sir) as well as *vomecê* (a polite form of *you*) and *o patrão* (boss), while Huck always addresses Jim as *tú*. In Kunst's view, these asymmetries in address "constantly undercut . . . scenes of love and reunion whenever they occur."[131] However, in a Portuguese translation published in São Paulo by Monteiro Lobato the following year, Huck and Jim address each other with the same term—the "familiar but not intimate '*você*.'"[132] In Persian translations published in Tehran by Parviz Najm al-Dini (1984) and by Shahram Puranfar (1991), as Behnam M. Fomeshi notes, Huck and Jim address each other with the informal and friendly second-person singular form *to* rather than the more formal term *shoma*.[133]

In Hughes's early French translation, Jim addresses Huck using the formal *vous* form, while Huck sticks to the more familiar *tu* form. Ronald Jenn notes that "this imbalance seriously disrupts the egalitarian relationship the two characters come to develop."[134] Suzanne Nétillard's translation from 1948, published by the communist publishing house Les Éditions Hier et Aujourd'hui, departed from this pattern, having both Jim and Huck use *tu*, recognizing the camaraderie that had developed between them. Although in most countries there is a move to more symmetrical forms of address between Huck and Jim as racial attitudes become more progressive over time, the shift is often far from linear. While Nétillard's translation tried to do justice to the egalitarian camaraderie of the original, André Bay's often-reissued translation from 1960, in which Huck addresses Jim as *tu* while Jim addresses Huck as *vous*, requires Jim to address Huck with more respect than Huck accords *him*.[135] But the pattern would be reversed again in the translations published by Bernard Hoepffner in 2008 and Freddy Michalski in 2009. Jenn and Channaut note that "both Hoepffner and Michalski use the informal '*tu*' form when Jim addresses Huck and vice versa, reinforcing their egalitarian relationship and Jim's role as a father figure to the boy."[136] The pendulum swung back yet again in Philippe Jaworski's French translation in 2015, in which Jim addresses Huck as *vous*, while Huck address Jim as *tu*.[137]

Just as contemporary translators tend to seek ways of presenting Jim's speech as "different" but not "deficient," they also, for the most part, increasingly show a preference for having Huck and Jim using symmetrical forms of address when speaking to each other—a sign, one hopes, of an increasing reluctance to encode a racial hierarchy in their relationship that Twain's novel does its best to undermine.[138] But the shift is neither consistent nor complete.

Some twenty-first-century translators are tackling these challenges head-on by incorporating prefaces and copious notes into their translations, embracing the opportunity to engage with the daunting complexities of language and power that help make this book so thought-provoking and complicated and that make their task so hard.

Hamada Kassam plans to make Jim a significant focus of the extended preface that will introduce his vernacular Arabic translation of the novel. It will discuss Jim's social background and voice as an American slave and his importance to Twain's attack on slavery. "My audience should know about all these significant points because the slavery of color that Twain presents does not exist" in Arab societies.[139] "Unlike in the USA," he notes, "slavery in Syria was not based on color throughout the course of history. People from different races and continents were captured in wars and enslaved, including white people from Europe."[140] As Abdulmalik notes in her dissertation on previous Arabic translations, "Slave, in Arabic, refers to Armenian, Asian, African and any non-Muslim who is captured during war. . . . [Previous Arabic] translators did not provide any explanation" to clarify the dynamics of color in American slavery.[141] Kassam's preface will correct that omission, making sure that Arab readers of his translation have a clear understanding of the role of color in shaping Jim's experience and status in American society.

Other contemporary translators have shared Kassam's appreciation of the value of explanatory paratextual materials such as critical introductions and annotations to help non-English speakers grasp the subtleties of this complex and challenging book—perhaps no one as fully as An-chi Wang. With its 387 explanatory footnotes, 104-page critical introduction dealing with scholarship on the book and its reception history, and 67-page bibliography (as well as a preface by a leading literary scholar), the acclaimed translation by An-chi Wang, published in Taiwan in 2012, is recognized as the most complete version of the book in Chinese—superior to the ninety previous Chinese translations that have been identified.[142]

From the start, Wang urges her "readers to pay close attention to Jim."[143] To that end, at the beginning of chapter 2 when Jim first appears in the book, Wang flags him (in her annotations) as the "main character who is going to be the most important influence in Huck's life." Wang includes some thirty footnotes concerning Jim, to remind readers "that he is not merely a 'foil' character." She explains, for example, that Jim may be "superstitious, but some of his beliefs contain folk wisdom inherited from his generations of ancestors. Jim is naive, but he has his own logical way of thinking." Wang hopes to convey in her introduction and notes that Twain's novel, in her view, is the most important indictment of slavery that America has produced. Wang, who has taught American literature for many decades to college students in Taiwan, makes sure to "keep racism as a central issue" in her impressive edition of *Huckleberry Finn* and in her classroom.

In her introduction Wang reminds readers that the fact that we see Jim only from Huck's perspective leads many readers to

underrate him and dismiss him as stereotypical. She emphasizes "Jim's role as Huck's surrogate father who initiates him into
human integrity," in contrast to pap, who does nothing but exploit him. Wang tells us that she does not "cut or add any of Jim's
lines." "I explain whatever is hidden between the lines with abun-
dant footnotes," she says, maintaining her "translation principle":
"Stick to the original text, and complement with annotations."[144]

Wang includes in her introduction a discussion comparing Jim
with the early Confucian philosopher Mencius, an approach that
she believes can help her students appreciate Jim's character. It
explores Jim's moral significance in the context of virtues associated with Mencius as well as Jim: "sympathy and humane-
ness."[145] One can only hope that Wang's methods will become
influential in future translations of *Huck Finn* in all languages.
How the non-anglophone world comes to understand Jim, *Huckleberry Finn*, Mark Twain, and the way that race is represented in
America's most important and influential novel depends on it.

CHAPTER 7

Afterlives

Jim in the High School Classroom

OES JIM HAVE A PLACE in American high schools? Although the book's repeated use of an offensive racial slur usually figures in attempts to remove it from the classroom, the characterization of Jim is often also central to these protests.

An editorial in the *Baltimore Afro-American* in 1965 argued that Jim did not belong in the nation's classrooms on the grounds that *"Huckleberry Finn* pictures colored people in their days of humiliation."[1] The editorial resonates with a comment David Bradley made a half century later when he suggested that from the late 1950s through the present, what underlies the protests over *Huckleberry Finn* "is shame. Americans are, not unreasonably, ashamed that there ever was chattel slavery in this country, and have employed all kinds of repressive strategies to deny its nature and continuing effects."[2] In 1966, some Black students at the University of Massachusetts walked out of class when the character Jim was mentioned, arguing that "the book gave a distorted image of colored people" that they found "embarrassing."[3] One Black student said, "The book reinforces prejudice, reinforces the belief that all Negroes shuffle, eat watermelon and giggle."[4] A *Chicago*

Defender article about the protest in 1966 reported that students found "the famous character known as 'Nigger Jim' [*sic*] ... particularly offensive."[5]

Protests continued in the decades that followed. In an affluent suburb of Houston in 1984, school officials spent three months addressing complaints from about a dozen Black parents and students that the novel "presented blacks 'in a negative light.'"[6] In 1994, Texas state senator Royce West, who had sponsored a bill in the legislature that would have prevented any state funds from being spent on *Huckleberry Finn,* told me that "the characterization of Jim" contributed to parents' opposition to having their children read the book in school: "If you continue to tell people, particularly young impressionable minds, that they come from a long line of individuals that are quote unquote 'no good,' that have always been in subservient positions, do you just kind of reinforce that and continue to deflate their self-esteem, or should you be about building positive self-esteem?"[7] In 1998, Kathy Monteiro, the white mother of a Black teenager in Tempe, Arizona, was so determined to remove the book from her daughter's classroom at McClintock High School that she disrupted a talk by a visiting African American Twain scholar, Jocelyn Chadwick, and had to be removed by security. A picket sign she held in front of the school—while rather cryptic—makes clear the source of her distaste for the book: it read, "We're tired of Nigger Jim sittin' in."[8] In 2003, Twain's "portrayal of blacks" was cited when the book was challenged near Seattle, Washington. ("I believe the book is degrading and denigrating toward African Americans," a student at Renton High School told the Associated Press.)[9] In 2006, in a book-length brief on why *Huckleberry Finn* should not be taught, Sharon Rush argued that "Twain depicts Jim as a slave who lacks agency, and who is beholden to Huck, a young teenager," and who "passively submits to Huck's decisions and never strikes out on his own." Rush, who, like Monteiro, is the white mother of a Black daughter, maintained that neither white nor Black students identify with Jim.[10] In 2019, two New Jersey General Assembly members initiated a resolution to prevent the book from being taught in the state, noting that it "can cause students to feel upset, marginalized, or humiliated."[11]

The presence of Jim in the nation's classrooms has been challenged since the late 1950s across the country in Arizona, California, Connecticut, Florida, Illinois, Iowa, Kansas, Maryland, Massachusetts, Michigan, Minnesota, Mississippi, New Jersey, New York, Oklahoma, Oregon, Pennsylvania, Texas, Virginia, Washington, and elsewhere. The novel has often made the American Library Association's list of the most frequently banned books.[12] Parents challenging the book argue that Jim is not the kind of role model they want for their children; that he is an inferior, diminished, childlike figure who perpetuates stereotypes about Blacks; that he is an embarrassment who makes students uncomfortable; and that encountering him in the classroom can hurt Black students' self-esteem and encourage racist attitudes on the part of their white peers. They may be right—if the book is poorly taught. Sadly, it often is.

Huckleberry Finn may be the fugu fish of the American literature classroom. The fugu is a great delicacy highly prized in Japanese, Korean, and other Asian cuisines, but if not carefully prepared by people who know what they're doing, it can be lethal. Studying *Huckleberry Finn* can be a powerful, transformative experience for students, a high point of their studies—but like the fugu fish, it requires careful preparation by teachers with the training and the confidence to deal with the thorny historical, literary, and social issues it engages. No teacher should be forced to teach this book. Teaching it poorly can make it toxic. Teachers should not bring Jim into their classroom if they are not prepared to engage the history of American racism that informs the novel and that continues to derail American ideals of equality. They should not bring Jim into their classroom if they are unequipped to deal with Twain's decision to satirize racism by telling the story through the eyes of a child too innocent to recognize what's wrong with the society in which he lives. They should not bring Jim into their classroom if their students are too immature to grapple with these complexities. They should not bring Jim into their classroom if they are unwilling to address the presence of the offensive racial slur that appears more than two hundred times in the book. And they should not bring Jim into their classroom if his voice is the only Black voice on the syllabus. In an appendix, I suggest some strategies that might be helpful to teachers.

It pains me greatly that a book which could be positive and empowering for both Black and white students has led, in some cases, to hurt and humiliation instead. But when the book is taught well, informed by the history of racism in America and by an awareness of how Twain's irony works—in short, if a teacher is prepared to teach the book in all its complexity—is it still too hard for high school students to understand? Are high school students by definition too young to grasp what Twain's satire is trying to convey about who Jim is, to recognize the ways in which Jim demolishes the legitimacy of arguments for white superiority? Can they appreciate Jim as a character Twain admired and wanted the reader to admire as well?

It takes an unusually well-prepared, well-informed, and sensitive high school teacher to teach this book in a way that avoids the minefields that have dogged it in the classroom for decades. Such teachers may be relatively rare, but they should be honored and cherished. A chorus of comments from high school students who were fortunate enough, over the years, to have just such teachers suggests that high school students—Black as well as white—are capable not only of understanding the book but also of articulating insightful responses to it.

Julia Rosenbloom, who is Black and Jewish, read the novel in Ben Benskin's sophomore English class at Georgetown Day School in Washington, DC, in 1994. Although she remembers having been "a little worried" about how people would react to the presence of a hateful racial epithet that still retains its power to hurt, she ended up convinced that the book was important for all students to encounter in high school. As she said at the time, she believes that Twain creates a hierarchy of moral actors in the novel, with Tom at the bottom, Huck in the middle, and Jim on top. She also noted that Twain's irony underscores the fact that "the society he describes in the book condemns the person who is most admirable from a moral perspective to the most base condition socially, physically, and legally." The point is that "Twain is ridiculing the society that treats Jim this way." The novel provoked a host of interesting discussions—in class and in the lunchroom and the halls—about racism, about how an avowedly Christian society justified slavery, and about what happened in the post-Reconstruction North. The book, she believes, has an important lesson to teach: "what it really means to behave morally."[13]

To explore these questions further, let's take a few moments to look in depth at how students experienced the book in Ann Lew's classroom at Phillip and Sala Burton High School in San Francisco in 1993 and in John Pascal's classroom at Seton Hall Preparatory School in West Orange, New Jersey, in 2022 and 2023.

When Ann Lew first presented *Huckleberry Finn* to her eleventh-grade American literature class in a minority-majority public high school in San Francisco in 1990, she writes, "several of my African American students were so offended that they did not want to deal with the text at all." Lew and her students "all survived that semester," but shortly thereafter when Lew served on the text-book selection committee of the San Francisco Unified School District, she and another teacher suggested that the book be removed from the required reading list. Neither the committee nor the English Department chairs of the district's high schools agreed: the book "remained the one required text for eleventh-grade English." Despite the mandate, Lew still wasn't sure she would teach the book. "I had to be absolutely convinced that Twain had important things to say to my classes of multiethnic, multilingual teenagers," Lew writes. "If there was one iota of stereotyping in Twain's characterization of Jim, I decided, the novel had no place in my curriculum."[14]

That summer Lew took a class at the Bread Loaf School of English where *Huckleberry Finn* was a required text. The class encouraged her to think about issues that might help her teach the book again. "With the voices of my students still ringing in in my ears," Lew writes, "I decided to do a close study of Jim." Lew examined every episode in the book involving Jim and reached some conclusions that surprised her:

> Writing a paper that focused on these episodes, I put to rest any doubts I had about Twain's portrayal of Jim. Contrary to the charges of negative stereotyping, Jim is consistently shown to be smart, assertive, and compassionate. In his quiet, gentle way, he boldly violates the behavior code of the slave as prescribed by the white system. He emerges as a superior character who not only teaches Huck morality but who himself rises above the brutalizing effects of slavery. It became apparent to me that through this character Twain registers his own opposition to the societal values he deems immoral and wages his own war against slavery.

Lew realized how important it would be for her to "present the novel in its historical context." Before jumping into the text with her class, she knew she would need to "lay the groundwork for addressing the race issue by placing Twain firmly in mid-nineteenth-century America, a time when the religious, social, and economic institutions of society supported slavery and the accompanying notion of the inferiority of African Americans." She knew that "the fact that these ideas found support and legitimacy in scientific and intellectual communities" would be crucial to convey.[15]

From that summer on, each year that she prepared to teach *Huckleberry Finn,* Lew reread portions of an invaluable book that had been introduced to her in her summer class: *Race: The History of an Idea in America* by the literary scholar Thomas Gossett.[16] Drawing on Gossett's classic work, Lew would "spend one or two class periods discussing nineteenth-century theories of race" before jumping into *Huckleberry Finn.* At the start of their discussion of the novel, Lew writes that she asks her students

> to pay close attention to what Jim says and does before deter-
> mining whether or not, he is stereotyped. We brainstorm traits
> associated with slaves: ignorant, passive, childlike, dependent,
> primitive, inferior, and the like. As for the offensive language,
> I ask students to watch closely the relationship between the
> word "nigger" and Twain's characterization of Jim, and ask
> what this label has to do with him as a person. I also ask
> students to keep in mind that the big debate among nine-
> teenth-century anthropologists was not whether blacks and
> whites should be treated as equal members of the human
> race, but whether the nonwhites belonged to the human
> race at all.

Lew would also share the evolution of her own relationship to the book as a required text, even showing them the paper that she had written during the summer and the drafts that preceded it. (Her students enjoyed seeing that even their teacher made spelling errors in her first draft!)[17]

Lew discusses the early episode in the novel where Tom and Huck play a trick on Jim and Jim turns the experience into a story that other slaves pay him to keep retelling—and that allows him to dodge questions about where the five-cent piece actually came from. "What does this episode show about Jim?" she asks. One student replies, "He sounds stupid, believing in witches." Another says, "He's smart. He's making money." "We don't know whether Jim really believes he is bewitched," Lew tells the class, "but he shrewdly turns the boys' trick to his advantage. He capitalizes on another opportunity when he dupes Huck into paying him a quarter for the hairball to tell him where his Pap is." Her students "appreciate Jim's quick wit and his ability to make a fast buck—or a quarter, in this case." Lew writes that

> my students, most of whom come from cultures rich in folklore, have an intuitive understanding of Jim's frame of reference. The Filipino American students tell stories of people in their families being visited by ghosts. The Chinese American youngsters are admonished each year not to sweep the floor on Chinese new year because they would be sweeping away good luck. The African American students with grandparents from the South report stories of people being able to foretell the future by one sign or another. One student has a grandmother who, like Jim, can forecast rain according to the way the birds fly.

She asks the class what point they think Twain is making about superstition in the book. Although some say "it's rather silly," others "think there may be something to it since they also live with superstitious beliefs." Is religion, as presented in the book, a more valid system of belief than superstition, she asks? Or are both equally valid—and equally flawed? Someone "inevitably points out that in San Francisco there is no 13th Avenue or 13th Street" and that there are no thirteenth floors in the high rises downtown.[18]

What does the dialogue between Huck and Jim about Solomon reveal about Jim? Lew asks her class. A student observes that "Jim probably identifies with the powerlessness of the child who is being fought over and certainly not with the powerful king who, like a slaveowner, can order lives to be sacrificed." And what of the Frenchman colloquy? The class "decided that perhaps Jim is making a pitch for the unity of the human race. People should stand together as a human race, not as members of distinct language groups."[19] After their close examination of Jim, her students see that "he violates every stereotype we have about slaves. What Jim says and does in the course of the novel consistently shows him to be smart, assertive, humane, independent, dignified. And superior. He is the only decent adult male in the novel; all others are violent, foolish, drunk, corrupt, cowardly, or hypocritical."[20] By about halfway through the discussion of the novel, the mismatch between traits associated with the offensive racial epithet and Twain's characterization of Jim becomes clear. "Is this irony?" one student asks. ("Thank goodness," Lew says to herself. "One person was paying attention!") Lew notes that Twain "repeatedly points out this contradiction between the language we use and the reality it is meant to convey," translating that contradiction "into art and then an indictment against society."[21]

Lew writes that "one student of mixed-race parentage (black and white) commented, 'Before I read *Huck Finn*, I thought that it was a racist book, out to degrade black people. My mother, who is white, told me that. So did my black friends. But when I read the book, I found out that that wasn't true at all.'" Jim, this student continued, "'has a mind of his own. No way does Twain put Jim down.'"[22]

Even though she once lobbied to get the book removed from San Francisco classrooms, Lew became convinced that "Jim is a good role model with a rich cultural heritage to offer teenagers of the '90s." Lew saw evidence every day of the difficulties that "nonwhite males continually face" in our society and believes the book can offer a respite to her students. "They, like Jim, are having to find the resources within themselves to cope with the world, to turn situations to their advantage. They must reject negative labels that others still try to impose on them, refrain from buying into negative stereotypes and viewing themselves as victims. . . . They, like Jim, must achieve their own self-definition." Lew notes that the book prompts her students to recall "experiences of prejudice or racism" that they have faced themselves: "African American males frequently talk about mistreatment by the police. Asian males tell of being beaten up by one or another ethnic group. One bright Latina tells of how she was diagnosed as retarded in the fourth grade because she did not speak English." Lew has concluded that "reading *Huck Finn* with students opens rich opportunities for discussions about race."[23]

Three decades and close to three thousand miles separate Ann Lew's classes taught in early 1990s San Francisco from the classes that John Pascal taught in the early 2020s in West Orange, New Jersey. Lew's school, Burton High, a minority-majority public high school, was established in 1984 as the result of a consent decree between the City of San Francisco and the NAACP. Pascal's private school, Seton Hall Preparatory School, whose student body is approximately one-third minority and all-male, is New Jersey's oldest Catholic college preparatory school and dates back to 1856. But Lew and Pascal are both remarkably dedicated and engaged teachers determined to make Jim live and breathe for their students, and both seem to have achieved that goal, despite the differences in their institutional settings.

In Pascal's classroom, framed sketches of Mark Twain by students and others sit atop a bookshelf filled with books by and about Twain. A table displays the three hefty volumes of Twain's *Autobiography* and a small model of a steamboat that might have plied the Mississippi in Twain's day, a gift that a colleague and friend of Pascal's spotted in an antiques store. Pascal, who has published articles on Twain in scholarly journals himself, teaches *Huckleberry Finn* in two American literature classes. Juniors in his honors English class read Zora Neale Hurston's *Their Eyes Were Watching God*, with its strong Black female character and its all-Black world, the summer before they begin to study Twain. Before they take this class, all that most of the students know about Twain is that there is a diner named for him nearby. But by the time they're done, most of them have an impressive understanding of the book, of its author, and of Jim.

Pascal, who has just finished his twenty-third year at Seton Hall Prep, is admirably humble: he has taught the required junior English course since 2007. But he says that he did not begin to have students focus on *Huckleberry Finn* "in depth until 2019 because I wasn't confident that I could teach it correctly."[24] Pascal introduces the book by giving students a biographical slideshow that notes some key points marking Twain's odyssey of growth and change on the subject of race: his childhood in a slaveholding society; his father's service on a jury that sent abolitionists to the state penitentiary; the influence of the Langdon family; his friendship with Frederick Douglass; the financial help that Twain gave Warner T. McGuinn, one of the first Black law students at Yale; his support of Booker T. Washington's fundraising efforts; the trip down the Mississippi that Twain took in 1882 while he was writing *Huckleberry Finn*. Pascal notes that *Huckleberry Finn* and its author have been "accused of being racist because of the N-word," a charge with which he disagrees but which he recognizes is important to address. He gives the students copies of the entries on "nigger" and "African Americans" in R. Kent Rasmussen's *Critical Companion to Mark Twain* and discusses those materials with them. While noting the ubiquity of the word in Black popular culture, Pascal sketches the "awful history" it represents and tells them that the word is not to be voiced in his classroom.[25] He tells the class they will be spending six weeks on the novel, and he gestures to the bookcase filled with books by and about Twain that students are free to browse.

Then he hands out the books. After much thought, Pascal decided that it would be important for his students to read the definitive edition prepared by the editors of the Mark Twain Project and published by the University of California Press, a book whose extensive explanatory notes detail the history of slavery that informs the book and clarify many of the obscure references.[26] The accuracy of the text is unparalleled; the edition also includes facsimile manuscript pages and maps, in addition to copious annotations and a glossary. Pascal, who had previously used a Signet Classics paperback, bought the books himself as his "gift to the Prep." He writes that the notes and glossary were hugely important for the students: "The difference was like night and day!"[27] Pascal gives them detailed worksheets after each class discussion to assess their understanding of each section.[28] Jim figures prominently in the students' papers and exams.

In her book *Huck Finn's "Hidden" Lessons*, Sharon Rush argues that scholars who see Jim as being "strong and savvy" often "arrive at this interpretation through sophisticated literary techniques and rhetorical devices," which realistically high school teachers cannot be expected to deploy.[29] John Pascal resorts to no "sophisticated literary techniques and rhetorical devices" in his classroom. He relies instead on the old-fashioned virtue of close reading.

Rush also doubts that any white students would identify with Jim and maintains that Black students do not identify with Jim either. (The book, she charges, leaves Black students feeling "devalued, excluded, angry, resentful and betrayed.")[30] But the papers and exams that Pascal's students wrote—Black students as well as white—suggest otherwise. Let me share some of their comments on the discussion between Huck and Jim about Solomon, on Jim's decision to cover pap's body, on the trick Huck plays on Jim during the fog and its aftermath, on the story Jim tells about his daughter, and on various dimensions of the Evasion portion of the novel. Finally, I'll quote from their general comments on the role Jim plays in the book, on how they feel about him, and on how they'd respond to those who want to take the book out of their classroom because Jim "isn't a good role model" (a phrase used by Texas state senator Royce West).[31] When I quote from their 2022 and 2023 papers and exams here, I am intentionally not cleaning up their writing, leaving minor infelicities and lapses in punctuation, spelling, and grammar in place. The words I quote are the words they wrote, and I have permission to use them here.

Andrew Merklinger and Daniel Lowe both observe that the qualities of mind that Jim shows in his discussion with Huck about Solomon and the ways of kings run counter to the prevailing racial ideology of the time. Merklinger notes that "rational-minded thinking" was not expected of slaves. "The questions that Jim was asking were legitimate questions," he tells us, "and yet Huck ruins it at the end by thinking, 'you can't learn a n-word to argue,' which is a completely moronic thing for Huck to say because Jim did nothing wrong." He doesn't "fault Huck too much because of his upbringing in a racist society," but he still finds the exchange "infuriating." The "intellectual conversation" between Jim and Huck in chapter 14, he tells us, "shows the side of slaves that people did not want to accept," that is, their intelligence. In a similar vein, Lowe writes that "Jim's questions and confusions are valid" and show "his innate intelligence that Huck doesn't recognize."

What do they think motivated Jim's decision to cover pap's body? Logan Brzozowski is convinced that "Jim was a father-like figure to Huck by protecting him from seeing death at such a young age." In a similar vein, Reed Bienstock says the episode shows "Jim's care for Huck and thoughtfulness regarding Huck." Andrew Merklinger, Patrick Quinn, and Danny Easter are also convinced that Jim covered pap's body to protect Huck.

What about the trick Huck plays on Jim during the fog and what occurs afterward? William Kahney describes the scene like this: "Jim gets serious and stares Huck dead in the eye. Jim follows with a paragraph about what type of people pull these tricks and how hurt he was by this. Huck realizes his mistake, and after 15 minutes he goes over to Jim to rectify what he had done. . . . A white child apologizing to a slave? Are you kidding me? Jim just staring at Huck is considered an offense worthy of punishment. Then Huck gets shamed enough by a slave that he wants to go over and kiss his feet! If this is not an ironic way of showing how stupid racism is then I do not know what is." Meanwhile Sean Murphy maintains that at this point in the book, "the power dynamic switches because an escaped slave indirectly called a white boy trash, which was unheard of for this time." For Murphy, "This scene is one of the most powerful moments and biggest defiance of racial boundaries in the novel. Despite being astonished that a slave just talked to him in such manner, Huck feels the need to apologize to Jim. However, because of the racial boundaries that have been engrained in Huck's mind, it took him fifteen minutes to build up the courage to apologize to Jim. Twain wants the reader to be enraged that Huck needs so much time to apologize to a black person. Huck was not even aware that blacks could have feelings."

William Kahney finds a similar dynamic at work in the scene in which Jim tells the story about his daughter 'Lizabeth, a scene that he believes shows that slaves "are capable of unconditional love and emotion. Contrary to the trendy beliefs of this period, the slaves shared the same feelings and emotions as white people. Huck even admits to Jim having similar feelings to white people, although it does not feel normal to him." Of this scene, Devin Campana, who is Black, writes that "because of the racist mindset that Huck has, he can't believe Jim is thinking the way that a 'white person' does." Twain cannot let Huck, "a product of the racist south, come out and say that Jim is his best friend," but that fact becomes clear to the reader. For Campana, "Jim is the most important character in this entire story.... Jim is Huck's father, brother, priest, caretaker, and best friend, but Twain doesn't tell us that." He lets us see it for ourselves.

The students do a credible job of analyzing the infamous final portion of the book (chapter 32 to the end, known as the Evasion), the section where, as Daniel Lowe puts it, "Tom prolongs Jim's freedom by making elaborate plans and pointless adventures." Isaiah Shoyombo, another Black student, writes, "While Twain was writing this book, America was still recovering from the Civil War. Twain had seen 'Reconstruction' play out. He noticed how despite white people of the south had been promising to free slaves, and that slaves had all the rights that white people had, none of it was actually true." "Instead of immediately giving slaves the rights and freedom they deserved," Shoyombo adds, "the whole concept of black freedom was dragged out. In *Adventures of*

Huckleberry Finn, Twain uses both Tom and Huck to address and attack this situation that was present in America." In the book, Shoyombo continues, "Tom represented the white man during Reconstruction. Tom dragging out the freedom of Jim is exactly like what was present during reconstruction at that time. Even though Jim was already rightfully free, he was still kept captive and held in slavery." Anthony James ("AJ") Bicksler, a varsity football player, had a more visceral response to the final portion of the novel during a class discussion; as John Pascal wrote me, Bicksler said: "I want to tackle Tom to the ground for what he's put Jim AND US THROUGH!"[32]

Of Jim's decision to give up his freedom to stay with a wounded Tom Sawyer while Huck went to fetch a doctor, Andrew Merklinger is struck by the fact that "Jim was willing to risk his freedom for a man who was basically using him as a toy." Joaquin Niehenke writes, "Jim is a free man at this point in the novel, which means he is jeopardizing his liberty to stay with Tom. Twain's use of irony to blitz racism here is that Jim is sacrificing his freedom for a white man who pre-empted his liberation with four weeks of suffering."

Devin Campana quotes the doctor who implores those assembled at the Phelps farm: "'Don't be no rougher on him than you're obleeged to, because he ain't a bad n-word.' . . . an n-word like that is worth a thousand dollars—and kind treatment, too." Devin writes, "Jim risked his freedom to get help for Tom, and then he is given a price tag." He adds, "And while the doctor does say that Jim should get better treatment, he says this after saying how much Jim would be worth, which is ironic."

What is Jim's function in the novel? In Alex Andia's view, "Twain uses Jim in this novel to change his readers' perspectives." Twain's goal, he believes, is to get "readers to understand the complexities of the normalized racist society in which Twain

Alex Andia in John Pascal's classroom at Seton Hall Preparatory School. He believes that "Twain uses Jim in this novel to change his readers' perspectives," to get "readers to understand the complexities of the normalized racist society in which Twain wrote this book." Photo by John Pascal.

wrote this book." (His comment resonates with that of Twain scholar Joe Fulton, who maintains that "reading *Adventures of Huckleberry Finn,* the reader engages in a personal act of ethical becoming and rises from the narrative with new perspectives and attitudes.")[33] In a similar vein, Casey O'Sullivan writes that Twain uses Jim's character "to flip racial stereotypes. Through the characters of the Duke, the King and Pap he attacks the white community by showing how white people were uncivilized and barbaric themselves yet they believed they were better than Black people."

Lucah Benitez, who is Black, concurs, arguing that "Twain uses Jim's characterization to challenge stereotypes about Black people." Benitez writes that "Jim is selfless, innocent, loyal, honest, and kind." He argues that Twain's portrayal of Jim is "ironic because . . . at that time African Americans were typically portrayed as simple-minded, lazy, animal-like, and violent. Giving Jim these positive traits humanized his character in a way that was uncommon for the time." Despite having seen and "felt all of the atrocities that were inflicted on his race at the hands of white people," Benitez adds, "Jim ironically allows himself to trust, respect and befriend a white person when most would expect his character to be bitter towards the white race in its entirety." Twain contrasts Jim, with all of his positive qualities, with "a large number of white characters who are hypocrites, liars, [and] murderers." In Benitez's view, "Twain does this deliberately to show the often unseen negative sides of white society." The king and duke, for example, "are liars and thieves" who "care about personal gain, regardless of the cost or how it affects those around them," while "Pap is a jealous, mean, racist, abusive, and alcoholic father, who has nothing going for him in life, other than making Huck's life miserable." Benitez is struck by the irony of the fact that these characters are "the perfect embodiment of white trash yet they view themselves as superior to Black people." Isaiah Shoyombo writes that "over and over again Twain attacks white society at the time and repeatedly exposes the true nature of it." The bottom line for Shoyombo is this: "Instead of shoving this country's evil history in a corner, we should proclaim it, face it, and then learn from it, and grow together as a society."

Two of the Black students in Pascal's American literature class, Devin Campana and Lucah Benitez, had been skeptical about reading Twain before they took the class in their junior year. But although Benitez had initially been resistant to the idea of reading Twain at all, he ended up being the student who always volunteered first to provide a chapter summary. Indeed, Benitez and Campana both got so interested in Twain that by the end of the term they wanted more: they both signed up for Pascal's Twain seminar after the required English III class ended.[34] (Campana's intense sense of connection with the author stemmed in part from Twain's support of Yale law student Warner T. McGuinn, who

Devin Campana on a class field trip to the Mark Twain Home & Museum in Hartford, Connecticut. He told John Pascal that he signed up for his Mark Twain seminar at Seton Hall Preparatory School after studying *Huckleberry Finn* in his American literature class because "he wanted to find out how a kid born in a slave-owning home, neighborhood, and region grew up eventually to condemn slavery." Photo by John Pascal.

became a key mentor to Thurgood Marshall, the lead attorney in *Brown v. Board of Education* (1954), which held that segregation in public schools was unconstitutional, and who became the first African American justice on the Supreme Court. Campana wrote poignantly in a response to the readings on April 28, 2023, "If it weren't for Mark Twain, I probably wouldn't have been able to attend a school of mostly white kids.") Campana told Pascal that he signed up for the Twain seminar "because he wanted to find out how a kid born in a slave-owning home, neighborhood, and region grew up eventually to condemn slavery."

Sharon Rush quotes with approval critics Fredrick Woodard and Donnarae McCann, who argue that Jim "gives no sign of perceiving himself as anything but a child among children."[35] But Pascal's students didn't see him that way at all. Jaysen Lim writes that

Southern society tries its absolute hardest to suppress Jim and make him look like a foolish nobody. Whether intentional or not, a multitude of characters toy around with Jim's dignity and *life,* as if they have no value at all. . . . Some readers may look at Jim valuing himself at a measly $800 or agreeing to the most ridiculous "Arab" outfit and see Jim as nothing but a hateful and stereotypical depiction of a slave during the first half of the 1800s. However, with an understanding of how Southern society and norms often restricted Jim and the knowledge of Jim's daring and loving personality in spite of those norms, Jim becomes one of the most unsung heroes in literature.

Taylor Mason writes that "Jim is my favorite character in the novel, & that still stands. . . . I genuinely cannot think of a reason why anyone would ever say Jim is not a good role model."

Several students comment on the many positive character traits they associated with Jim, including his intelligence. Alex Gitto writes that "although Jim is uneducated, he is very logical and uses his brain," while Jack Tierney wrote that "Jim is undoubtedly not perfect. He is ignorant and sometimes makes mistakes, but that is what makes him a realistic and admirable role model. Him being imperfect does not make him a bad role model, it makes him human." Admirable qualities Gitto associates with Jim include "care, love, humor, common sense, humbleness, & humility." Reed Bienstock writes, "Jim is compassionate, thoughtful, and is a family man." For Kevin Jiratatprasot, "The most important qualities of Jim's character is that he sees the good in people while knowing his self value." Michael Kelly particularly values Jim's loyalty. Alex Tran appreciates Jim's composure. For Casey O'Sullivan, Jim's "many important qualities" include "how much he cares, level head, his selflessness." Gitto asserts that Jim "would stop at nothing to protect his own. Jim is a better man than everyone in the novel."

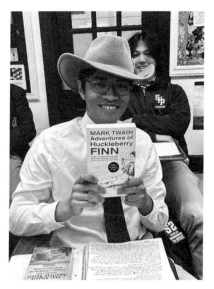

Jaysen Lim in John Pascal's classroom at Seton Hall Preparatory School. He wrote that "some readers may look at Jim valuing himself at a measly $800 or agreeing to the most ridiculous 'Arab' outfit and see Jim as nothing but a hateful and stereotypical depiction of a slave during the first half of the 1800s. However, with an understanding of how Southern society and norms often restricted Jim and the knowledge of Jim's daring and loving personality in spite of those norms, Jim becomes one of the most unsung heroes in literature." Photo by John Pascal.

In Connor Schmit's view, Jim is "everything a white racist would assume Jim not to be. . . . I would argue to someone who wants to ban the book because Jim is not a good role model for students, that they aren't reading deep enough into the text. . . . Twain presents all white characters with underlying/straight up racism, violence, and lack of morality, while presenting Jim as the only good and moral person. . . . If Twain were to sugar coat the reality of racism at the time," Schmit continues, "it would do injustice to the situation and downplay the truth."

For O'Sullivan, "Jim is truly the only good person in the story." Benitez writes, in a similar vein, "Jim is the best person in the book; he is kind, brave, patient, and calm . . . [and] has always protected Huck whenever he needs it. . . . I have always liked Jim's character, he was always the one that made the right choices." Although Rush insists that Black students do not identify with Jim, Lucah Benitez would disagree: "One way that I respond to his character is in awe," Benitez writes. "I have always worked to

Connor Schmit in John Pascal's classroom at Seton Hall Preparatory School. He wrote, "If Twain were to sugar coat the reality of racism at the time it would do injustice to the situation and downplay the truth." Photo by John Pascal.

emulate Jim's personality," Benitez adds, particularly his loyalty and patience. He believes that Jim "would be a perfect role model for younger people."

In Matthew Corr's view, Jim is an "undercover role model, and does not get the praise for it. . . . He is always there to help, whether it be moral decisions or knowing what to do he is always there. Jim is a very strong character, both mentally and physically. . . . The people that want this book to be banned, just are either racist themselves or are not smart enough to see how much of a role Jim plays."

For Nicholas Lapczynski, "Jim embodies what a human being should be."

Some students are surprised at how their view of Jim changed over the course of reading the novel. For example, Aryan Kapoor writes, "Mr. Pascal, when I first started reading the book and as we progressed, I thought of Jim as someone who served one purpose—to help Huck, a white boy, develop morally." But he came

Matthew Corr in John Pascal's classroom at Seton Hall Preparatory School. He wrote that Jim is an "undercover role model, and does not get the praise for it. . . . He is always there to help, whether it be moral decisions or knowing what to do he is always there. Jim is a very strong character, both mentally and physically. . . . The people that want this book to be banned, just are either racist themselves or are not smart enough to see how much of a role Jim plays." Photo by John Pascal.

Nicholas Lapczynski in John Pascal's classroom at Seton Hall Preparatory School. "Jim embodies what a human being should be." Photo by John Pascal.

to believe that "Jim is soooooo much more than that." He writes that Jim, who is "treated as subhuman" through much of the novel, is someone who is "exceedingly intelligent and logical," that he is "a father," "a loving human," and someone who "grows and changes" over the course of the book. In his view, Jim is "a GREAT MODEL for people. . . . " He even adds, "I love him. I want to give him a hug."

While this comment may strike readers as perhaps over the top, it is consistent with other remarks students made. Mark Lubiak writes that "Jim isn't just a character, he is a symbol of good in an evil world." Michael Kelly writes that "Jim is somebody that I would want as a friend and role model. . . . Jim cared for and protected Huck as best as he could, like a true friend would. I would tell whoever thinks Jim is not a good role model that they are completely wrong. I would also tell them to go read the book more closely and try to find where Jim is not a good role model. Spoiler alert there is none." Matthew Touchard writes, "Jim makes me want to be a better person." Julian Gray sums Jim up like this: "Jim's qualities make him the only person in the story who you can look up to. He is a kind, genuine, and practical man. I would say that Jim is not only a good role model he is the only one in the novel. Jim should be looked up [to] by all students. He never lies and always treats others with kindness and respect. He also never acts like he is better than anyone in the novel even though he is."

While Sharon Rush believes that teaching the novel contributes to "a culture of disrespect" in the classroom, John Pascal's students express a very different view. William Kahney writes, for example, that "I value a society where all are treated equally with respect and dignity. Understanding how Twain attacks racism can

Julian Gray in John Pascal's classroom in Seton Hall Preparatory School. He wrote that "Jim's qualities make him the only person in the story who you can look up to. He is a kind, genuine, and practical man. I would say that Jim is not only a good role model he is the only one in the novel. Jim should be looked up [to] by all students. He never lies and always treats others with kindness and respect. He also never acts like he is better than anyone in the novel even though he is." Photo by John Pascal.

help us achieve this. We can use this book to look into the past, to see how dreadful things were. With a clear view of how things used to be, we can put all our energy into getting our society the furthest away from what Twain's society was. If Mark Twain attacked racism in a time when you could be lynched for supporting blacks, why can we not attack it now?"

Devin Campana also finds the book relevant to issues our society is still struggling with now: "As an African-American myself," he writes, "I can say that there are still people around who act like some of the white people in the story, an example being the murder of George Floyd. He was murdered, and the police officer that murdered him was not being stopped by people around him, and it even took our justice system an entire year before they decided to act against him, showing that there are still racial injustices now that've been around for centuries, and it is something that seems like it will never go away."

John Pascal (in white suit) with his students in the class of 2024 at Seton Hall
Preparatory School holding their copies of *Adventures of Huckleberry Finn* on
March 3, 2024. The other students quoted in this chapter graduated in 2023.
All were taught the novel during their junior year. *Front row from left to right,*
left side of the Pirate: Anthony James "AJ" Bicksler, Jack Tierney, Michael Kelly,
Connor Schmit. *Back row from left to right, left side of the Pirate:* Mark Lubiak,
Julian Gray, Kevin Jiratatprasot, Matthew Touchard, Alex Tran. *Front row*
from left to right, right side of the Pirate: Luke Brzozowski, Nicholas Lapczynski,
Alex Gitto, Jaysen Lim, Taylor Mason. *Back row from left to right, right side*
of the Pirate: Danny Easter, Reed Bienstock, Casey O'Sullivan, Alex Andia,
Matthew Corr, Aryan Kapoor, Patrick Quinn. Photo by John Pascal.

Toni Morrison wrote in 1996, "The 1880s saw the collapse of
civil rights for blacks as well as the publication of *Huckleberry
Finn.* This collapse was an effort to bury the combustible issues
Twain raised in his novel. The nation, as well as Tom Sawyer, was
deferring Jim's freedom in agonizing play. *The cyclical attempts to*
remove the novel from classrooms extend Jim's captivity into each gen-
eration of readers."[36] John Pascal's students would clearly agree.

The insights raised by the high school students quoted here
from Washington, DC, San Francisco, and West Orange, New Jersey, suggest that Jim can have a place in American high schools
when the book is taught by teachers with the skills, the training,
and the desire to teach it. The evidence from John Pascal's classroom and those of Ann Lew and Ben Benskin suggests not that

every teacher should teach this book but that teachers prepared to help their students grapple with the challenging, powerful, beautiful, rich, sad, and profound issues that Jim raises should not be denied the opportunity to do so.

AFTERWORD

———

"**Y**OUR BOOK IS ABOUT RACISM,**" my friend Min Jin Lee
told me on the phone recently. I immediately knew she
was right. An award-winning writer of color herself who,
I sometimes think, understands me better than I understand
myself, she added: "It's what you've been writing about all your
life."

Her comments clarified for me just how much this book is
about how racism distorts our understanding of the past, of the
present, and of each other. About the myopia that stops us from
recognizing each other's humanity, from appreciating each other's
virtues, from grasping the brutal nature of the racist roadblocks
(subtle and unsubtle, intentional and unintentional, small and
large) that prevent so many from living their best lives.

I have, indeed, been writing and teaching about racism for
decades—racism toward African Americans, toward the Chinese,
toward Japanese Americans, Mexican Americans, Native Americans, Jews, and others. But when I try to figure out what set this
agenda in motion, I realize that it all began with Jim.

I had begun my education in Brooklyn, New York, in a school
in which about a third of the students were Black. I first read
Huckleberry Finn as a junior in a nearly all-white high school in

Westport, Connecticut. The Civil Rights Movement was picking up steam—along with opposition to it. The opposition made no sense to me. How could people be against equality in a nation founded on the ideal that "all men are created equal"? Then I read *Huckleberry Finn* my junior year. I recall recognizing that Jim was the most admirable character in the book. And I remember being appalled that he had the same rights as the cattle he tended for his mistress. I was fascinated by how Twain refrained from having any character in the book recognize that there was anything wrong with what was clearly an indefensible status quo. Including Huck. Respectable folks like the Phelpses acquiesced to all the bigotry of their world, and reinforced it. Even Huck, who had come to see Jim as a friend, didn't generalize from their friendship to recognize that the system that kept his friend enslaved was wrong. Twain's irony made the book's critique of racism incredibly powerful. Being asked to write about how Twain used irony to attack racism in *Huckleberry Finn* is what propelled me into the field of literature in the first place.

I am filled with humility when I realize that even a writer as gifted as Mark Twain had such trouble getting his fellow Americans to look at themselves in the mirror. The more I study American history, the more I am persuaded that *Huckleberry Finn* evokes—perhaps as only a work of art can—both the boldness of founding a nation on the ideals laid out in the Declaration of Independence and the brazen hypocrisy that allowed those ideals to be violated so fully from the start. It is perhaps unsurprising that the persistence of racism in our world has fostered a myopia that has prevented many—including myself—from recognizing Jim's full humanity until now.

After immersing myself in the historical conditions surrounding Jim's life, the experiences Twain had that led him to challenge prevailing myths about race in the novel, the debates among critics about who Jim really is, the ways in which actors and directors have portrayed him on stage and screen, how his words and his character have been depicted in some of the sixty-seven languages in which we can encounter him, and the controversies surrounding him in the nation's high school classrooms, I find myself returning to the text itself with fresh eyes.

I am awed by Jim's astute ability to weigh the complexities of any situation. By his compassion. By his sense of justice. By his creativity. By his generosity. By his strength. By his integrity. By his refusal to let a world that denies that he is even human constrain his ability to love.

And I am still stunned by Twain's daring experiment of presenting Jim only through the eyes of a child with such a limited understanding of what he is seeing.

And then I realize what trust Twain had in us, his readers. He trusted in our ability to read between the lines and understand things that Huck never did. He trusted us to see through the whitewashed history of America's racist past that was being presented as truth even at the time he wrote and that has continued to be foisted on each new generation ever since. He trusted us to read the story he placed before us and to recognize the phenomenon that he would later call the "lie of silent assertion"—"the silent assertion that there wasn't anything going on in which humane and intelligent people were interested . . . and are engaged by their duty to try to stop."[1]

Do we have the courage to honor that trust, to be the readers he hoped we could be? The jury is still out.

APPENDIX

Notes for Teachers

This appendix does not pretend to be a comprehensive teaching guide. Rather, it gathers ideas that have proven helpful to teachers trying to address the major challenges posed by *Huckleberry Finn* in the classroom. Part One focuses on the challenge of dealing with the offensive racial epithet; the challenge of contextualizing the history of race and racism in America as background for the novel; and the challenge of teaching Mark Twain's use of irony to attack racism. Part Two includes two scenes from Ralph Wiley's unproduced screenplay, *Spike Lee's Huckleberry Finn*, and a description of how to use them for staged readings in class. I have had my students stage these scenes for two decades, and the results have been remarkable. Part Three contains full citations for works mentioned in Parts One and Two that are not included in the endnotes, as well as suggestions for further reading.

Part One

THE CHALLENGE OF DEALING WITH THE OFFENSIVE RACIAL EPITHET THAT RUNS THROUGH THE BOOK

Teachers often cite the ubiquity in the book of an offensive racial epithet as a reason not to teach *Adventures of Huckleberry Finn*. Teachers should not teach it if they are not prepared to have a discussion about this word before their students begin reading the novel.

Some of the points made in the "Explanatory" that precedes the table of contents in this book bear repeating. The notorious racial slur that appears more than two hundred times in *Huckleberry Finn* has been used for centuries in the United States to vilify and stigmatize Black people. Spoken by a non-Black individual, the word immediately identifies the speaker with the ideology of white supremacy, and with it the history of dehumanization, disparagement, and defamation to which Black people have been subjected from the beginnings of racial slavery through the present. While seeking to represent the authentic speech of his characters on the page as accurately as possible, Mark Twain recognized that the word denied the humanity of the people it was used to describe, enabling and embodying the racist norms that prevailed in the world in which he lived.[1] Although no character in the novel challenges those norms directly, Twain makes those norms the object of his lacerating satire in an effort to push his readers to recognize and reject them on their own.

Teachers might note that although the word can bring to mind the hateful practices that have fostered anti-Black hostility from Twain's day to our own, a sizable number of Black people have used—and use—the word themselves in a range of contexts, sometimes repurposing it in ways that diminish its stigma. But the slur's historical use by white people to maintain an unjust racial order associates it with a history of violence and insult that remains and that can still provoke anger and cause pain.

Before teaching the book, teachers should inform themselves about the history of the word and how it came to derive the power that it wields in American culture. Randall Kennedy's book *Nigger: The Strange Career of a Troublesome Word* (2003) is a good place to start.[2] For students, a shorter text by Kennedy could be assigned: "A Note on the Word 'Nigger,'" which appears on the website of the National Park Service's Park Ethnography Program, along with the entry on the word in R. Kent Rasmussen's *Critical Companion to Mark Twain*.[3] Teachers might also find helpful Jabari Asim's book *The N Word: Who Can Say It, Who Shouldn't, and Why*.[4] Teachers should be willing to discuss the power that the word retains today to demean and diminish Black people while also being reclaimed by some Black people as a term of affection when referring to each other. To clarify these issues, I highly recommend having students watch an excellent Peabody Award–winning documentary written and directed by Todd Williams and produced by executive producer Nelson George, *The N-Word*, released June 26, 2004.[5]

Teachers might engage students in a discussion of why Twain repeatedly used a word that at the time was an offensive epithet as well as the word normally used to refer to Black people. In their efforts to convey Twain's recognition of the power of the word to almost single-handedly transform Black people into the "other," I recommend that teachers assign Twain's satire from 1869 about a lynching in Memphis in which an innocent man lost his life. It is called "Only a Nigger," and in the piece, Twain mockingly impersonates the Memphis lynchers justifying and minimizing the importance of their actions by saying that "only a 'nigger'" was killed by their mistake. Twain puts the term in quotation marks, making clear that he viewed it as part of how the lynchers turned the murdered Black man into someone whose life didn't matter.[6]

Teachers might also consider assigning short stories by nineteenth-century Black writers that are set, like *Huckleberry Finn*, in antebellum times, in which the offensive epithet appears. For example, teachers might assign "The Ingrate" by Paul Laurence Dunbar and "The Passing of Grandison" by Charles W. Chesnutt. Both of these writers use the word for the same reasons that Mark Twain does: to accurately portray the speech of a particular time and place and to convey the ways in which the word helps portray Black people as hopelessly "other."[7]

As I wrote in my "Explanatory," given the pain that the word inflicts, I believe there is no need to read the word aloud in the classroom.[8] The word is offensive—but so, too, are slavery and racism. We can no more hide from this painful word than we can from America's painful past. But it is helpful to provide students with a context for understanding its destructive power by exposing them to some of the resources outlined here, as well as strategies to avoid saying the word out loud.

The idea of having students read aloud from *Huckleberry Finn* in class is controversial. Personally, I'd discourage this, but some teachers have found the practice constructive. In any case, I'd encourage teachers to tell their students that the offensive epithet should not be said aloud in class. If portions of the book containing the word need to be quoted in class, students and teachers might substitute a euphemism of their choice (such as *n-word* or simply substituting the letter *n*).[9] Teachers should note that students should never use the word when writing in their own voices in their essays and research papers. However, teachers may decide whether to give students the option of using the word in writing when quoting from the text; alternatively, they might substitute something like [n—]. A trigger warning noting the presence of the offensive epithet in the book might be included in the syllabus, or it could be written on the blackboard before students start reading the book, along with a statement along the lines indicated above about how the word should be handled.

Teachers might also find the following sources helpful on this topic: Alan Carey-Webb's "Racism and 'Huckleberry Finn': Censorship, Dialogue, and Change" (1993); Shelley Fisher Fishkin's "Take the N-Word Out of 'Huck Finn'? It's an Insult to Mark Twain—and to American History" (2011); David E. E. Sloane's "The N-Word in *Adventures of Huckleberry Finn* Reconsidered" (2014); Jocelyn Chadwick's "We Dare Not Teach What We Know We Must: The Importance of Difficult Conversations" (2016); Jocelyn Chadwick's "When Will We Listen? Mark Twain through the Lenses of Generation Z" (2018); and David A.

Gorlewski's "Scholars Weigh In on Teaching *Adventures of Huckleberry Finn*" (2022).[10]

College teachers might consider assigning David Bradley's essay "Eulogy for Nigger," winner of the international Notting Hill Editions Essay Prize in 2015. It was written originally on the occasion of the NAACP's decision to hold a funeral for the word. The text of the essay was reprinted in London when it won the prize.[11]

THE CHALLENGE OF CONTEXTUALIZING THE HISTORY OF RACE AND RACISM IN AMERICA

Exposing students to slave narratives and essays by Black writers can help them understand the conditions that inform the novel. Having students read slave narratives (or portions of them) by Frederick Douglass, William Wells Brown, Harriet Jacobs, and others, as well as selections from WPA Federal Writers' Project interviews with individuals who were formerly enslaved in Missouri, can give them a useful grounding in the situation in which Jim finds himself in the novel. All of these are readily available online and are not difficult to understand, although they can be emotionally painful to confront.[12] Recollections of people enslaved in Missouri may be found at the website of Missouri State Parks.[13] In addition, Frederick Douglass's essay "What to the Slave Is the Fourth of July?" is powerful and clearly argued, as well as profound, and can deepen any discussion of race in the classroom.[14]

Teachers might share the myths about race that dominated the world in which both Huck and Mark Twain lived that I outline in the first section of chapter 2 of this book and ask students to think about whether Jim embodies or subverts those myths. Take the myth about Black lack of intelligence. Ask students to read the book starting with the assumption that Jim is smart. How does that shape the way we read various scenes that might, on the surface, appear to cast him as a minstrel show figure? Do the same with the myths about Black lack of creativity or the ability of Black people to feel pain and grief. Discussions of whether—and how—Jim subverts popular stereotypes about race might be enhanced by having students watch the Emmy-winning documentary about stereotypes by Marlon Riggs titled *Ethnic Notions* (1987).[15]

One novel intervention that some teachers found helpful in recent years was taking their classes to a stage adaptation of *Huckleberry Finn* called *Splittin' the Raft*, by Scott Kaiser.[16] In this play, Frederick Douglass acts as Greek chorus of sorts, delivering excerpts from his speeches as asides to the audience that serve as commentaries on the action. (This option is viable only if a local theater group or high school or college theater club is willing to present the play.)

Reading accessible works on race and racism can help a teacher prepare for issues that may come up in discussions. Some useful works in this category include Ibram X. Kendi, *Stamped from the Beginning: The Definitive History of Racist Ideas in America* (2016); Thomas H. Gossett, *Race: The History of an Idea in America* (1997); George M. Fredrickson, *The Arrogance of Race: Historical Perspectives on Slavery, Racism, and Social Inequality* (1988); Toni Morrison, *The Origin of Others* (2017); and George M. Fredrickson, *Racism: A Short History* (rpt., 2015).[17]

Examining American culture's discomfort with facing issues of race and racism as they relate to Twain can also help prepare a teacher for controversies surrounding the book. Two works that do this are my book *Lighting Out for the Territory: Reflections on Mark Twain and American Culture* (2002) and my essay "Mark Twain and Race" (2002).[18]

THE CHALLENGE OF TEACHING MARK TWAIN'S USE OF IRONY TO CRITIQUE RACISM

The materials that follow come out of programs I've presented over the past three decades in Austin and Dallas, Texas; in Greenwich and Hartford, Connecticut; in Stanford, California; at the National Humanities Center in Research Triangle Park, North Carolina, and elsewhere to help high school teachers teach this book.

"Teaching *Adventures of Huckleberry Finn*," a ninety-minute webinar of a teachers' institute that I conducted in 2015 for the National Humanities Center's "Humanities in the Classroom" Webinar Series, can be helpful. It addresses questions such as how to help students recognize how Twain's irony works and what led him to choose the risky strategy of creating a narrator who fails to understand so much of the world around him. I discuss, among other things, the value of preceding discussions of *Huckleberry Finn* with discussions of some of Twain's widely available earlier satires on racism that feature narrators too innocent or too bigoted to grasp what is wrong with the racism that their society widely normalizes—works such as "What Have the Police Been Doing?," "Disgraceful Persecution of a Boy," and the "Goldsmith's Friend Abroad Again" letters.[19]

My essay "Teaching Mark Twain's *Adventures of Huckleberry Finn*," published in 1999 by PBS in connection with the film *Born to Trouble: Adventures of Huckleberry Finn* (part of its *Culture Shock* series) can be useful to teachers as well, along with a six-part teachers' guide developed in connection with the film.[20]

A paper topic that was assigned during my American literature class during my junior year in high school—"Write a paper on how Mark Twain uses irony to attack racism in *Huckleberry Finn*"—has proven useful to John Pascal in his classes at Seton Hall Preparatory School for the past three years.

Part Two

To dramatize the ironic gap between the action of the book as Huck narrates it and the action of the book as Jim perceives it, I have found it helpful to have students do a staged reading of two scenes from *Spike Lee's Huckleberry Finn* by Ralph Wiley. The first involves the prank Tom plays on Jim at the start of the book, and the second centers on the prank Huck plays on Jim after the fog.

Wiley, who died in 2004, was an influential sports journalist and iconoclastic satirist who was also an appreciative and insightful reader of Mark Twain. His books include *Dark Witness: When Black People Should Be Sacrificed (Again)* (1996), as well as *Why Black People Tend to Shout: Cold Facts and Wry Views from a Black Man's World* (1991) and *What Black People Should Do Now: Dispatches from Near the Vanguard* (1993).[21] Wiley had wanted to subtitle *Dark Witness* "In Homage to Mark Twain," but his publisher refused. When Wiley gave the book to friends, he sometimes pasted a yellow sticky note with his preferred subtitle on the cover (he gave me a copy with such a sticky note in 1999). Wiley wrote the screenplay in the 1990s and hoped to persuade his good friend Spike Lee to produce it. Wiley, who was coauthoring *By Any Means Necessary: The Trials and Tribulations of Making Malcolm X* with Lee at the time, also hoped to persuade the actor Denzel Washington, then starring in the Malcolm X film, to play Jim.[22] Wiley shared his script with me, sought my advice, and enlisted my help. The movie was never made—but Spike Lee spent a day with Wiley and me in his Brooklyn studio discussing *Huckleberry Finn*, Jim, and why both Ralph and I cared so much about this book. Wiley gave me permission to publish several scenes from the unproduced screenplay in the *Mark Twain Circular*, encouraging teachers to have their students do staged readings of them. I published the scenes in 1999. For more than twenty years, I have been having students do staged readings of them in class, as have many other teachers around the country. The results have been nothing less than transformative.

In this screenplay, Huck's voiceover narration stays close to the story as Huck tells it in the novel, while the camera shows us the action from Jim's perspective. In addition to casting students as Jim, Huck, and Tom, teachers who want to have students stage these two scenes should cast a student to read the part of "Narrator" and another to read the "stage directions." Excerpts from the screenplay follow.[23] My article about the screenplay, "In Praise of *Spike Lee's Huckleberry Finn* by Ralph Wiley" (*Mark Twain Circular* 13, no. 4 [1999]), may be accessed at this link: https://marktwaincircle.org/ralph-wiley-huck-finn.

SCENES FROM *SPIKE LEE'S HUCKLEBERRY FINN*
BY RALPH WILEY

7. EXT. WIDOW DOUGLAS HOME. REAR. NIGHT. — *Huck scrambles out of the window onto the roof of attached shed. He jumps down and crawls back among the trees and underbrush behind the house and there is Tom, grinning. They tiptoe along a path among the trees. Passing the back of the corral, where Jim sits, using an awl on what appears to be a doll's head. Huck steps on a dry branch and it snaps. At this sound, Jim surreptitiously puts away the doll-object and picks up a rack of tallow candles; his head comes up as he begins to snap them off.*

JIM

Who dah?

The boys bend over, stock-still, grimacing, then hide behind separate trees. We can see that Jim catches a glimpse of them. Jim walks back into the foliage with two candles, and stops in a space between the two trees. Only a fool would not have seen the boys. So Jim pretends to be one.

JIM

Say—who is you? Whar is you? Well, I knows what I's gon' do. I's gon' set down heah . . . ahh! . . . and listen till I hears it agin.

Jim sits down on a natural seat under the tree. Huck is on the other side. Huck shuts his eyes tight. Jim settles into a comfortable position, puts his hat on the ground and sighs contentedly.

7A. EXT. MOON SHOT. SILVERY RIVER. NIGHT.

8. EXT. TREES. NIGHT. — *Huck hears heavy breathing from the other side, begins to peer around the tree. We see Jim, eyes slitted open, obviously awake, feigning sleep, as he continues to make the sound of a man deep in slumber. Tom Sawyer's cap begins to emerge from the other side of the opposite tree. Jim's eyes close effortlessly. Tom makes a sign to Huck; he and Huck creep away on their hands and knees in opposite directions away from the trees.*

9. EXT. MEDIUM SHOT. JIM UNDER TREE. NIGHT. — *Through the foliage we can see Jim, Huck and Tom's profiles enter from opposite sides of the shot, close-up. They look at each other, then back at Jim, then back to each other.*

TOM

Let's tie him to the tree.

HUCK

No, let's don't. S'pose he wakes up? It's my bust, not yourn.

TOM

Go on ahead. I'll happen to borrow some 'a them candles from Jim.

Huck slips off.

NARRATOR

Nothing would do Tom but he must crawl to where Jim was, and play something on him. Tom didn't borry the candles, he left Jim a nickel for them . . . he also slipped Jim's hat on a limb.

Tom creeps up to Jim and picks up the candles and leaves a nickel, turns to go, but is unable to resist a trick. He picks up Jim's hat and places it on the limb of a tree, and then, with a look of glee, races off to catch Huck. As he goes, Jim smiles and opens his eyes, looks down and smiles at the nickel even more affectionately. He palms the nickel; then calmly looks up and takes his hat off the limb of the tree, puts it on his head, and walks away, all action as Narrator says . . .

NARRATOR

Afterwards, Jim said witches bewitched him, put him in a trance and rode him all over the State, and then set him under the tree again and hung his hat on a limb to show who done it. Next time Jim told it, he said they rode him down to New Or-leans. Next time it was all the way 'round the world. Strange niggers came from miles away to hear Jim talk about it. Jim, he was most ruined for a servant, he got so stuck up, on account of having seen the Devil . . .

10. EXT. HILLSIDE. NIGHT. — *Seven boys, including Huck and Tom, run along the hillside, in the moonlight. Tom stops and howls like a wolf at the silvery moon.*

NARRATOR

. . . and been rode by witches.

61. EXT. RIVER RAFT. NIGHT. — *Jim is "sitting there with his head down between his knees, asleep, with his right arm hanging over the steering oar. The other oar was smashed off. The raft was littered with leaves and branches and dirt. So she'd had a rough time." Huck paddles up silently, quietly, makes the canoe fast, boards the raft, lies down under Jim's nose, "and begun to gap, and stretched my fists out against Jim and says":*

HUCK

Hello, Jim, have I been asleep? Why didn't you stir me up?

JIM

Huck? En you ain' dead—you ain' drowned? Lemme look at you, lemme see . . .

Jim touches Huck's shoulders and arms. Near tears with relief.

JIM

. . . no, you'se back, d'same ole Huck . . . thanks to goodness.

HUCK

What's the matter with you, Jim. You been a-drinking?

JIM

. . . Has I had a chance to be drinkin'?

HUCK

Well then, what makes you talk so wild?

JIM

How does I talk wild?

JIM

How? Talkin' about me coming back and all that stuff, as if I'd been gone away?

JIM

Huck. Huck Finn. You look me in d'eye; *look me in d'eye; Ain't* you been gone away?

HUCK

Gone away? I hain't been gone anywheres. Where would I go to?

Jim pauses for a few seconds; decides to string along, affects a slightly stronger dialect.

JIM

Well . . . looky here, boss, dey's sumf'n wrong, dey is. Is I *me*, or who *is* I? Is I *heah*, or whah is I?

HUCK

Well, you're here plain enough, but I think you're a tangle-headed old fool, Jim.

JIM

(*unamused*) I is, is I? Didn't you tote out d'line in d'canoe fer to make fast to d'tow-head?

HUCK

Tow-head? What tow-head? *I* hain't seen no tow-head.

JIM

Didn' d' line pull loose, en de raf' go hummin' down d' river, en leave you en d'canoe behind in d'fog?

HUCK

What fog?

JIM

De fog. En didn' you whoop, en didn't I whoop? En didn' I bus' up agin a lot er dem islands en have a turrible time en mos' get drowned? Ain't dat so—boss?

HUCK

It's too many for me, Jim. I hain't seen no fog, nor no islands, nor no troubles, nor nothing. *You* been dreaming.

Jim "didn't say nothing for about five minutes, but he set there studying it over. Then he says":

JIM

... Well, den ... reck'n I *did* dream it, Huck ... never had no dream
b'fo' dat's tired me like dis one.

HUCK

That's all right, because a dream does tire a body like everything,
sometimes. Tell me about it, Jim, about your dream.

Jim purses his lips, knits his brow, then eases his features and speaks:

JIM

... well, d'fust tow-head mus' stan' for a man who gon' try t'do us
some good; den d'curren's is 'nuther man dat'll get us 'way from d'
good man. D'whoops is warnin's dat gon' come t'us ever now en den,
'long d'way. D'tow-heads is troubles en all kine o' mean folk, but ef
we mine's our bidness, don' talk back en aggravates 'em, we'll pull
thoo en gits to de big clear river, d'O-hi-o.

*Huck's face clouds up tiring of Jim's facility with the lie Huck himself had started, and
not wanting to think about losing his companion at the Ohio. Huck's face then becomes
smug.*

HUCK

Oh, well, that's all 'terpreted well enough, as far as it goes, Jim (*points
to dirt on raft*). But what does these things stand for?

*Jim looks at the detritus, then at Huck, levelly, emotionlessly, then back to the sticks,
leaves and dirt; one side of his face—the side away from Huck—lifts in a fatalistic half-
smile. He turns back to Huck looking at him steadily, without smiling, and says:*

JIM

What do dey stan' for? I's gon' tell you ... When I got all wore out
wid work, en wid callin' for you, my heart was most broke because
you was los' en I didn' k'yer no mo' what become er me en d'raf'. En
when I wake up en fine you back agin, all safe en soun' ... en all you
wuz thinkin' 'bout wuz how you could make a fool uv ole Jim wid a lie.
(*points to detritus on the raft, speaks calmly, clearly*). . . . **Dat truck dah
is trash; en trash is what people is dat puts dirt on de head er dey
fren's en makes 'em ashamed.**

Jim slowly rises and enters the wigwam. Huck watches him, then looks out over the river, as if he is too proud to care. But then, he looks down.

61a. INT. WIGWAM. NIGHT. — *Jim sits, pensively. It seems Huck is no different from the "witches and devils" that have ridden him in his days of bondage. Huck enters wigwam. Jim recoils, but holds it in. Huck gets on his haunches, looks at Jim, looks down. Looks up.*

HUCK

Jim, I . . . *(inhales, exhales deeply)* I'm sorry, Jim.

And with that, a crack in Jim's soul is patched. Huck looks down again as Jim regards him with slightly knitted brows. His face softens. He reaches out with the flat palm of his hand—hesitates, then rubs the boy's bowed head. Huck looks up, so thankfully, his eyes shining wet.

Part Three

In addition to the works cited throughout, the following may provide teachers with useful background.

SELECTED BIBLIOGRAPHY

Berlin, Ira. *Generations of Captivity: A History of African-American Slaves.* Cambridge, MA.: Belknap Press of Harvard University Press, 2003.

Bird, John. "'Like Setting Down on a Kag of Powder and Touching It Off Just to See Where You'll Go To': Reflections on Forty Years of Teaching *Huckleberry Finn.*" *Mark Twain Annual* 21 (2023): 135–42.

Bird, John, ed. *Mark Twain in Context.* Cambridge: Cambridge University Press, 2020.

Blight, David W. *Race and Reunion: The Civil War in American Memory.* Cambridge, MA: Belknap Press of Harvard University Press, 2001.

Bordewich Fergus M. *Bound for Canaan: The Epic Story of the Underground Railroad, America's First Civil Rights Movement.* New York: HarperCollins, 2005.

Botkin, B. A., ed. *Lay My Burden Down: A Folk History of Slavery.* 1945. Reprint, Athens: University of Georgia Press, 1989.

Bradley, David. "Eulogy for Nigger." *Independent,* October 8, 2015. www.independent.co.uk/news/world/world-history/eulogy-for-nigger-the-provocative-title-that-has-been-printed-verbatim-a6687016.html.

Bradley, David, and Shelley Fisher Fishkin, eds. *Encyclopedia of Civil Rights in America.* 3 vols. New York: M. E. Sharpe, 1997.

Budd, Louis J. *Mark Twain: Social Philosopher.* 1962. Columbia: University Press of Missouri, 2001.

Budd, Louis J., ed. *New Essays on "Huckleberry Finn."* Cambridge: Cambridge University Press, 1985.

Camfield, Gregg, ed. *The Oxford Companion to Mark Twain.* New York: Oxford University Press, 2004.

Chadwick [Chadwick-Joshua], Jocelyn. *The Jim Dilemma: Reading Race in "Huckleberry Finn."* Jackson: University Press of Mississippi, 1997.

Champion, Laurie, ed. *The Critical Response to Mark Twain's "Huckleberry Finn."* New York: Greenwood, 1991.

Davis, David Brion. *Inhuman Bondage: The Rise and Fall of Slavery in the New World.* Oxford: Oxford University Press, 2006.

Dempsey, Terrell. *Searching for Jim: Slavery in Sam Clemens' World.* Columbia: University of Missouri Press, 2003.

Doyno, Victor A. *Writing "Huck Finn": Mark Twain's Creative Process.* Philadelphia: University of Pennsylvania Press, 1991.

Fishkin, Shelley Fisher. *Was Huck Black? Mark Twain and African-American Voices.* New York: Oxford University Press, 1993.

Foner, Philip S. *Mark Twain: Social Critic.* New York: International Publishers, 1958.

Franklin, John Hope, and Evelyn Higginbothom. *From Slavery to Freedom: A History of African Americans.* [originally published 1941] 10th ed. Boston: McGraw-Hill, 2000.

Franklin, John Hope, and Loren Schweninger. *Runaway Slaves: Rebels on the Plantation.* New York: Oxford University Press, 1999.

Frederickson, George M. *The Black Image in the White Mind: The Debate on Afro-American Character and Destiny, 1817–1914.* Middletown, CT: Wesleyan University Press, 1971.

Fry, Gladys-Marie. *Night Riders in Black Folk History.* 1975. Reprint, Athens: University of Georgia Press, 1991.

Fulton, Joe B. *Mark Twain's Ethical Realism: The Aesthetics of Race, Class, and Gender.* Columbia: University of Missouri Press, 1997.

Gates, Henry Louis Jr., ed. *The Classic Slave Narratives.* New York: Penguin, 1987.

Gates, Henry Louis Jr., et al., eds. *The Norton Anthology of African American Literature.* 3rd ed. 2 vols. New York: W. W. Norton, 2014.

Goodheart, Lawrence, Richard D. Brown, and Stephen G. Rabe, eds. *Slavery in American Society.* Lexington, MA: D. C. Heath, 1992.

Gribben, Alan. *Mark Twain's Literary Resources: A Reconstruction of His Library and Reading.* Vol. 1. Athens: University of Georgia Press, 2019.

Gribben, Alan. *Mark Twain's Literary Resources: A Reconstruction of His Library and Reading.* Vol. 2. Montgomery, AL: NewSouth Books, 2022.

Hearn, Michael Patrick. *The Annotated Huckleberry Finn.* New York: W. W. Norton, 2001.

Horton, James Oliver, and Lois E. Horton. *Slavery and the Making of America.* New York: Oxford University Press, 2005.

Hughes, Langston, and Arna Bontemps, eds. *The Book of Negro Folklore.* New York: Dodd, Mead, 1958.

Inge, M. Thomas, ed. *Huck Finn among the Critics.* Frederick, MD: University Publications of America, 1985.

Johnson, Charles Richard, Patricia Smith, and WGBH Series Research Team. *Africans in America: America's Journey through Slavery.* New York: Harcourt Brace, 1998.

Johnson, Claudia Durst. *Understanding "Adventures of Huckleberry Finn": A Student Casebook to Issues, Sources, and Historical Documents.* Westport, CT: Greenwood, 1996.

Jordan, Winthrop. *The White Man's Burden: Historical Origins of Racism in the United States.* New York: Oxford University Press, 1993.

Leonard, James S., ed. *Making Mark Twain Work in the Classroom.* Durham, NC: Duke University Press, 1999.

Leonard, James S., Thomas A. Tenney, and Thadious M. Davis, eds. *Satire or Evasion? Black Perspectives on "Huckleberry Finn."* Durham, NC: Duke University Press, 1992.

Levine, Lawrence W. *Black Culture and Black Consciousness: Afro-American Folk Thought from Slavery to Freedom.* Oxford: Oxford University Press, 1977.

Lott, Eric. *Love and Theft: Blackface Minstrelsy and the American Working Class.* New York: Oxford University Press, 1993.

Mac Donnell, Kevin, and R. Kent Rasmussen, eds. *Mark Twain and Youth: Studies in His Life and Writings.* London: Bloomsbury, 2016.

Merritt, Keri Leigh. *Masterless Men: Poor Whites and Slavery in the Antebellum South*. Cambridge: Cambridge University Press, 2017.

Messent, Peter, and Louis J. Budd, editors. *A Companion to Mark Twain*. Oxford: Blackwell, 2005.

Mintz, Steven, ed. *African American Voices: The Life Cycle of Slavery*. St. James, NY: Brandywine, 1993.

Pettit, Arthur G. *Mark Twain and the South*. Lexington: University of Kentucky Press, 1974.

Powers, Ron. *Dangerous Water: A Biography of the Boy Who Became Mark Twain*. Boston: Da Capo, 1999.

Powers, Ron. *Mark Twain: A Life*. New York: Free Press, 1996.

Raboteau, Albert J. *Slave Religion: The "Invisible Institution" in the Antebellum South*. 1978. Updated ed. Oxford: Oxford UP, 2004.

Rasmussen, R. Kent. *Critical Companion to Mark Twain: A Literary Reference to His Life and Work*. 2 vols. New York: Facts on File, 2007.

Rasmussen, R. Kent. *Mark Twain A to Z*. New York: Facts on File, 1995.

Rickford, John R. *African American Vernacular English: Features, Evolution, Educational Implications*. Oxford: Blackwell, 1999.

Rickford, John Russell, and Russell John Rickford. *Spoken Soul: The Story of Black English*. New York: John Wiley and Sons, 2000.

Robinson, Forrest G. *In Bad Faith: The Dynamics of Deception in Mark Twain's America*. Cambridge, MA: Harvard University Press, 1986.

Sattelmeyer, Robert, and J. Donald Crowley, eds. *One Hundred Years of "Huckleberry Finn": The Boy, His Book, and American Culture: Centennial Essays*. Columbia: University of Missouri Press, 1985.

Sloane, David E. E. "Comic Attack: Mark Twain and the N-word in the Classroom." *Mark Twain Annual*, vol. 21 (2023): 123–34.

Sloane, David E. E. "*Huck Finn* and Race: A Teacher's Toolbox." In *Huck Finn: The Complete Buffalo and Erie County Public Library Manuscript-Teaching and Research Digital Editions*. Buffalo and Erie County [NY] Public Library, 2003.

Smitherman, Geneva. *Talkin That Talk: Language, Culture and Education in African America*. London: Routledge, 2000.

Toll, Robert C. *Blacking Up: The Minstrel Show in Nineteenth-Century America*. New York: Oxford University Press, 1974.

Wells-Oghoghomeh, Alexis. *The Souls of Womenfolk: The Religious Cultures of En-slaved Women in the Lower South*. Chapel Hill: University of North Carolina Press, 2021.

Wieck, Carl F. *Refiguring Huckleberry Finn*. Athens: University of Georgia Press, 2000.

NOTES

Explanatory

1. "EXPLANATORY. In this book a number of dialects are used, to wit: the Missouri negro dialect; the extremest form of the backwoods Southwestern dialect; the ordinary 'Pike County' dialect; and four modified varieties of this last. The shadings have not been done in a haphazard fashion, or by guesswork; but pains-takingly, and with the trustworthy guidance and support of personal familiarity with these several forms of speech. I make this explanation for the reason that without it many readers would suppose that all these characters were trying to talk alike and not succeeding. THE AUTHOR." Mark Twain, *Adventures of Huckleberry Finn*, edited by Victor Fischer and Lin Salamo with Harriet Elinor Smith and the late Walter Blair, from the Mark Twain Project, Robert H. Hirst, general editor (1885; Berkeley: University of California Press, 2003), xxxiii.

2. Mark Twain, "Fenimore Cooper's Literary Offenses" (1895), in *Mark Twain: Collected Tales, Sketches, Speeches, and Essays, 1891–1910*, edited by Louis J. Budd (New York: Library of America, 1992), 181.

3. Twain made this word central to the title of an antilynching satire he published in the *Buffalo (NY) Express* in 1869 that he called "Only a Nigger." In this satire, the "honorable" men of Memphis use the word to justify their having lynched an innocent man. The miscarriage of justice they have perpetrated does not trouble them because "only 'a nigger'" lost his life as a result. Mark Twain, "Only a Nigger" (1869), in *Mark Twain at the "Buffalo Express,"* edited by Joseph McCullough and Janice McIntire-Strasburg (DeKalb: Northern Illinois University Press, 1999), 22–23.

4. For more on the history of the word and its role in American culture,

see Randall Kennedy, "A Note on the Word 'Nigger,'" Park Ethnography Program, National Park Service, www.nps.gov/ethnography/aah/aaheritage/intro_furthRdg1 .htm; and Randall Kennedy, *Nigger: The Strange Career of a Troublesome Word* (New York: Knopf Doubleday, 2003). See also the Peabody Award–winning documentary directed by Todd Williams and produced by Nelson George, *The N-Word,* released June 26, 2004, www.youtube.com/watch?v=v3Z9dudFGLQ. The appendix at the end of this book addresses this issue, as well.

5. Black writer David Bradley disagrees (as I do) with those who want to eliminate the word from the book. See his comments on this point on CBS's *Sixty Minutes* in "*Huckleberry Finn* and the N-Word," *Sixty Minutes,* June 12, 2011, www .youtube.com/watch?v=nW9 qcc1m9o. Bradley, a Pen/Faulkner award-winning novelist, responded to the NAACP's decision to hold a public burial for the word by writing a memorable essay that won the top international essay prize, the biennial £20,000 Notting Hill Prize in 2015. Emily Dugan, "Eulogy for Nigger Author Wins Notting Hill Prize," *Independent,* October 8, 2015, www.independent .co.uk/news/people/david-bradley-eulogy-for-nigger-author-wins-notting-hill -editions-essay-prize-a6686996.html. The piece became the title essay in a new anthology, *A Eulogy for Nigger and Other Essays: The Second Notting Hill Editions Essay Prize Winners* (London: Notting Hill Editions, 2015), and was republished in the *Independent.* David Bradley, "Eulogy for Nigger," *Independent,* October 8, 2015, www.independent.co.uk/news/world/world-history/eulogy-for-nigger-the -provocative-title-that-has-been-printed-verbatim-a6687016.html.

Introduction

1. The book was published in London in 1884 but did not appear in the United States until 1885. The title page in both editions reads *Adventures of Huckleberry Finn (Tom Sawyer's Comrade),* and it is to this full title that the title of the book at hand alludes. It is worth noting that the character Jim in *Huckleberry Finn* is a completely different character than the enslaved child named Jim in *The Adventures of Tom Sawyer* (1876).

2. The town of St. Petersburg in the book is based on the town of Hannibal, MO, in which Samuel Clemens grew up. He would adopt the pen name "Mark Twain" in 1863.

3. Mark Twain, *Autobiography of Mark Twain,* vol. 1, edited by Harriet Elinor Smith with Benjamin Griffin, Victor Fischer, Michael B. Frank, Sharon K. Goetz, and Leslie Diane Myrick, from the Mark Twain Project, Robert H. Hirst, general editor (Berkeley: University of California Press, 2010), 212.

4. Leo Marx, "Mr. Eliot, Mr. Trilling, and 'Huckleberry Finn,'" *American Scholar* 22, no. 4 (1953): 430.

5. Fredrick Woodard and Donnarae MacCann, "Minstrel Shackles and Nineteenth-Century 'Liberality' in *Huckleberry Finn*," in *Satire or Evasion? Black Perspectives on Huckleberry Finn*, edited by James S. Leonard, Thomas A. Tenney, and Thadious M. Davis (Durham, NC: Duke University Press, 1992), 142.

6. Mark Twain, "EXPLANATORY," in *Adventures of Huckleberry Finn*, edited by Victor Fischer and Lin Salamo with Harriet Elinor Smith and the late Walter Blair, Mark Twain Library, from the Mark Twain Project, Robert H. Hirst, general editor (1885; Berkeley: University of California Press, 2003), xxxiii. Twain cites among the "rules governing literary art" the rule that "when personages of a tale deal in conversation, the talk shall . . . be talk such as human beings would be likely to talk in the given circumstances." Mark Twain, "Fenimore Cooper's Literary Offenses" (1895), in *Mark Twain: Collected Tales, Sketches, Speeches, and Essays, 1891–1910*, edited by Louis J. Budd (New York: Library of America, 1992), 181.

7. Percival Everett, *James: A Novel* (New York: Doubleday, 2024).

8. Gerry Brenner, "More Than a Reader's Response: A Letter to 'De Ole True Huck,'" *Journal of Narrative Technique* 20, no. 2 (1990): 221–34; E. E. Burke, *Taming Huck Finn (New Adventures)* (self-pub., 2018); Jon Clinch, *Finn* (New York: Random House, 2007); Robert Coover, *Huck Out West* (New York: W. W. Norton, 2018); Tim DeRoche, *The Ballad of Huck and Miguel* (Los Angeles: Redtail Press, 2018); Wil Haygood, *Two on the River* (New York: Atlantic Monthly Press, 1988); Scott Kaiser, *Splittin' the Raft* (self-pub., CreateSpace, 2017); John Keene, "Rivers," in *Counternarratives* (New York: New Directions, 2015); Norman Lock, *The Boy in His Winter* (New York: Bellevue Literary Press, 2014); Gina Logan, *The Autobiography of Miss Huckleberry Finn* (self-pub., CreateSpace, 2013); Greg Matthews, *The Further Adventures of Huckleberry Finn* (New York: Crown, 1988); Edward Morgan, *Sounding the River (Huck Finn Revisited)* [play at Milwaukee Rep, 2001] (unpub.); Mark Twain and Lee Nelson, *Huck and Tom among the Indians* (Springville, UT: Cedar Fort, 2010); Phong Nguyen, *The Adventures of Joe Harper* (San Francisco: Outpost19, 2016); Nancy Rawles, *My Jim* (New York: Crown, 2005); Bernard Sabath, *The Boys in Autumn* [play on Broadway, 1986] (Woodstock, IL: Dramatic Publishing, 1986); Sam Sackett, *Huckleberry Finn Grows Up* (self-pub., iUniverse, 2012); Martí Sales, *Huckleberry Finn: Poems*, translated by Elisabet Ràfols and Ona Bantjes-Ràfols (Toronto: Book*Hug Press, 2015); John Seelye, *The True Adventures of Huckleberry Finn* (Evanston, IL: Northwestern University Press, 1970); Julie Smith, *Huckleberry Fiend* (New York: Mysterious Press, 1987); Mark Time, *Black Lives Matter Too: My Adventures with Huckleberry Finn* (Chatham, NJ: Bowker, 2018); Mark Time, *Black Lives Matter Too, Two: The Death of Huckleberry Finn* (N.p.: John/Zavez, 2020); Dan Walker, *Huckleberry Finn in Love and War* (self-pub., CreateSpace, 2015); David F. Walker and Marcus Kwame

Anderson, *Big Jim and the White Boy* (Berkeley: Ten Speed Graphic / Ten Speed Press, 2024); Robert Wells, *Passing through to the Territory* (self-pub., 2019); Clement Wood, *More Adventures of Huckleberry Finn* (Cleveland, OH: World Publishing, 1940); *Tom Sawyer Abroad/Tom Sawyer, Detective*, edited by John C. Gerber and Terry Firkins (Berkeley: University of California Press, 2011); *Mark Twain, Huck Finn and Tom Sawyer Among the Indians and Other Unfinished Stories*, edited by Dahlia Armon, Paul Baender, and Walter Blair, with William M. Gibson and Franklin R. Rogers (Berkeley: University of California Press, 2011).

9. John H. Wallace, ed., *The Adventures of Huckleberry Finn Adapted* (Falls Church, VA: John H. Wallace and Sons, 1985); Alan Gribben, ed., *Mark Twain's Adventures of Tom Sawyer and Huckleberry Finn: The NewSouth Edition* (Montgomery, AL: NewSouth Books, 2011); Mark Twain, with Gabriel Diani and Etta Devine, *Adventures of Huckleberry Finn: Robotic Edition* (Los Angeles: Diani and Devine Press, 2011); and Mark Twain, with W. Bill Czolgosz, *Adventures of Huckleberry Finn and Zombie Jim* (self-pub., CreateSpace, 2015). See also Jill Pantozzi, "Interview: The Adventures of Huckleberry Finn, the Robotic Edition," *The Mary Sue*, April 12, 2012, www.themarysue.com/huckleberry-finn-robotic-edition/; E. D. W. Lynch, "Adventure of Huckleberry Finn [Robotic Edition] by Diani & Devine," *Laughing Squid*, December 9, 2011, https://laughingsquid.com/adventures-of -huckleberry-finn-robotic-edition-by-diani-devine/; and Mark Medley, "Can't Wait for Censored Version of Huck Finn? Read Adventures of Huckleberry Finn and Zombie Jim," *National Post*, January 5, 2012, https://nationalpost.com/after word/cant-wait-for-censored-version-of-huck-finn-read-adventures-of-huckle berry-finn-and-zombie-jim.

10. For my discussions of the evolution of Mark Twain's thinking about race, see Shelley Fisher Fishkin, "Mark Twain and African Americans," in *Mark Twain in Context*, edited by John Bird (Cambridge: Cambridge University Press, 2019), 192–202; Fishkin, "Black and White Youth in Mark Twain's Hannibal," in *Mark Twain and Youth: Studies in His Life and Writings*, edited by Kevin Mac Donnell and R. Kent Rasmussen (London: Bloomsbury, 2016), 223–37; Fishkin, "Mark Twain and Race," in *A Historical Guide to Mark Twain*, edited by Shelley Fisher Fishkin (New York: Oxford University Press, 2002), 127–62; and Fishkin, *Lighting Out for the Territory: Reflections on Mark Twain and American Culture* (New York: Oxford University Press, 1996), 13–114.

11. Fishkin, "Mark Twain and African Americans."

12. Mark Twain, *Following the Equator*, The Oxford Mark Twain, edited by Shelley Fisher Fishkin (1897; New York: Oxford University Press, 1996), 213.

13. Kerry Driscoll, *Mark Twain among the Indians and Other Indigenous Peoples* (Oakland: University of California Press, 2019).

14. In 1985 the *Christian Science Monitor* asserted that many people, Black and white, believed that Jim was "not only the most noble character of the book but also the first Black hero in American fiction." Hilary DeVries, "At 100, 'Huck Finn' Is Still Causing Trouble," *Christian Science Monitor*, March 15, 1985. It is more accurate to call Jim "one of the first" rather than "the first," although the list of Black heroes in American fiction before 1885 is a short one. There are innumerable Black heroes in the slave narratives that were published throughout the nineteenth century but just a handful when it comes to fiction. The list of Black heroes in American fiction before 1885 might include Archy Moore in the early antislavery novel by Richard Hildreth, *The Slave; or, Memoirs of Archy Moore* (1836); Uncle Tom as well as George Harris in Harriet Beecher Stowe's *Uncle Tom's Cabin* (1852); Madison Washington, the hero of the only work of fiction Frederick Douglass ever wrote, a story entitled "The Heroic Slave" (1852); William, the central Black male character in William Wells Brown's novel *Clotel; or, The President's Daughter: A Narrative of Slave Life in the United States* (1853); Mr. Walters, a wealthy Black real estate investor in Frank J. Webb's novel *The Garies and Their Friends* (1857); and Henry Blake, an escaped slave who plans a slave insurrection in Martin Delany's novel *Blake; or, The Huts of America*, which was serialized between 1859 and 1862.

CHAPTER 1. Contexts and Conditions

1. Diane Mutti Burke, *On Slavery's Border: Missouri's Small-Slaveholding Households, 1815–1865* (Athens: University of Georgia Press, 2010), 3.

2. Albert J. Raboteau, *Slave Religion: The "Invisible Institution" in the Antebellum South*, updated ed. (New York: Oxford University Press, 2004), cxiv. Toni Morrison has noted that for her and for Black people that she knew, "in addition to the very shrewd, down-to-earth, efficient way in which they did things, there was this other knowledge or perception, always discredited but nevertheless there, which informed their sensibilities and clarified their activities." Morrison tells us that she grew up in a house in which people had "some sweet, intimate connection with things that were not empirically verifiable. . . . Without that, I think I would have been quite bereft because I would have been dependent on so-called scientific data to explain hopelessly unscientific things and also I would have relied on information that even subsequent objectivity has proved to be fraudulent." Quoted in Christina Davis and Toni Morrison, "Interview with Toni Morrison," *Présence Africaine*, n.s. (1st trimester 1988): 144.

3. Raboteau, *Slave Religion*, 275, 286; William Wells Brown, *My Southern Home; or, The South and Its People* (Boston: A. G. Brown, 1880), 70, at Documenting the American South, https://docsouth.unc.edu/neh/brown80/menu.html.

4. Daniel Hoffman, *Form and Fable in American Fiction* (Charlottesville: University Press of Virginia, 1994), 339.

5. Alexis Wells Oghoghomeh, *The Souls of Womenfolk: The Religious Cultures of Enslaved Women in the Lower South* (Chapel Hill: University of North Carolina Press, 2021), 147, 155–56, 158, 160, 192.

6. Richard Kimmons, Lawrence County, MO, slave narrative in "Individual Slave Narratives at Missouri State Museum," Missouri State Parks, https://mo stateparks.com/page/58373/individual-slave-narratives.

7. Mark Twain, *Adventures of Huckleberry Finn*, edited by Victor Fischer and Lin Salamo with Harriet Elinor Smith and the late Walter Blair, Mark Twain Library, from the Mark Twain Project, Robert H. Hirst, general editor (1885; Berkeley: University of California Press, 2003), 201–2.

8. Tishey Taylor, Poplar Bluff, MO, slave narrative in "Individual Slave Narratives at Missouri State Museum," Missouri State Parks, https://mostate parks.com/page/58373/individual-slave-narratives.

9. Terrell Dempsey, *Searching for Jim: Slavery in Sam Clemens's World* (Columbia: University of Missouri Press, 2003), 78; Brown, *My Southern Home*, 15, 20, 25, 26, 27.

10. Brown, *My Southern Home*, 15, 20, 25, 26, 27.

11. Mark Twain, "Jane Lampton Clemens," posthumously published memoir in *Mark Twain's Hannibal, Huck and Tom*, edited by Walter Blair (Berkeley: University of California Press, 1969), 49; Mark Twain, *Following the Equator* (1897; New York: Oxford University Press, 1996), 352; Sam Clemens, typescript of notebook 28b, 22–23, quoted in Arthur G. Pettit, *Mark Twain and the South* (Lexington: University Press of Kentucky, 1974), 15.

12. Mary Armstrong, St. Louis, MO, and Emma Knight, Florida, MO, slave narratives in "Individual Slave Narratives at Missouri State Museum," Missouri State Parks, https://mostateparks.com/page/58373/individual-slave-narratives.

13. Bill Simms, Osceola, MO, slave narrative in "Individual Slave Narratives at Missouri State Museum," Missouri State Parks, https://mostateparks.com/page /58373/individual-slave-narratives.

14. Twain, "Jane Lampton Clemens," 49.

15. Dempsey, *Searching for Jim*, 185.

16. Dempsey, *Searching for Jim*, 83.

17. Clay Smith, Hannibal, MO, slave narrative, Western Historical Manuscripts Collection, University of Missouri, Columbia, reprinted in *The American Slave: A Composite Autobiography*, series 1, vol. 2: *Arkansas, Colorado, Minnesota, Missouri, and Oregon and Washington Narratives*, edited by George P. Rawick (Westport, CT: Greenwood, 1977), 263; Hurley J. Hagood and Roberta Hagood, "Hannibal's Underground Railroad," *Hannibal (MO) Courier-Post*, June 22, 1991.

18. Dempsey, *Searching for Jim*, 218–19; "Memoir of Franklin Harriman," quoted in Dempsey, *Searching for Jim*, 220.

19. Twain, "Jane Lampton Clemens," 49; William Wells Brown, *Narrative of William W. Brown, a Fugitive Slave* (Boston: Anti-Slavery Office, 1947), 33–34.

20. Dempsey, *Searching for Jim*, 87.

21. Charlie Richardson, Warrenburg, MO, slave narrative in "Individual Slave Narratives at Missouri State Museum," Missouri State Parks, https://mostate parks.com/page/58373/individual-slave-narratives; Dempsey, *Searching for Jim*, 88.

22. Dempsey, *Searching for Jim*, 11; "The History of Slavery in St. Louis: Slavery and the Law," National Park Service, www.nps.gov/articles/000/slavery -and-the-law.htm; "Laws Concerning Slavery in Missouri: Territorial to 1850s," Missouri's Early Slave Laws: A History in Documents, Missouri Digital Heritage, www.sos.mo.gov/archives/education/aahi/earlyslavelaws/slavelaws.asp; "Slave Stampedes on the Southern Borderlands," National Park Service Network to Freedom / House Divided Project at Dickinson College, https://housedivided.dick inson.edu/sites/stampedes/the-1856-hannibal-stampede/screen-shot-2021 -06-21-at-7-29-58-am/.

23. Dempsey, *Searching for Jim*, 12.

24. "Laws Concerning Slavery in Missouri"; Nelson Allyn, "Nat Turner's Rebellion, 1831," History Resources, Gilder Lehrman Institute of American History, www.gilderlehrman.org/history-resources/spotlight-primary-source/nat -turner's-rebellion-1831.

25. "Laws Concerning Slavery in Missouri"; CPI Inflation Calculator, www .officialdata.org (accessed July 23, 2024).

26. Mark E. Neely Jr., *The Last Best Hope of Earth: Abraham Lincoln and the Promise of America* (Cambridge, MA: Harvard University Press, 1993), 82, cited in James Tackach, "Why Jim Does Not Escape to Illinois in Mark Twain's *Adventures of Huckleberry Finn*," *Journal of the Illinois State Historical Society* 97, no. 3 (2004): 218.

27. Dempsey, *Searching for Jim*, 176.

28. Esther Easter, Westport, MO, slave narrative, in Federal Writers' Project, *Slave Narrative Project*, vol. 13, *Oklahoma*, 88, available at http://hdl.loc.gov /loc.mss/mesn.130; Twain, "Jane Lampton Clemens," 49. Indeed, Joseph P. Ament, owner of the Hannibal *Missouri Courier*, worked as an agent for a company that offered "Insurance on Negroes" at the time that Sam Clemens worked for him as a printer's apprentice. Dempsey, *Searching for Jim*, 143.

29. Mark Twain, *Mark Twain's Autobiography*, edited by Albert Bigelow Paine, 2 vols. (New York: Harper and Brothers, 1924), 1:101; "Runaway Slave Laws," in "Laws Concerning Slavery in Missouri"; Dempsey, *Searching for Jim*, 46, 170.

30. "Missouri v. Celia," Slavery and the Making of America, 2004, www
.thirteen.org/wnet/slavery/experience/legal/feature2c.html.

31. Explanatory notes, in Mark Twain, *Adventures of Huckleberry Finn*, edited
by Victor Fischer and Lin Salamo with Harriet Elinor Smith and the late Walter
Blair, Mark Twain Library, from the Mark Twain Project, Robert H. Hirst, general
editor (1885; Berkeley: University of California Press, 2001), 394; S. L. C., "To the
Muscatine *Tri-Weekly Journal*," February 24-26, 1855, *Mark Twain's Letters*, vol. 1:
1853-1866, edited by Edgar Marquess Branch, Michael B. Frank, Kenneth M. Sand-
erson, the Mark Twain Project, Robert H. Hirst, general editor (Berkeley: University of California Press, 1988), 51.

32. Explanatory notes in Twain, *Adventures of Huckleberry Finn,* 392-93;
Donald H. Welsh, "Sam Clemens' Hannibal," *Midcontinent American Studies Journal* 3, no. 1 (1962): 38; S. L. C., "To the Muscatine *Tri-Weekly Journal*"; "Free Black
People Must Apply for a License to Remain in Missouri," March 14, 1835, A History of Racial Injustice, Equal Justice Initiative, https://calendar.eji.org/racial-in
justice/mar/14.

33. "Missouri's Dred Scott Case, 1846-1857," Missouri Digital Heritage,
www.sos.mo.gov/archives/resources/africanamerican/scott/scott.asp. See also
Paul Finkelman, *Dred Scott v. Sandiford: A Brief History with Documents* (Boston:
Bedford/St. Martin's, 2016). The Court held that people of African descent "are
not included, and were not intended to be included, under the word 'citizens' in
the Constitution, and can therefore claim none of the rights and privileges which
that instrument provides for and secures to citizens of the United States. On the
contrary, they were at that time considered as a subordinate and inferior class
of beings, who had been subjugated by the dominant race, and, whether emanci-
pated or not, yet remained subject to their authority, and had no rights or privileges but such as those who held the power and the government might choose
to grant them." "Dred Scott v. Sandford (1857)," Milestone Documents, National
Archives, www.archives.gov/milestone-documents/dred-scott-v-sandford.

34. Dempsey, *Searching for Jim,* 23, 26.

35. Twain, "A Scrap of Curious History," quoted in Dempsey, *Searching for
Jim,* 27.

36. "An Act in Relation to the Marital Rights and Children of Colored Persons," February 20, 1865, cited in "Timeline of Missouri's African American History," Missouri Digital Heritage, www.sos.mo.gov/mdh/curriculum/africanamer
ican/timeline/timeline3.

37. Fannie Barrier Williams, "A Northern Negro's Autobiography," in *The
New Woman of Color: The Collected Writings of Fannie Barrier Williams, 1893-1918,*
edited by Mary Jo Deegan (DeKalb: Northern Illinois University Press, 2002), 5-13.

38. Deegan, *New Woman of Color*, xiii–lx.

39. "Racial Terror and Reconstruction: A State Snapshot," Reconstruction in America, Equal Justice Initiative, https://eji.org/report/reconstruction-in-amer ica/documenting-reconstruction-violence/#racial-terror-and-reconstruction-a -state-snapshot.

40. "He foresaw himself writing a major treatise on lynching, perhaps as large as six volumes, 'to be called "History of Lynching in America" or "Rise and Progress of Lynching," or some such title,' but then decided against the idea." L. Terry Oggel, quoting Clemens's letter to Frank Bliss, August 29, 1901, in "Speaking Out about Race: 'The United States of Lyncherdom' Clemens Really Wrote," *Prospects: An Annual of American Cultural Studies* 25 (October 2000): 129.

41. "FRED DOUGLASS! His Great Speech Yesterday . . . ," *Elmira (NY) Advertiser*, August 4, 1880. For more on Douglass's speech and Twain's almost certain awareness of it, see Matt Seybold's persuasive article, "Even If He Weren't My Friend: Frederick Douglass and Mark Twain," Center for Mark Twain Studies, August 2, 2021, https://marktwainstudies.com/freddouglassmarktwain/. Twain himself would have witnessed some of the impacts of the erosion of these rights during the trip down the Mississippi that he took in 1882 when he was researching *Life on the Mississippi*.

42. Jim's Journey: The Huck Finn Freedom Center, www.jimsjourney.org; Faye Dant, *Hannibal's Invisibles*, introduction by Shelley Fisher Fishkin (Cleveland, OK: Belt, 2024). For more on Jim's Journey, see Shelley Fisher Fishkin, *Writing America: Literary Landmarks from Walden Pond to Wounded Knee* (New Brunswick, NJ: Rutgers University Press, 2015), 5–6, 122–25; and Fishkin, "Black and White Youth in Mark Twain's Hannibal," in *Mark Twain and Youth: Studies in His Life and Writings*, edited by Kevin Mac Donnell and R. Kent Rasmussen (London: Bloomsbury, 2016), 223–37.

CHAPTER 2. Myths and Models

1. Thomas Jefferson, *Notes on the State of Virginia* (1785), query 14, available at Documenting the American South, https://docsouth.unc.edu/southlit/jefferson /jefferson.html; "Racial Stereotypes of the Civil War Era," American Antiquarian Society, www.americanantiquarian.org/Freedmen/Intros/questions.html.

2. George M. Fredrickson, *The Arrogance of Race: Historical Perspectives on Slavery, Racism, and Social Inequality* (Middletown, CT: Wesleyan University Press, 1988).

3. Some of the earliest letters Sam Clemens wrote his family as a teenager away from home for the first time were peppered with racist comments reflecting the ideology of Black inferiority to which he had been exposed since birth. See

Shelley Fisher Fishkin, "Mark Twain and Race," in *A Historical Guide to Mark Twain,* edited by Shelley Fisher Fishkin (New York: Oxford University Press, 2002), 127, 130.

4. Mark Twain, "Consistency" (1887), in *Mark Twain: Collected Tales, Sketches, Speeches, and Essays, 1852–1890,* edited by Louis J. Budd (New York: Library of America, 1992), 909.

5. Philip S. Foner, *Mark Twain: Social Critic* (New York: International Publishers, 1958), 288–89.

6. For a detailed discussion of the relationship between Clemens and Adolph Sutro, see Shelley Fisher Fishkin, "A Fresh Look at Mark Twain and the Jews," *Journal of Foreign Languages and Cultures* 1, no. 1 (2017): 11–27; and Fishkin, "Mark Twain and the Jews," *Arizona Quarterly: A Journal of American Literatures, Culture and Theory* 61, no. 1 (2005): 137–66.

7. Samuel L. Clemens (hereafter cited as SLC) to Charles Erskine Scott Wood, January 22, 1885, in Mark Twain, *Autobiography of Mark Twain,* edited by Benjamin Griffin and Harriet Elinor Smith with Victor Fischer, Michael B. Frank, Sharon K. Goetz, and Leslie Diane Myrick, vol. 2, from the Mark Twain Project, Robert H. Hirst, general editor (Berkeley: University of California Press, 2013), 607.

8. "Readers of *Harper's Monthly,* the *New York World, Century Magazine, McClure's,* and the *Chicago Daily Tribune* . . . were familiar with his distaste for anti-Semitism. He had published a searing exposé of anti-Semitism in the Austro-Hungarian empire and had minced no words denouncing pogroms in Russia. He had condemned French anti-Semitism in the Dreyfus Affair on numerous occasions, and in a widely-read essay called 'Concerning the Jews' had provided his own analysis of the roots of anti-Semitism. Would he want his daughter to marry one? Absolutely. When Clara Clemens did just that in 1909, Twain embraced his Jewish son-in-law, the pianist and conductor, Ossip Gabrilowitsch, with affection." Fishkin, "Fresh Look," 12.

9. See Fishkin, "Mark Twain and Race," 135–36.

10. My line of argument here builds on David Lionel Smith's argument in his seminal essay "Huck, Jim, and American Racial Discourse," in *Satire or Evasion? Black Perspectives on Huckleberry Finn,* edited by James S. Leonard, Thomas Tenney, and Thadious M. Davis (Durham, NC: Duke University Press, 1992), 103–20; and on that of Jocelyn Chadwick-Joshua, *The Jim Dilemma: Reading Race in "Huckleberry Finn"* (Jackson: University Press of Mississippi, 1998). (Note: although the book was published under the name Chadwick-Joshua, the author has used the name "Chadwick" for over two decades—and asked the publisher to change the way she is listed. She will be identified as Chadwick from this point on in this book.)

11. Richard H. Colfax, *Evidence against the View of the Abolitionists Consisting of Physical and Moral Proofs, of the Natural Inferiority of the Negroes* (New York: James T. M. Bleakley, 1833), 26. See also Colfax quoted in "Racial Stereotypes of the Civil War Era: 19th Century Claims That Science Proved the Inferiority of African-Americans," Northern Visions of Race, Region and Reform, American Antiquarian Society, www.americanantiquarian.org/Freedmen/Intros/questions.html.

12. Samuel George Morton, *Crania Americana; or, A Comparative View of the Skulls of Various Aboriginal Nations of North and South America; To Which Is Prefixed an Essay on the Varieties of the Human Species* (Philadelphia: J. Dobson, 1839). See also "Racial Stereotypes of the Civil War Era."

13. Michael E. Ruane, "A Brief History of the Enduring Phony Science That Perpetuates White Supremacy," *Washington Post,* April 30, 2019. For an overview of these theories, see also Ibram X. Kendi, *Stamped from the Beginning: The Definitive History of Racist Ideas in America* (New York: PublicAffairs, 2016).

14. Yasuko I. Takezawa, "Gobineau's Essay on the Inequality of Human Races," *Encyclopedia Britannica,* www.britannica.com/topic/race-human/Gobineaus-Essay-on-the-Inequality-of-Human-Races; Thomas H. Gossett, *Race: The History of an Idea in America,* new ed. (New York: Oxford University Press, 1997), 342–57.

15. George S. Sawyer, *Southern Institutes; or, An Inquiry into the Origin and Early Prevalence of Slavery and the Slave-Trade: With an Analysis of the Laws, History, and Government of the Institution in the Principal Nations, Ancient and Modern, from the Earliest Ages Down to the Present Time; With Notes and Comments in Defence of the Southern Institutions* (Philadelphia: J. P. Lippincott, 1858), 192; Howard Dodson, "Needed: A New Perspective on Black History," *Humanities* 2, no. 1 (1981): 2; L. Scott Miller, "The Origins of the Presumption of Black Stupidity," *Journal of Blacks in Higher Education,* no. 9 (1995): 78–82.

16. Mark Twain, *The Innocents Abroad,* The Oxford Mark Twain, edited by Shelley Fisher Fishkin (1869; New York: Oxford University Press, 1996), 5–6, 118–24, 163–64, 183.

17. Twain, *Innocents Abroad,* 240–42.

18. SLC to Olivia L. Langdon, December 15 and 16, 1869, in *Mark Twain's Letters,* vol. 3: *1869,* edited by Victor Fischer, Michael B. Frank, and Dahlia Armon, from the Mark Twain Project, Robert H. Hirst, general editor (Berkeley: University of California Press, 1992), 426.

19. For the story of how Twain got to know and support Warner T. McGuinn, see Shelley Fisher Fishkin, *Lighting Out for the Territory: Reflections on Mark Twain and American Culture* (New York: Oxford University Press, 1997), 100–108; Shelley Fisher Fishkin, "Black and White Youth in Mark Twain's Hannibal,"

in *Mark Twain and Youth: Studies in His Life and Writings,* edited by Kevin Mac Donnell and R. Kent Rasmussen (London: Bloomsbury, 2016), 228–30; and Edwin MacDowell, "From Twain, a Letter on Debt to Blacks," *New York Times,* March 14, 1885. For McGuinn's intellectual and political talent, see Tanya Koshy, "Remodeling Resistance: Black Civil Society and the Battle Against Baltimore's Residential Segregation Ordinances (1910–1918)" (honors thesis, American Studies Program, Stanford University, May 2006).

20. Charles Dudley Warner, "The Education of the Negro," in *Complete Works of Charles Dudley Warner,* vol. 14 (Hartford, CT: American Publishing, 1904), 384.

21. Mark Twain, "A Family Sketch," in Mark Twain, Livy Clemens, and Susy Clemens, *A Family Sketch and Other Private Writings,* edited by Benjamin Griffin, from the Mark Twain Project, Robert H. Hirst, general editor (Oakland: University of California Press, 2014), 18–29; Benjamin Griffin, "Unveiling MT's 'Family Sketch,'" *Mark Twain Annual* 11 (2013): 109–12; Bonnyeclaire Smith-Stewart, "Interview with Bonnyeclaire Smith-Stewart about George Griffin, Hartford Butler of Mark Twain," *Mark Twain Journal* 53, no. 1 (2015): 114–21; Kevin Mac Donnell, "George Griffin: Meeting Mark Twain's Butler Face-to-Face," *Mark Twain Journal* 62, no. 1 (2024): 10–58.

22. See Shelley Fisher Fishkin, *Was Huck Black? Mark Twain and African-American Voices* (New York: Oxford University Press, 1993), 124; and Twain, "Family Sketch," 24, 20.

23. Twain, "Family Sketch,"13.

24. Constance Neyer, "The Butler behind Mark Twain: George Griffin Was a Part of Samuel Clemens' Family and Remains a Key Figure in Hartford's African-American Heritage," *Hartford (CT) Courant,* February 6, 1994; Arthur G. Pettit, *Mark Twain and the South* (Lexington: University Press of Kentucky, 1974), 103–4.

25. Notice and explanatory notes, in Mark Twain, *Adventures of Huckleberry Finn,* edited by Victor Fischer and Lin Salamo with Harriet Elinor Smith and the late Walter Blair, Mark Twain Library, from the Mark Twain Project, Robert H. Hirst, general editor (1885; Berkeley: University of California Press, 2001), 376.

26. Twain, "Family Sketch," 20.

27. Twain, "Family Sketch," 22. Benjamin Griffin notes that "Governor Robinson" was "Mayor of Hartford from 1872–1874. . . . Although Connecticut Republicans twice nominated him for office, he was never governor." Griffin, "Biographical Directory," in Twain, Clemens, and Clemens, *Family Sketch and Other Private Writings,* 184.

28. Twain, "Family Sketch," 23. For more on George Griffin, as well as the

only extant photograph of him, see Kevin Mac Donnell's excellent article, "George Griffin: Meeting Mark Twain's Butler Face-to-Face." Mac Donnell presented his research at a program at the Mark Twain House and Museum on May 14, 2024, that may be accessed at this link: www.youtube.com/watch?v=Y3XYs3UagBg.

29. SLC to Edward Bok, editor, *Ladies' Home Journal*, July 17, 1904, quoted in Sharon D. McCoy, "No Evading the Jokes: *Adventures of Huckleberry Finn*, Mark Twain, and Male Friendship across Racial and Class Lines," *Mark Twain Annual* 12 (2014): 51.

30. SLC to John Brown, August 25 and 27, 1877, Elmira, NY, Mark Twain Project, https://www.marktwainproject.org/letters/ucclo1473/.

31. Chadwick, *Jim Dilemma*, 20.

32. Jefferson, *Notes on the State of Virginia*, query 14. It was also widely believed that Black people were less sensitive to physical pain. See Joanna Bourke, "Pain Sensitivity: An Unnatural History from 1800 to 1965," *Journal of Medical Humanities* 35, no. 4 (2014): 301–19.

33. Mark Twain, "A True Story, Repeated Word for Word as I Heard It," *Atlantic Monthly*, November 1874, reprinted in Twain, Clemens, and Clemens, *Family Sketch and Other Private Writings*, 45–50.

34. David Blight, *Race and Reunion: The Civil War in American Memory* (Cambridge, MA: Belknap Press of Harvard University Press, 2001), 220–31.

35. Paul Laurence Dunbar was engaged in an analogous project. See Shelley Fisher Fishkin, "Race and the Politics of Memory: Mark Twain and Paul Laurence Dunbar," *Journal of American Studies* 40, no. 2 (2006): 283–309.

36. A South Carolinian, "South Carolina Society," *Atlantic Monthly*, June 1877, quoted in Rayford W. Logan, *The Betrayal of the Negro from Rutherford B. Hayes to Woodrow Wilson* (1954; New York: Da Capo, 1997), 252.

37. This section draws on descriptions of Cord and "A True Story" in Shelley Fisher Fishkin, *Writing America: Literary Landmarks from Walden Pond to Wounded Knee* (New Brunswick, NJ: Rutgers University Press, 2015), 133–38; and Fishkin, *Was Huck Black?*, 8–9, 151n22. David E. E. Sloane and Terry Conroy have tracked down external confirmation that the story that Mary Ann Cord told Twain actually happened, much as she described it. Terry Conroy and David E. E. Sloane, "'A True Story' Confirmed: How a Slave Mother Found Her Lost Son," *Studies in American Humor*, n.s., 3, no. 22 (2010): 147–54.

38. Fishkin, *Was Huck Black?*, 8–9, 151n22.

39. William Dean Howells to SLC, September 17, 1874, in *Mark Twain–Howells Letters: The Correspondence of Samuel L. Clemens and William Dean Howells: 1872–1910*, vol. 1, edited by Henry Nash Smith and William M. Gibson (Cambridge, MA: Belknap Press of Harvard University Press, 1960), 24–25; William

Dean Howells, "Recollections of an Atlantic Editorship," *Atlantic Monthly*, November 1907, 601.

40. "Negro," in *The American Cyclopædia: A Popular Dictionary of General Knowledge*, edited by George Ripley and Charles Anderson Dana, 16 vols. (New York: D. Appleton, 1873–76), 12:216. Twain had referred to the *Cyclopædia* as "that steadfast friend of the editor all over the land." Quoted in Alan Gribben, *Mark Twain's Literary Resources: A Reconstruction of His Library and Reading*, vol. 2 (Montgomery, AL: NewSouth Books, 2022), 21. Gribben notes that Twain donated his complete set of this edition of the *Cyclopædia* to the Redding Library in Connecticut, but Twain clearly ignored or rejected this particular entry.

41. Lucinda H. McKethan, "Huck Finn and the Slave Narratives: Lighting Out as Design," *Southern Review* 20, no. 2 (1984): 253–54.

42. Mark Twain, *Autobiography of Mark Twain*, vol. 1, edited by Harriet E. Smith with Benjamin Griffin, Victor Fischer, Michael B. Frank, Sharon K. Goetz, and Leslie Diane Myrick, from the Mark Twain Project, Robert H. Hirst, general editor (Berkeley: University of California Press, 2010), 390.

43. Deborah A. Lee, "Love and Debt: A True Story of Mary Ann Cord, John T. Lewis, and Mark Twain at Quarry Farm," *Mark Twain Journal* 54, no. 2 (2016): 97–134.

44. SLC to Olivia L. Langdon, December 15 and 16, 1869, Pawtucket, RI, and Boston, in *Mark Twain's Letters*, vol. 3: *1869*, edited by Victor Fischer and Michael B. Frank, with Dahlia Armon, the Mark Twain Project, Robert H. Hirst, general editor (Berkeley: University of California Press, 1988), 426.

45. For more on the friendship between Twain and Lewis, see Robert Paul Lamb, "John T. Lewis and Mark Twain: A Friendship," August 28, 2023, Center for Mark Twain Studies, https://marktwainstudies.com/john-t-lewis-mark-twain-a-friendship.

46. Jefferson, *Notes on the State of Virginia*, query 14.

47. *Autobiography of Mark Twain*, 1:389.

48. *Autobiography of Mark Twain*, 1:399–400. Daniel Quarles's most memorable ghost story may have been "The Golden Arm," the tale written in Black dialect that is featured in Mark Twain's essay "How to Tell a Story." Mark Twain, "How to Tell a Story," in *How to Tell a Story and Other Essays*, The Oxford Mark Twain, edited by Shelley Fisher Fishkin (New York: Oxford University Press, 1996), 3–15.

49. Mark Twain, "Corn-Pone Opinions" (1901), in *Mark Twain: Collected Tales, Sketches, Speeches, and Essays, 1891–1910*, edited by Louis J. Budd (New York: Library of America, 1992), 507–11.

50. This section draws on Fishkin, *Was Huck Black?*, 54–59, 173–74n6. Robert Paul Lamb notes that Jerry's impact on Twain may have gone beyond opening

his eyes to the power of satire: Twain would adopt Jerry's philosophy of human behavior as his own. Lamb notes that the same year Twain published *Huckleberry Finn* he wrote a piece on "The Character of Man" which centered on ideas about conformity to which Jerry had introduced him. Robert Paul Lamb, "Mark Twain's New Method of Cultural Critique: Authorial Double-Voiced Speech in *Adventures of Huckleberry Finn,*" *American Literary Realism* 52, no. 1 (2019): 21n27.

51. Hildegard Cummings, "The Hartford Artist," in *Charles Ethan Porter, 1847?–1923,* edited by Helen K. Fusscas (Marlborough, CT: Connecticut Gallery, 1987), 62.

52. H. W. French, *Art and Artists in Connecticut* (New York: Charles T. Dillingham, 1879), 160.

53. Shelley Fisher Fishkin, Afterword, in Mark Twain, *Is He Dead? A Comedy in Three Acts,* edited by Shelley Fisher Fishkin (Berkeley: University of California Press, 2003), 158, 212–13n32; Fusscas, *Charles Ethan Porter,* 38; Thomas P. Riggio, "Charles Ethan Porter and Mark Twain," in Fusscas, *Charles Ethan Porter,* 78; and James Miller, "Charles Ethan Porter and the Hartford Black Community," in Fusscas, *Charles Ethan Porter,* 88–95.

54. *San Francisco Chronicle,* March 15, 1885, cited in Victor Fischer, "Huck Finn Reviewed: The Reception of 'Huckleberry Finn' in the United States, 1885–1897," *American Literary Realism, 1870–1910* 16, no. 1 (1983): 24.

55. Chadwick, *Jim Dilemma,* x.

56. Mark Twain, "A Fable" (1909), in *The Complete Short Stories of Mark Twain,* edited by Charles Neider (New York: Alfred A. Knopf, 2012), 633–34.

CHAPTER 3. The Debates

1. "Some of Mark Twain's Fun; He and Mr. Cable Amuse an Audience by Turns," *New York Sun,* November 19, 1884.

2. There is also no evidence that Twain ever called Jim by this name in his public readings. When the epithet appears in newspapers, it is never a direct quotation from Twain.

3. As was the case with the papers that ran the episode under the headline "Nigger Jim's Story," the excerpt ran over the byline Mark Twain but without any reference to the novel.

4. *Buffalo (NY) Evening Telegraph,* May 23, 1885; *Larned (KS) Chronoscope,* March 6, 1885; "Nigger Jim's Story," *Crawford Avalanche* (Grayling, MI), April 30, 1885; "Didn't Shut the Door; Nigger Jim's Little Deaf and Dumb Daughter—How He Punished Her and Why He Couldn't Forgive Himself—A Pathetic Story," *Parsons (KS) Palladium,* March 18, 1885; *Placer Herald* (Rocklin, CA), April 25, 1885; *Santa Maria (CA) Times,* May 9, 1885.

5. Albert Bigelow Paine, *Mark Twain: A Biography*, 4 vols. (New York: Harper and Bros., 1912), available at www.gutenberg.org/cache/epub/2988/pg2988 -images.html; Albert Bigelow Paine, *The Boys' Life of Mark Twain* (New York: Harper and Bros., 1916), 7; Ernest Hemingway, *Green Hills of Africa* (New York: Scribner, 1935), 23; Bernard DeVoto, *Mark Twain's America* (1932), edited by M. J. Gallagher (Lincoln: University of Nebraska Press, 1997), 52, 236, 292, 302; Norman Mailer, "*Huckleberry Finn*, Alive at 100," *New York Times*, December 9, 1984; Leslie Fiedler, "Viewpoint: Subversive Mark Twain," *Viewpoint* (Center for Inquiry) (Summer 1983): 56; Leslie Fiedler, *Love and Death in the American Novel* (1960) (reprint, Dallas, TX: Dalkey Archive Press, 1997), 196, 271, 279, 367; C. Vann Woodward, *The Burden of Southern History* (1960) (reprint, Baton Rouge: Louisiana State University Press, 2008), 181, 295; Mel Watkins, *Stepin Fetchit: The Life and Times of Lincoln Perry* (New York: Knopf Doubleday, 2010), 92.

6. Malcolm Bradbury, "*Huckleberry Finn*: An Epic of Self Discovery," *UNESCO Courier* 35, no. 6 (1982): 16; Josef Skvorecky, "Huckleberry Finn: Or, Something Exotic in Czechoslovakia," *New York Times*, November 8, 1987; Perry Miller, *Nature's Nation* (Cambridge, MA: Harvard University Press, 1967), 269, 270, 282; Edward L. Ayers, *The Promise of the New South: Life after Reconstruction* (New York: Oxford University Press, 1992), 538; Hilton Als, "More Harm Than Good: Surviving the N-Word and Its Meanings," *New Yorker*, February 3, 2002; Russell Baker, "Observer: The Only Gentleman," *New York Times*, April 14, 1982; Michiko Kakutani, "Light Out, Huck, They Still Want to Sivilize You," *New York Times*, January 6, 2011; Donald Bogle, *Blacks in American Films and Television: An Encyclopedia* (New York: Garland, 1988), 490; "Louis C.K.: Live at the Comedy Store (2015)," transcript, May 4, 2017, https://scrapsfromtheloft.com/comedy /louis-c-k-live-at-the-comedy-store-2015-transcript/; "Opie and Anthony—Louis CK on the Removal of Nigger Jim," *Bilibili*, September 21, 2017, www.bilibili.com /video/BV1gx411G7S4/.

7. Harold Beaver, "Run, Nigger, Run: *Adventures of Huckleberry Finn* as a Fugitive Slave Narrative," *American Studies* 8, no. 3 (1974): 339; Gladys Bellamy, *Mark Twain as a Literary Artist* (1950; reprint, Norman: University of Oklahoma Press, 2012), 52, 321, 338, 342, 361, 372; Kenneth S. Lynn, *Mark Twain and Southwestern Humor* (Boston: Little, Brown, 1959), 240; Kenneth S. Lynn, "Huck and Jim," *Yale Review* 47, no. 3 (1958): 428; Leo Marx, "Mr. Eliot, Mr. Trilling, and 'Huckleberry Finn,'" *American Scholar* 22, no. 4 (1953): 424; Arthur G. Pettit, *Mark Twain and the South* (Lexington: University Press of Kentucky, 1973), 46, 55–56, 77, 95, 103, 104, 105; Tom Quirk, *Coming to Grips with Huckleberry Finn* (Columbia: University of Missouri Press, 1993), 64, 66, 67, 73, 74, 75, 114, 127; Dixon Wecter, *Sam Clemens of Hannibal* (Boston: Houghton Mifflin, 1952), 44, 100; Dixon Wec-

ter, "Introduction: One More Word," in Mark Twain, *Adventures of Huckleberry Finn* (New York: Harper and Row, 1963), xi.

8. Beverly Goldberg, "On the Line for the First Amendment: A 1995 Interview with Judith Krug, Director of the ALA's Office for Intellectual Freedom," *American Libraries,* May 27, 2009, https://americanlibrariesmagazine.org/2009 /05/27/on-the-line-for-the-first-amendment/; Ralph Ellison, *Shadow and Act* (1964; New York: Knopf Doubleday, 2011), 50, 58.

9. Joe B. Fulton, *Mark Twain's Ethical Realism: The Aesthetics of Race, Class, and Gender* (Columbia: University of Missouri Press, 1997), 56.

10. "Mark Twain's New Story," *New York Sun,* February 15, 1885.

11. Sterling Brown, *The Negro in American Fiction* (1937; New York: Arno, 1968), 68.

12. T. S. Eliot, "Introduction to *Huckleberry Finn* (Chanticleer Press, 1950)," in *The Mark Twain Anthology: Great Writers on His Life and Works,* edited by Shelley Fisher Fishkin (New York: Library of America, 2010), 239.

13. Leo Marx, "Mr. Eliot, Mr. Trilling, and 'Huckleberry Finn,'" *American Scholar* 22, no. 4 (1953): 430.

14. John Strausbaugh, *Black Like You: Blackface, Whiteface, Insult, and Imitation in American Popular Culture* (New York: Jeremy P. Tarcher/Penguin, 2006), 225.

15. Strausbaugh, *Black Like You,* 227.

16. Christina Melton, "Baton Rouge Bus Boycott," 64 Parishes, https://64par ishes.org/entry/baton-rouge-bus-boycott, updated March 9, 2022. See also Adam Fairclough, *Race and Democracy: The Civil Rights Struggle in Louisiana, 1915–1972* (Athens: University of Georgia Press, 1995).

17. Ellison, "Change the Joke and Shift the Yoke" (1958), in *Shadow and Act,* 50.

18. Eric Lott, *Love and Theft: Blackface Minstrelsy and the American Working Class* (New York: Oxford University Press, 1993).

19. Lott, *Love and Theft,* 4.

20. There were occasional exceptions, as Sharon D. McCoy observes. The song "Pass down de Centre," performed by the San Francisco Minstrels, for example, "is hardly the nostalgic longing for the 'good old days' that we expect from a blackface 'plantation' number. [The song] is instead an ambiguous and ambivalent mixture of hope, anger, agency, burlesque, possibility and despair." And, as McCoy notes, minstrel shows in the 1870s often addressed topics removed from life on the plantation, satirizing the contemporary corruption, for example, of a political figure like New York City's William Magear "Boss" Tweed. Sharon D. McCoy, "'The Trouble Begins at Eight': Mark Twain, the San Francisco

Minstrels, and the Unsettling Legacy of Blackface Minstrelsy," *American Literary Realism* 41, no. 3 (2009): 237, 243–44.

21. David Bradley, personal communication, March 30, 2023.

22. In Hannibal, Twain saw minstrels in Spalding and Rogers' Floating Palace (a showboat that stopped at the steamboat landing) and Dan Rice's Circus; he saw the San Francisco Minstrels in both San Francisco and New York, and he saw the New Christy Minstrels in St. Louis. Anthony J. Berret, "Huckleberry Finn and the Minstrel Show," *American Studies* 27, no. 2 (1986): 37–38. See also McCoy, "'Trouble Begins at Eight,'" 233.

23. Samuel L. Clemens (hereafter cited as SLC) to Tom Hood and George Routledge and Sons, March 10, 1873, in *Mark Twain's Letters*, vol. 5: *1872–1873*, edited by Lin Salamo and Harriet Elinor Smith, the Mark Twain Project, Robert H. Hirst, general editor (Berkeley: University of California Press, 1996), 315.

24. Mark Twain, *Autobiography of Mark Twain*, edited by Benjamin Griffin and Harriet Elinor Smith with Victor Fischer, Michael B. Frank, Sharon K. Goetz, and Leslie Diane Myrick, vol. 2, from the Mark Twain Project, Robert H. Hirst, general editor (Berkeley: University of California Press, 2013), 294.

25. The distance between Black life and representations of it on the minstrel stage was the focus of many scholars in the late twentieth century who noted that "the minstrel show was neither about authentic black life nor about an authentic South. Alexander Saxton, David Roediger, and Eric Lott have . . . argued that blackface performance was a fantasy of northern white performers, largely from middle-class homes who knew little or nothing of nothing of black life." W. T. Lhamon, *Raising Cain: Blackface Performance from Jim Crow to Hip Hop* (Cambridge, MA: Harvard University Press, 1998), 6.

26. Mark Twain, "EXPLANATORY," in *Adventures of Huckleberry Finn*, edited by Victor Fischer and Lin Salamo with Harriet Elinor Smith and the late Walter Blair, Mark Twain Library, from the Mark Twain Project, Robert H. Hirst, general editor (1885; Berkeley: University of California Press, 2001), xxxiii. Unless otherwise indicated, this is the edition of the novel to which all notes refer.

27. The term *racial counterfeit* comes from Lott, *Love and Theft*, 38. For a nuanced discussion of the complexities of Twain's attraction to minstrel shows, see Henry B. Wonham, *Playing the Races: Ethnic Caricature and American Literary Realism* (New York: Oxford University Press, 2004), 69–100.

28. SLC to William Dean Howells, September 20, 1874, in *Mark Twain's Letters*, vol. 6: *1874–1875*, edited by Michael Frank and Harriet Elinor Smith, the Mark Twain Project, Robert H. Hirst, general editor (Berkeley: University of California Press, 2002), 233.

29. Sterling Brown, *The Negro in American Fiction* (1937; New York: Arno, 1968), 68.

30. David Lionel Smith, "Black Critics and Mark Twain," in *The Cambridge Companion to Mark Twain*, edited by Forrest G. Robinson (Cambridge: Cambridge University Press, 1995), 119.

31. Langston Hughes, Milton Meltzer, and Charles Eric Lincoln, *A Pictorial History of the Negro in America* (New York: Crown, 1968), 235.

32. Twain, *Adventures of Huckleberry Finn*, 6–8.

33. Chadwick Hansen, "The Character of Jim and the Ending of 'Huckleberry Finn,'" *Massachusetts Review* 5, no. 1 (1963): 46.

34. Fredrick Woodard and Donnarae MacCann, "Minstrel Shackles and Nineteenth-Century 'Liberality' in *Huckleberry Finn*," in *Satire or Evasion? Black Perspectives on Huckleberry Finn*, edited by James S. Leonard, Thomas A. Tenney, and Thadious M. Davis (Durham, NC: Duke University Press, 1991), 145.

35. Andrew Silver, *Minstrelsy and Murder: The Crisis of Southern Humor, 1835–1925* (Baton Rouge: Louisiana State University Press, 2006), 96.

36. See Shelley Fisher Fishkin, "In Praise of 'Spike Lee's Huckleberry Finn' by Ralph Wiley," *Mark Twain Circular* 13, no. 4 (1999): 1–8, available at www.marktwaincircle.org/ralph-wiley-huck-finn. Both scenes from Wiley's screenplay, which are reprinted in the *Mark Twain Circular* and in the "Appendix: Notes for Teachers" at the end of this book, may be reproduced for classroom use.

37. Twain, *Adventures of Huckleberry Finn*, 6.

38. James M. Cox first suggested this possibility in 1966. Cox, *Mark Twain: The Fate of Humor* (Princeton, NJ: Princeton University Press, 1966), 319.

39. David L. Smith, "Huck, Jim, and American Racial Discourse," in Leonard, Tenney, and Davis, *Satire or Evasion?*, 109.

40. Smith, "Huck, Jim, and American Racial Discourse," 109.

41. Smith, "Huck, Jim, and American Racial Discourse," 109–10.

42. Carl F. Wieck, *Refiguring Huckleberry Finn* (Athens: University of Georgia Press, 2000), 25, 109.

43. Lamb, "Mark Twain's New Method of Cultural Critique," 5.

44. Lamb, "Mark Twain's New Method of Cultural Critique," 5.

45. Hansen, "Character of Jim," 47.

46. Smith, "Huck, Jim, and American Racial Discourse," 110–11.

47. Forrest G. Robinson, "The Characterization of Jim in *Huckleberry Finn*," *Nineteenth-Century Literature* 43, no. 3 (1988): 372.

48. Wieck, *Refiguring Huckleberry Finn*, 165.

49. Victor A. Doyno, "Huck's and Jim's Dynamic Interactions: Dialogues, Ethics, Empathy, Respect," *Mark Twain Annual* 1 (2003): 21–22. Edward Kemble's illustration for chapter 4 (p. 37, first American edition) of Jim listening to the hair ball has probably contributed to the view that this episode is redolent of minstrelsy. Jim might be wearing the typical stage makeup of blackface minstrelsy,

given his exaggerated lips. Some other images of Jim are problematic, as well. However, other pictures of Jim are respectful and neutral (e.g., "We turned in and slept," chap. 13, p. 108; "On the Raft," chap. 12, p. 93; and "Asleep on the Raft," chap. 15, p. 105). Twain said the pictures "will just barely do— & that is the best I can say for them." Twain qtd. in Samuel Charles Webster, ed., *Mark Twain, Business Man* (Boston: Little, Brown, 1946), 415. For more on Kemble's drawings as ethnic caricature, see Wonham, *Playing the Races*, 89–99.

50. Woodard and MacCann, "Minstrel Shackles," 145.

51. Elaine Mensh and Harry Mensh, *Black, White, and Huckleberry Finn: Re-imagining the American Dream* (Tuscaloosa: University of Alabama Press, 2000), 39.

52. Twain, *Adventures of Huckleberry Finn*, 283.

53. Sterling Stuckey, *Slave Culture: Nationalist Theory and the Foundations of Black America* (New York: Oxford University Press, 1987), 109, 43.

54. Langston Hughes and Arna Bontemps, eds., *The Book of Negro Folklore* (New York: Dodd, Mead, 1958), 191.

55. Twain, *Adventures of Huckleberry Finn*, 57; Mensh and Mensh, *Black, White, and Huckleberry Finn*, 48.

56. Wieck, *Refiguring Huckleberry Finn*, 165; Silver, *Minstrelsy and Murder*, 102.

57. Donald B. Gibson, "Mark Twain's Jim in the Classroom," *English Journal* 57, no. 2 (1968): 196, emphasis in original.

58. Twain, *Adventures of Huckleberry Finn*, 94–96.

59. Woodard and MacCann, "Minstrel Shackles," 145. In a similar vein, Andrew Silver writes that this "minstrel dialogue" involves Huck taking on "the role of a minstrel dandy to Jim's end man." Silver, *Minstrelsy and Murder*, 109. Berret, "Huckleberry Finn and the Minstrel Show," 40.

60. Neil Schmitz, "The Paradox of Liberation in *Huckleberry Finn*," *Texas Studies in Literature and Language* 13 (Spring 1971): 32.

61. Mensh and Mensh, *Black, White and Huckleberry Finn*, 50. As Jocelyn Chadwick puts it, "By assuming the persona of Solomon and thereby appropriating Solomon's voice and authority," Jim rejects his subservient role and manages to break, in the process, "the conventional boundaries between masters and slaves in the old South." Jocelyn Chadwick, *The Jim Dilemma: Reading Race in "Huckleberry Finn"* (Jackson: University Press of Mississippi, 1998), 51.

62. Wieck, *Refiguring Huckleberry Finn*, 23–24.

63. For Douglass's visit backstage, see Guy A. Cardwell, *Twins of Genius* (London: Neville Spearman, 1962), 22. For the presence of "Sollermun" on the program, see Fred W. Lorch, "Cable and His Reading Tour with Mark Twain in

1884–1885," *American Literature* 23, no. 4 (1952): 475; and Albert Bigelow Paine, *Mark Twain: A Biography,* 4 vols. in 2 (New York: Harper and Brothers, 1912), 2:785. Wieck has written at length about resonances between Douglass's *Narrative* and *Huckleberry Finn.* He suggests that "the influence was stronger and more profound than has hitherto been understood." Wieck, *Refiguring Huckleberry Finn,* 20–39, quotation at 39. For more on the relationship between Twain and Douglass, see Matt Seybold, "Even if He Weren't My Friend: Frederick Douglass and Mark Twain," Center for Mark Twain Studies, August 2, 2021, https://marktwainstudies.com/freddouglassmarktwain/.

64. Twain, *Adventures of Huckleberry Finn,* 97–98.

65. Berret, "*Huckleberry Finn* and the Minstrel Show," 39.

66. Fredrick Woodard and Donnarae MacCann, "Huckleberry Finn and the Tradition of Blackface Minstrelsy," *Interracial Books for Children Bulletin* 15, no. 1–2 (1984): 5.

67. Brown (*Negro in American Fiction,* 68), summarized in Smith, "Black Critics and Mark Twain," 120–21.

68. Hansen, "Character of Jim," 50–51.

69. Steven Mailloux, *Rhetorical Power* (Ithaca, NY: Cornell University Press, 1989), 74; Smith, "Huck, Jim, and American Racial Discourse," 111; Pettit, *Twain and the South,* 112–13; Chadwick, *Jim Dilemma,* 53.

70. Betty Jones, "Huck and Jim: A Reconsideration," in Leonard, Tenney, and Davis, *Satire or Evasion?,* 155. See also Mensh and Mensh, *Black, White, and Huckleberry Finn,* 53–54.

71. M. J. Sidnell, "Huck Finn and Jim: Their Abortive Freedom Ride," *Cambridge Quarterly* 2, no. 3 (1967): 204; Woodard and MacCann, "Minstrel Shackles," 145.

72. Winston Kelley reads this scene the same way as Wiley, noting that "when Huck fails to back down, Jim gives him the minstrel-like performance Huck seems to demand, fabulating an extravagantly dramatic account of what happened." Winston Kelley, "How German Translations of 'Trash' in Chapter 15 of *Huckleberry Finn* Facilitate Misunderstanding the Whole Novel," Special Forum on "Global Huck," edited by Shelley Fisher Fishkin, Tsuyoshi Ishihara, Ronald Jenn, Holger Kersten, and Selina Lai-Henderson, *Journal of Transnational American Studies* 12, no. 2 (2021): 92.

73. Twain, *Adventures of Huckleberry Finn,* 103.

74. From *Spike Lee's Huckleberry Finn* by Ralph Wiley. Copyright © 1997 Ralph Wiley. ALL RIGHTS RESERVED. Printed with permission of the author. May be reproduced for classroom use only. WGA-E Registered #107314-00. Emphasis in original. The scene, along with Fishkin, "In Praise of 'Spike Lee's Huckleberry

Finn,'" appears at https://marktwaincircle.org/ralph-wiley-huck-finn and in the "Appendix: Notes for Teachers" at the end of this book. For over two decades my students have done staged readings of this scene in class and have found that it profoundly shapes their understanding of Jim's character.

75. Twain, *Adventures of Huckleberry Finn*, 105.

76. Stephen Railton, "Jim and Mark Twain: What Do Dey Stan' For?," *Virginia Quarterly Review* 63, no. 3 (1987): 398.

77. Silver, *Minstrelsy and Murder*, 122; E. L. Doctorow, *New Yorker*, June 26, 1995, 132.

78. Marx, "Mr. Elliot, Mr. Trilling, and 'Huckleberry Finn,'" 429–30. Similarly, Woodard and MacCann write that "infantile reactions on Jim's part are multiplied and intensified in the last fifth of the novel when he acquiesces completely to Tom's escape plan." Woodard and MacCann, "Minstrel Shackles," 146.

79. Hansen, "Character of Jim," 59–60; Pettit, *Twain and the South*, 119; Joseph Sawicki, "Authority/Author-ity: Representation and Fictionality in *Huckleberry Finn*," *Modern Fiction Studies* 31 (1985): 698.

80. Twain, *Adventures of Huckleberry Finn*, 289.

81. Twain, *Adventures of Huckleberry Finn*, 296–97.

82. Twain, *Adventures of Huckleberry Finn*, 309.

83. Twain, *Adventures of Huckleberry Finn*, 309, 310.

84. Twain, *Adventures of Huckleberry Finn*, 323, 325; Chadwick, *Jim Dilemma*, 125.

85. Peaches Henry, "The Struggle for Tolerance: Race and Censorship in *Huckleberry Finn*," in Leonard, Tenney, and Davis, *Satire or Evasion?*, 33, 38.

86. Chadwick, *Jim Dilemma*, 122–23, 124.

87. Twain, *Adventures of Huckleberry Finn*, 327, 328.

88. Twain, *Adventures of Huckleberry Finn*, 354.

89. Smith, "Huck, Jim, and American Racial Discourse," 114–15.

90. Smith, "Huck, Jim, and American Racial Discourse," 115.

91. Matthew Seybold, "Even If He Weren't My Friend: Frederick Douglass and Mark Twain," Mark Twain Studies, August 2, 2021, https://marktwainstudies.com/freddouglassmarktwain/.

92. Scholars who suggest that the last portion of the novel is a commentary on race relations in the 1880s include Harold Beaver, *Huckleberry Finn* (London: Allen and Unwin, 1987); Louis J. Budd, "Southward Currents under Huck Finn's Raft," *Mississippi Valley Historical Review* 46, no. 2 (1959): 222–37; Stephen Clarke, "Huckleberry Finn's Conscience: Reckoning with the Evasion," *Journal of Ethics* 24, no. 4 (2020): 485–508; Victor A. Doyno, *Writing "Huck Finn": Mark Twain's Creative Process* (Philadelphia: University of Pennsylvania Press, 1992); Shelley

Fisher Fishkin, *Was Huck Black? Mark Twain and African-American Voices* (New York: Oxford University Press, 1993), 68–95; Shelley Fisher Fishkin, "Race and the Politics of Memory: Mark Twain and Paul Laurence Dunbar," *Journal of American Studies* 40, no. 2 (2006): 283–309; Richard Gollin and Reta Gollin, "Huckleberry Finn and the Time of the Evasion," *Modern Language Studies* 9 (Spring 1979): 5–15; Lawrence B. Holland, "A 'Raft of Trouble': Word and Deed in *Huckleberry Finn*," in *American Realism: New Essays*, edited by Eric Sundquist (Baltimore: Johns Hopkins University Press, 1982), 66–81; Andrew Levy, *Huck Finn's America* (New York: Simon and Schuster, 2015); Stacey Margolis, "Huckleberry Finn or Consequences," *PMLA* 116, no. 2 (2001): 329–43; Stephen Mailloux, "Reading Huckleberry Finn: The Rhetoric of Performed Ideology," in *New Essays on "Adventures of Huckleberry Finn,"* edited by Louis J. Budd (New York: Cambridge University Press, 1985); Charles H. Nilon, "The Ending of *Huckleberry Finn*: 'Freeing the Free Negro,'" in Leonard, Tenney, and Davis, *Satire or Evasion?*; Neil Schmitz, "The Paradox of Liberation in *Huckleberry Finn*," *Texas Studies in Language and Literature* 13, no. 1 (1971): 125–36; Neil Schmitz, "Twain, *Huckleberry Finn*, and the Reconstruction," *American Studies* 12, no. 1 (1971): 59–67; Kevin Michael Scott, "'There's More Honor': Reinterpreting Tom and the Evasion in *Huckleberry Finn*," *Studies in the Novel* 31, no. 2 (2005): 187–207; Tony Tanner, *Reign of Wonder: Naivety and Reality in American Literature* (Cambridge: Cambridge University Press, 1965); and Wieck, *Refiguring Huckleberry Finn*, 56–69. For a corrective to some imprecise or misleading dimensions of discussions of Reconstruction in these works, see Brook Thomas, "*Adventures of Huckleberry Finn* and Reconstruction," *American Literary Realism* 50, no. 1 (2017): 1–24.

93. Robert Paul Lamb, "America Can Break Your Heart: On the Significance of Mark Twain," in *A Companion to American Fiction, 1865–1914*, edited by Robert Paul Lamb and G. R. Thompson (Oxford: Blackwell, 2005), 484.

94. Toni Morrison, "Introduction," in Mark Twain, *Adventures of Huckleberry Finn*, The Oxford Mark Twain, edited by Shelley Fisher Fishkin (New York: Oxford University Press, 1996), xxxvi.

95. Robinson, "Characterization of Jim," 370.

96. Robinson, "Characterization of Jim," 365; Cox, *Mark Twain*, 318–19; Lamb, "Twain's New Method of Cultural Critique," 2–3.

97. Robinson, "Characterization of Jim," 363.

98. Morrison, "Introduction," xxxv.

99. Wecter, "Introduction," xxiii.

100. See an overview of this trend in Shelley Fisher Fishkin, "New Perspectives on 'Jim' in the 1990s," *Mark Twain Review* (Korea) 4 (Winter 1999): 5–19.

101. Chadwick, *Jim Dilemma*, xii.

102. Smith, "Huck, Jim, and American Racial Discourse," 112.

103. See work by Smith, Chadwick, Ellison, Robinson, and Fishkin cited above, as well as Lawrence Howe, "Property and Dialect Narrative in 'Huckleberry Finn': The 'Jim Dilemma' Revisited," *Mark Twain Annual* 7, no. 1 (2009): 7.

104. Lamb, "America Can Break Your Heart," 480.

105. Hilton Obenzinger, "Going to Tom's Hell in *Huckleberry Finn*," in *A Companion to Mark Twain*, edited by Peter Messent and Louis J. Budd (Oxford: Blackwell, 2005), 412.

106. Robinson, "Characterization of Jim," 391.

107. Robinson, "Characterization of Jim," 369.

108. Morrison, "Introduction," xxxviii.

109. Twain, *Adventures of Huckleberry Finn*, 125.

110. Lamb, "Twain's New Method of Cultural Critique," 2; Lamb, "America Can Break Your Heart," 482.

111. Lamb, "America Can Break Your Heart," 482.

112. Twain, *Adventures of Huckleberry Finn*, 51; Doyno, "Huck's and Jim's Dynamic Interactions," 23.

113. Twain, *Adventures of Huckleberry Finn*, 104; Morrison, "Introduction," xxxiii.

114. Lamb, "America Can Break Your Heart," 481.

115. Lamb, "Twain's New Method of Cultural Critique," 2.

116. See the satirical letter that Clemens published under the pseudonym Thomas Jefferson Snodgrass in *Keokuk (IA) Saturday Post*, November 1, 1856, available at www.twainquotes.com/Keokuk/18561101.html.

117. Twain, *Is Shakespeare Dead?*, in Mark Twain, *"1601," and "Is Shakespeare Dead?,"* The Oxford Mark Twain, edited by Shelley Fisher Fishkin (New York: Oxford University Press, 1996), 5.

118. Gary Scharnhorst, "Mark Twain's Lost 'Burlesque *Hamlet*,'" *American Literary Realism* 52, no. 3 (2021): 272–77.

119. See, e.g., the ghosts in *Hamlet, Julius Caesar, Macbeth*, and *Richard III*. See also Ben Lauer, "Shakespeare's Top 5 Spookiest Ghosts," *Shakespeare and Beyond*, October 25, 2019, Folger Shakespeare Library, www.folger.edu/blogs/shakespeare-and-beyond/top-5-spookiest-ghosts/.

120. Scharnhorst, "Mark Twain's Lost 'Burlesque *Hamlet*,'" 276.

121. One scholar has noted other resonances of *Hamlet* in the novel—including the fact that the first line Jim speaks in the book—"Who dah?"—(which also happens to be "the first phrase of directly uttered speech" in the novel) repeats

the first line of *Hamlet*—"Who's there?" Benedict J. Whalen, "Mark Twain's Reading of Shakespeare in *Adventures of Huckleberry Finn*," *Mark Twain Journal*, 61, no. 2 (2023): 127.

122. Mark Twain, *Adventures of Huckleberry Finn: Text of the First Edition, Sources, Criticisms*, edited by Hamlin Hill and Walter Blair (Scranton, PA: Chandler, 1962), 400, 405.

123. Dan De Quille (William Wright), *History of the Big Bonanza: An Authentic Account of the Discovery, History, and Working of the World Renowned Comstock Lode of Nevada* (Hartford, CT: American Publishing, 1876); Dan De Quille, "Sketches of Indian Life" (from *History of the Big Bonanza*), in *The Art of Huckleberry Finn: Text, Sources, Criticisms*, edited by Hamlin Hill and Walter Blair (Scranton, PA: Chandler, 1962), 400, 405.

124. De Quille, *History of the Big Bonanza*, 411–16.

125. See Fishkin, *Was Huck Black?*, 86–87.

126. Pettit, *Twain and the South*, 128.

127. SLC to James R. Osgood, March 4, 1882, Mark Twain Project, https://legacy.marktwainproject.org/xtf/view?docId=letters/UCCL02561.xml;query=Osgood;searchAll=;sectionType1=;sectionType2=;sectionType3=;sectionType4=;sectionType5=;style=letter;brand=mtp#1.

128. *Huck Finn* manuscript quoted in Victor A. Doyno, *Writing "Huck Finn": Mark Twain's Creative Process* (Philadelphia: University of Pennsylvania Press, 1992), 122.

129. *Huck Finn* MS, 209–10, quoted in Doyno, *Writing "Huck Finn,"* 122.

130. *Huck Finn* MS, quoted in Doyno, *Writing "Huck Finn,"* 122.

131. White, *Every-day English*, 195–96, quoted in Gavin Jones, *Strange Talk: The Politics of Dialect Literature in Gilded Age America* (Berkeley: University of California Press, 1999), 46–47.

132. John R. Rickford, *African American Vernacular English: Features, Evolution, Educational Implications* (Malden, MA: Blackwell, 1999), 4–9; Geneva Smitherman, *Talkin That Talk: Language, Culture and Education in African America* (New York: Routledge, 2000), 19–28. For an early investigation of Twain's use of AAVE, see Lee A. Pederson, "Negro Speech in the *Adventures of Huckleberry Finn*," *Mark Twain Journal* 13, no. 1 (1965–66): 1–4.

133. Lisa Cohen Minnick, *Dialect and Dichotomy: Literary Representations of African American Speech* (Tuscaloosa: University of Alabama Press, 2004), 67, 66–67, 73.

134. Ann Ryan, "Speak Softly, but Carry a Big Stick: Tom Sawyer and Company's Quest for Linguistic Power: A Sociolinguistic Analysis of Mark Twain's

The Adventures of Tom Sawyer, Adventures of Huckleberry Finn, and *Tom Sawyer Abroad"* (MA thesis, Liberty University, 2010), 16.

135. Holger Kersten, "The Creative Potential of Dialect Writing in Later-Nineteenth-Century America," *Nineteenth-Century Literature* 55, no. 1 (2000): 95.

136. This manuscript page is reproduced by the Mark Twain Project in "Appendix D: Manuscript Facsimiles," *Adventures of Huckleberry Finn* (2003), 564. Twain changed *of* to *er* twenty-two times and *of* to *o'* five times. (Twain would also sometimes replace *of* with *uv* or *un.*)

137. SLC to William Dean Howells, September 20, 1874, Mark Twain Project, in *Mark Twain's Letters,* vol. 6: *1874–1875,* edited by Michael Frank and Harriet Elinor Smith, the Mark Twain Project, Robert H. Hirst, general editor (Berkeley: University of California Press, 2002), 233.

138. "The Pass-word," in *Brudder Bones's Nigger Dialogues; Containing Most Laughable Drolleries and Funny Stories, Abounding in Wit, Humour, and Sarcasm, for Representation by Two Delineators of Ethiopian Character at Public or Private Entertainments* (Glasgow: Cameron and Ferguson, 1869), 41; "The Sham Doctor," in *The Darkey Drama: A Collection of Approved Ethiopian Acts, Scenes, Interludes, etc. etc.; Now First Printed; As Played with Complete Success by the Christy's, Bryant's, Wood's, Charley White's, Buckley's, Morris and Pell's, Duprez and Green's, Hooley's, Sharpley's, "Iron Clads," Birch's, Leon and Kelly's, and Other First-Class Negro Minstrel Troupes,* edited by Henry L. Williams Jr. (London: Thomas Hailes Lacy, 1867), 54. Similarly, in "Box and Cox," Cox refers to "de wool off ob a black sheep" and "de last peck ob coal." See also *Darkey Drama,* 3, 4, 6, 12.

139. "We'll All Make a Laugh" quoted in Berret, "Huckleberry Finn and the Minstrel Show," 37; "Going a Journey" in *Brudder Bones,* 33; "Happy Uncle Tom" in *Brudder Bones,* 25. In the same vein, "Happy Uncle Tom" has a line that reads, "Oh, just gib me some ob dat" (*Brudder Bones,* 25).

140. "Sleepy Tom" in *Brudder Bones,* 43; "Spirit Rappings" in *Brudder Bones,* 36.

141. "Old Times Gone By" in *Brudder Bones,* 38; "The Three Black Smiths" in *Darkey Drama,* 31; "Ring, Ring de Banjo" and "Oh! Susanna" quoted in Lott, *Love and Theft,* 202, 211; "A Tough Boarding-House" in *Brudder Bones,* 10; "Grasshoppers" in *Brudder Bones,* 49; "Jenny, Put de Kettle On" in *White's New Illustrated Melodeon Song Book, Containing a Variety of All the New and Most Popular Songs, Jokes, Conundrums, Burlesque Lectures, etc.; Embracing the Choicest Collection as Sung by White's Band of Serenaders, The Christys, Campbells, and Sable Brothers* (New York: H. Long and Brother, 1865), 2; "Dandy Broadway Swell" in *White's New Illustrated Melodeon,* 43.

142. Doyno, "Huck's and Jim's Dynamic Interactions," 23.

143. "Electric Shocks" in *Brudder Bones,* 52; "The Grand Burlesque Lecture on Phrenology!" in *White's New Illustrated Melodeon,* 81; "Patent Safe" in *Brudder Bones,* 46; "Suke ob Tenisee" in *White's New Illustrated Melodeon,* 17; "The Dinner Horn" in *White's New Illustrated Melodeon,* 19; "Slap Jack" in *Brudder Bones,* 13. Other examples include the lines, "Sixty dollars for a ting like dat" in "Happy Uncle Tom"; "tink ob frens he luff behind" in "The Dinner Horn"; and "I tink I'm goin' to heben, Jane!" in "Going a Journey."

144. "Sleepy Tom," *Brudder Bones,* 43; "The Fall," *Brudder Bones,* 47; "A Tough Boarding-House," 10.

145. John Russell Rickford and Russell John Rickford, *Spoken Soul: The Story of Black English* (New York: John Wiley, 2000), 30.

146. "The Senator, or Atlantic Cable" in *Brudder Bones,* 44; "I Can't Help Dat," quoted in Christian McWhirter, *Battle Hymns: The Power and Popularity of Music in the Civil War* (Chapel Hill: University of North Carolina Press, 2023), 140.

147. "Burlesque Political Stump Speech" in *Brudder Bones's Stump Speeches and Burlesque Orations; Containing also Humorous Lectures, Negro Drolleries, and Comic Recitations, Interspersed with Racy Yankee Stories* (Glasgow: Cameron and Ferguson, 1868), 10.

148. In "Mark Twain's Representation of Negro Speech," James Nathan Tidwell notes that Twain "shows his linguistic sense by using 'eye dialect' in only five words: ben (been), b'fo' (first syllable), han's, wuz, and um. . . . By not re-spelling words for eye dialect, Twain makes Jim's conversation easy reading." James Nathan Tidwell, "Mark Twain's Representation of Negro Speech," *American Speech* 17, no. 3 (1942): 173. Tidwell should have included *uv* for *of,* and *shore* for *sure,* as well.

149. "Electric Shocks" in *Brudder Bones,* 52.

150. "Wonderful Eggs" in *Brudder Bones,* 15; "The Bet" in *Brudder Bones,* 16.

151. Doyno writes that Twain dropped a "manuscript sentence of Huck giving orders about breakfast preparations. Twain was gradually figuring out what the relationship could be like; originally Huck had given Jim orders about the fire, contradicted Jim, and demanded, 'No, you follow me, and bring some brands along.' (MS 170) Without this explicitly bossy sentence, the two characters still do get to have a fire nearer the river, but without having a boss/servant stratification." Doyno, "Huck's and Jim's Dramatic Interactions," 23.

152. Jones, *Strange Talk,* 165, 177.

153. Booker T. Washington, "Tributes to Mark Twain," *North American Review,* June 1910, 829.

154. Minnick, *Dialect and Dichotomy,* 68.

155. John McWhorter, *Talking Back, Talking Black: Truths about America's Lingua Franca* (New York: Bellevue Literary Press, 2016), 26.

156. McWhorter, *Talking Back, Talking Black*, 25–26.

157. They write, "Without the awareness of AAVE's systematicity or its legitimate status as a rule-governed dialect, one might assume that the occurrence of such speech patterns in someone's speech marks both a lack of grammaticality and intelligence. However, as shown above, Jeantel displays a deep understanding of the dialect's grammar and its associated patterns. Unfair judgment of Jeantel's language skills is demonstrated in public comments on news articles published covering the trial: 'She is a dullard, an idiot, an individual who can hardly speak in coherent sentences'—Jim Heron, Appalachian State. 'This lady is a perfect example of uneducated urban ignorance' . . . —Sheena Scott." King and Rickford note that questions raised by jurors along with public comments such as those cited here "raise questions about the potential consequences of producing stigmatized speech in legal settings and the role that dialect plays in attributions of credibility or trustworthiness." Sharese King and John R. Rickford, "Language on Trial," *Daedalus* 152, no. 3 (2023): 181–82.

158. Kenneth E. Eble, *Old Clemens and W.D.H.: The Story of a Remarkable Friendship* (Baton Rouge: Louisiana State University Press, 1985), 66.

159. James A. Miller made this comment during a public talk at the Mark Twain Memorial in Hartford, Connecticut, in the fall of 1989 and reaffirmed it in conversation during the summer of 1990 (personal communication).

160. Rickford and Rickford, *Spoken Soul*, 195.

161. Rickford and Rickford, *Spoken Soul*, 6.

162. Vernon E. Jordan Jr., quoted in Rickford and Rickford, *Spoken Soul*, 185.

163. McWhorter, *Talking Back, Talking Black*, 59.

164. Fishkin, *Was Huck Black?*, 107.

165. Shelley Fisher Fishkin, "The Challenge of Teaching *Huckleberry Finn*," in *Making Mark Twain Work in the Classroom*, edited by James S. Leonard (Durham NC: Duke University Press, 1999), 191.

166. I was also wrong when I asserted, in the same book, that "like the minstrel show itself, Jim was an eclectic amalgam of authentic black voices and white caricatures of them" (*Was Huck Black?*, 92). I am now convinced that when Ellison wrote in 1958 that "Twain fitted Jim into the outlines of the minstrel tradition and it is from behind this stereotype mask that we see Jim's dignity and human capacity—and Twain's complexity—emerge," what he meant was that *on the surface* Twain fitted Jim into this tradition. The conversation I had with him in 1991 supports the idea that Ellison, who kept a photo of Twain next to his desk,

knew that apparent resemblances between Jim and minstrelsy dissolve on closer inspection.

167. High school juniors in John Pascal's class at Seton Hall Preparatory often expressed their admiration for and identification with Jim in their final exams in 2023 and 2024. For example, Michael Kelly wrote, "Jim is somebody I would want as a friend and role model." Casey O'Sullivan wrote, "Jim is truly the only good person in the story." Lucah Benitez wrote, "Jim is the best person in the book. . . . [H]e was always the one that made the right choices." Responses like these will be discussed in more detail in Chapter 7: "Afterlives: Jim in the High School Classroom."

168. Johnson, quoted in Rickford and Rickford, *Spoken Soul*, 18.

169. Brown, *Negro in American Fiction*, 68.

170. In this view, the minstrel show and the novel are both structured in three parts featuring an opening set of comic dialogues, an "olio" with novelty acts (such as those of the king and duke), and zany burlesque skits set on a southern plantation. Berret, "Huckleberry Finn and the Minstrel Show," 38, 44; Obenzinger, "Going to Tom's Hell," 403–5; Tracey E. Ryser, "'A White Man's Inadequate Portrait of a Slave': Minstrel Shows and *Huckleberry Finn*" (MA thesis, Youngstown State University, 2004), iii, 25–29, 42–61.

CHAPTER 4. Jim's Version

1. Archie Moore, "Why I Played Jim, the Slave; Huck Finn Movie Might Help, Rather Than Hurt Negroes, Says World Champ," *Ebony*, September 19, 1960, 43.

2. Archie Moore quoted in "Archie Moore Does All Right as Actor," *Escanaba (MI) Daily Press*, October 22, 1959, 1.

3. Ron Richardson quoted in Alvin Klein, "Theater; Ron Richardson of 'Big River' Takes Success in Stride, Faith," *New York Times*, April 4, 1985.

4. Ron Richardson quoted in Joe Brown, "Ron Richardson at High Tide," *Washington Post*, May 17, 1986.

CHAPTER 5. Jim on Stage and Screen

1. This chapter does not pretend to be comprehensive and does not address aspects of each adaptation that do not involve Jim. It deals with the following actors who played Jim on stage or screen (the list below includes their birthplaces and the year of the film, play, or television broadcast in which they played Jim): George Reed (from Macon, GA) (1920); Clarence Muse (from Bal-

timore) (1931); Wayland Rudd (from Lincoln, NE) (1936); Rex Ingram (from Cairo, IL) (1939); Archie Moore (from Benoit, MS) (1960); Serge Nubret (from Anse-Bertrand, Guadaloupe) (1968); Felix Imoukhuede (from Lagos, Nigeria) (1973); Meshach Taylor (from Boston) (1985); Ron Richardson (from Philadelphia) (1985); Samm-Art Williams (from Burgaw, NC) (1985); Courtney Vance (from Detroit, MI) (1993); Charles Dumas (from Chicago) (2000); and Jacky Ido (from Ouagadougou, Burkina Faso) (2012).

2. *Huckleberry Finn,* film directed by William Desmond Taylor; written by Julia Crawford Ivers and Mark Twain; featuring George Reed, Lewis Sargent, Katherine Griffith, Martha Mattox, Frank Lanning, and Gordon Griffith; produced by Famous Players-Lasky; cinematographer, Frank E. Garbutt; released by Paramount Pictures, February 22, 1920. Quotation from David Kiehn, "*Huckleberry Finn,*" San Francisco Silent Film Festival, 2011, https://silentfilm.org /huckleberry-finn/.

3. "'Huckleberry Finn' (1920)—Hidden Gem," Silent Hall of Fame, https:// silent-hall-of-fame.org/index.php/other-favorite-films/701-huckleberry-finn -1920-hidden-gem-10; R. Kent Rasmussen, "Film, Television, and Theatre Adaptations," in *Mark Twain in Context,* edited by John Bird (New York: Cambridge University Press, 2020), 333.

4. Brought from Kongo to America by enslaved people, patting juba involved creating complex rhythms by slapping hands and thighs.

5. Julia Crawford Ivers, *Huckleberry Finn,* incomplete scenario for silent film, May 22, 1919, MSSHM 83965, Archives and Manuscripts, Huntington Library, San Marino, CA, 6.

6. Ivers, *Huckleberry Finn,* 9.

7. *Huckleberry Finn,* film directed by Norman Taurog; written by Grover Jones, William Slavens McNutt, and Mark Twain; featuring Clarence Muse, Jackie Coogan, Junior Durkin, Mitzi Green, Jackie Searl, and Eugene Pallette; cinematographer, David Abel; released by Paramount Pictures, August 7, 1931. Christopher Gray, "Streetscapes: Harlem's Lafayette Theater; Jackhammering the Past," *New York Times,* November 11, 1990.

8. Donald Bogle, *Toms, Coons, Mulattoes, Mammies and Bucks: An Interpretive History of Blacks in American Films,* 4th ed. (New York: Continuum, 2002), 53.

9. Clyde V. Haupt, *Huckleberry Finn on Film: Film and Television Adaptations of Mark Twain's Novel, 1920–1993* (Jefferson, NC: McFarland, 1994), 27.

10. Clarence Muse, "The Dilemma of the Negro Actor" (self-pub., 1934), 2, available at https://search.alexanderstreet.com/preview/work/bibliographic _entity%7Cbibliographic_details%7C4391495.

11. Clarence Muse quoted in Gary Null, *Black Hollywood: The Negro in Motion Pictures* (New York: Citadel, 1977), 2.

12. Herb Boyd, "Clarence Muse, a Versatile Artist and Actor of Integrity," *New Amsterdam News*, January 24, 2020, https://amsterdamnews.com/news/2020/01/24/clarence-muse-versatile-artist-and-actor-integrity/.

13. Donald Bogle, *Blacks in American Film and Television: An Encyclopedia* (New York: Garland, 1988), 431–32.

14. *The Adventures of Huckleberry Finn*, film directed by Richard Thorpe; written by Hugo Butler, Waldo Salt, and Mark Twain; featuring Rex Ingram, Mickey Rooney, Walter Connolly, and William Frawley; produced by Joseph L. Mankiewicz; cinematographer, John F. Seitz; released by Metro-Goldwyn-Mayer, February 10, 1939.

15. *Huckleberry Finn*, film directed by Michael Curtiz; written by Mark Twain and James Lee; featuring Archie Moore, Tony Randall, Eddie Hodges, Neville Brand, Patty McCormick, Mickey Shaughnessy, Buster Keaton, and John Carradine; cinematographer, Ted D. Cord; produced by Sam Goldwyn Jr.; released by Metro-Goldwyn-Mayer, August 3, 1960.

16. "Emperor Ingram of 'Haiti,'" *New York Times*, July 24, 1938.

17. Jonathan Dewberry, "Black Actors Unite: The Negro Actors' Guild," *Black Scholar* 21, no. 2 (1990): 3.

18. "Rex Ingram Bankrupt; Negro Actor Who Played 'De Lawd' in Film Owes $9,511," *New York Times*, September 10, 1937.

19. Kate Dossett, *Radical Black Theatre in the New Deal* (Chapel Hill: University of North Carolina Press, 2020), 217–19, 221 (photo of Ingram as Christophe holding two guns).

20. Cairo is the town that Jim seeks in *Huck Finn*, where the Mississippi meets the Ohio River. After Cairo heading south, slave states lined both sides of the river. It was well known among slaves that Cairo presented their best bid for freedom, and one can only speculate whether this had anything to do with Ingram's claim.

21. "Rex Ingram: We Both Have Much to Learn," *The Skeins: Unraveling the "Ribbon of Dreams" in Classic Films and More*, February 15, 2010, http://moirasthread.blogspot.com/2010/02/rex-ingram-we-both-have-much-to-learn.html; Rex Ingram, "'I Came Back from the Dead': Actor Tells of His Determination to Return to Stardom after a Period of Disaster," *Ebony*, March 1955, 48–58.

22. Donald Bogle, *Hollywood Black: The Stars, the Films, the Filmmakers* (Philadelphia: Running Press, 2019), 49; Bogle, *Toms, Coons*, 70.

23. Bogle, *Blacks in American Film and Television*, 406.

24. Bogle, *Toms, Coons*, 70.

25. Bogle, *Toms, Coons*, 70.

26. Seth Abramovitch, "Oscar's First Black Winner Accepted Her Honor in a Segregated 'No Blacks' Hotel in L.A.," *Hollywood Reporter*, February 19, 2014.

27. Nicholas S. Patti, "Rex Ingram, 1894–1969," Encyclopedia.com, 2018, www.encyclopedia.com/people/literature-and-arts/film-and-television-biogra phies/rex-ingram#B.

28. *Newsweek*, for example, praised his "outstanding performance as Jim." Quoted in Haupt, *Huckleberry Finn on Film*, 57.

29. Haupt, *Huckleberry Finn on Film*, 47–48.

30. Moore would hold the title from 1952 to 1962, becoming the longest-reigning world champion in that class ever.

31. Archie Moore, *The Archie Moore Story* (New York: McGraw-Hill, 1960), 187.

32. Moore quoted in "Will 'Uncle Tom' Film Role Hurt Archie Moore? Actor to Make Film Debut," *Jet*, October 15, 1959, 52.

33. Darcy Demille, "Data 'n' Chatter," *St. Paul (MN) Recorder*, August 28, 1959.

34. "Will 'Uncle Tom' Film Role Hurt Archie Moore?," 52.

35. Uncle Tom was no "Uncle Tom" either. The character has been widely misunderstood. See, for example, Patricia Turner's comments in the NPR report "In Character: Why African-Americans Loathe 'Uncle Tom,'" NPR, July 30, 2008, www.npr.org/templates/story/story.php?storyId=93059468.

36. Moore, *Archie Moore Story*, 189.

37. Bob Thomas, "Archie Moore Discusses His Acting Job," *Denton (TX) Record-Chronicle*, October 22, 1959.

38. Archie Moore, "Why I Played Jim, the Slave; Huck Finn Movie Might Help, Rather than Hurt Negroes, Says World Champ," *Ebony*, September 1960, 43.

39. Moore, "Why I Played Jim," 43.

40. Moore, *Archie Moore Story*, 188.

41. Red Smith, "Archie Leaves Pro Actors Dead in 'Huckleberry Finn' Test," *Democrat and Chronicle* (Rochester, NY), October 11, 1959.

42. The scene from the script was reprinted verbatim in *Jet*. "Will 'Uncle Tom' Film Role Hurt Archie Moore?," 54–55.

43. Moore, *Archie Moore Story*, 191.

44. Alan K. Rode, *Michael Curtiz: A Life in Film* (Lexington: University Press of Kentucky, 2017), 533–34; "First-Class Showman: Archie Moore Is as Cagey on Stage as in the Ring," *Daily Intelligencer* (Doylestown, PA), October 21, 1959.

45. Moore, "Why I Played Jim," 43.

46. Moore, "Why I Played Jim," 43.

47. Moore, *Archie Moore Story*, 188.

48. Moore, "Why I Played Jim,"43.

49. "Archie Moore in *Huckleberry Finn*," *Life*, June 27, 1960, 113.

50. Bob Thomas, "Archie Moore Seeks Movie Career," *Record Searchlight* (Redding, CA), October 22, 1959.

51. Donald Ingram Ulin, "From *Huckleberry Finn* to *The Shawshank Redemption*: Race and the American Imagination in the Biracial Escape Film," *European Journal of American Studies* 8, no. 1 (2013), https://doi.org/10.4000/ejas.10026.

52. Moore, *Archie Moore Story*, 193.

53. "Despite Moore's stellar turn the script turned Twain's edgy adventure tale into a Disneylike family movie" (Rode, *Michael Curtiz*, 53–54); "Prizefighter Archie Moore Giving Moving Performance as Runaway Slave Jim," *Parents* 3, no. 1–6 (1961): 8; "Bright Debut of an Old Pro," *Life*, June 27, 1960, 113; "Films: Boxer *Archie Moore* Plays the Part of *Jim*, the Runaway Slave, in a Surprisingly Effective and Moving Performance," *America* 103 (April 1960): 522; "Films in Review," *Filmfacts* 3 (1960): 172.

54. "Entertainments: The Adventures of Huckleberry Finn," *Upper Hutt Leader* (Wellington, NZ), August 24, 1961, 2.

55. Perry Frank, "*Adventures of Huckleberry Finn* on Film," in *Huck Finn among the Critics: A Centennial Selection*, edited by M. Thomas Inge (Frederick, MD: University Publications of America, 1985), 298; R. Kent Rasmussen and Mark Dawidziak, "Mark Twain on the Screen," in *A Companion to Mark Twain*, edited by Peter Messent and Louis J. Budd (Malden, MA: Blackwell, 2005), 284.

56. Moore, "Why I Played Jim," 48.

57. Moore went on to say, "I believe that eventually total freedom will come as long as we Negroes continue to demand it without bringing discredit on ourselves." Moore, "Why I Played Jim," 49.

58. Margarita Marinova, "*Huck Finn*'s Adventures in the Land of the Soviet People," *Journal of Transnational American Studies* 12, no. 2 (2021): 119, 122, 124. Between 1918 and 1959, Marinova notes, nearly eleven million copies of Twain's works in twenty-five languages were published in the Soviet Union.

59. Mark Twain, *Приключения Геккельберри Финна и беглого негра Джима* (*Prikljuchenija Gekkel'berri Finna i beglogo negra Dzhima*) [Adventures of Huckleberry Finn and the Runaway Negro Jim] (Leningrad: Molodaia gvardia, 1926); Marinova, "*Huck Finn*'s Adventures," 120, 124; A. Sarukhanyan, "Mark Twain in Russia," 1959, Mark Twain Stormfield Project 1908–2012, https://twain project.blogspot.com/2010/07/russian-versions-of-mark-twains-books.html.

60. Interest in this film among Twain scholars has been ignited recently by the work of Cassio de Oliveira, who presented a paper on it at the Ninth Inter-

national Conference on the State of Mark Twain Studies in 2022 and published his research in the *Journal of Transnational American Studies* in 2023: Cassio de Oliveira, "Mark Twain on the Soviet Silver Screen: Stalinist Laughter and Antiracism in *Tom Soier*," *Journal of Transnational American Studies* 14, no. 2 (2023): 29–49.

61. S. Ani Mukherji, "'Like Another Planet to the Darker Americans': Black Cultural Work in 1930s Moscow," in *Africa in Europe: Studies in Transnational Practice in the Long Twentieth Century*, edited by Eve Rosenhaft and Robbie Aitken (Liverpool: Liverpool University Press, 2013), 135; Yevgeniy Fiks, ed., *The Wayland Rudd Collection* (Brooklyn, NY: Ugly Duckling Presse, 2021); Jonah Goldman Kay, "Art Books: The Wayland Rudd Collection: Propaganda Posters, Works of Art, and Other Pieces of Print Culture Reveal a Complex and at Times Incongruous Approach to Race," *Brooklyn Rail*, March 2022, https://brooklynrail.org/2022/03/art_books/The-Wayland-Rudd-Collection. Christopher E. Silsby, "African American Performers in Stalin's Soviet Union: Between Political Promise and Racial Propaganda" (PhD diss., City University of New York, 2018). Ira Aldridge had played Othello in London in the nineteenth century, and Paul Robeson began playing the role there in March 1930, a month before Rudd played it in the United States.

62. Meredith L. Roman, *Opposing Jim Crow: African Americans and the Soviet Indictment of U.S. Racism, 1928–1937* (Lincoln: University of Nebraska Press, 2012), 11; de Oliveira, "Mark Twain on the Soviet Silver Screen," 33. On March 9, 1932, New York's *Amsterdam News* ran the headline "Soviet Seeks Negroes to Make Film of Conditions Here," while on March 19 the *Chicago Defender* announced, "Russia to Produce Film of Race Life in America Soon," cited in Mukherji, "Like Another Planet," 121. See also Maxim Matusevich, "Blackness the Color of Red: Negotiating Race at the US Legation in Riga, Latvia, 1922–33," *Journal of Contemporary History* 52 no. 4 (2017): 832–52; Allison Blakely, *Russia and the Negro: Blacks in Russian History and Thought* (Washington, DC: Howard University Press, 1986), 102, 145–47; and Soviet screenwriter G. E. Grebner's preface to *Chernyi i belyi*, quoted in Mukherji, "'Like Another Planet,'" 121.

63. Jack El-Hai, "Black and White and Red," *American Heritage*, May–June 1991, www.americanheritage.com/black-and-white-and-red; Mukherji, "'Like Another Planet,'" 121; "Movie Players Leave for Moscow," *Amsterdam News* (New York), July 15, 1932; "Russia to Produce Film of Race Life in America Soon," *Chicago Defender*, March 19, 1932; "Stars Now on Way to Russia to Make Film," *Chicago Defender*, June 11, 1932; "To Make Photoplay in Soviet Russia," *Chicago Defender*, July 9, 1932; "Soviet Seeks Negroes to Make Film of Conditions Here," *Amsterdam*

News (New York), March 9, 1932; "21 Movie Players Leave for Moscow," *Amsterdam News* (New York), July 15, 1932.

64. Arnold Rampersad, *The Life of Langston Hughes*, vol. 1 (New York: Oxford University Press, 1996), 244-46.

65. El-Hai, "Black and White and Red"; Roman, *Opposing Jim Crow*, 137; Allison Blakely, "Foreword: Contested Blackness in Red Russia," *Russian Review* 75, no. 3 (2016): 363-64; Mukherji, "'Like Another Planet,'" 138.

66. Silsby, *African American Performers*, 88, 101-2; Langston Hughes, "Mixes Russian and Jazz on Soviet Stage," *Baltimore Afro-American*, February 25, 1933. Another veteran of the *Black and White* fiasco was also cast in the film: Lloyd Patterson, who would play a slave named George.

67. *Том Сойер* (*Tom Soier*) [Tom Sawyer, Russian], film directed by Lazar Frenkel and Gleb Zatvornitsky; written by Nikolay Shestakov and Mark Twain; featuring Wayland Rudd, Lloyd Patterson, Konstantin Kulchitsky, Nikolai Katsovich, Pyotr Svechnikov, and Nikolai Uspensky; cinematographer, Yuri Vovchenko; released by Ukrainfilm (Soviet Union), December 31, 1936.

68. De Oliveira, "Mark Twain on the Soviet Silver Screen," 31.

69. De Oliveira, "Mark Twain on the Soviet Silver Screen," 31.

70. Meredith Roman, "Anti-Racist Aspirations and Artifacts," in Fiks, *Wayland Rudd Collection*, 154.

71. Constantin Katsakioris, "The Lumumba University in Moscow: Higher Education for a Soviet–Third World Alliance, 1960–91," *Journal of Global History* 14, no. 2 (July 2019): 289; Beth Knobel, "Changing Lifestyles: Moscow's Marxist School Strives to Reinvent Itself," *Los Angeles Times*, February 16, 1993; Maxim Matusevich, "Probing the Limits of Internationalism: African Students Confront Soviet Ritual," *Anthropology of East Europe Review* 27, no. 2 (2009): 24; Maxim Matusevich, ed., *Africa in Russia, Russia in Africa: Three Centuries of Encounters* (Trenton, NJ: Africa World Press, 2007), 172; Maxim Matusevich, "Journeys of Hope: African Diaspora and the Soviet Society," *African Diaspora* 1, no. 1-2 (2008): 67-74; Maxim M. Matusevich, "Soviet Anti-Racism and Its Discontents," in *Alternative Globalizations: Eastern Europe and the Postcolonial World*, edited by James Mark, Artemy M. Kalinovsky, and Steffi Marung (Bloomington: Indiana University Press, 2020), 229-50; Everest Mulekezi, "I Was a Student at Moscow State," *Reader's Digest*, July 1961, 99-104; Olabisi Ajala, *An African Abroad* (London: Jarolds, 1963); Andrew Richard Amar, *An African in Moscow* (London: Ampersand, 1965); William Anti-Taylor, *Moscow Diary* (London: Robert Hale, 1967); Andrea Lee, *Russian Journal* (New York: Random House, 1981); Maxim Matusevich, "Black in the U.S.S.R.," *Transition*, no. 100 (2008): 56-75; Kimberly St.

Julian-Varnon, "The Racist Treatment of Africans and African Americans in the Soviet Union," *New Lines Magazine*, February 17, 2023, https://newlinesmag.com /essays/the-racist-treatment-of-africans-and-african-americans-in-the-ussr/; Julie Hessler, "Death of an African Student in Moscow: Race, Politics, and the Cold War," *Cahier du Monde Russe* 47, no. 1–2 (2006): 33–63; Peter Shearman, *Rethinking Soviet Communism* (London: Palgrave, 2015), 132; Riikkaman Johanna Muhonen, "'Good Friends' for the Soviet Union: The People's Friendship University in Soviet Educational Cooperation with the Developing World, 1960–1980" (PhD diss., Central European University, 2022), 23. Although the actor spells his name Felix Imoukhuede today, the film lists him as Feliks Imokuede.

72. *Совсем пропащий* (*Sovsem propushchiy*) [*Hopelessly Lost*, Russian], film directed by Georgiy Daneliya; written by Georgiy Daneliya, Viktoriya Tokareva, and Mark Twain; featuring Feliks Imokuede, Roman Madyanov, Yevgeny Leonov, Vladimir Basov, Vladimir Ivashov, and Vakhtang Kikabidze; cinematographer, Vadim Yusov; produced by Mosfilm and released August 27, 1973.

73. Daria Goncharova, "'Workers of the World Unite!': Huck, Jim, and the Cold War's Racial Tensions," in *Post45 vs. the World: Literary Perspectives on the Global Contemporary*, edited by William G. Welty (Wilmington, DE: Vernon Press, 2023), 55–76.

74. Alexander Federov, *Cinema in the Mirror of the Soviet and Russian Film Criticism*, 2nd ed. (Moscow: ICO Information for All, 2019), 32.

75. Goncharova, "'Workers of the World,'" 63–64; Theodore Shabad, "'Huck Finn' Put on Film in Soviet," *New York Times*, November 29, 1972.

76. Thomas Borstelmann, *The Cold War and the Color Line: American Race Relations in the Global Arena* (Cambridge, MA: Harvard University Press 2001), 106.

77. Goncharova, "'Workers of the World,'" 56–57.

78. Goncharova, "'Workers of the World,'" 59.

79. Goncharova, "'Workers of the World,'" 62.

80. Goncharova, "'Workers of the World,'" 73.

81. Goncharova, "'Workers of the World,'" 69.

82. On his return, Imokuede joined the Nigerian Agip Oil Company, where he worked for the rest of his career. He lives in Lagos today.

83. Oseomoje Imoukhuede confirmed that the street in Lagos was indeed named for his cousin Felix Imoukhuede.

84. "*Huckleberry Finn*: Literature or Racist Trash?," *Nightline* (broadcast February 4, 1985), transcript, including ABC Special Report, in *The Critical Response to Mark Twain's* Huckleberry Finn, edited by Laurie Champion (Westport, CT: Greenwood, 1991), 147.

85. "*Huckleberry Finn*: Literature or Racist Trash?," 148.

86. *"Huckleberry Finn:* Literature or Racist Trash?," 148.

87. *"Huckleberry Finn:* Literature or Racist Trash?," 149.

88. *"Huckleberry Finn:* Literature or Racist Trash?," 149.

89. Gordon and the Organic Theater Company had become known for a style of adapting works of literature that maintained total fidelity to an author's words. Stephen C. Gray, "A History of the Chicago Off-Loop Theatre Explosion: 1969 to 1989" (PhD diss., Ohio State University, 1997), 163.

90. Roger Dettmer, "The Organic Grows Up and Tackles *Huck Finn," Chicago Tribune,* February 2, 1975.

91. Gray, "History of the Chicago Off-Loop Theatre Explosion," 163.

92. Richard Christiansen, "'Huckleberry Finn' Triumphant," *Chicago Daily News,* February 6, 1975. See also Richard Christiansen, "'Huck Finn' at the Goodman," *Chicago Tribune,* February 3, 1985.

93. Earl Calloway, "Criticism Lashed upon Goodman's Provocative Huckleberry Finn," *Chicago Defender,* February 7, 1985.

94. "Kimball Art Center Presenting 'Huck Finn,'" *Summit County Bee* (Coalville, UT), September 16, 1976; Tony Halloway, "Reviewer: Play Well Done," *Pantagraph* (Bloomington, IL), May 3, 1976.

95. *Adventures of Huckleberry Finn,* stage play adapted by the Organic Theater Company; directed by Stewart Gordon; featuring Meshach Taylor, John Cameron Mitchell, and Tom Towles; opened February 4, 1985, Goodman Theatre, Chicago. Recorded by WTTW.

96. E. R. Shipp, "A Century Later, Huck's Still Stirring Up Trouble," *New York Times,* February 4, 1985.

97. Calloway, "Criticism."

98. Calloway, "Criticism."

99. See Shelley Fisher Fishkin, *From Fact to Fiction: Journalism and Imaginative Writing in America* (Baltimore: Johns Hopkins University Press, 1985), 65–66; Fishkin, "Mark Twain and Race," in *A Historical Guide to Mark Twain,* edited by Shelley Fisher Fishkin (New York: Oxford University Press, 2002), 135–36; and Fishkin, "Race and Ethnicity: African Americans," in Bird, *Mark Twain in Context,* 195.

100. Shelley Fisher Fishkin, "Twain in '85," *New York Times,* February 15, 1985.

101. SLC to Francis Wayland, December 24, 1885, boxed text of letter reprinted in Edwin McDowell, "From Twain, a Letter on Debt to Blacks," *New York Times,* March 14, 1885.

102. The desk in which the letter was found had belonged to one of Dean Wayland's descendants. See Francis Wayland to SLC, December 25, 1885, UCLC

24826, Mark Twain Project Online; and Philip Butcher, "Mark Twain's Install-ment on the National Debt," *Southern Literary Journal* 1, no. 2 (1969): 48–55.

103. See Shelley Fisher Fishkin, *Lighting Out for the Territory: Mark Twain and American Culture* (New York: Oxford University Press, 1997), 100–108; and Shelley Fisher Fishkin, "Changing the Story," in *People of the Book: Thirty Scholars Reflect on Their Jewish Identity*, edited by Jeffrey Rubin-Dorsky and Shelley Fisher Fishkin (Madison: University of Wisconsin Press, 1996), 47–68.

104. McDowell, "From Twain, a Letter." See also Mark Alden Branch, "Old Yale: A Civil Rights Champion," *Yale Alumni Magazine*, January–February 2024, 22–3.

105. This narrative of press responses to the McGuinn letter first appeared in Fishkin, *Lighting Out for the Territory*, 106–8.

106. *Big River*, musical directed by Des McAnuff; written by William Haupt-man and Mark Twain; original score by Roger Miller; choreographed by Janet Watson; featuring Ron Richardson, Daniel H. Jenkins, René Auberjonois, Bob Gunton, and John Goodman; opened 25 April 25, 1985, closed September 20, 1987, at the Eugene O'Neill Theatre on Broadway.

107. Nan Robertson, "'Big River's' Big Voice: Jim the Slave," *New York Times*, May 2, 1984.

108. Robertson, "'Big River's' Big Voice."

109. See, e.g., Frank Rich, "Stage: With Huck Finn on the 'Big River,'" *New York Times*, April 26, 1985.

110. Rich, "'Big River.'"

111. Richardson, quoted in Robertson, "'Big River's' Big Voice."

112. Richardson, quoted in Patrick Pacheko, "Huck Takes the Stage," *News-day* (Long Island, NY), April 14, 1985.

113. Akihiko Senda, "Experiments in Cross-Cultural Theater," *Japan Quar-terly* 36, no. 3 (1989): 311.

114. Robertson, "'Big River's' Big Voice."

115. Robertson, "'Big River's' Big Voice."

116. "Ron Richardson," *Variety*, April 10, 1995.

117. Alvin Klein, "Theater: Ron Richardson of 'Big River' Takes Success in Stride, Faith," *New York Times*, August 4, 1985.

118. John C. Thorpe, "Theatre," *Crisis* 92, no. 7 (1985): 15.

119. Klein, "Theater: Ron Richardson."

120. Klein, "Theater: Ron Richardson."

121. Joe Brown, "Ron Richardson at High Tide," *Washington Post*, May 17, 1986.

122. Brown, "Ron Richardson."

123. Richardson, quoted in Pacheko, "Huck Takes the Stage," 97. In 2010 William Hauptman would revise the script to decrease some of the instances of the word. Note from William Hauptman, March 1, 2010, in William Hauptman, Roger Miller, and Mark Twain, *Big River: The Adventures of Huckleberry Finn* (Nashville, TN: Concord Theatricals, 1985, 1986, 2010).

124. Klein, "Theater: Ron Richardson."

125. Robertson, "'Big River's' Big Voice."

126. Richardson, quoted in Robertson, "'Big River's' Big Voice."

127. Klein, "Theater: Ron Richardson."

128. For more on Twain's blending of Black and white rhetorical traditions, see Shelley Fisher Fishkin, *Was Huck Black? Mark Twain and African-American Voices* (New York: Oxford University Press, 1993).

129. Hauptman, Miller, and Twain, *Big River*, 78.

130. Hauptman, Miller, and Twain, *Big River*, 78.

131. Hauptman, Miller, and Twain, *Big River*, 78.

132. Hauptman, Miller, and Twain, *Big River*, 116–17.

133. Rasmussen and Dawidziak, "Mark Twain on the Screen," 280.

134. Hauptman, Miller, and Twain, *Big River*, 123.

135. Hauptman, Miller, and Twain, *Big River*, 124.

136. Hauptman, Miller, and Twain, *Big River*, 129.

137. Rasmussen, "Film, Television, and Theater Adaptations," 332.

138. Michael Bolanos, "The Journey behind 'A Journey in Open Diplomacy,'" *Soviet Life* 2 (February 1987): 60–61.

139. Richardson, quoted in Clyde Haberman, "An American in Japan's 'Big River,'" *New York Times*, March 19, 1988.

140. Haberman, "American in Japan's 'Big River.'"

141. Mel Gussow, "Ron Richardson Is Dead at 43; Won a Tony in 'Big River' Role," *New York Times*, April 6, 1995.

142. "Forget Dubbing, He'll Do the Role in Japanese," *Deseret News* (Salt Lake City, UT), May 13, 1988; Haberman, "American in Japan's 'Big River.'"

143. Haberman, "American in Japan's 'Big River.'"

144. *Big River*, musical translated by Yoji Aoi; directed by Michael Greif; music by Roger Miller; produced by Saburo Kitamura; featuring Hiroyuki Sanada and Ron Richardson; opened March 4, 1988, closed May 5, 1988, at the Aoyama Gekijo, Tokyo; opened May 10, 1988, closed May 29, 1988, at the Kintetsu Gekijo, Osaka. See Tsuyoshi Ishihara, "Mark Twain in Japan: Mark Twain's Literature and 20th Century Japanese Juvenile Literature and Popular Culture" (PhD diss., University of Texas at Austin, 2003), 231; and Haberman, "American in Japan's 'Big River.'"

145. "Forget Dubbing."

146. Haberman, "American in Japan's 'Big River.'"

147. Haberman, "American in Japan's 'Big River.'"

148. Senda, "Experiments in Cross-Cultural Theater," 311.

149. Haberman, "American in Japan's 'Big River.'"

150. For reviews of the original Japanese production of *Big River*, see Ishihara, *Mark Twain in Japan: The Cultural Reception of an American Icon* (Columbia: University of Missouri Press, 2005), 126–27.

151. Senda, "Experiments in Cross-Cultural Theater," 313. When he returned home to the United States, Richardson expressed his gratitude to the Japan Society for the help he was given by performing at a benefit for them with his Japanese costar, Hiroyuki Sanada.

152. Mel Gussow, "Ron Richardson Is Dead at 43."

153. For charges of minstrelsy, see Mark Royden Winchell, "'Huckleberry Finn' Suffers from Revision," *Newsday* (Long Island, NY), May 8, 1984; Barry Bearak, "Huck's Adventurous 100 Years," *Atlanta (GA) Constitution*, December 22, 1985; and John J. O'Connor, "TV Review: 4-Part 'Huckleberry Finn' Begins," *New York Times*, February 10, 1976. *Adventures of Huckleberry Finn*, DVD, directed by Peter H. Hunt; written by Guy Gallo and Mark Twain; produced by William P. Perry and Jane Iredale; music by William Perry; cinematographer, Walter Lassally; featuring Samm-Art Williams, Patrick Day, Jim Dale, Frederic Forrest, Anne Shropshire, Sada Thompson, and Eugene Oaks, with appearances by Butterfly McQueen and Lillian Gish; aired on PBS, *American Playhouse*, February 10, 1986.

154. "Williams, Samm-Art, 1946," Encyclopedia.com, www.encyclopedia.com/education/news-wires-white-papers-and-books/williams-samm-art-1946.

155. Mel Gussow, "The Theater: 'Cork,' by Samm-Art Williams," *New York Times, December 9, 1986.*

156. Trudier Harris, "Samm-Art Williams," in *Dictionary of Literary Biography: Afro-American Writers after 1955: Dramatists and Prose Writers*, edited by Thadious M. Davis and Trudier Harris, vol. 38 (Detroit, MI: Gale Research, 1985), 305; Steve Lawson, "An Unsung Civil War Heroine Lives Again on the Home Screen," *New York Times*, February 24, 1985.

157. *Adventures of Huckleberry Finn*, directed by Peter H. Hunt.

158. O'Connor, "TV Review."

159. Toni Morrison, "Introduction," in Mark Twain, *Adventures of Huckleberry Finn*, The Oxford Mark Twain, edited by Shelley Fisher Fishkin (New York: Oxford University Press, 1996), xxxiii.

160. Robert Paul Lamb, "The Roots of Huck Finn's Melancholy: Sam Clemens, Mark Twain, and a World of Pain," *Mississippi Quarterly* 72, no. 2 (2019): 166.

As Lamb reminds us, Henry Nash Smith had noted that "Huck's character is the product of Mark Twain's own lifelong depressiveness, loneliness, morbidity, and haunting sense of guilt." Henry Nash Smith, *Mark Twain: The Development of a Writer* (Cambridge, MA: Belknap Press of Harvard University Press, 1962), 130–32, cited in Lamb, "Roots of Huck Finn's Melancholy," 169.

161. Gary Scharnhorst, *The Life of Mark Twain: The Early Years, 1835–1871* (Columbia: University of Missouri Press, 2018), 22, cited in Lamb, "Roots of Huck Finn's Melancholy," 171.

162. Ron Powers, *Dangerous Water: A Biography of the Boy Who Became Mark Twain* (New York: Da Capo, 2001), 57, 97–117.

163. Guy Gallo, quoted in Hebert Mitgang, "Televising the Dark Side of 'Huck Finn,'" *New York Times*, February 9, 1986.

164. Morrison, "Introduction," xxxiv, xxxv.

165. Williams, quoted in Fred Rothenberg, "'Huckleberry Finn' Starts on PBS Tonight," *News* (Frederick, MD), February 10, 1986. His comment is echoed by that of screenwriter Guy Gallo: "Here were two outcasts, a Black slave and a troubled white boy oppressed by his ignorant father, on a journey to freedom. Every time their raft touched ground—touched the United States—they got into trouble. The 'white trash' boy, who has inherited the prejudices of his father and the community, and the Black slave come to love each other. The journey is of their growing affection." Gallo quoted in Mitgang, "Televising the Dark Side of 'Huck Finn.'"

166. O'Connor, "TV Review"; Owen McNally, "'Huck Finn' Is Pleasant to Watch but a Bit Long," *Hartford (CT) Courant*, July 2, 1985.

167. O'Connor, "TV Review."

168. Haupt, *Huckleberry Finn on Film*, 142.

169. Mitgang, "Televising the Dark Side of 'Huck Finn.'" The *Hartford Courant* commended director Hunt for having dealt "realistically with the sordid side of life along the river, including violence, racism and fraud," adding that "screen writer Guy Gallo's adaptation is commendably true in letter and spirit to Mark Twain's masterpiece." McNally, "'Huck Finn' Is Pleasant to Watch."

170. Haupt, *Huckleberry Finn on Film*, 123.

171. Quoted in Haupt, *Huckleberry Finn on Film*, 146.

172. Rothenberg, "Huckleberry Finn." In a similar vein, the *New York Times* observed that "this Jim, played by Samm-Art Williams, is a man of unquestioned dignity." O'Connor, "TV Review." McNally, "'Huck Finn' Is Pleasant to Watch."

173. Rasmussen and Dawidziak, "Mark Twain on the Screen," 287–88. In 2001 Michael Patrick Hearn argued that this production was still "the most ambitious and faithful production" yet. Hearn, *The Annotated Huckleberry Finn* (New

York: W. W. Norton, 2001), cxxxiv. Similarly, in 1994 Haupt had declared this production to be "the most sensitive and intelligent rendition [of *Huckleberry Finn*] made to date." Haupt, *Huckleberry Finn on Film*, 113. See also E. Hulse, "Adventures of Huckleberry Finn," Video Librarian, July 11, 2007, https://video librarian.com/reviews/film/adventures-of-huckleberry-finn/.

174. The multitalented Williams continues to have a thriving career both as a playwright and as an actor and producer in film and television and has been nominated for a Tony and two Emmys.

175. Lia Chang, "Backstage Pass with Lia Chang: Remembering Meshach Taylor, 1947–2014," https://liachang.wordpress.com/profiles/meshach-taylor/. Taylor's hundred-year-old mother, Hertha Ward Taylor, told this to his friend Joe Mantegna shortly before Taylor's funeral, as Mantegna noted in the eulogy that he delivered at a memorial service at the Old North Church at Forest Lawn–Hollywood Hills in Los Angeles on July 6, 2014.

176. Caroline B. Hubbard, "Vance '82: Mass. Ave to Broadway," *Harvard Crimson*, September 20, 2013, www.thecrimson.com/article/2013/9/20/courtney -b-vance-82-in-conversation/; *The Adventures of Huck Finn*, film directed by Stephen Sommers; produced by Laurence Mark; written by Mark Twain and Stephen Sommers; featuring Courtney Vance, Elijah Wood, and Robbie Coltrane; released by Disney, April 2, 1993.

177. Courtney Vance, quoted in Henry Sheehan, "'Huck' Player Brings Dignity to Slave Character," *Fort Worth* (TX) *Star-Telegram*, April 18, 1993.

178. Courtney Vance quoted in "'Huckleberry Finn' Actor's Input Protects Dignity of His Character," *Orlando* (FL) *Sentinel*, April 22, 1993.

179. Vance quoted in "'Huckleberry Finn' Actor's Input Protects Dignity of His Character."

180. Stephen Sommers, quoted in Bernard Weinraub, "Huck Finn Adventure for a Mississippi River Boy," *New York Times*, March 25, 1993.

181. Sheehan "'Huck' Player."

182. Sheehan, "'Huck' Player."

183. Weinraub, "Huck Finn Adventure."

184. Allen Carey-Webb, "Racism and 'Huckleberry Finn': Censorship, Dialogue, and Change," *English Journal* 82, no. 7 (1993): 26.

185. Carey-Webb, "Racism and 'Huckleberry Finn,'" 26.

186. Carey-Webb, "Racism and 'Huckleberry Finn,'" 26.

187. Sheehan, "'Huck' Player."

188. Robert W. Butler, "'Huckleberry Finn' Actor Finds Dignity in Difficult Role," *Kansas City* (MO) *Star*, April 9, 1993.

189. Terry Orme, "'Huck Finn' Has Same Charm, Pluck of Twain," *Salt Lake (UT) Tribune*, April 2, 1993.

190. Patrick Bibby, "'Huckleberry Finn' Still an Endearing Tale," *Greenville (SC) News*, May 7, 1993; Gannett News Service, "Twain Classic Is Watered Down," *Lansing (MI) State Journal*, April 1, 1993.

191. David Kehr, "'Finn' de Siècle: New 'Huck' Slows Twain's River Down to a Trickle," *Chicago Tribune*, April 2, 1993.

192. David Ansen, "Rites of Passage," *Newsweek*, April 4, 1993.

193. Brownstein, "Straying from the Classic Disney Formula."

194. Joshua Chu, "Retired Penn State Professor, Actor, Writer Charles Dumas Reflects on Lifetime of Social Justice," *Daily Collegian* (Penn State University), January 22, 2021, www.psucollegian.com/culture_lifestyle/retired-penn-state -professor-actor-writer-charles-dumas-reflects-on-lifetime-of-social-justice /article_b6d211e0-5c45-11eb-ad82-c3510b44f404.html; Layli Maria Miron, "Charles Dumas, JD: Actor, Activist, Writer," Public Writing Initiative, Penn State University, July 21, 2020, https://pwi.psu.edu/2020/07/21/charles-dumas/.

195. Edward Morgan went on to say, "It grew from there. Given the conceit that these two geezers were somehow magically alive—it seemed to me they could use magic to 'conjure up' a young Jim and Huck, and all the other necessary spirits. And once they were in charge, then there might be ways that OLD HUCK and OLD JIM would try to monkey with the story. And before long, the two men were off on a new kind of adventure." Morgan, comments in "Prologue," news-letter of the Milwaukee Rep, quoted in Shelley Fisher Fishkin, "World Premiere of *Sounding the River (Huck Finn Revisited),*" Mark Twain Forum blog, March 11, 2001, https://listserv.yorku.ca/cgi-bin/wa?A2=TWAIN-L;519b1924.0103.

196. Edward Morgan, email to author, July 28, 2023.

197. Morgan email.

198. *Sounding the River (Huck Finn Revisited),* stage play directed by Edward Morgan; written by Edward Morgan and Mark Twain; featuring Charles Dumas, Raphael Peacock, Jim Baker, Sean McNally, James Pickering, La Shawn Banks, Paul Bentzen, Mark Corkins, Olivia D. Dawson, Rose Pickering, and Laura Gordon; music arranger and director, Chic Street Man; music performed by Cedric Turner and Scott Wakefield; opened February 21, 2001, closed April 1, 2001, at the Milwaukee Repertory Theater. I am grateful to Edward Morgan for having shared the script with me and given me permission to quote from it.

199. Morgan, *Sounding the River*, 15, 17.

200. Morgan, *Sounding the River*, 22, 24–25.

201. Morgan, *Sounding the River*, 25–26.

202. Morgan, *Sounding the River*, 34, 35, 36, 38–39.

203. Morgan, *Sounding the River*, 52–54, 78, 74.

204. Edward Morgan, email to author, July 27, 2023; Morgan, *Sounding the River*, 206.

205. Morgan, *Sounding the River*, 100, 104, 118–19.

206. Morgan email, July 27, 2023.

207. Edward Morgan, Prologue, *Newsletter of the Milwaukee Repertory Company*, Twainweb, March 11, 2001, https://listserv.yorku.ca/cgi-bin/wa?A2=TWAIN-L;519b1924.0103&FT=&P=&H=&S=b.

208. A reviewer for *Backstage* wrote that as "Huck and the escaped slave Jim" are "reunited as senior citizens" who "travel back in time" with the help of an old lamp from Twain's home, "the old fellows observe the trip from the fringes of the action, commenting on it from the perspective of their advanced years. With those comments, Morgan . . . establishes the irony employed by Twain in writing about the partnership between a racist white boy and a runaway slave fleeing oppression together." *Backstage*, March 16, 2001, quoted on the website of playwright and director Edward Morgan, www.edward-morgan.com/sounding-the-river-1. The *Milwaukee Journal Sentinel* called the production "beautifully produced and well-acted." "Perhaps because [Morgan] was not trying to write a straightforward adaptation of the book, the play works much better than many attempts to transfer the page to the stage." The reviewer also noted "a fluidity largely due to Morgan's shrewd use of period music—old country, blues and spirituals—to connect the scenes." The reviewer believed that the "sharp, clear and sure-handed acting from the entire cast provides the richly colored portrait of river life created by Twain and recreated by Morgan." *Milwaukee Journal Sentinel*, quoted at www.edward-morgan.com/sounding-the-river-1.

209. The film was produced on the cusp of the social and cultural change that the student demonstrations of 1968 in Germany would help set in motion. At the time it was made, however, mainstream cultural productions could still count on being received by "a general German audience which basically did not question the validity of the historical representations of racial and class differences. It is only in the 1970s that a more general change of attitude sets in and enters cultural productions. It is the airing of the American TV series *Kunta Kinte* (the adaptation of Alex Haley's *Roots*, 1976) in 12 episodes in 1978 which brings about a different perception of slavery and of African Americans." Alfred Hornung, email to the author, February 4, 2024.

210. Ingrid Gessner notes that "the works of Berlin filmmaker Branwen Okpako about the Afro-German detective Sam Meffire in the award-winning documentary *Dreckfresser* (2001) or in the feature film *Tal der Ahnungslosen* (2003) took up lived Black history in (East) Germany in the 2000s. They can be read both as

cultural criticism and as poetic inscriptions that (might) have led to a new interpretation of Jim as we see it in Huntgeburth and Arango's *Die Abenteuer des Huck Finn* (2012)." Gessner, email to the author, February 4, 2024.

211. "Steve McQueen, the British director of *12 Years a Slave*, commented when his film was shown in 2013, that the slave trade is a cinematic subject whose time has come, and he called this 'the Obama Effect.'" Andrew Anthony, "*12 Years a Slave* and the Roots of America's Shameful Past," *Observer*, January 5, 2014, quoted in Paul Giles, "Obama, Tarantino, and Transnational Trauma," in *Obama and Transnational American Studies*, edited by Alfred Hornung (Heidelberg: Universitätsverlag, 2016), 257.

212. Richard Dyer, "The White Man's Muscles," in *Race and the Subject of Masculinities*, edited by Harry Stecopoulos and Michael Uebel (Durham, NC: Duke University Press, 1997), 286.

213. *Un gosse de la butte* [alternative title *Rue de cascades*, French], film directed by Maurice Delbez; written by Robert Sabatier, Maurice Delbez, and Jean Cosmos; featuring Serge Nubret, Madeleine Robinson, and René Lefèvre; cinematographer, Jean-Georges Fontenelle; produced by Edmond Lemoine; released by Les Films de Mai (France), December 2, 1964.

214. *Tom Sawyers und Huckleberry Finns Abenteuer* (Tom Sawyer's and Huckleberry Finn's Adventures), episode 4 of four-part mini-series made for German television by French, German, and Romanian production companies (Franco London Films, Office de Radiodiffusion Télévision Français [ORTF], Deropa Films, Studioul Cinematografic Bucuresti); directed by Wolfgang Liebeneiner; screenplay by Walter Ulbrich; featuring Serge Nubret (Jim), Marc di Napoli (Huck), Roland Demongeot, Robert Hecker, Lina Carstens, and Marcel Peres; narrated by Ernst Fritz Fürbringer; produced by Stefan Barcava, Henry Deutschmeister, Ulrich Picard, and Walter Ulbrich; premiered on ZDF, January 12, 1968.

215. John E. Davidson, "Working for the Man, Whoever That May Be: The Vocation of Wolfgang Liebeneiner," in *Cultural History through a National Socialist Lens: Essays on the Cinema of the Third Reich*, edited by Robert Charles Reimer, (Rochester, NY: Camden House, 2000), 242.

216. Ingrid Gessner observes that Liebeneiner's series from 1968 "was produced and broadcast as what was called Weihnachts-Vierteiler (Christmas four-part series), which explains its enormous popularity." At a time when there were only two channels—the networks ARD and ZDF—these four movie-length episodes that aired every Sunday during Advent (between December 1 and December 22) constituted "a real event back then" that "had the whole family sitting in front of the TV" (Gessner, email to the author, February 1, 2024). See also "Tom Sawyers und Huckleberry Finns Abenteuer," TV Wunschliste, www.wunschliste .de/serie/tom-sawyers-und-huckleberry-finns-abenteuer.

217. *Die Abenteuer des Huck Finn* (*The Adventures of Huckleberry Finn*) [German], film directed by Hermine Huntgeburth; written by Sascha Arango and Mark Twain; featuring Jacky Ido, Leon Seidel, Louis Hofmann, and August Diehl; music by Niki Reiser; produced by Boris Schönfelder for Schönhauser Film Production; distributed by Majestic Filmverleih, released December 20, 2012. Ingrid Gessner notes that the screenwriter, Arango, "is himself a person of color. Arango is also known as Sascha Arango Bueno and as Arturo Arango. The son of a German mother and a Colombian father, Sascha Arango was born in December 1959 and grew up with his brother Tonio in Berlin-Wilmersdorf. Besides screenplays, he has also written several radio and theater plays and has been awarded the Adolf Grimme Prize [a prestigious award for German television] several times" (Gessner email). "Sascha Arango," www.filmportal.de/person/sascha-arango_533c763f73604bf7a99a7d787937b7a9.

218. *Die weisse Massai* (*The White Masai*) [German], film directed by Hermine Huntgeburth; written by Corinne Hofmann, Johannes W. Betz, and Nadia Fares; featuring Nina Hoss, Jacky Ido, and Katja Flint; cinematography by Martin Langer; produced by Günter Rohrbach; released September 15, 2005.

219. Jacky Ido interviewed on *One on One with Steve Adubato*, November 7, 2014, www.youtube.com/watch?v=V8Z4GsAT3hQ.

220. "Jacky Ido," TVSA: South Africa's TV Website, www.tvsa.co.za/actors/viewactor.aspx?actorid=16877.

221. Sophie Charlotte Rieger, "Die Abenteuer des Huck Finn," film review, Filmstarts, www.filmstarts.de/kritiken/196411/kritik.html.

222. Limits of space prevented me from dealing with other laudable performances. For example, I regret that there was not room to discuss Paul Winfield's portrayal from 1974 of Jim as a caring husband and father seeking freedom to keep his family whole or Brock Peters's portrayal from 1981 of a Jim who is more confident and playful than he is in other productions.

CHAPTER 6. Jim in Translation

1. Selina Lai-Henderson, *Mark Twain in China* (Stanford, CA: Stanford University Press, 2015), 106.

2. Much of this chapter draws on essays that appeared in a Special Forum of the *Journal of Transnational American Studies* in 2021, edited by Shelley Fisher Fishkin, Tsuyoshi Ishihara, Ronald Jenn, Holger Kersten, and Selina Lai-Henderson. "Special Forum: Global Huck: Mapping the Cultural Work of Translations of Mark Twain's *Adventures of Huckleberry Finn*," *Journal of Transnational American Studies* 12, no. 2 (2021): 7–287, hereafter cited as *Global Huck*.

3. Ronald Jenn, "Global Jim: Translating African American Voices in Mark

Twain's *Adventures of Huckleberry Finn* Worldwide," *Revue Française d'Études Américaines*, no. 174 (2023): 92. This excellent article by Jenn, with whom I have collaborated for years on projects related to *Huck Finn*'s global travels, addresses many of the issues I explore in this chapter in a manner parallel to my own.

4. Kuni Sasaki, trans., *Hakkuruberī monogatari* [The story of Huckleberry] (Tokyo: Seika shoin, 1921); Tsuyoshi Ishihara, *Mark Twain in Japan: The Cultural Reception of an American Icon* (Columbia: University of Missouri Press, 2005), 24.

5. Ishihara, *Mark Twain in Japan*, 26.

6. For more on the history of racism in Japan, see Hiroshi Fukurai and Alice Yang, "The History of Japanese Racism, Japanese American Redress, and the Dangers Associated with Government Regulation of Hate Speech," *Hastings Constitutional Law Quarterly* 45, no. 3 (2018): 533–75.

7. Tsuyoshi Ishihara writes, "Sasaki's distortions of Jim seem to reflect Japanese people's deep-seated prejudices against blacks at the time. It was not black America but white America that Japan had recognized as its model since its encounter with America in the mid-nineteenth century. As a result, the Japanese assimilated white American racism toward blacks." Ishihara, *Mark Twain in Japan*, 26.

8. Ishihara, *Mark Twain in Japan*, 27.

9. For details on Kenzaburō Ōe's crediting *Huckleberry Finn* with having sparked his excitement about literature, see Shelley Fisher Fishkin, *Lighting Out for the Territory* (New York: Oxford University Press, 1996), 190, 194. When I met Ōe in Austin, Texas, in 1996 and asked him whether I was correct in my suspicion that his first book, *The Catch*, was responding directly to *Huckleberry Finn*, Ōe answered yes.

10. Winston Kelley "How German Translations of 'Trash' in Chapter 15 of *Huckleberry Finn* Facilitate Misunderstanding the Whole Novel," in *Global Huck*.

11. Mark Twain, *Las aventuras de Huckleberry Finn* [The adventures of Huckleberry Finn], translated by M. Teresa Monguió (Barcelona: Juventud, 1957); Mark Twain, *Die Abenteuer des Huckleberry Finn* [The adventures of Huckleberry Finn], translated by Rainer Lübbren (Stuttgart: Blüchert, 1956). Arthur Egon Kunst identifies these scenes as omitted from these Spanish and German translations in Kunst, "Twenty-Four Versions of *Huckleberry Finn*: Studies in Translation" (PhD diss., Indiana University, 1961), 228–29.

12. Mark Twain, *Abenteuer und Fahrten des Huckleberry Finn* [Adventures and travels of Huckleberry Finn], translated by Henny Koch (Stuttgart: Robert Lutz, 1892); *Die Abenteuer des Huckleberry Finn* [The adventures of Huckleberry Finn], translated by Ulrich Johannsen (part 1) and Marie Schloss (part 2), in *Die Abenteuer des Tom Sawyer und Huckleberry Finn* [The adventures of Tom Sawyer

and Huckleberry Finn] (1913; Leipzig: Josef Singer, 1923), 302–615; Fred Wübben, trans., *Fahrten und Abenteuer* [Trips and adventures] (Heidelberg: Kemper, 1951); Mark Twain, *Les aventures de Huck Finn, l'ami de Tom Sawyer* [The adventures of Huck Finn, Tom Sawyer's Friend], translated by William-Little Hughes (Paris: Hennuyer, 1886) [note: the translator's name appears to have been William Little Hughes, but it appears as "William-L." on the title page of *Les aventures de Huck Finn, l'ami de Tom Sawyer*]; Kunst identified these scenes as missing in these early German and French translations (Kunst, "Twenty-Four Versions," 228–29). It is also missing from a Korean translation from 2008 by Kim Uk Dong: Mark Twain, 허클베리 핀의 모험 (*Hŏk'ŭlberi P'in ŭi Mohŏm*) [Adventures of Huckleberry Finn], translated by Kim Uk Dong (Kyŏnggi-do P'aju-si, South Korea: P'urŭn Sup Chuniŏ, 2008). I am indebted to Chris Suh for confirming that these scenes are missing in this edition.

13. Kunst, "Twenty-Four Versions," 83.

14. Mark Twain, *Huckleberry Finn*, translated by Franz Geiger (Vienna: Ibis, 1952); Mark Twain, 哈克贝利·芬历险记 (*Hake Beili Fen lixianji*) [Adventures of Huckleberry Finn], translated by Ren Aoshuang (Tianjin: Tianjin People's Publishing, 2003); Kim, *Hŏk'ŭlberi P'in ŭi Mohŏm*.

15. Mark Twain, *Huckleberry Finn*, translated by Wolfram Gramowski (Cologne: Agrippina, 1954); Mark Twain, *Huckleberry Finns äventyr* [Huckleberry Finn's Adventures], translated by Olav Angell (Oslo: Kagge, 2003); Mark Twain, مغامرات هكلبري فن [Adventures of Huckleberry Finn], translated by Shawqi Alameer (Cairo: International Company for Publication–Longman, 1992); *Huck Finn, el negro y Tom Sawyer* [Huck Finn, the Negro, and Tom Sawyer], vol. 2 of *Las cinco mejores obras de Mark Twain*, 5 vols., edited by José Castellano and translated by Simón Santainé (Barcelona: Mateu, 1957); Mark Twain, *Приключения Гекльберри Финна* (*Priklyucheniya Gekl'berri Finna*) [Adventures of Huckleberry Finn], edited by Korneĭ Chukovsky (Moscow: Molodaia gvardia, 1933); Mark Twain, فين هاكلبيري مغامرات [Adventures of Huckleberry Finn], translated by Kawthar Mahmoud Mohammad (Cairo: Hindawi Foundation for Education and Culture, 2012); Mark Twain, مغامرات هكلبري فن [Adventures of Huckleberry Finn], translated by Nasr Abdulrahman (Cairo: Al-Hay'ah Al-Amah li Qusor Al-Aaqafa GOCP, 2015).

16. Ronald Jenn, "From American Frontier to European Borders: Publishing French Translations of Mark Twain's Novels *Tom Sawyer* and *Huckleberry Finn* (1884–1963)," *Book History* 9, no. 1 (2006): 238.

17. Jenn, "From American Frontier," 248.

18. Judith Lavoie, "Traduire pour aseptiser: *Huck Finn* revu et corrigé par W. L. Hughes," *Babel* 48, no. 3 (2002): 194.

19. Mark Twain, *Adventures of Huckleberry Finn*, edited by Victor Fischer

and Lin Salamo with Harriet Elinor Smith and the late Walter Blair, Mark Twain Library, from the Mark Twain Project, Robert H. Hirst, general editor (1885; Berkeley: University of California Press, 2001), 150.

20. Lavoie, "Traduire pour aseptiser," 199 (translation mine).

21. Lavoie, *Mark Twain et la parole noire* (Montreal: Presses Universitaires de Montreal, 2002), 24 (translation mine).

22. Jenn, "From American Frontier," 252; Mark Twain, *Les aventures de Huckleberry Finn* [The adventures of Huckleberry Finn], translated by Suzanne Nétillard (Paris: Hier et Aujourd'hui, 1948).

23. Mark Twain, हकलबरी फनि [Huckleberry Finn], 5th ed., translated by Omkar Sharad (New Delhi: Radhakrisha Prakashan, 2018).

24. Seema Sharma, "*Huck*'s Adventures in India: Cultural Conversation in Select Hindi Adaptations," in *Global Huck*, 206.

25. Twain, *Adventures of Huckleberry Finn*, 105.

26. Sharad, *Huckleberry Finn*, 35 (translation Sharma's); Sharma, "*Huck*'s Adventures in India," 207.

27. Sharma, "*Huck*'s Adventures in India," 207.

28. Kunst, "Twenty-Four Versions," 83–84 (translation mine).

29. Kelley, "German Translations of 'Trash,'" 99.

30. Lai-Henderson, *Mark Twain in China*, 112. Their version of Jim's story, Lai-Henderson writes, "deprives the readers of a more complete picture of the slave trade and the inhumanity of slavery."

31. Twain, *Adventures of Huckleberry Finn*, 57; Chris Suh, personal communication, May 2023.

32. Cassio de Oliveira, email to the author, September 11, 2023.

33. Julia Lin, "Children's Literature, Translation and Censorship: The Spanish Translations of *Adventures of Huckleberry Finn* under Franco's Dictatorship (1939–1975)" (MA thesis, University of Sydney, 2015).

34. Lin, "Children's Literature," 58–62.

35. Lin, "Children's Literature," 62.

36. Mark Twain, مغامرات‡هكلبري [Adventures of Huckleberry Finn], translated by Mahir Naseem (Cairo: Maktabat Misr, 1958).

37. Mariam Abdulmalik, "The *Adventures of Huckleberry Finn* in Arabic Translations: A Case Study" (PhD diss., SUNY Binghamton, 2016), 147.

38. Mark Twain, مغامرات‡هكلبري‡فن [Adventures of Huckleberry Finn], translated by Nasr Abdulrahman (Cairo: Al-Hay'ah Al-Amah li Qusor Al-Aaqafa GOCP, 2015). See also Hamada Kassam, "Arabic Huck: *Adventures of Huckleberry Finn* in Vernacular Arabic," in *Global Huck*, 71–90.

39. Abdulmalik, "*Adventures of Huckleberry Finn* in Arabic Translations," 74.

40. Kassam, "Arabic Huck," 75.

41. Raphael Berthele, "Translating African-American Vernacular English into German: The Problem of 'Jim' in Mark Twain's *Huckleberry Finn*," *Journal of Sociolinguistics* 4, no. 4 (2000): 603.

42. Koch quoted in Berthele, "Translating African-American Vernacular English," 603.

43. Johannsen and Schloss quoted in Berthele, "Translating African-American Vernacular English," 603.

44. Robert W. Kestling, "Blacks under the Swastika: A Research Note," *Journal of Negro History* 83, no. 1 (1998): 84–99.

45. Eugen Fischer quoted in Kestling, "Blacks under the Swastika," 87. Kestling cites Christian Pross and Goetz Aly, *The Value of the Human Being: Medicine in Germany, 1918–1945* (Berlin: Hentrich, 1991), 98–99; Michael Burleigh and Wolfgang Wippermann, *The Racial State: Germany, 1933–1945* (Cambridge: Cambridge University Press, 1991), 129–30; Benno Mueller-Hill, *Murderous Science: Elimination by Scientific Selection of Jews, Gypsies, and Others, Germany, 1933–1945* (Oxford: Oxford University Press, 1988), 10–12, 30, 138; and Keith L. Nelson, "The 'Black Horror on the Rhine': Race as a Factor in Post–World War I Diplomacy," *Journal of Modern History* 42, no. 4 (1970): 606–27.

46. Kestling, "Blacks under the Swastika," 85, citing Robert N. Proctor, *Racial Hygiene: Medicine under the Nazis* (Cambridge, MA: Harvard University Press, 1988), 114.

47. Hughes quoted in Lavoie, "Traduire pour aseptiser," 194 (translation mine).

48. Mark Twain, *Las aventuras de Huck* [The adventures of Huck], 2 vols., translated by Carlos Peyrera and Fernando de la Milla (Madrid: Caro Raggio, 1923), quoted in Kunst, "Twenty-Four Versions," 36 (translation mine).

49. Cassiano Teixeira de Freitas Fagundes, "Retraduções de variedades linguísticas da literatura de língua inglesa: O polissistema brasileiro em transformação Florianópolis" (MA thesis, Universidade Federal de Santa Catarina, Florianópolis, 2016), 121; Mark Twain, *As aventuras de Huck* [The adventures of Huck], translated by Monteiro Lobato (São Paulo: Brasiliense, 1957).

50. Lavoie, "Traduire por aseptiser," 195 (translation mine).

51. Lavoie, "Traduire por aseptiser," 197 (translation mine).

52. Lavoie, "Traduire por aseptiser," 200.

53. Judith Lavoie, "Mark Twain vs. William-Little Hughes: The Transformation of a Great American Novel," in *In Translation: Reflections, Refractions, Transformations,* edited by Paul St.-Pierre and Prafulla C. Kar (Amsterdam: John Benjamins, 2007), 101.

54. Lavoie, "Mark Twain vs. William-Little Hughes," 101, 105.

55. William B. Cohen, *The French Encounter with Africa: White Response to Blacks, 1530–1880* (Bloomington: Indiana University Press, 2003), 244, 291.

56. Mark Twain, *Pustolovščine Huckleberryja Finna* [Adventures of Huckleberry Finn], translated by Pavel Holeček (Ljubljana, Slovenia: Mladinska knjiga, 1948), discussed in Janko Trupej, "Translating Racist Discourse in Slovenia during the Socialist Period: Mark Twain's *Adventures of Huckleberry Finn*," in *Translation and the Reconfiguration of Power Relations: Revisiting Role and Context of Translation and Interpreting*, edited by Beatrice Fischer and Matilde Nisbeth Jensen (Graz, Austria: LIT, 2012), 96–101.

57. Twain, *Huckleberry Finn*, 100.

58. Trupej, "Translating Racist Discourse in Slovenia," 99.

59. Trupej, "Translating Racist Discourse in Slovenia," 99.

60. Trupej, "Translating Racist Discourse in Slovenia," 100.

61. Trupej, "Translating Racist Discourse in Slovenia," 100.

62. Trupej, "Translating Racist Discourse in Slovenia," 100.

63. Mark Twain, *Prigode Huckleberryja Finna* [Adventures of Huckleberry Finn], trans. Janez Gradišnik (Ljubljana, Slovenia: Mladinska knjiga, 1962), discussed in Trupej, "Translating Racist Discourse in Slovenia," 101–2.

64. Trupej, "Translating Racist Discourse in Slovenia," 104–5.

65. Sharad, *Huckleberry Finn*, 86, discussed in Sharma, "*Huck*'s Adventures in India," 206–7.

66. Sharma, "*Huck*'s Adventures in India," 207–8.

67. Berthele, "Translating African-American Vernacular English," 592.

68. Berthele, "Translating African-American Vernacular English," 608.

69. Berthele, "Translating African-American Vernacular English," 601.

70. Berthele, "Translating African-American Vernacular English," 600.

71. Mark Twain, *Le avventure di Huckleberry Finn* [The adventures of Huckleberry Finn], translated by Gabriele Musumarra (1964; reprint, Milan: Biblioteca Universale Rizzoli, 2000), discussed in Iain Halliday, *Huck Finn in Italian, Pinocchio in English: Theory and Praxis of Literary Translation* (Madison, NJ: Fairleigh Dickinson University Press, 2009), 93.

72. Berthele, "Translating African-American Vernacular English," 602.

73. Lai-Henderson, *Mark Twain in China*, 111.

74. An-chi Wang, email to author, August 21, 2023.

75. Jenn, "Global Jim," 96.

76. Jenn, "Global Jim," 96, citing Masoud Sharififar and Seyed A. Enjavi Nejad, "A Study of African American Vernacular Dialect Translation into Persian in *The Adventures of Huckleberry Finn*," *Iranian EFL Journal* 9, no. 1 (2013): 495.

77. B. J. Epstein, "Are There Blacks in Europe? How African-American Characters Are (Or Are Not) Translated," in *True North: Literary Translation in the Nordic Countries*, edited by B. J. Epstein (Cambridge: Cambridge Scholars Press, 2014), 90, 95.

78. Epstein, "Are There Blacks in Europe?," 96.

79. Berthele, "Translating African-American Vernacular English," 603.

80. Berthele creates a table that shows how thirteen German translators from 1890 to 1997 used sixteen strategies of marking speech for African American English in German. Categories such as using colloquial words, regional words, dialectical syntax, and double negation are in the "difference" category, while mistakes in congruence, genus, and case, along with wrong word order and missing articles, are in the "deficit" category. Although spelling mistakes are included in the "deficit" category, sound/syllable loss is in the "difference" grouping. Berthele, "Translating African-American Vernacular English," 604.

81. Berthele, "Translating African-American Vernacular English," 605; Mark Twain, *Huckleberry Finns Abenteuer*, translated by Sybil Countess Schönfeldt (Würzburg, Germany: Arena, 1978).

82. Berthele, "Translating African-American Vernacular English," 605.

83. Berthele, "Translating African-American Vernacular English," 588. Berthele examined about forty German translations from some thirty translators over the past century. His analysis focused on thirteen of these translations in detail.

84. Berthele, "Translating African-American Vernacular English," 609.

85. Berthele, "Translating African-American Vernacular English," 607. Berthele cites Herbert Graf and Eike Schöenfeld, *Black American English: Vorläufiges Glossar und andere Arbeitsergebnisse einer Fortbildungstagung* (Straelen, Germany: Straelener Manuskripte, 1983).

86. See work cited above by Abdulmalik (Arabic), Berthele (German), Jenn and Channaut (French), Epstein (Danish, Norwegian, Swedish), Halliday (Italian), Ishihara (Japanese), Jenn (French), Kassem (Arabic), Kunst (French, German, Portuguese, Russian, Spanish), Lai-Henderson (Chinese), Lin (Spanish), Marinova (Russian), and Sharma (Hindi). For Czech, see Tereza Šedivá, "*Huckleberry Finn* in Czech: Comparative Analysis of Translations" (MA thesis, Masayyk University, Brno, 2011). For Chinese and Spanish, see José Manuel Rodríguez Herrera, "The Reverse Side of Mark Twain's Brocade: *The Adventures of Huckleberry Finn* and the Translation of Dialect," *European Journal of English Studies* 18, no. 3 (2014): 278–94. For Vietnamese, see Hoang Thi Diem Hang, "An Assessment of the Vietnamese Translation of *The Adventures of Huckleberry Finn*," *VNU Journal of Foreign Studies* 35, no. 1 (2019): 35–54. For Spanish, see also Miguel Sanz

Jiménez, "The Problem of the Explanatory: Linguistic Variation in Twenty-First-Century Spanish Retranslations of *Huckleberry Finn*," in *Global Huck*, 77–99. For Assamese, Korean, Urdu, and Yiddish, I am indebted to personal communication with scholars and curators Aruni Kashyap (Assamese), Chris Suh (Korean), C. Ryan Perkins (Urdu), and Eitan Lev Kensky (Yiddish), who examined translations in these languages at my request. This list, of course, barely scrapes the surface of a very small number of critical studies of translations of *Huckleberry Finn*. To date, the novel has been translated into sixty-seven languages.

87. Epstein, "Are There Blacks in Europe?," 89; Angell, *Huckleberry Finns äventyr*, 12.

88. Korneĭ Chukovsky, *The Art of Translation: Korneĭ Chukovsky's "A High Art,"* translated and edited by Lauren G. Leighton (Knoxville: University of Tennessee Press, 1984), 127–28, quoted in Marinova, "Huck Finn's Adventures," 91. See also Chukovsky, *Priklyucheniya Gekl'berri Finna* [Adventures of Huckleberry Finn].

89. Ishihara, *Mark Twain in Japan*, 12.

90. Sanz Jiménez, "Problem of the Explanatory." See also Rodríguez Herrera, "Reverse Side," 278–94.

91. Abdulmalik, "Adventures of Huckleberry Finn in Arabic Translations," 43.

92. Twain, *Huck Finn*, 22.

93. Abdulmalik, "Adventures of Huckleberry Finn in Arabic Translations," 45. Kassam, email to the author, February 21, 2024.

94. Šedivá, *Huckleberry Finn in Czech*, 53; Mark Twain, *Dobrodružství Huckleberryho Finna* [Adventures of Huckleberry Finn], translated by František Gel (1953; reprint, Prague: Albatros, 1986); Mark Twain, *Dobrodružství Huckleberryho Finna* [Adventures of Huckleberry Finn], translated by Jana Mertinová (Prague: Albatros, 2007).

95. Šedivá, *Huckleberry Finn in Czech*, 74.

96. Marinova, "Huck Finn's Adventures," 128. See also Mark Twain, *Приключения Гекльберри Финна* (*Priklyucheniya Gekl'berri Finna*) [Adventures of Huckleberry Finn], translated by Nina Daruzes (Moscow: Detgiz, 1955).

97. Marinova, "Huck Finn's Adventures," 128.

98. Meta Grosman, *Književnost v medkulturnem položaju* [Literature in an intercultural situation] (Ljubljana, Slovenia: Znanstveni inštitut Filozofske fakultete, 2004), 147–48, quoted in Trupej, "Translating Racist Discourse in Slovenia," 102.

99. Rodríguez Herrera, "Reverse Side," 281.

100. Rodríguez Herrera, "Reverse Side," 286; Mark Twain, *Las aventuras de*

Huckleberry Finn [The adventures of Huckleberry Finn], translated by J. A. de Larrinaga (1974; reprint, Barcelona: Mondadori, 2006).

101. Lai-Henderson, *Mark Twain in China*, 113.

102. Selina Lai-Henderson, "Translation and International Reception," in *Mark Twain in Context*, edited by John Bird (Cambridge: Cambridge University Press, 2020), 322.

103. Lai-Henderson, *Mark Twain in China*, 113; Mark Twain, 哈克你贝利·费恩历险记(*Hakeni Beili Feien lixianji*) [Adventures of Huckleberry Finn], translated by Cheng Shi (Taipei: Guangfu, 1989); 哈克你贝利·芬历险记 (*Hakeni Beili Fen lixianji*) [Adventures of Huckleberry Finn], translated by Xu Ruzhi (Nanjing: Yi Lin, 1995).

104. Lai-Henderson, *Mark Twain in China*, 114.

105. Lai-Henderson, *Mark Twain in China*, 114.

106. Rodríguez Herrera notes, as an example, the translator's use of "the wrong character布 instead of the right one 不 (a negation mark) to translate the informal expression 'ain't going to forget you.'" Rodríguez Herrera, "Reverse Side," 294, 289.

107. Lai-Henderson, *Mark Twain in China*, 114–15. Xu, *Hakeni Beili Fen lixianji* [Adventures of Huckleberry Finn]. Xu also "provides over 150 footnotes with details about American history, geography, race relations, language, and culture that are necessary for a thorough understanding of the novel, especially for readers who have little knowledge of the United States" (Lai-Henderson, *Mark Twain in China*, 115).

108. Šedivá, *Huckleberry Finn in Czech*, 53.

109. Šedivá, *Huckleberry Finn in Czech*, 53.

110. Ronald Jenn and Véronique Channaut, "Translations of *Adventures of Huckleberry Finn* in France (1886–2015)," in *Global Huck*, 56, 60.

111. Rodríguez Herrera, "Reverse Side," 282.

112. Vanessa Lopes Lourenço Hanes, review, "*As aventuras de Huckleberry Finn de Mark Twain*, tradução de Rosaura Eichenberg," *Cadernos de Tradução* 2, no. 28 (2011): 243–48. See also Vera Lucía Ramos, "Mark Twain: The Making of an Icon through Translations of *Huckleberry Finn* in Brazil," in *Global Huck*, 149–71.

113. Kassam, "Arabic Huck," 73.

114. Kassam, "Arabic Huck," 79–80.

115. Hamada Kassam, email to the author, August 5, 2023.

116. Kassam, "Arabic Huck," 80.

117. Sharma, "*Huck*'s Adventures in India," 209.

118. Mark Twain, *Aventuras de Huckleberry Finn* [Adventures of Huck Finn],

in *Selección de obras de Mark Twain,* edited by Bernard DeVoto and translated by Andrés M. Mateo (Mexico City: Limusa Wiley, 1967), 207–542.

119. Gonzalo Aguirre Beltrán, *Cuijla: Esbozo etnográfico de un pueblo negro* (Mexico City: Fondo de Cultura Económica, 1958), 9–11; Jessica M. Harris, "When the Right Word Is Not Enough: Spanish-Language Translations of *Huck Finn*" (Plan II honors thesis, University of Texas at Austin, 2001), 47–48. Harris summarizes in detail the linguistic characteristics Beltrán observes among the Cuijleños and their relationship to the ways in which Mateo translates Jim's speech in the novel. See also Shelley Fisher Fishkin, "Transnational Mark Twain," in *American Studies as Transnational Practice: Turning toward the Pacific,* edited by Yuan Shu and Donald E. Pease (Hanover, NH: Dartmouth College Press, 2015), 120.

120. Beltrán, *Cuijla,* 208.

121. Beltrán, *Cuijla,* 253–56; Mateo, *Aventuras de Huckleberry Finn* [Adventures of Huck Finn], 318, 322, 597.

122. Twain, *Adventures of Huckleberry Finn,* chap. 14.

123. In addition, they might say *parriba* for *para arriba,* or *patrás* for *para atrás.* Also *pal* for *para él, namás* for *nada más,* and *l'amigo* for *el amigo.* Beltrán, *Cuijla,* 207.

124. Beltrán, *Cuijla,* 253, 255, 257; Mateo, *Aventuras de Huckleberry Finn* [Adventures of Huck Finn], 293, 296, 322. He also says *salvao* for *salvado, sabé* for *saber,* and *onde estoy* for *dónde estoy* (323).

125. Beltrán, *Cuijla,* 226.

126. Harris, "When the Right Word," 51.

127. Mark Twain, *As aventuras de Huckleberry Finn* [The adventures of Huckleberry Finn], translated by Francisco José Tenreiro, 2nd ed. (Lisbon: Inquérito, 1973). I am grateful to Isabel Caldeira for bringing this translation to my attention and to Isabel Oliveira Martins for having shown it to me in the exhibit she produced with Maria de Deus Duarte at the Biblioteca Nacional de Portugal on October 9, 2010. See the exhibition catalog *Mark Twain em Portugal* (Lisbon: Biblioteca Nacional de Portugal/Centro de Estudios Anglisticos de Universidade de Lisboa/Fundaçao para Ciéncia e Tecnologia, 2010).

128. See Maria dulce de Oliveira Almada, *Cabo Verde: Contribuição para o estudo do dialecto falado no seu arquipélago* (Lisbon: Junta de Investigações do Ultramar, Centro de Estudos Políticos e Sociais, 1961); Carlos Alberto Delgado, *Crioulo de Cabo Verde: Situação linguistica da sona do barlavento* (Praia, Cape Verde: Instituto da Biblioteca Nationale do Livro, 2008); and António Carreira, *Crioulo de Cabo Verde: Surto e expansão* (Lisbon: n.p., 1982). See also "Cape Verdean Cre-

ole," Indiana University, https://celt.indiana.edu/portal/cape-verdean-creole /index.html.

129. Tenreiro, *Aventuras de Huckleberry Finn* [Adventures of Huckleberry Finn], 63, 76.

130. Jenn, "Global Jim," 98.

131. Ricardo A. Fernandes, *Aventuras de Huckleberry Finn* [Adventures of Huckleberry Finn] (Lisbon: Portugália, 1956), cited in Kunst, "Twenty-Four Versions," 76.

132. Mark Twain, *As aventuras de Huckleberry Finn* [The adventures of Huckleberry Finn], translated by Monteiro Lobato (São Paulo: Editora Nacional, 2005), cited in Kunst, "Twenty-Four Versions," 76.

133. Behnam M. Fomeshi, email to the author, August 13, 2023. Mark Twain, *Hakelberifin* [Huckleberry Finn], translated by Parviz Najm al-Dini (Tehran: Tusan, 1984); *Majara-haye Hakelberifin* [Adventures of Huckleberry Finn], translated by Shahram Puranfar (Tehran: Mahtab, 1991).

134. Jenn, "From American Frontier," 242.

135. Mark Twain, *Les aventures d'Huckleberry Finn* [The adventures of Huckleberry Finn], translated by André Bay (Paris: Livre Club du Libraire, 1960); Jenn, "From American Frontier," 253.

136. Jenn and Channaut, "Translations," 53.

137. Jenn and Channaut, "Translations," 61. Jenn and Channaut see this aspect of Jaworski's approach here as "a major setback" that relegates Jim, once again, "to a subordinate position" (53). Of course, it could also be read as a nod to Jim's awareness of his position in a world in which he could be severely punished for disrespecting a white person—of any age.

138. Fishkin, "Transnational Mark Twain," 120.

139. Kassam email.

140. Kassam email. See also Kassam, "Arabic Huck," 71–89.

141. Abdulmalik, "*Adventures of Huckleberry Finn* in Arabic Translations," 47.

142. Mark Twain, 赫克歷險記 (*Hake lixianji*) [Adventures of Huckleberry Finn], edited and translated by An-chi Wang (Taipei: Linkingbooks, 2012), 133–52.

143. An-chi Wang, email to the author, August 9, 2023. Also Wang, "Translation Processes and Cultural Critique in My Annotated Chinese Translation of Huckleberry Finn" *Journal of Transnational American Studies* 12, no. 2 (2021): 242–71.

144. Wang email. In a long, laudatory preface to Wang's translation, leading translation studies scholar Te-hsing Shan commends Wang's success in having placed Twain's novel in both American and Chinese literary traditions and cultural contexts.

145. Jung H. Lee, "The Moral Power of Jim: A Mencian Reading of *Huckleberry Finn*," *Asian Philosophy: An International Journal of the Philosophical Traditions of the East* 19, no. 2 (2009): 101–18.

CHAPTER 7. Jim in the High School Classroom

1. "Take Them Off the List: An Editorial," *Afro-American* (Baltimore), February 13, 1965.

2. Moriah Gibson, Tyson Hardnett, and Andy Stevens, "An Interview with David Bradley," The Censorship Files, https://thecensorshipfiles.wordpress.com /an-interview-with-david-bradley/.

3. "'Huckleberry' 'Hit,'" *Afro-American* (Baltimore), December 17, 1966.

4. "Negro Students Protest Reading 'Huckleberry Finn,'" *New York Times*, December 7, 1966.

5. "Required Reading?," *Chicago Defender*, December 22, 1966.

6. "Huck Finn Floats a Troubled Raft," *Park Forest (IL) Star*, June 28, 1984.

7. Texas state senator Royce West, interview with the author, October 10, 1995, Dallas.

8. *Monteiro v. Tempe Union High School Dist.*, 158 F.3d 1022 (9th Cir. 1998). The disruption of Jocelyn Chadwick's talk was filmed in the documentary *Born to Trouble: Adventures of Huckleberry Finn*, directed by Jill Janows (2000, WGBH). Picket sign quoted in Jocelyn Chadwick, *The Jim Dilemma: Reading Race in "Huckleberry Finn"* (Jackson: University Press of Mississippi, 1998), xi.

9. Melanthia Mitchell, "NAACP to Investigate Treatment of 'Huckleberry Finn' Opponent," *Chronicle* (Centralia, WA), December 11, 2003.

10. Sharon E. Rush, *Huck Finn's "Hidden" Lessons: Teaching and Learning across the Color Line* (Lanham, MD: Rowman and Littlefield, 2006), 48, 108–9.

11. See resolution titled NJ ACR225. Jennifer Anandanayagam, "Why the Adventures of Huckleberry Finn Became a Banned Book," The List, www.thelist .com/1045098/the-real-reason-the-adventures-of-huckleberry-finn-became-a -banned-book. The book was challenged, for example, in Duluth, MN, in 2018 and in Burbank, CA, in 2020; Dorany Pineda, "Off the Reading List: Burbank's School District Sets Aside Five Novels Challenged as Racist, including 'To Kill a Mockingbird,' as Parents and Students Debate," *Los Angeles Times*, November 12, 2020. See also Brett Busang, "Let Us Sit and Consider These 'Old Bones," *Richmond (VA) Times-Dispatch*, February 23, 2018; and Tony Norman, "Read the Great Books That Use the Worst Slur," *Pittsburgh Post-Gazette*, February 13, 2018.

12. "Banned Books 2022—*The Adventures of Huckleberry Finn*," Marshall University Libraries, www.marshall.edu/library/bannedbooks/the-adventures-of -huckleberry-finn/.

13. Julia Rosenbloom, telephone interviews with the author, December 1994 and April 1996, quoted in Shelley Fisher Fishkin, *Lighting Out for the Territory: Reflections on Mark Twain and American Culture* (New York: Oxford University Press, 1997), 195–96.

14. Ann Lew, "Teaching 'Huck Finn' in a Multiethnic Classroom," *English Journal* 82, no. 7 (1993): 16–21, 17.

15. Lew, "Teaching 'Huck Finn,'" 17.

16. Lew used the first edition of the book, which came out in 1963. A new edition of the book, published in 1997 in Oxford's Race and American Culture series, is still in print. Thomas Gossett, *Race: The History of an Idea in America* (1963), introduction by series editors Shelley Fisher Fishkin and Arnold Rampersad, new afterword by Thomas Gossett, and bibliographic essay by Maghan Keita (New York: Oxford University Press, 1997).

17. Lew, "Teaching 'Huck Finn,'" 17–18.

18. Lew, "Teaching 'Huck Finn,'" 18, 19.

19. Lew, "Teaching 'Huck Finn,'" 19.

20. Lew, "Teaching 'Huck Finn,'" 20.

21. Lew, "Teaching 'Huck Finn,'" 20.

22. Lew, "Teaching 'Huck Finn,'" 21.

23. Lew, "Teaching 'Huck Finn,'" 21. Lew adds, "I would like to be able to say that all of my students were enthralled with our reading of *Huck Finn*. Some were, and raced through the book, ahead of everyone else. But most of them said that it was just 'all right.' Some didn't like it because it was 'boring.' What was important to me, however, was that no one walked away from it saying that Twain was racist or that he made them feel bad about themselves" (21).

24. John Pascal, personal communication, June 13, 2023.

25. R. Kent Rasmussen, "nigger," in *Critical Companion to Mark Twain: A Literary Reference to His Life and Work*, 2 vols. (New York: Facts on File, 2007), 2:815; Rasmussen, "African Americans," in *Critical Companion to Mark Twain*, 2:565–70. Although before 2020 John Pascal used to allow students to say the word aloud when quoting from the book—while noting it was not acceptable to use in any other context—he changed that policy in the wake of the murder of George Floyd, and the word has not been read aloud in his classroom since. Pascal adds that he tells students that "we won't read [the slur] aloud, except to either jump over it or just say 'N-word.' No student has ever had a problem with this." John Pascal, email to the author, August 19, 2023.

26. Mark Twain, *Adventures of Huckleberry Finn*, edited by Victor Fischer and Lin Salamo with Harriet Elinor Smith and the late Walter Blair, Mark Twain

Library, from the Mark Twain Project, Robert H Hirst, general editor (1885; Berkeley: University of California Press, 2001).

27. John Pascal, personal communication (telephone), fall 2023.

28. Pascal often invites a couple of Twain scholars to his honors elective on Mark Twain to respond to the students' questions on Zoom. During the many such sessions I have had with his students over the years, I've been impressed by the astute and well-formulated queries that they've posed and by the depth of their engagement with the novel.

29. Rush, *Huck Finn's "Hidden" Lessons*, 47. Rush is referring to the deployment of literary techniques and rhetorical devices such as "logomachal frames," "metatasis," and "Menippean symposium"—terms that Jocelyn Chadwick discusses in *The Jim Dilemma*.

30. Rush, *Huck Finn's "Hidden" Lessons*, 111.

31. West interview.

32. John Pascal, typed notes on exchange that took place in his period G class in June 2023. Email to the author, July 17, 2023.

33. Joseph B. Fulton, *Mark Twain's Ethical Realism: Aesthetics of Race, Class, and Gender* (Columbia: University Press of Missouri, 1998), 87.

34. Pascal notes that "Lucah was sad to have to drop the Twain course because it would not fit into the rest of his revised course schedule. Fortunately Devin could take the course." Indeed, the following year when Devin Campana entered the University of Utah, he went to the university library and asked where the Twain books were. He wrote Pascal that "they have a pretty complete collection, but he will suggest getting a 'complete' set." He sent his old teacher a photo of himself bundled up for a Utah winter and smiling while holding up a copy of *Roughing It*. Pascal shared the photo with me. John Pascal, email to the author, February 25, 2024.

35. Rush, *Huck Finn's "Hidden" Lessons*, 146.

36. Toni Morrison, "Introduction," in Mark Twain, *Adventures of Huckleberry Finn*, The Oxford Mark Twain, edited by Shelley Fisher Fishkin (New York: Oxford University Press, 1996), xxxvi, emphasis added.

Afterword

1. Mark Twain, "My First Lie and How I Got Out of It" (1899), in *Mark Twain: Collected Tales, Sketches, Speeches, and Essays, 1891–1910*, edited by Louis J. Budd (New York: Library of America, 1992), 440, 441. Twain restates his definition of the concept twice in the essay, referring to it as "the silent assertion that there wasn't anything going on in which humane and intelligent people were

interested" and "the silent assertion that nothing is going on which fair and intelligent men are aware of and are engaged by their duty to try to stop."

Appendix

1. Twain made this word central to the title of an antilynching satire he published in the *Buffalo* (*NY*) *Express* in 1869 that he called "Only a Nigger." In this satire, the "honorable" men of Memphis use the word to justify their having lynched an innocent man. The miscarriage of justice they have perpetrated does not trouble them because "only 'a nigger'" lost his life as a result. Mark Twain, "Only a Nigger" (1869), in *Mark Twain at the "Buffalo Express,"* edited by Joseph McCullough and Janice McIntire-Strasburg (DeKalb: Northern Illinois University Press, 1999), 22–23.

2. Randall Kennedy, *Nigger: The Strange Career of a Troublesome Word* (New York: Knopf/Vintage, 2003).

3. Randall Kennedy, "A Note on the Word 'Nigger,'" National Park Service, Park Ethnography Program, https://www.nps.gov/ethnography/aah/aaheritage/intro_furthRdg1.htm; R. Kent Rasmussen, "nigger," in *Critical Companion to Mark Twain: A Literary Reference to His Life and Work,* 2 vols. (New York: Facts on File, 2007), 2:815.

4. Jabari Asim, *The N Word: Who Can Say It, Who Shouldn't, and Why* (Boston: Houghton Mifflin, 2007).

5. *The "N" Word,* Todd Williams, writer/director; Nelson George, executive producer; Helena Echegoyen, producer; Nelson George, producer; Peter Ochs and Brad Katz, editors; released June 26, 2004. https://www.imdb.com/title/tt0417003/.

6. Twain, "Only a Nigger," 22–23. See also Joseph A. Alvarez, "High Toned Injustice and Samuel L. Clemens' 'Only a Nigger,'" *South Atlantic Review* 75, no. 2 (2010): 35–43.

7. Students in my classes have found both of these stories very engaging. Paul Laurence Dunbar, "The Ingrate," in Paul Laurence Dunbar, *The Sport of the Gods and Other Essential Writings,* edited by Shelley Fisher Fishkin and David Bradley (New York: Modern Library, 2005), 107–14; Charles W. Chesnutt, "The Passing of Grandison," AmericanLiterature.com, https://americanliterature.com/author/charles-w-chesnutt/short-story/the-passing-of-grandison.

8. For a discussion of the pros and cons of teaching the book Twain wrote versus Alan Gribben's NewSouth books expurgated version, see "*Huckleberry Finn* and the N-Word," *Sixty Minutes,* June 12, 2011, www.youtube.com/watch?v=nW9-qee1m9o.

9. These substitutions, of course, still require students to imagine the word they do not voice, in the process, perhaps, giving it even more power. However, the atmosphere in American schools today make it inadvisable to say the word aloud unless one wants to court controversy. See, for example, Professor Jonathan Rieder's experience at Barnard as described in Alex Morey and Nadine Strossen, "Who's Allowed to Teach 'Culture in America'? Inside One Barnard Professor's Fight over Who Decides," *Fire,* April 25, 2023, www.thefire.org/news /whos-allowed-teach-culture-america.

10. Alan Carey-Webb, "Racism and 'Huckleberry Finn': Censorship, Dialogue, and Change," *English Journal* 82, no. 7 (1993): 22–34; Shelley Fisher Fishkin, "Take the N-Word Out of 'Huck Finn'? It's an Insult to Mark Twain—and to American History," *New York Daily News,* January 5, 2011, www.nydailynews .com/2011/01/05/take-the-n-word-out-of-huck-finn-its-an-insult-to-mark-twain -and-to-american-history/; David E. E. Sloane, "The N-Word in *Adventures of Huckleberry Finn* Reconsidered," *Mark Twain Annual* 12, no. 1 (2014): 70–82; Jocelyn Chadwick, "We Dare Not Teach What We Know We Must: The Importance of Difficult Conversations," *English Journal* 106, no. 2 (2016): 88–91; Jocelyn Chadwick, "When Will We Listen? Mark Twain through the Lenses of Generation Z," Center for Mark Twain Studies, March 7, 2018, https://marktwainstudies.com /when-will-we-listen-mark-twain-through-the-lenses-of-generation-z/; David A. Gorlewski, "Scholars Weigh In on Teaching *Adventures of Huckleberry Finn,*" *English Journal* 112, no. 2 (2022): 23–24.

11. David Bradley, "Eulogy for Nigger," *Independent,* October 8, 2015, www .independent.co.uk/news/world/world-history/eulogy-for-nigger-the-provocative -title-that-has-been-printed-verbatim-a6687016.html.

12. Documenting the American South, https://docsouth.unc.edu/docsouth data/.

13. "Individual Slave Narratives at Missouri State Museum," Missouri State Parks, https://mostateparks.com/page/58373/individual-slave-narratives.

14. Frederick Douglass, "What to the Slave Is the Fourth of July?," oration delivered in Corinthian Hall, Rochester, on July 5, 1852, available at National Endowment for the Humanities, https://edsitement.neh.gov/student-activities /frederick-douglasss-what-slave-fourth-july.

15. *Ethnic Notions,* documentary film directed and produced by Marlon Riggs, distributed by California Newsreel, 1987.

16. Scott Kaiser, *Splittin' the Raft* (self-pub., CreateSpace, 2017). For a detailed description of high school students' responses, see the following article by the play's director about a tour in Georgia: Harrison Long, "'We're Not Ready

for Huck Finn': An Important Story Struggles to Be Told" (2014), Faculty Publications 3353, Kennesaw State University, https://digitalcommons.kennesaw.edu/facpubs/3353.

17. Ibram X. Kendi, *Stamped from the Beginning: The Definitive History of Racist Ideas in America* (New York: PublicAffairs, 2016); Thomas H. Gossett, *Race: The History of an Idea in America,* reprint ed. with a new afterword by Gossett, an introduction by Arnold Rampersad and Shelley Fisher Fishkin, and a bibliography by Maghan Keita (New York: Oxford University Press, 1997); and George M. Fredrickson, *The Arrogance of Race: Historical Perspectives on Slavery, Racism, and Social Inequality* (Middletown, CT: Wesleyan University Press, 1988); Toni Morrison, *The Origin of Others,* foreword by Ta-Nahisi Coates (Cambridge, MA: Harvard University Press, 2017); George M. Fredrickson, *Racism: A Short History,* reprint ed., foreword by Albert Camarillo (Princeton, NJ: Princeton University Press, 2015).

18. Shelley Fisher Fishkin, *Lighting Out for the Territory: Reflections on Mark Twain and American Culture* (New York: Oxford University Press, 1996); Shelley Fisher Fishkin, "Mark Twain and Race," in *Historical Guide to Mark Twain,* edited by Shelley Fisher Fishkin (New York: Oxford University Press, 2002), 127–62.

19. Shelley Fisher Fishkin, webinar on "Teaching *Adventures of Huckleberry Finn,*" conducted for the National Humanities Center "Humanities in the Classroom" program, 2015, https://nationalhumanitiescenter.org/education-material/teaching-adventures-of-huckleberry-finn/; Mark Twain, "What Have the Police Been Doing?," *Territorial Enterprise* (Virginia City, NV), January 16–18, 1866, www.twainquotes.com/18660118t.html; Mark Twain, "Disgraceful Persecution of a Boy," *Galaxy Magazine,* May 1870, www.twainquotes.com/Galaxy/187005e.html; Mark Twain, "Goldsmith's Friend Abroad Again" letters: *Galaxy,* October 1870, www.twainquotes.com/Galaxy/187010b.html; *Galaxy,* November 1870, www.twainquotes.com/Galaxy/187011c.html; *Galaxy,* January 1871, www.twainquotes.com/Galaxy/187101e.html.

20. Shelley Fisher Fishkin," "Teaching Mark Twain's *Adventures of Huckleberry Finn,*" Website of PBS "Culture Shock" series, 2015, www.pbs.org/wgbh/cultureshock/teachers/huck/essay.html. The six-part teacher's guide to *Born to Trouble: Adventures of Huckleberry Finn* comes out of a "*Huck Finn* in Context" curriculum developed in Cherry Hill, NJ. Website of PBS "Culture Shock" series, 2015, www.pbs.org/wgbh/cultureshock/teachers/huck/howto.html, www.pbs.org/wgbh/cultureshock/teachers/index.html. For the origins and development of the Cherry Hill curriculum by group of parents, teachers, administrators, and students, see www.pbs.org/wgbh/cultureshock/teachers/huck/controversy.html and www.pbs.org/wgbh/cultureshock/teachers/article2.html.

21. Ralph Wiley, *Why Black People Tend to Shout: Cold Facts and Wry Views from a Black Man's World* (New York: Birch Lane, 1991); Ralph Wiley, *What Black People Should Do Now: Dispatches from Near the Vanguard* (New York: Ballantine Books, 1993); and Ralph Wiley, *Dark Witness: When Black People Should Be Sacrificed (Again)* (New York: One World, Ballantine, 1996). Other books by Ralph Wiley include *Serenity: A Boxing Memoir* (Lincoln: University of Nebraska Press, 2000); *Growing Up King: An Intimate Memoir,* with Dexter Scott King (New York: Grand Central, 2003); and *Born to Play: The Eric Davis Story,* with Eric Davis (New York: Viking, 1999). For more on Wiley, see Matt Schudel, "Sportswriter Ralph Wiley Dies; Essays Probed Black Life," *Washington Post,* June 16, 2004; and Jon Thurber, "Ralph Wiley, 52; Sportswriter and Author of Books on Race," *Los Angeles Times,* June 16, 2004.

22. Spike Lee and Ralph Wiley, *By Any Means Necessary: The Trials and Tribulations of Making Malcolm X* (New York: Hyperion, 1992). Wiley also wrote *Best Seat in the House: A Basketball Memoir,* with Spike Lee (New York: Three Rivers Press, 1998).

23. Excerpts from *Spike Lee's Huckleberry Finn* by Ralph Wiley, c/o Heygood Images Productions, Inc. Copyright © 2025 Estate of Ralph Wiley. Reprinted with permission.

ACKNOWLEDGMENTS

———

Many people helped make this book happen, and I'm delighted to be able to express my gratitude to them here.

This book would not exist had I not gotten a phone call two years ago from Henry Louis Gates Jr. inviting me to write it for the new series on Black Lives that Yale was launching with three outstanding scholars at its helm: Skip himself, along with David Blight and Jacqueline Goldsby. That phone call turned my research agenda—and my life—completely upside down, and I am very glad that it did! It is an honor to a part of an enterprise led by scholars I so greatly admire. I am grateful to Skip Gates not only for this opportunity but for having been such a font of support and good advice—as well as a dear friend—for so many years.

And I am incredibly fortunate that Yale University Press invited Robert Paul Lamb to be a reader of my manuscript. He was the perfect choice. His remarkably insightful, meticulous, erudite, and astoundingly detailed comments were enormously helpful and shaped every chapter of the book, as well as its structure, in myriad ways.

My editor at Yale, Jessie Kindig, was the kind of editor scholars dream of but rarely get. She offered astute page-by-page suggestions informed by her deep knowledge of both history and literature that made this a much better book. Her sense (which Twain would have appreciated) of the importance of using the right word and not its second cousin informed all of her edits. I am greatly in her debt. I am also grateful for the help that Yale's Ash Lago and Ann-Marie Imbornoni gave in preparing the manuscript and the extra distance Ash went to secure photographs.

I am still amazed by the generosity of two friends and colleagues who volunteered to read my manuscript in its entirety—Arnold Rampersad, with whom I coedited Oxford's Race and American Culture book series for a decade, and Hilton Obenzinger, with whom I once I cotaught a course on Mark Twain. The guidance they provided was invaluable.

This book builds on the work of a group of stellar scholars and writers who have helped me think through issues at the core of this book and whose friendship I value greatly. Discussions with the late Ralph Wiley (z"l) in person in Austin, Baltimore, New York, Stanford, and Washington, DC, and on email and in letters helped set in motion for me approaches to *Huckleberry Finn* that culminated in the book at hand—approaches that were also explored in groundbreaking ways by David L. Smith, Jocelyn Chadwick, and Terrell Dempsey. Conversations with David Bradley helped clarify my thinking on a broad range of issues: with patience and his trademark iconoclasm he helped give me the courage to grapple with tough topics.

The "Explanatory" with which this book opens was a special challenge. Although it is just four paragraphs long, those paragraphs are filled with land mines. I was fortunate, indeed, to have a group of scholars and friends whose judgment I trust weigh in suggesting edits, proposing links, and helping those paragraphs hit their mark without exploding en route. I thank Lisa Cardyn, Harry Elam, Michele Elam, Kevin Gaines, Skip Gates, Bob Lamb, Shirley Geok-lin Lim, Lerone Martin, Nina Morgan, Hilton Obenzinger, Carla Peterson, Jessica Schairer, Lauri Scheyer, Sam Stol-off, Alexis Wells-Oghoghomeh, and Rafia Zafar for their great suggestions. (But any problems in the final version that appears in the book are on me, not them.)

Chapter 1, "Contexts and Conditions," benefited from conversations with my colleague Alexis Wells-Oghoghomeh and was informed, as well, by conversations I had in years past with the late Sterling Stuckey (z"l) and the late Robert Farris Thompson (z"l). Bill Ferris introduced me in graduate school to the importance of paying serious attention to the folk beliefs that figure prominently in this section. Faye Dant, founder of Jim's Journey: The Huck Finn Freedom Center, an important Black history museum in Hannibal, Missouri, and author of *Hannibal's Invisibles* (2024), has long been a source of inspiration, and never more so than when I was writing this book. She had an important influence on this chapter.

Chapter 2, "Myths and Models," is indebted to the late Charles T. Davis (z"l), who told me with a knowing smile back in graduate school that I had to read "A True Story" (I'm so very glad I took his advice!). My many visits to the Mark Twain House and Museum in Hartford, Connecticut, helped me understand Twain's special relationship with George Griffin and his appreciation of the work of Charles Ethan Porter, and my many visits to Quarry Farm in Elmira, New York, helped me appreciate the scene where Twain interacted with both Mary Ann Cord and John T. Lewis. I am grateful to the staff of both institutions for preserving and celebrating the memory of these individuals. A visit to Jim's Journey in Hannibal gave me the opportunity to learn more about Daniel Quarles and meet one of his descendants.

Chapter 3, "The Debates," was shaped by what I learned from three brilliant writers no longer with us whom it was my pleasure and honor to know: Hal Holbrook (z"l), Ralph Ellison (z"l), and

Toni Morrison (z"l). Each of them indelibly influenced my understanding of what mattered most about Twain. Their encouragement and support of my work meant the world to me. A number of wonderful fellow Twain scholars and friends who have passed on also left their mark on this chapter—including Louis Budd (z"l), Vic Doyno (z"l), and Jim Miller (z"l). My research assistant at Stanford, Constantia Katerina Georgiou, made key contributions to this chapter, as well as to chapter 5, and I am grateful for her excellent help.

Chapter 4, "Jim's Version: An Interpretive Exercise," was inspired in large part by my conversations over the years with Ralph Wiley, whose unproduced screenplay and whose dedication to the project of letting us see the world through Jim's eyes opened up new perspectives on familiar terrain. Arnold Rampersad, Hilton Obenzinger, Jessie Kindig, Myrial Holbrook, and the inimitable Bob Lamb had perceptive responses that improved the final result.

Chapter 5, "Afterlives: Jim on Stage and Screen," benefited greatly from R. Kent Rasmussen's willingness to read it in manuscript, offering corrections and helpful advice based on his encyclopedic knowledge of film adaptations of Twain's works (I regret that limits of space required me to cut a discussion of the portrayal of Jim by one of his favorite actors, Brock Peters). I owe a debt to Cassio de Oliveira for having introduced me to the two Soviet films I discuss in this chapter and for having pointed me toward useful sources. Lina Belitski translated Russian title cards for me. Ingrid Gessner and Alfred Hornung both offered helpful insights into the cultural context of the two German films I discuss. I am grateful to playwright and director Edward Morgan for having invited me to see a production of his play *Sounding the River (Huckleberry Finn Revisited)* in Milwaukee in 2001 and participate in a symposium about it, and for having shared the unpublished script with me, allowing me to quote from it in this book—as well as for the extended conversations we had about it on email. I thank Mike McKee of WTTW in Chicago for giving me access to his station's Emmy-winning recording of the Goodman Theatre's production from 1985 of *Huckleberry Finn* featuring Meshach Taylor. I am also grateful to Olamide Udoma-Ejorh, a Lagos-based city planner, for having responded to my query about whether the street in Lagos was, in fact, named for Felix Imoukhuede and for having gone the extra distance in locating his cousin, Oseomoje Imoukhuede, who helped me learn what Felix Imoukhuede did after starring in a Soviet film as a graduate student.

Chapter 6, "Afterlives: Jim in Translation," is deeply indebted to the talented colleagues with whom I had the privilege of co-editing a Special Forum in the *Journal of Transnational American Studies* on "Global Huck": Tsuyoshi Ishihara, Ronald Jenn, Holger Kersten, and Selina Lai-Henderson. I also thank the outstanding contributors to that Special Forum, whose research figures prominently in this chapter: Veronica Channaut and Ronald Jenn (who wrote on French versions), Behnam Fomeshi (on Persian versions), Miguel Sanz Jiménez (on Spanish versions), Winston Kelley (on German versions), Margarita Marinova (on Russian versions), Vera Lucia Ramos (on Brazilian Portuguese versions), and Seema Sharma (on Hindi versions), as well as two stellar translators featured in the special forum: Hamada Kassam (Arabic) and An-chi Wang (Chinese). Ronald Jenn and Judith Lavoie were gracious enough to read this chapter in manuscript. Ramit Goyal identified translations of which I had not been previously aware in Punjabi and Gujarati. I am grateful to the following for having examined versions in languages I do not read and for having done their best to answer questions I had about them and provide me with useful information about them: Teresa Alves (Portuguese), Teresa Cid (Portuguese), Aruni Kashyap (Assamese), Eitan Lev Kensky (Yiddish), C. Ryan Perkins (Urdu), and Chris Suh (Korean). I thank Amel Fraisse for all she did to help identify translations in under-resourced languages for our work together on the Rosetta Project. Conversations with my colleagues on the Editorial Board of the *Journal of Transnational American Studies* helped me appreciate the importance of the transnational perspectives on American culture that were key to chapters 5 and 6. I thank Erika Doss, Kevin Gaines, Alfred Hornung, Hsuan Hsu, Shirley Geok-lin Lim, Nina Morgan, Jennifer Reimer, Brian Russell Roberts, Greg Robinson, Takayuki Tatsumi, and Pia Wiegmink—as well as Vanessa Evans, Sabine Kim, Selina Lai-Henderson, Mahshid Mayar, Aiko Takeuki-Demirci, and Mai Wang—for all they've taught me.

Chapter 7, "Afterlives: Jim in the High School Classroom," relied heavily on the willingness of John Pascal to share the "secret sauce" that makes him such an effective teacher as well as the wonderful papers and exams that his students at Seton Hall Preparatory School wrote—papers and exams that were impressive, engaging, and a genuine pleasure to read. I thank his students for giving me permission to quote from them, and I'm immensely grateful to John for his Herculean efforts to get signed releases from each of them, including students who had graduated. I also thank his wife, Nelly Patricia Pascal, for having scanned all their releases and gotten them to us as promptly as she did. Conversations with John Pascal reminded me of how lucky I was to have had an equally dedicated teacher myself when I was in high school, the late Anthony Arciola (z"l), the Staples High School teacher who introduced me to *Huckleberry Finn*. Julia Rosenbloom was good enough to reflect on her high school experience with the novel years ago, and I remain in debt to her for that.

A conversation with Min Jin Lee prompted me to write the Afterword and brilliantly clarified for me what my aspirations in this book had been.

The "Appendix: Notes for Teachers" was shaped at its core by my students at Stanford—and earlier at the University of Texas at Austin and at Yale. They taught me to appreciate the challenges of grappling with the gnarly legacies of racism in American culture and their impact on how we understand Mark Twain. The Appendix also reflects things I learned from colleagues who joined me in making presentations for high school teachers and local communities around the country about *Huck Finn* and/or theatrical adaptations of it (David Bradley in Dallas, Greenwich, Hartford, Milwaukee, Seattle, and Stanford; Jocelyn Chadwick in Dallas, Seattle, and Stanford; and Hilton Obenzinger in Stanford). It also benefited from my discussions with teachers who participated in the webinar I conducted for the National Humanities Center and from what I learned teaching a course at Stanford with my esteemed colleague Allyson Hobbs on "Race and Reunion: Slavery and the Civil War in American Memory" for many years (and an earlier version of the course that I taught with Bryan Wolf). I am enormously grateful to Cole Wiley for giving me permission to reprint scenes from his father's screenplay in the Appendix to this book. I also want to thank James W. Leonard, editor of the *Mark Twain Circular*, for updating the link to my article about *Spike Lee's Huckleberry Finn* that first appeared in the *Circular* in 1999.

Sam Stoloff, my agent, is always a source of good advice and guidance. Robin McClish managed to be miraculously on call to solve the innumerable computer problems I had while writing this book. Laura Daly and Laura Jones Dooley provided expert copy editing. Barry Moser graciously let me use his stunning illustrations.

My friend and neighbor Michael Keller runs the best university library on the planet, and without the assistance of the spectacularly effective interlibrary loan department at Stanford, as well as Stanford's American literature and American history curators, Rebecca Wingfield and Ben Stone, this book would look very different. I am also grateful to my Yale classmate Karen Lawrence for making the Huntington Library such an inviting place to do research; the Huntington's rare manuscripts collection was important to chapter 5, and the library's excellent collection of critical works about Twain played a key role in my research for chapter 3. I am grateful to my longtime friend Robert H. Hirst for his stellar stewardship of the Mark Twain Papers and Project at the Bancroft Library, UC-Berkeley, and for welcoming me and my students every year; the Project's excellent collection of translations and secondary sources was very helpful to my research for this book. Mark Twain Project Online is a superb boon for scholars and was also essential to my research.

Many colleagues, friends, and former students offered feedback, encouragement, and helpful leads at a number of points as I incubated research that became this book: Molly Antopol, Terri Apter, Mita Banerjee, Michele Barry, Dorothy Bender, Adrienne Bitar, David Bradley, Jørn Brøndel, Lisa Cardyn, Gordon H. Chang, King-kok Cheung, Catherine Ceniza Choy, Joyce Cohen, Steve Courtney, Laura Daly, Mark Dawidziak, Jodi DeBruyne, Cassio de Oliveira, Michele and Harry Elam, Bill Ferris, Estelle Freedman, Maurene Fritz, Ingrid Gessner, Brian Goodman, Benjamin Griffin, Ina Habermann, Robert H. Hirst, Allyson Hobbs, Alfred Hornung, Mallory Howard, Hsinya Huang, Ronald Jenn, Gavin Jones, Van Jordan, Rose Hsiu-li Juan, Clara Juncker, James Kardon, Michael Keller, David Kennedy, Bob and Nan Keohane, Selina Lai-Henderson, Paul Lauter, Judith Lavoie, Carol Lawrence, Min Jin Lee, Shirley Geok-lin Lim, Jay Lipner, Kevin Mac Donnell, Lerone Martin, Elaine Tyler May, Nina Morgan, Patricia Parker, Carla Peterson, Jean Pfaelzer, Peggy Phelan, Beth Piatote, Ato Quayson, Vaughn Rasberry, Kent Rasmussen, Jeanne Campbell Reesman,

Jon Rieder, Brian Russell Roberts, Greg Robinson, Jessica and John Schairer, Lauri Scheyer, Matt Seybold, Yuan Shu, Gail Slocum, Mitch Slomiak, Werner Sollors, Chris Suh, Alexis Wells-Oghoghomeh, Cole Wiley, Nathaniel Williams, Richard Yarborough, Connie Young Yu, and Rafia Zafar. Also Debbie Bernick, Mary Chitty, Meg Custer, Cornelia "Nene" Emerson, Alexis Krasilovsky, Anne Magoun, Becky Newan, Mary Pearl, Catherine Ross, Jan Roth, Connie Royster, Lydia Temoshok, Susan Yecies, Alice Young, and other members of my First Women at Yale group.

I was fortunate to be asked by Matt Seybold and Joe Lemak to be cochair with Tracy Wuster of the Ninth International Conference on the State of Mark Twain Studies as I was working on this book. Our program committee and the attendees at the conference in 2022 stimulated my thinking about issues in this book at a particularly fortuitous juncture. It was also extremely helpful to have an intense multihour seminar-on-wheels driving to and from the Elmira conference from New Haven with legendary Twain scholar David E. E. Sloane.

Being awarded the Olivia Langdon Award for Scholarly Creativity and Innovation from the Mark Twain Circle of America in 2022 and the Carl Bode-Norman Holmes Pearson Award for Lifetime Achievement and Outstanding Contribution to American Studies from the American Studies Association in 2023 as I worked on this book helped spur me on; I am grateful to both organizations for their recognition of my work.

I want to thank to Judith Richardson for having taken the helm of American Studies at Stanford during my sabbatical and Maritza Colon, An Truong Nguyen, Beth Kessler, Nancy Child, and Leah Chase for all they did to make it possible for me to write a book while directing Stanford's American Studies Program. And I thank my deans, Gabriella Safran and Debra Satz, for the support they offer faculty in the humanities and for all they've done to make those of us involved in doing research in the humanities believe that what we do matters.

My wonderful sons, Joey and Bobby, cheered me on from the start. Creative and talented in their own right, they have been constant sources of inspiration. Other family members have also offered encouragement that helped push me to the finish line— the late Carol Plaine Fisher (z"l), David and Jill Fishkin, Cary Franklin, Betti-Sue Hertz, Joan Perrin, Leonard Plaine (z"l), Moss Plaine, Lynne Breger Tag, and Georgia Witkin. The voices of my late parents, Renée and Milton Fisher (z"l)—both elegant writers and demanding editors—echoed in my ears as I wrote each page; their guidance from beyond the grave made this a better book. The hope that my grandchildren, Sasha and Anna, will have the opportunity to study *Huckleberry Finn* when they are in high school helped propel me to write this book. In fact, the chance to shape how their generation will understand who Jim is and why he does what he does has been a driving force.

My extraordinary husband, Jim Fishkin, has shared his home with this other Jim with more grace and patience than I had any right to expect. Carefully stepping over the piles of books that invaded every corner of our house and taking precious time away from the important book he is finishing himself, he was always ready to be a helpful sounding board and a constant source of encouragement and support. I owe him my greatest debt and dedicate this book to him.

INDEX